BRITISH IMPERIAL POLICY AND DECOLONIZATION, 1938–64

British Imperial Policy and Decolonization, 1938–64

Volume 1, 1938–51

A. N. Porter
Reader in History
King's College, London

and

A. J. Stockwell
Senior Lecturer in History
Royal Holloway and Bedford New College,
University of London

St. Martin's Press New York

Scholarly & Reference Division,
St. Martin's Press, Inc., 175 Fifth Avenue, New York, NY
10010

First published in the United States of America in 1987

Printed in Hong Kong

ISBN 0–312–00554–7

Library of Congress Cataloging-in-Publication Data
Porter, A. N. (Andrew N.)
British imperial policy and decolonization,
1938–64.
Bibliography: v. 1, p.
Includes index.
Contents: v. 1. 1938–51
1. Great Britain—Colonies—Administration—
History. 2. Decolonization—History. I. Stockwell,
A. J. II. Title.
JV1018.P66 1987 325'.31'41 87–4272
ISBN 0–312–00554–7 (v. 1)

Contents

Contents

List of Documents

Abbreviations

CAB	Cabinet Records, at the Public Record Office, Kew.
CDAC	Colonial Development Advisory Committee
CEAC	Colonial Economic Advisory Committee
CMB	Committee on Malaya and Borneo
CO	Colonial Office Records, at the Public Record Office, Kew.
DO	Dominions Office (Commonwealth Relations Office) Records, at the Public Record Office, Kew.
DOC	Document
FO	Foreign Office
HMG	His Majesty's Government
ODC	Overseas Defence Committee of the Cabinet
OEEC	Organization for European Economic Co-operation
PP	British Parliamentary Papers
PREM	Prime Minister's Office Records, at the Public Record Office, Kew.
SEAC	South East Asia Command
T	Treasury Records, at the Public Record Office, Kew.
UNRRA	United Nations Relief and Recovery Agency

Acknowledgements

As is common among historians, we have between us incurred many debts to both institutions and colleagues while at work on this volume. We are particularly grateful to the staff of the Public Record Office at Kew, to the pressures of whose work we have added inordinately of late. Imperial and Commonwealth historians will always remain heavily reliant, as we have been, on the goodwill of the Librarian and staff of Rhodes House Library, Oxford. Working in London, we are also indebted to the staff at the Institute of Historical Research, the University Library at Senate House, and the library of the School of Oriental and African Studies. Not only the resources of the library at the Institute of Commonwealth Studies, but the continual stimulus provided by its research seminars, have been invaluable. To King's College and to Royal Holloway and Bedford New College our thanks are due for financial assistance in the preparation of documents; and for a great deal of practical help to that same end, we have depended heavily on the generous assistance of Miss June Walker, Mrs Doris Lovell, and Mrs Rita Townsend. Finally we must express our gratitude to Dr Robert Pearce, Mr A. H. M. Kirk-Greene, and especially Dr Robert Holland.

A. N. PORTER
A. J. STOCKWELL

Preface

'Too many documents!' This is already the cry of archivists charged with the storage of twentieth-century records, and is frequently also that of scholars faced with the task of encompassing the complexity of modern government activity. It may well also be the first reaction of imperial or commonwealth historians who have seen a succession of documentary collections come their way: A. B. Keith; R. M. Dawson; N. Mansergh (*Documents and Speeches*); Madden and Fieldhouse; James Eayrs; and recently the incomparable series on the transfers of power in India and Burma. There are others still – by Cumpston, Newbury, and Pandey – each with their particular problem, period, or patch of empire.[1] Why then add another? It is not only the sceptic who regards published collections of documents as the academic's device for avoiding the issues, who will ask this question.

Our decision was influenced by several considerations. It arose in part from our experience as teachers of undergraduates, which has made us conscious of the widespread interest in twentieth-century history. It stemmed too from our awareness, as scholars involved in research in imperial and commonwealth history, of the extremely interesting work now being done in the field of decolonization. Finally it reflected our continuing conviction that the history of Britain and of her one-time colonial territories cannot properly be understood in isolation from each other. It therefore seemed a good idea when the opportunity arose to mount a special course for final-year students in which these various interests would be combined. One of the major transformations of the modern world could be examined in some depth through focusing on the British experience of decolonization.

We required a manageable yet suitably varied collection of source material to provide a documentary basis for our teaching. Nothing of the kind existed in print, although printed sources relevant to the theme are obviously already plentiful, and unpublished materials in vast quantities are steadily becoming available as British government papers are released under the 'thirty-year rule'. Thus we faced the task of compiling our own working collection. Based as we are in London, this has at least been possible: for scholars elsewhere, notwithstanding similar interests in teaching and research, the task would have been much more difficult. We therefore thought it would be useful to make more widely available a selection of the material we have gathered. This is the first of two volumes which together will span roughly the period 1938–64.

Having remarked on its origin and general purpose, we should perhaps set out the principles of selection which we have tried to follow and reconcile with each other in deciding on its contents. Of course, we have had constantly in mind the occurrences and themes which, from a reading of secondary literature as well as primary material, seem to us to be of particular importance. Along with this, and in addition to the perennial limitations of space, there have been two important practical considerations. We have thought it essential to include material which would be of particular illustrative value, material which would reveal the uncertainty, untidiness and conflicts in government, or which would provoke questions, as well as that which recorded apparently inevitable outcomes or beautifully-rounded justifications of policy not in fact so clearly conceived at the time of formulation. A preference has also been given to the most inaccessible material, both as a convenience to other teachers and in order to emphasise how little as yet has been drawn together from the sources which exist despite the labour of many scholars. In the selection therefore we have for the most part avoided contemporary printed source material. We have also taken it for granted that scholars will have the possibility of access to other recently-published collections, and we have severely restricted references, for example, to India. Finally, we have concentrated our attention in particular on unpublished material from British government sources in the Public Record Office at Kew.

In presenting the documents, we have been guided by the historian's need to have the form of the originals reproduced as closely and as fully as possible. Minutes and memoranda were written often in haste; they are frequently eccentric or inconsistent, and are sometimes wrong. Yet for those wishing to study, in this case, how governments worked, these 'blemishes' are telling and important; equally illuminating are the conventions of the day. We have therefore retained the original forms of dating and punctuation, with the sole exception of the then customary full point after 'Mr'. No alterations have been made to the wording of documents, but in instances where the original was illegible or seemed bizarre, editorial interpolations have been placed inside square brackets.

No collection of this kind can hope to please everyone. Ours may well irritate area specialists, leaving them with the feeling that their corner of the world, if not omitted altogether, has been insufficiently (although we hope not falsely) represented. It will disappoint others by its failure to give weight to particular themes, for example the development of non-European nationalism. To such complaints there are reasonable responses. It would be quite impossible to provide a connected account of many separate examples of colonies moving to independence. For the handling of many questions we are as far removed from relevant sources as other scholars may be from those we have been able to use. Moreover, this is a collection concerned not with decolonization *tout court* but with British imperial policy and decolonization. This is perhaps amenable to closer definition but is at the same time broader in scope than any formal process of decolonization.

Even from this perspective other issues still have been neglected. The focus and the sources are predominantly metropolitan, and are intentionally so. We hope that it is fairly illustrative of the most important themes in the making of British imperial policy during the period covered. We have tried to convey something of the different levels at which decisions were taken, and an impression of the numerous arenas in which courses of action were discussed and 'policy' formulated. In so far as we consider changing international circumstances, or the growth of colonial nationalist movements, they appear as forces exerting pressure on Britain, as constraints perceived with more or less clarity by British officials when considering their future and the possibilities open to them. Particular colonies surface from time to time and will do so more often in the second volume, but our aim is to convey above all something of the relative importance which individually they had for contemporaries, either in themselves or as representatives of a type of problem which had to be faced.

A. N. PORTER
A. J. STOCKWELL

Part I
Introduction

1 Decolonization and Patterns of Historical Explanation

In the modern history of British expansion overseas there have been three great periods of change, each distinguished by uncommonly concentrated and far-reaching alterations in the shape of Britain's formal empire. Between the outbreak of the American War of Independence in 1776 and the end of the Napoleonic Wars in 1815, Britain lost thirteen American colonies, acquired the heart of a new empire in India, and established a significant presence in numerous other areas as geographically distant and culturally diverse as Quebec, Trinidad, the Cape of Good Hope, and New South Wales. A second sea-change took place in the late nineteenth century; most notably, between 1870 and 1900 some two-thirds of Africa was claimed as British territory. Finally, since 1945, there has occurred the dissolution of that territorial empire, the process of Britain's formal decolonization, commencing with the independence of India and Pakistan in 1947 and largely complete by 1964.

Intellectual curiosity as to the causes, course, and consequences of these major metamorphoses has always been strong. They are, after all, important not only for Britain's own history but for that of many once-colonial peoples, and are inseparable from the pattern of relations between the world's sovereign states. Britain's decolonization was affected by and contributed to changes in the global balance of power; it was also part of an international transformation in which the lesser empires of the Belgians, French, Portuguese and Dutch were also dismantled. Although, unlike earlier alterations to Britain's empire, decolonization is only now beginning to be viewed with that detachment and sense of proportion essential to historical understanding, explanations have never been lacking. By way of introduction, some of these are worth recollection.

Many people have held the view that the British always

intended eventually to relinquish their colonies. The British were committed, it was said, to a liberal democratic culture and to representative institutions. Having burnt their fingers in eighteenth-century America, they discovered the wisdom of intervening as little as possible in local colonial concerns, and thereafter habitually extended powers of self-government to white colonists. The nineteenth century witnessed the British confidently asserting that their institutions held the key to political stability and economic prosperity, and committed to the duty of transmitting the same to uncivilized or barbaric non-Europeans. Colonial rule was synonymous with education, development, and progress: when the process was complete decolonization represented the fulfilment of the imperialists' purpose. Where white dominions like Australia first trod, colonies of non-European subjects naturally followed. The timing of Britain's withdrawal was to be explained largely as the result of conscious intention and planning.

This 'liberal commonwealth' tradition is seriously misleading in so far as it attributes to successive imperial governments degrees of clear-sightedness, benevolent or selfless intention, and firm control over initiatives or the pace of change, which square ill with the reality. Sceptics point to the fact that in the 1930s there was much evidence of disillusionment with the equation of empire and progress, and little sign of preparation for the rapid developments occurring after 1945. They ask why decolonization should have taken place so rapidly, and at much the same time, despite the great diversity of circumstances within different colonies.

Nationalists above all have argued that the British did not plan to go. Instead, they were pushed out of their empire by the increasingly effective organization and cumulative resistance of colonial peoples. This type of explanation was widely favoured in the 1960s, with protagonists pointing to Indian threats of non-co-operation and British fears of anarchy, to states of emergency in Malaya, Kenya, and Cyprus, to African protest in the Central African Federation, as evidence that imperial rulers could no longer cope. Like the 'liberal commonwealth' argument, this 'nationalist' interpretation often served an historical function, in this case assisting new leaders to establish their credentials and claims to authority as the successors of the British.

Others have seen as crucial the contribution of the newly-emergent super-powers, with their willingness to put pressure on colonial rulers to relax controls and withdraw. Of particular importance to such analyses is the ending – through involvement in the Second World War – of the previously isolationist temper of Americans and of US foreign policy. Conscious of American strength, the Roosevelt and Truman administrations were determined to influence the new post-war world order. Championship of self-government and colonial independence was designed to win friends abroad and break into what Americans saw as the closed imperial systems of European states. The USSR can be assigned a less positive role, with decolonization being seen as a device developed in the context of the Cold War for the purpose of maintaining the allegiance of the non-European world for the capitalist West.

These explanations all contain elements of truth, but also leave important questions unanswered. Why, one might ask, was British control of her colonies so weak that local protest forced her to retreat? Had it always been difficult to assert imperial authority, or had control only suddenly begun to collapse? Why was it difficult for Britain to resist international criticism and pressure from, for example, the USA? Part of the solution may be found in the nature of colonial rule and in the particular development of individual colonies. One could perhaps highlight the fact that imperial control has always depended on a measure of co-operation or collaboration between colonial rulers and influential local interest groups. Establishing such collaborative relations has always required considerable political skills on both sides. Periodically relations broke down, and new alliances had to be constructed; eventually, however, the British exhausted the possibilities available to them, albeit at different times in different places.

Answers may also lie in Britain itself. Decolonization may be seen as a simple response to Britain's comparative economic decline in the world. With relatively reduced resources and a declining proportion of world trade, the costs for Britain of running and defending her empire were simply too great. Withdrawal enabled British governments to cut their losses. It has also been suggested, by contrast, that the problem for Britain was not economic but psychological: the resources were there but the political will to rule was less and less apparent. The election of Labour governments, especially in 1945, was only one of the more striking signs of the evaporation of imperial spirit. Taken singly, these arguments are hardly satisfactory, but if the economic and political slants are combined it is possible to see the basis for a more sophisticated explanation. Britain certainly operated under growing material constraints, but remained nevertheless one of the world's richest nations; the resources necessary for an imperial power lay to hand, but were being diverted to other ends as a result of domestic political choice. It was impossible both to run an empire and meet an open-ended commitment to a welfare state. After 1951 Conservative governments did not dare to dismantle what Labour had established in an excess of optimism. Decolonization therefore became inevitable.

So far, we have indicated three broad approaches to the basic question 'how are historians to explain decolonization?' In one way or another Britain decided that she would no longer retain her formal empire; Britain was forced out of individual colonies by the pressure of local events; Britain was edged towards a renunciation of empire by international pressures. These might be taken individually, but this documentary collection reflects the view that a pluralist explanation is inescapable, and it recognizes that the balance of factors involved varies with time and place. It also emphasizes the importance of political conflict and compromise in a situation where the discussions of Cabinets, the debates of Whitehall bureaucrats, the perceptions of colonial administrators, the ambitions of colonial nationalists, the instincts of voters everywhere, frequently shifted and were often divided if not undecided.

For some historians economic determinants undoubtedly carry most weight. In the long run, it has been argued, Britain's empire represented the legacy of her nineteenth-century position as the world's most powerful industrial economy. Once that position was lost Britain's empire could not be sustained, and the USA which succeeded to Britain's pre-eminent position naturally played a major role in the history of Britain's decolonization. An alternative view rests on the extent to which the existence of Britain's empire had long served the interests of other nations, especially through her re-export trades and her financial institutions. Once other nations developed the wish and the machinery to secure these interests for themselves, Britain's role as middleman was no longer necessary. Britain's own tendency to trade increasingly with more-developed economies also made empire redundant.

These arguments grounded in 'political economy' are attractive but still present difficulties. They can easily blur the distinction between economic developments and political events, leaving unanswered the question as to how precisely the political decisions associated with decolonization can be linked to the coincidental economic patterns of the same period. For many a neo-Marxist this difficulty is resolved by arguing that decolonization has never been achieved. A transfer of political power took place, but it was merely the function of new leaders to continue the task of the imperial rulers, that of organizing local economies in ways which serve the interests of the capitalist world rather than their own.

2 The Machinery of Government and Policy-Making

Who ran the colonial empire? Constitutionally it was the Secretary of State for the Colonies who was answerable to Cabinet in the first instance and ultimately to Parliament. But, however impressive the political authority or departmental ability enjoyed by some Colonial Secretaries, in the examination of imperial policy it is necessary to probe beyond his office and consider inter-departmental relations within Whitehall, the internal organization of the Colonial Office and relations between London and colonial governments. The Colonial Secretary had always had the dual task of upholding HMG's policy in the colonies and protecting colonial interests from excessive metropolitan demands. Between the wars the Colonial Office was able to operate with minimal contact with other departments; only Palestine, Kenya and the West Indies were sources of occasional embarrassment to the Secretary of State in Cabinet or Parliament. During the 1940s, however, tension between British and colonial interests became more pronounced and there was a corresponding growth in inter-departmental consultation at both official and ministerial levels. For example, the Colonial Office liaised with the Ministries of Food and Supply and the Board of Trade on the mobilization of colonial resources for the war effort and post-war rehabilitation of the British economy (DOC 54); with the Foreign Office on the colonial implications of Allied strategy (DOC 16); with the War Office and the service ministries on the conduct of war and the re-occupation of fallen territories (DOC 26); with the India Office on the implications of a 'colonial charter' (DOC 17); with the Treasury on the UK contribution to colonial development and welfare and, conversely, colonial assistance to Britain at times of economic crisis (DOCs 27 and 44); and with the Dominions Office (from 1947 the Commonwealth Relations Office) on the questions of Central Africa

(DOCs 57 and 61) and constitutional status as, starting with Ceylon, colonies progressed towards Commonwealth membership.

The outcome of such exchanges, however, was often governed less by the Colonial Office's particular knowledge or formal responsibilities than by its political weakness. In the Cabinet hierarchy the Colonial Office did not rank with the 'great offices of state' like the Treasury, Foreign Office and Home Office. While there were a few Secretaries of State, such as Cranborne, Lyttelton and Macleod, whose skill and clout were respected by their Prime Ministers, the post was often occupied by political light-weights, like Malcolm MacDonald, or by elder (if not superannuated) statesmen like George Hall and James Griffiths. Even Creech Jones who has been called 'the most influential Colonial Secretary since Joseph Chamberlain'[1], was unimpressive in the House of Commons, was, like his predecessor, increasingly pre-occupied by the Palestine issue where the Foreign Secretary called the British tune, and was later regarded by Attlee as 'one of my mistakes'.

Even within his own Department the Colonial Secretary could not be in full control of policy-making. The nature of office organization and the variety of the colonies prevented this. Until the Second World War the Office was structured largely on a geographical basis; thus the West Indies (Public Record Office reference series CO 318), West Africa (CO 554), Nigeria (CO 583), Tanganyika (CO 691), Northern Rhodesia (CO 795), and so on. Most governors' in-coming despatches were matters of routine, frequently dealt with by the relevant territorial section without reference to the Secretary of State or his Parliamentary Under-Secretary. In 1927–8 a committee chaired by the Permanent Under-Secretary recommended the creation of 'Subject' departments to complement the work of the existing General division (CO 323) in the co-ordination of territorial administrations and in the provision of technical advice. Thus began regional series such as East Africa (CO 822), Eastern which included South-east Asia, Indian Ocean and the Far East (CO 825), and Africa (CO 847), and subject series like Economic (CO 852). CO 537, which had petered out in the late 1920s, was revived in the last years of the war;

covering all colonial territories, this series is central to the study of imperial policy in the years 1943–51 and its importance belies its original title 'Supplementary'.

C. N. Parkinson, in expounding his 'law' of bureaucratic expansion, has wryly cited Colonial Office activity under the aegis of his namesake, Sir Cosmo Parkinson, as a case in point.[2] More recently, however, historians have argued that the mushrooming of files and personnel and the spawning of Subject and Regional sections during the 1940s indicate a real growth of work and coherence of organization and policy which derived more from the Colonial Office's own creative response to war than from the *dirigisme* of the subsequent Labour government. Crucial, indeed, to the initiation of progressive departures in the fields of development, African administration and South-east Asian reconstruction were sectional heads, notably S. Caine, A. B. Cohen and G. E. Gent, not the Permanent Under-Secretaries, none of whom in the period from the late 1930s to the mid-1950s represented the new generation of radical thinking. Yet refreshing ideas on their own did not make for change; any policy which impinged on the interests of other Whitehall departments, as did imperial defence or expenditure on development and welfare, required Cabinet approval while the implementation of all new schemes depended upon the co-operation and capacity of departmental colleagues and colonial governments.

The original arrangement of Colonial Office business on geographic lines had reflected the variety of dependencies, as had the separate traditions of each colonial administration. Orthodoxy had held that the Colonial Office (Home Civil Service) and Colonial Services performed different functions, and careers in each had been differentiated accordingly. Moreover, individual colonial governments had acquired their own conditions of service, linguistic expertise, *esprit de corps* and tribal suspicion of 'outsiders' transferred from other colonies or seconded from Whitehall. In the 1930s recruitment to colonial administrations was placed on a uniform footing and 'beachcombing' (that is, the exchange of personnel between London and the locality) became more frequent. During the war London wrested much in the conduct of affairs from the man on the spot; this was no time to be unduly sensitive to customary practices and precedent. If the morale of some services, such as the Malayan and Nigerian, suffered as a result, this centralization strengthened links between governors and London and between the governments within different regions, while the Devonshire Scheme (1945–6) marked an advance in the recruitment and training of cadet field officers.

Though the balance of advantage swung in London's favour during the Second World War, imperial organization fell far short of becoming monolithic. As Cranborne told the Chinese Ambassador in September 1942, 'it was almost impossible to lay down a cut and dried policy applicable to all colonies alike'.[3] Moreover, after 1945 the high-tide of metropolitan direction ebbed. Whitehall placemen, like Gent in Malaya, Creasy in the Gold Coast and later Cohen in Uganda, were deflected from the routes mapped out in London; exponents of the 'local tradition', like Sir Philip Mitchell in Kenya, were once again vociferous. Furthermore, indigenous movements and the autochthonous developments of Afro-Asian societies placed immense strains upon the manipulative skills of metropolitan and local authorities alike.

3 The Colonial Empire in the 1930s

The history of colonial policy, especially as seen from the Colonial Office, has been marked by the tension between two general considerations. The view that colonial management should contribute significantly to Britain's strength and well-being has commonly confronted another which has emphasized Britain's moral or humanitarian obligation to promote the material welfare and general progress of colonial subjects. Frequently, of course, colonial affairs were settled without reference to such principles. The assumption that they were in harmony with each other, or required little effort of reconciliation, had a respectable intellectual pedigree; it was also a convenient resort for the unimaginative, the timid or precedent-ridden, and the majority of men who welcomed a quiet life. In the 1930s, however, such optimism or complacency was difficult to sustain. It became increasingly clear that, despite administrative reorganization in Whitehall, colonial policy in practice often lacked momentum or direction and served neither principle effectively.

The condition of Britain between the wars was such as to encourage statesmen to eye colonial resources with a view to their exploitation for metropolitan benefit, this being justified as the necessary pre-condition for advance in the colonies themselves. However, the persistence of worldwide economic depression and Britain's own economic malaise following the events of 1929–31 did much to emphasize how slender was the support which the empire – self-governing as well as colonial – either could or would give to metropolitan recovery. Official interest outside the Colonial Office became increasingly fitful. Similarly, most colonies found the terms of imperial trade turning against them and gained little obvious benefit from the first Colonial Development Act (1929). Not only had it been conceived with the interests of British industry in mind, but reduced local revenues and shortages of staff or expertise stifled colonial government attempts to take advantage of it. As growing colonial populations strained available employment, swelled the towns, and exacerbated the fall in agricultural incomes or labourers' wages, so shortages, taxes, and the relative success of white settlers or expatriate firms in obtaining financial reliefs, were felt more keenly. Everywhere there existed significant sectors of colonial opinion which felt deprived of adequate political opportunities either to voice their complaints or to influence administrative responses. The emergence of rudimentary trade unions and Western-style political associations indicated such needs and contributed to their definition, but were rarely capable of providing satisfaction.

It is therefore not surprising to find that popular discontents gave rise to vigorous protest. In the late 1920s, south-eastern Nigeria witnessed violent riots against the extension of colonial taxation; in 1930–1, and again in 1937–8, Gold Coast cocoa-farmers combined to withhold crops from the market in order to force higher prices from buyers; West African railway workers frequently went on strike, and in 1935 serious unrest spread widely among mineworkers on the copper belt in Northern Rhodesia. The decade had opened dramatically with the Indian Civil Disobedience movement, but most persistent were the disturbances in the West Indies, especially Jamaica, between 1935 and 1938.

These events gradually increased the attention given to colonial affairs beyond the innermost circles of the Colonial Office and the Colonial Service. Government responses were inescapable if only to maintain law and order, but there was great uncertainty and divided opinion as to the forms they should take. Although in India a broad strategy for containing local conflicts had been evolved – one which mixed economic inducements with political concession and a measure of repression – nevertheless agreement on balance and timing was still extremely difficult to achieve, as the extended prelude to the Government of India Act (1935) or discussion of Indian finances both illustrated. In other parts of the empire, particularly the African colonies, even the strategy to be employed was obscure. Too often experience gained in the colonies and the information accumulating slowly in London seemed to reveal problems without illuminating answers. Systems of 'indirect rule' using native authorities seemed, after the experience even of an enthusiast like Cameron in Tanganyika, far less capable and adaptable to wider responsibilities than had once been thought; their coexistence in the same territories with Legislative and Executive Councils often inhibited political development altogether. Labour problems, the results of unrestricted commodity production, the need for education and welfare provision, all evidently required tackling – somehow.

The mixture of routine response, resignation, uncertainty, and active search for more positive policies, with which the Colonial Office approached its tasks in the later 1930s is well-illustrated in the case of the West Indies. From one angle the problems of these colonies seemed insoluble. Excessively dependent on sugar as their export staple, the West Indies were the victims of world over-production, falling prices, and their inability to attract investment. With low wages and standards of living, little taxable wealth and poor education, they offered limited prospects for successful economic diversification. A growing population, and despairing or incompetent local politicians, threatened simply to intensify their stagnation. This diagnosis differed little from that made in the 1890s, and in the 1930s there seemed no more likelihood than before that Britain either could or would provide the very large, almost certainly continuing, financial support which alone was capable of bringing sustained improvement. Whitehall's further investigation of the sugar industry in 1930, subsequent attempts at protection and manipulation of the sugar market, and local enquiries into the unrest, only confirmed departmental conventional wisdom that 'solutions' were no more than wishful thinking (DOC 1). However, there were others less familiar with local precedents and possessing their own specialized skills who were prepared to challenge such views. Administrative changes in the Colonial Office, and eventually the interest of a new Secretary of State, stimulated fresh debate, as the Financial and Economic Adviser's reaction to the West Indies' troubles shows (DOC 2). In these quarters, the idea that the imperial government might do no more than endorse the limited findings of colonial enquiries into the immediate circumstances of riots in Barbados or Trinidad, was unacceptable. By June 1938 the argument for a complete re-examination of West Indian problems, on the assumption that a strong case could be made for more finance to be provided by the British government, had been thoroughly discussed and accepted within the Colonial Office.

Undoubtedly motives inside the office were mixed. Against the background of disturbances, officials had a sense that constructive suggestions were politically necessary, not least if departmental credibility was to be preserved. However, they were also responding sympathetically to other more general pressures for reappraisal and action. The West Indian disturbances had excited attention in Labour Party and trade-union circles, which in turn gave added point to the Colonial Office's decisions between 1936 and 1938 to appoint a Labour Adviser and to establish its own Social Services department. Not only were influential unofficial critics like W. M. Macmillan making the case for newly-constructive approaches to the West Indies. Other publications like R. L. Buell's *The Native Problem in Africa* (1928) and S. H. Frankel's *Capital Investment in Africa* (1938) were indicative of a more widespread concern to give direction to colonial policies. This culminated, again in 1938, with the publication in November of Lord Hailey's *An African Survey*. The production of three years' travel and research, it emphasized the pace of change in Africa, the urgent need for economic development, the growth of African demands for all manner of social services, and the administrative and political inadequacy of indirect rule. Before long Hailey's *Survey* was being recommended within the Colonial Office as the starting-point for thinking about colonial Africa's problems.

However, on this as on many other occasions, the Colonial Office had little power of its own for effective action, dependent as it was on the calibre, co-operativeness, and political skills of local colonial administrators, and the ambitions or political weight of other home departments as reflected in the priorities established by the Cabinet. Progress in West Indian policy, especially with its financial implications, hinged not least on Treasury agreement and Prime Ministerial approval. To the satisfaction of the Colonial Office,MacDonald's case for a general enquiry was accepted (DOC 3). Quite as notable as the rapidity of the Cabinet's decision to appoint a Royal Commission, especially in view of the tactical opportunities which this presented for delay, was the speed with which it was set up. Its members, carefully selected, were appointed in August 1938, and from October 1938 to March 1939 were at work in the Caribbean.

MacDonald's commitment to a better deal for the colonial empire was not confined to the West Indies. He began at once to review the workings of the Colonial Development Act, and by December had decided to incorporate the outcome of the West Indian enquiry into a much broader scheme for the whole empire. Clearly it is necessary at this point to consider a number of factors, the extent not only of the Secretary of State's genuine warm-heartedness but also his political ambitions, as well as the part played by the Office's own momentum as distinct from MacDonald's personal ability to enthuse his officials. Recent research suggests that his influence was considerable; yet the key to this lay less in personal advocacy than with circumstances favourable to his case. Reports from the Colonial Development Advisory Committee on the workings of the 1929 arrangements, as well as Hailey's influence, observation of colonial trouble-spots, and complaints from colonial governors like Bourdillon in Nigeria, all pointed not just to the limitations of existing methods of promoting colonial prosperity but to the artificiality of separating economic development from maintenance costs of projects and social welfare.

In the past this was the issue on which the Treasury had stood firm: the inclusion of welfare expenditure would undermine the imperial government's traditional insistence on colonial self-sufficiency, and would open the UK's Exchequer to unlimited demands for funds. The worsening international situation and rising defence costs meant that the Chancellor's unwillingness either to abandon that principle or respond generously to whatever the West India Royal Commission might recommend, increased. Nevertheless, throughout 1939 MacDonald and his senior officials developed undeterred their plans to enlarge considerably the sums available for development, to set up a Colonial Research Fund, admit welfare projects, and to restore Colonial Office control over the expenditure.

Enthusiasm for colonial development thus revived in the late 1930s, in response to various dissatisfactions, political necessity and public embarrassment. It was associated with a pronounced concern for popular welfare, and for the first time the insistence that this must be locally-funded was muted. It would be wrong to conclude, however, that decisive or irreversible changes of direction in colonial policy had occurred. Evidence of hard thinking about the political future of most colonies was still conspicuous by its absence; and in India the leisurely implementation of the 1935 Act through the elections of 1937 conveyed neither enthusiasm nor sense of momentum. The reassertion of principles of imperial trusteeship remained mixed with metropolitan self-interest. This was indicated occasionally in plans to use colonial territory as currency for exchange in the diplomatic appeasement of Germany. The general lack of sympathy for such schemes on the British side was perhaps informed by a feeling that the ancient dream of complementarity might still have something in it. Of Britain's total imports, those from empire and commonwealth sources increased from 24.5 percent in 1931 to 37.3 percent in 1937; their share of British exports rose from 32.6 percent to nearly 40 percent. In 1937, the Secretary of State for the Colonies saw fit to establish a Colonial Empire Marketing Board, confirming the fact that the empire's importance to British trade was rising steadily at this time.

4 The Outbreak of the Second World War and the Mobilization of Colonial Resources

The outlook for any general reshaping of colonial policy in the summer of 1939 was, however, as uncertain as the international situation was tense. Not only had the 'moral disarmament' of empire not reached the point where the 'dilemmas of trusteeship' were easily resolved; it was still far from clear whether or to what extent the banner of colonial development and welfare being embroidered in the Colonial Office would prove an acceptable standard for the Cabinet when the costs of unfurling it came to be counted. Very soon, however, decisions had to be made. The declaration of war against Germany on 3 September 1939 not only seemed to jeopardize any hope of sustaining MacDonald's recent initiatives but threatened to disrupt very seriously routine administration and day-to-day life throughout the empire. No territory could be considered invulnerable. All expenditure at once became liable to scrutiny in the light of its contribution to the war effort, and, following the precedents of 1914–18, it rapidly became clear that colonial policy would now be dictated in many respects by metropolitan needs. Not only were colonial troops, like the King's African Rifles and the Royal West African Frontier Force, mobilized and placed under War Office control; meetings of the Colonial Development Advisory Committee were suspended, and the Treasury took steps to halt all existing colonial development schemes as well as the implementation of new ones unless wartime demands justified otherwise.

Two questions are here of particular importance to historians. What demands did the imperial government make on its colonies as the war unfolded? What impact did these have on colonial administrations and their subjects? Detailed answers of course vary greatly between territories, but it was in these same general terms that Colonial Office officials addressed colonial governors in September 1939 as they tried to establish the principle of 'business as usual' and anxiously anticipated the problems likely to arise (DOCs 4 and 5). These early circular telegrams show the Colonial Office already very conscious of the part it had to play throughout the war as an intermediary between sometimes insensitive partners. On the one hand it faced the demands of metropolitan departments and the expectations of British taxpayers, who felt themselves at the centre of the war and entitled to every possible support. On the other, it was familiar with colonial difficulties and complaints, and was concerned to protect legitimate local interests as well as the colonial administrative service's achievements and conditions of work.

It was partly this Janus-like awareness which enabled MacDonald to develop arguments strong enough to safeguard pre-war plans. He was, however, aided by the West India Royal Commission, whose report was submitted to him in December 1939. As anticipated, its recommendations sketched out a comprehensive development plan for the islands. The newly-grown wisdom of the Colonial Office was much in evidence in the emphasis placed on the interdependence of social welfare and economic growth. An interventionist future for colonial administration was seen as essential, with the reform of landholding systems and the development of efficient, self-sufficient peasant agriculture being encouraged as the corollary of controlled production and marketing of principal export crops. The report advocated the establishment of a regional fund, to be placed, with the entire planning exercise, under a new Comptroller directly responsible to the Secretary of State.

If these recommendations implied a great deal, the report itself was openly critical. Together with the evidence submitted to Lord Moyne and his colleagues, it was regarded in Whitehall as an embarrassing indictment of past inefficiency and neglect by the imperial government. The result was an inter-departmental debate early in 1940 as to the wisdom of publication in circumstances where it might provide enemies with telling propaganda and alienate the sympathies of potential allies, notably the USA (DOC 6). Given the publicity received by the Commission and the interest in its outcome, it was politically impossible even in wartime to brush it aside.

Eventually the caution of the Foreign Office triumphed and the Cabinet kept back the full report until the end of the war. However, the arguments from wartime expediency could work both ways, and the Colonial Office's belief that colonial development and welfare itself had considerable practical and propaganda value was widely shared. As the head of the Africa Division, Sir Arthur Dawe, observed 'Politically the whole point is that we should make a big thing of the welfare side. Economic Development on its own would be construed as a means of exploiting the colonies for the war effort'.[4] The recommendations of the West India Commission were therefore published in February 1940 alongside a new Colonial Development and Welfare Act, as testimony to the values for which Britain was fighting and a sign of her confidence in victory. MacDonald's enthusiasms were taken up by colleagues now convinced that this commitment of imperial interest and funds would at least check colonial unrest, refurbish Britain's reputation as a colonial power, and help to ward off anti-colonial pressures for change when the war was over (DOC 7).

Made in the period of the 'phoney war', this commitment was increasingly difficult to live up to, and the Treasury persistently tried to limit the provision of funds. The West Indies, under the regime of Sir Frank Stockdale (Comptroller from 1 September 1940), were the principal beneficiaries. It is unclear quite how much this owed to American ambitions and interest in the region, so evident in the Anglo-American Caribbean Commission set up in March 1942 and in the subsequent West Indian Conference. Commitments to the West Indian colonies under the Act had reached £8.7m by 31 March 1945, more or less equalling the total spent on the empire between 1929 and 1940.[5] Sums such as these, however, were insignificant in the scale of wartime finance. They were often barely memorable for most colonial subjects in the face of more immediate pressures, however striking they seemed to metropolitan imaginations.

After defence, the principal task of government in the colonial empire was to reconcile the maintenance of normal economic activity and an acceptable standard of living with the conservation of resources and, increasingly, their mobilization for the war effort. The result was that exchange controls, restrictions on trade with non-sterling countries, import and export quotas, price control, and rationing, all proliferated. Colonial administrative staff stretched themselves still more thinly, and co-opted unofficials to run the new control boards and regional organizations. Inevitably there occurred far-reaching changes in relations between the governors and the governed.

Colonial primary producers almost at once found their markets seriously disturbed. Boards were therefore established to purchase crops in bulk and to dispose of them at guaranteed prices. Seychelles copra, Palestinian citrus fruit, and Jamaican bananas were all handled in this way. Most important was the West African Cocoa Control Board, established in 1940 and reconstituted in 1942 as the West African Produce Board to include vegetable oils and groundnuts. Along with overseas markets, foreign supplies were disrupted, whether through loss of alien suppliers, the diversion of UK manufacturing capacity, shipping shortages, or American export controls after August 1941. Stockpiling of foodstuffs, and attempts to curb black markets or speculation involved further administrative devices such as the British West Indies Food Conference; they were complemented by the promotion of local industry to provide import-substitutes.

Indian and colonial production became steadily more important to the war effort as UK stocks and dollar reserves ran out. Indian industry expanded enormously to provide vast supplies of munitions, steel, chemicals, tents and shoes, while tropical raw materials acquired vital strategic importance after the Japanese victories in South-east Asia (DOCs 10 and 11). Inevitably the conscription of labour followed. For the production of Tanganyika's sisal and pyrethrum, numbers of conscripts rose from about 8500 or 3.3 percent of the labour force late in 1942 to an authorized 30–35 000 by spring 1945. The Nigerian administration conscripted in all nearly 93 000 labourers for periods of up to four months in the tin mines. Volunteers and conscripts swelled the numbers available for military service. Local military forces in the colonial empire on the eve of the war totalled 43 000 and by May 1945, 473 000; nearly 79 percent were Africans. Institutions were created to organize these demands. The Eastern Group Supply Council with regional offices in the Middle East and East Africa was established under the auspices of the Government of India, while from 1942 a Resident Minister in West Africa linked the West African War Council with the War Cabinet's Africa Committee in London.

Colonial finance also fuelled the war, first of all by direct monetary contributions. Northern Rhodesia, for example, by 31 December 1943 provided an estimated £3.46m in direct loans, Post Office savings, War Stocks, War Savings Certificates, and military contributions, compared with its estimated total annual revenue in 1942 of £2.6m. The Sultan of Johore in 1940–1 made gifts of £750 000. Support also came in the form of Sterling Balances. Purchases of war materials from India, the colonies, and other members of the Sterling Area, were paid for immediately by local governments while the British government credited sterling securities to colonial accounts in London. These totalled £2 723m at the end of the war; the colonies (together with Syria, Lebanon, and Iraq) held £607m and India a colossal £1 138m.

Indian and colonial contributions were thus very great, and it was against this background that the Colonial Office tried to keep alive its progressive vision. Presenting the department's estimates in June 1942, the Under-Secretary of State argued that from this co-operation in war would inevitably flow a continuing partnership in the future development of the empire and Commonwealth. The 1940 Act was the principal sign of Britain's commitment to, and her chief means of, cementing this relationship (DOC 12). This new language of partnership was significant, but, while acknowledging that colonial war efforts deserved tangible recognition, Macmillan's speech ignored the many colonial citizens unimpressed by the offer of the 1940 Act as a *quid pro quo*.

Co-operation in the war was frequently unwilling, resistance to its demands commonplace, and resentment of its impact lasting. Protest was greatest in India where Congress ministries in the provincial governments resigned over the Viceroy's failure to consult Indian leaders on declaring war.

Non-co-operation escalated until eventually in August 1942 the Congress party launched its 'Quit India' campaign, whereupon its leaders were interned. An Indian National Army was organized to assist the Japanese against the British. Elsewhere the imprisonment of political activists, such as radical leaders of the Malayan Kesatuan Melayu Muda, and banning of political organizations, like the Kikuyu Central Association, were also not uncommon. Nevertheless, colonial authorities were very aware of the frustrations which existed, and colonial populations, like that in Britain, were the objects of a sustained propaganda campaign by the imperial government designed to uphold morale. Conscription and requisitioning were understandably unpopular, and could seriously affect the civilian population: a combination of military demands and drought, for example, turned Kenya from an exporter into an importer of maize by 1943. Inflation was everywhere a worry, creating hardship as costs of living rose faster than wages, and it fed on itself. Rising government expenditure on wartime requirements increased money supplies in the absence of sufficient consumer goods or determined taxation to absorb surplus funds. Amid the administrative quandaries and shortages, crises like the famine in Bengal during 1943, when between three and four million died, were doubly difficult to manage.

Grievances and losses were, however, far from the whole story of the war. Steps taken to prevent profiteering were often unsuccessful; industrial and agricultural producers of commodities in short supply were frequently able to look after their own. Willing collaboration with colonial administrations, and even opposition, often brought political if not material advantages. Thus the Muslim League moved in to fill the vacuum created by Congress' non-co-operation; settler farmers in East and Central Africa used the economic and political opportunities to repair the ravages of the 1930s and to entrench their position; West African politicians and trade unionists, in particular, made the most of popular grievances and began to widen their support.

The growth of towns and urban employment, involvement in a modern economy and contact with colonial government, awareness of a wider world experienced not least through military service, technical training, and political consciousness, were all enhanced by the war and often multiplied critics of both colonial rulers and those associated with them. Yet colonial governments were not necessarily weaker because they faced rapidly-changing circumstances and more complicated tasks. There is no doubt that the colonial service suffered from overwork, too few recruits, and lack of material incentives; but the war also brought new challenges and opportunities. Many administrative lessons were learnt, the range of state activity and powers was greater than ever before, and wartime mobilization – in many ways hugely successful – spawned new political alliances as well as reinforcing others. How to continue the adjustment of colonial policies to serve the objects of both metropolitan well-being and trusteeship was an open question in the later years of the war. The answers were crucially dependent on both international developments and metropolitan decisions.

5 The Second World War: International Relations and Colonial Policy

The Second World War heightened both the harsh reality and the rhetoric of imperial commitments. On the one hand it revealed Britain's inability to defend a two-hemisphere empire, plunged the country deeper into debt, encouraged nationalist resistance and subjected Britain to American anti-imperialism. On the other hand, the concept of 'trusteeship' was refurbished in the fashionable language of 'partnership' and the government pledged itself not only to the welfare of colonial peoples but also to their eventual self-government. Under the impact of war the British people, as A. J. P. Taylor has put it, 'ceased to believe' in empire.[6] Yet this view of the relationship between war and decolonization must be qualified not least by the fact that the governing élite had other ideas. Churchill, for one, had not become the King's first minister to preside over the liquidation of the British Empire. Clearly, imperial resources, outposts and troops were being harnessed to the world-wide effort. Imperial solidarity, indeed, was both a war aim and a means to that end. After the fall of France (June 1940) Britain and her Empire stood alone against the Axis – 'this was their finest hour'.

However, the Empire alone did not hold the key to eventual victory; US support was equally important. Appeals for assistance were answered in the Lend–Lease Act of March 1941. Though the volume of aid before Pearl Harbor was small compared with what later crossed the Atlantic and though the transaction was not without its advantages for America, by the time the USA entered the war in December 1941 Britain was heavily dependent upon her. This reliance on America, it became increasingly clear, was not to be without its cost: aid to Britain was always to an important degree conditional, for, although there was no coherent American view on British imperialism, there was a general mistrust of it. It was felt to obstruct free trade, prevent self-determination and reinforce the worst features of Britain's class-ridden society. By demonstrating Britain's vulnerability, war soon provided America with the opportunity to press for change in return for her support. The first real sign of this came when, after their meeting off Newfoundland in August 1941, Churchill and Roosevelt issued a statement affirming their solidarity of purpose and nobility of principle in the face of Axis propaganda. Article 3 of this Atlantic Charter seemed to many observers to commit both men to self-government for all peoples (DOC 8).

At the time the Atlantic Charter was drafted the issue of self-determination appeared less explosive than did the economic aspects of British imperialism. Americans were eager to exploit Britain's difficulties in order to strengthen their position in the Caribbean and to establish interests in the Middle East, India and South-east Asia which had hitherto lain largely within the European sphere. Nonetheless, the Colonial Office, which had not been consulted by those who drew up the Charter, had misgivings about Article 3's implications of precipitate and uniform decolonization; British 'trusteeship' meant paternalism, gradualism and respect for variety of tradition and circumstance. Reporting to the House of Commons on 9 September 1941, Churchill too took pains to exclude the British Empire from the purview of Article 3 which, he said, applied to 'the States and nations of Europe now under the Nazi yoke' (DOC 9). Yet the Prime Minister's statement did not settle the question of Britain's intentions for her Empire.

To Churchill's relief, Japan's attack on Pearl Harbor (7/8 December) brought the USA into the war; victory was assured. To his dismay the loss of Singapore (15 February 1942) exposed both India and Australia to invasion; the empire was in greater jeopardy than ever. American assistance was essential for the recovery of lost territories but Americans were in no mood to fight for reactionary objectives. The fall of Singapore unleashed on both sides of the Atlantic an onslaught of criticism of Britain's imperial record while the aspirations of Gandhi and the Indian National Congress provided progressives with a cause.

The transfer of power to India and Pakistan lies beyond the scope of this collection of documents. However, Indian developments and their effects on Anglo-American relations have an important bearing on British attitudes to the rest of the Empire. Pressed by his Labour partners in the coalition and by liberal opinion within the US administration, Churchill despatched Stafford Cripps to negotiate with Indian political leaders in March 1942. In effect, Cripps offered them independence after the war in return for their co-operation during it. Between them, Prime Minister, Viceroy and Congress ensured Cripps' failure. Nevertheless the Raj succumbed neither to the 'Quit India' rebellion nor to the Japanese attack, while Britain's stock in America rose as a result of the Mission since, as a member of Cripps' staff reported from the USA '[it] demonstrated that the Indian problem was not simple and that it was more a problem within India than between Britain and India'.[7]

Meanwhile Cranborne also indicated the widespread determination to retain imperial control when he took up the cudgels on behalf of British rule in South-east Asia and the Far East (DOC 13). Gent of the Eastern Department lamented Foreign Office 'defeatism' and its apparent subservience to 'the supposed American policy of preventing the restoration of British sovereignty in Malaya, Hong Kong, and possibly Burma too'.[8] The different approaches of Attlee, Cranborne, Eden and Amery to the Far Eastern question are illustrated in the record of their inter-departmental meeting held on 10 September 1942 (DOC 16). Before the month was out the Foreign and Colonial Offices had agreed that Britain should regain her dependencies after the war but should develop their resources, ensure their security and prepare them for eventual self-government, in accordance with the principles of the Atlantic Charter and within the framework of some Pacific Regional Council (about which the Colonial Office was less enthusiastic than the Foreign Office). Cranborne took pride in the conduct of his countrymen overseas and was keen to restate in more relevant terms Britain's concept of colonial trusteeship if only to counter US proposals for the international trusteehip of all European dependencies in the area.

Harold Macmillan's speech on 24 June 1942 also has its place here, in the context of calculated adjustments to imperial policy under international pressure. He reiterated the orthodoxy of gradualism – for example, 'self-government without security means nothing' – but he also declared 'the governing principle of the Colonial Empire' to be 'the principle of partnership between the elements composing it'. 'Within the fabric of the Commonwealth lies the future of the Colonial territories' (DOC 12). This intentionally ill-defined, ambiguous concept of 'partnership' whetted the appetitite of the Fabian Colonial Bureau whose members included Dr Rita Hinden, Professor W. A. Lewis, Professor W. M. Macmillan, Margery Perham and Leonard Woolf. Formed in 1940, the Bureau had been pressing for a Colonial Charter and on 1 July 1942 its chairman, Creech Jones, extracted from Harold Macmillan a promise to issue 'a comprehensive set of declarations' substantiating Churchill's brief statement about the imperial implications of the Atlantic Charter. In compiling such a portfolio Colonial Office staff were embarrassed to discover that such declarations as had been made were vague and non-committal. Obviously it would have been 'dangerous and foolish' to publish a White Paper based on such slender evidence (DOC 14), and the Colonial Office looked for ways out of the difficulty.

First, Creech Jones was partially disarmed by the government. The Labour MP, like many of his colleagues, had no wish to destroy the Empire; his brand of constructive colonialism sought to convert Empire into Commonwealth to the benefit of all concerned. Both Creech Jones and Lord Hailey attended the Conference of the American-based Institute of Pacific Relations at Mont Tremblant, Quebec, in December 1942. Although it was a non-governmental gathering, Whitehall briefed the British members and between them this representative of the working-man and the intellectual patrician presented an acceptable face of imperialism to North American critics; in stressing the notion of 'partnership' they won a battle in the propaganda war.

Cranborne also suggested, though without much confidence, a change of tack away from a unilateral Colonial Charter and towards a joint Anglo-American declaration, an idea which the British Ambassador in Washington had already discussed with the US Secretary of State (DOC 15). Given the British purpose, to educate British public opinion and to appease opposition, this was thought promising and officials went ahead. On 9 December 1942 the War Cabinet approved the despatch of a draft joint-declaration to the Dominions and the Ambassador at Washington. Viceroy Linlithgow was also kept informed. Like Cranborne, Linlithgow felt that the best form of defence was attack; he argued that it was 'essential to avoid adopting an apologetic attitude and equally essential to avoid allowing United States of America to come in on field of which they have no experience' (DOC 17). As the result of Dominion comments, inter-departmental discussions and the deliberations of a Cabinet Committee (Attlee, Eden, Cranborne and the new Secretary of State for Colonial Affairs, Stanley (DOC 18), the draft was revised and the final version was handed to Cordell Hull by Halifax in early February 1943. The principal features of the British draft were paternalism, gradualism and international co-operation through regional machinery. Britain welcomed United Nations participation in regional defence but insisted upon her sole right to administer her colonies; and while she declared that it was 'the duty of "Parent" or "Trustee" States to guide and develop the social, economic and political institutions of the Colonial peoples until they are able without danger to themselves and others to discharge the responsibilities of government', the draft refrained from mentioning independence, let alone a timetable for political advance.[9]

By contrast Cordell Hull's version, called 'Draft of a Declaration by the United Nations on National Independence' (9 March 1943), asserted the applicability of the Atlantic Charter 'to all nations and to all peoples', made great play with the word 'independence' (not used in the Atlantic Charter itself), insisted on fixing dates for its achievement and proposed the formation of an International Trusteeship Administration (like the 1919 Mandates system) to guard the interests of those peoples as yet unprepared for full independence.[10] The American and British positions appeared irreconcilable – there were, as Lord Hailey put it rather mildly, 'difficulties both of substance and of form' (DOC 20) – and the British hoped that the enterprise to issue a joint declaration would die a natural death, though Hull persisted with it at least until the end of 1943.

By this time, however, the Colonial Office was less afraid

that US sentiment would be foisted upon it by the Foreign Office. It had met the challenges of wartime mobilization and office reorganization; it had also weathered the storm of criticism that had been brewing since August 1941 and had broken in early 1942. It had emerged with a fresher image and renewed confidence. This mood was conveyed in the debate on Colonial Supply on 13 July 1943 when Stanley issued what amounted to a unilateral declaration of intent (DOC 21). In themselves his pledges were unremarkable; each had its antecedents in earlier pronouncements and their reiteration was not designed to place colonial policy on a new course. Nonetheless, their combination in a single statement suggested change and this startled those outside his immediate circle of advisers. Indeed, in combating American strictures, Colonial Office officials had at last been obliged to supply their masters with an intellectually coherent justification of that gradualist strategy which had, in earlier and calmer times, been taken for granted if not ignored. They had not merely dug in on old lines of defence but had advanced their position in significant ways. In response to what they regarded as the loose ideology of 'national self-determination', Colonial Office staff now argued that the material progress of colonies through planned development and welfare programmes was a prerequisite for political concessions. To counter what they took to be the injudicious proposal of Great Power Trusteeship, they argued that the regional co-ordination of somewhat disparate colonial territories and international co-operation particularly in defence would contribute to world peace, British interests and the viability of future self-governing successor states.

As hopes for a joint declaration withered from late 1943 and as planning the new world order took on real meaning at Cairo, Dumbarton Oaks, Yalta and San Francisco, so the inferiority of the Colonial Office in the Whitehall hierarchy and its impotence in international affairs were again revealed. It is true that US anti-imperialism grew more muted as the war proceeded but British resistance and Colonial Office polemic were less influential in curbing the enthusiasm of Americans for Afro-Asian independence than the Americans' own exercise of world power and their anticipation of the profits of free-trade imperialism after the war.

Still, the exercise in public relations between the summer of 1942 and the summer of 1943 had at least clarified the ideological context in which political planning for the colonies would be conducted.

6 The Second World War and the Planning of Political Development

1942–5 was the era of the 'master plan' both in war and on the home front but, as it mapped out the future, the Colonial Office was not moved by any general directive from the Cabinet or the Secretary of State embracing the empire as a whole. Proposals arose rather from divisional initiatives and were often affected by factors other than the recast ideology of trusteeship. Constitutional plans more particularly were a mixture of responses to Britain's wartime and post-war requirements and to circumstances and commitments inherited from the 1930s. Although hostilities appeared to wipe the slate clean in some countries, for example in the Far East, and thus tempted London officials to build *a priori*, and though the results were often more consistent than the botching of the previous decade when metropolitan and local interests had offset each other, yet wartime planners for all territories grappled to a greater or lesser degree with the legacies of indirect rule, race relations, plural societies and regional co-ordination. Some of the centre's schemes were also drastically modified by pressures on the periphery when, on the outbreak of peace, the time came for their implementation. Political planning during the war was essentially an administrative exercise and was often little influenced by indigenous colonial or 'nationalist' demands. Progress towards self-government, it was held, depended upon economic advance which in turn necessitated improvements in the machinery of the colonial state. The integration of divided societies was one aspect of such administrative reform; another was the closer association of territories in regional groups.

Space has not, of course, allowed the inclusion of documents relating to every territory for which the Colonial Office had responsibility. One omission is Ceylon which was still regarded as the blue-riband colony, played a pivotal role in the campaign against Japan and gained independence in 1948. However, the island was well on the way to self-government by the time our period starts; the decisive break-through came in 1938–9 when a cabinet form of government was achieved. Thereafter the run to independence within the Commonwealth was, in the words of K. M. de Silva, 'smooth and peaceful'.[11] What political excitement there was, occurred not in Anglo-Ceylonese relations but within Ceylonese politics.

As regards the lands further east, however, the Second World War marks a watershed in imperial policy. In the 1930s Britain's disparate empire in South-east Asia had consisted of the colony of the Straits Settlements (Penang, Malacca and Singapore), nine protected Malay states (four of which formed the Federated Malay States) and three Borneo protectorates of which one was the kingdom of the White Rajahs of Sarawak, another was administered by the North Borneo Company and the third was the Brunei sultanate. In the Malayan peninsula Britain recognised the sovereignty of the Malay Rulers, the autonomy of the Malay states and the special position of the Malay people as distinct from the immigrant Chinese and Indians. For progressives such arrangements were inefficient and socially divisive. The fall of Singapore offered a chance for change; imperial strategy, the economic importance of Malaya and the contrasting backwardness of Borneo precluded a return to the *status quo ante*. Under the leadership of G. E. J. Gent, who had grown increasingly impatient with pre-war constraints, the Eastern Department recommended a fresh approach to South-east Asia and, in conjunction with the War Office (since on its reoccupation the region would first be administered by the military), drafted directives for an initial Civil Affairs Administration which would dovetail with a long-term policy. They proposed (i) a Malayan Union of the nine Malay States, Penang and Malacca, (ii) the separate colony of Singapore, and (iii) negotiations with Rajah Vyner Brooke and Company Directors with a view to establishing Crown Colony government in Sarawak and North Borneo. Cruel to be kind, the British would assert direct rule; instead of shoring up historic sultanates they would work towards a system of government for the region as a whole in which all races might participate. As a step towards the eventual creation of a self-governing Dominion of South-east Asia they proposed the appointment of a Governor-General (after 1948, Commissioner-General) to co-ordinate the policies of the various colonial administrations. Malay sovereignty was an especially sensitive issue; the Malayan Union involved new treaties with the Sultans by which the Crown would acquire at least 'a scintilla of sovereignty'. In the Cabinet Committee, 22 March 1944, which considered the principles of policy to be followed after the war, Attlee was concerned lest 'the expression of an intention to re-negotiate treaties with the rulers might commit us to reinstate them whatever we or the people might wish'. Radical though its Malayan proposals were, the Colonial Office was not prepared to abolish the institution of sultanate and Stanley pointed out that 'actions which seemed democratic and progressive in the West might be very differently interpreted in the East'. The Committee decided that the directive to planners be rewritten in order to keep options open on the future status of the Malay Rulers.[12] On 31 May the War Cabinet approved the Report of the Committee (DOC 26) and authorized the Secretary of State to proceed accordingly.

Thereafter the plans for the military's Civil Affairs Administrations and for the subsequent civilian governments in Malaya and Borneo grew more and more detailed and inflexible. Absence from South-east Asia and wartime secrecy afforded officials in London huge advantages; on the other hand they were unable to test reactions as they went along. Given the local disruption during and immediately after the Japanese occupation, it is not surprising that British schemes, particularly the Malayan Union, provoked opposition. Retired Malayan civil servants, whom the Colonial Office had deliberately kept in the dark, were enraged. More significant was the campaign mounted by the 'politically quiescent' Malays who, fearing that Britain's new-found interest in democracy would lead to the supremacy of the Malayan Chinese, forced the British to replace the Malayan Union with a Federation (February 1948) guaranteeing the Sultans' sovereignty and the special position of the Malays. Nevertheless, there could be no return to normalcy and the principles of multiracialism and regionalism remained to guide Britain's Malayan strategy in the following years even though local circumstances necessitated caution and compromise.

Africa did not experience the dislocation of war as dramatically as did Asia but planning its political future was no less complicated for that. War added to the momentum of discussion triggered off by Hailey's *An African Survey* (1938). At the Carlton Hotel in October 1939 Secretary of State MacDonald launched a major review of African policy. One result was the report by Hailey, assisted by F. J. Pedler of the Colonial Office, on *Native Administration and Political Development in British Tropical Africa*.[13] Circumspectly Hailey advised the association of educated Africans in the political institutions and central administration of West African colonies. At the same time he warned against 'premature "constitution-mongering" in Africa', again stressed the prime importance of economic development and welfare and called for parallel progress of the 'native authorities in the sphere of local government'. On the basis of Hailey's report, O. G. R. Williams drafted 'a very rough tentative plan of political development' proceeding in five stages from municipal councils through legislative councils towards self-government, though he studiously avoided the issue of executive councils and the trap of an explicit timetable (DOC 22). Commenting on this paper at a meeting with the Secretary of State in July 1943, Hailey seemed to advance his position and, with the impact of the First World War upon India in mind, suggested that HMG should issue a statement in favour of responsible government and that Africans should be brought into the governors' executive councils in a semi-ministerial capacity (DOC 23). However, both suggestions were felt at the time to be unrealistic and Hailey himself was uneasy when Burns (Governor, Gold Coast) and Bourdillon (Governor, Nigeria) succeeded in opening their Executive Councils to African unofficials; he was further dismayed when the post-war constitutions for those dependencies placed unofficial majorities in their Legislative Councils. Yet these changes were not intended to 'sell the pass' to nationalist politicians, still less to smooth the pillow of the dying empire; rather they were attempts to project traditional leaders from local administration into central government and territory-wide politics. Indeed, governors, London officials and Lord Hailey were at one in assuming self-government to be generations distant, in regarding the chief as central to political advance and in subordinating constitutional issues to those of economics. With regard to the affairs of British West Africa as a whole, policy was co-ordinated at a high level first through the Resident Minister (Lord Swinton, 1942–4) and later through the West African Council (created in November 1945) but any advance towards federating the four territories was obstructed by the discrepant political maturity of the Gold Coast and Nigeria on the one hand, and Sierra Leone and the Gambia on the other.

In Central and East Africa, where settler communities made West African models of little relevance, there was less room for a Colonial Office initiative during the Second World War. On the contrary, the metropolitan need for raw materials had aggravated the tension between settler ambitions and HMG's commitment to native interests, and had enhanced the former's self-importance and bargaining position. The Bledisloe Commission (1939) had recommended the long-term British objective in Central Africa to be the closer union of the Rhodesias and Nyasaland provided that African interests were safeguarded. Some members of Churchill's coalition sympathized with the settler desire for amalgamation; officials in the Colonial Office, recognizing its economic and strategic sense, sought a formula which would protect the position of the African in Northern Rhodesia and Nyasaland, improve that of the Southern Rhodesian African and keep at bay both liberal criticism and South African northward expansionism. Like Williams on West Africa, G. F. Seel took Hailey's Report as his starting-point (DOC 19); but, owing to the fact that the Colonial Office possessed fewer cards in Central Africa, his proposals were not developed. By March 1944 the Cabinet decided against the amalgamation of the three dependencies and on 18 October the Secretary of State declared in Parliament that it was impracticable 'under existing circumstances'. The political complications of regionalization in Central Africa were as worrisome as the economic benefits were attractive, and so it was made clear that the Central African Council (October 1944) was designed to foster co-operation but not as a stepping-stone to federation. Similarly in East Africa, while in 1943 the Governor of Kenya presented a scheme for the amalgamation of Kenya, Uganda and Tanganyika, the Colonial Office commitment to 'native paramountcy' ensured its defeat and when, at the end of 1945, an East African High Commission was announced, care was taken to stress that its object was the promotion of economic links through, say, common services, and not the region's political union.

One fragmented area of the tropical empire with a chequered history of federal experiments was the West Indies. There had been, for example, the federation of the Leeward Islands in 1871, the abortive attempt in 1875–6 to link Barbados more closely with the Windwards from which Barbados was separated in 1885, the merger of St Kitts, Nevis and Anguilla in 1882, and that of Trinidad and Tobago in 1899. The Moyne Commission, too, looked forward to the eventual emergence of a West Indian federation and recommended immediate steps towards the union of the Leewards and Windwards although its report focused on development and welfare. From 1943, however, Colonial Office staff became convinced, partly as a result of the experiences of the Comptroller's organization, that the local and imperial benefits arising from federation would outweigh any objections that might be voiced by Americans to British interference in their backyard or by local élites more interested in the political advance of their separate islands. Without the complication of powerful white-settler communities, regionalism here provided a politically-acceptable defence against external pressure from the USA.

Nevertheless, the autonomy enjoyed by individual West Indian governments, mistrust of the Bahamas for the 'West Indian colonies proper', inter-island rivalry and the suspicion of Jamaica and Trinidad felt by smaller islands, race and the presence in Trinidad and British Guiana of large East Indian communities, and the fact that several colonies had already made significant moves towards internal self-government (for example, the Jamaican constitution of November 1944) all complicated the 'regionalization' of the British West Indies. In a despatch to West Indian governors in March 1945, Stanley declared his desire for West Indian federation and called for the views of the Caribbean legislatures. Almost a year later P. Rogers of the West India Department summarized the case for federation and the local reactions to it – Rogers felt that the economic and financial arguments were 'more doubtful' than the political need to break down the 'extreme parochialism' of British West Indian islands – and he went on to draft the basis of a conference agenda (DOC 34). There was sufficient support for closer association for Creech Jones to convene a conference at Montego Bay, Jamaica, in September 1947. Here the principle of federation was accepted and a Standing Closer-Association Committee was set up to examine the practicalities of unification.

Finally we should note the colonies deemed incapable of achieving and maintaining independence either on their own or in combination with others. These were the scattered island-fortresses and city-states like Malta, Gibraltar, Cyprus, Aden, St Helena, the Falklands and others, to which the embattled empire owed so much. Although Malta, for example, was the subject of a constitutional commission in 1946 as a result of which full responsible government (abolished in 1936) was restored, it was the defensive role of these islands and not the question of their self-determination that preoccupied the government during the war. It was not until late 1948, when political developments elsewhere in the empire made their predicament more obvious, that the Attlee administration tackled the issue of constitutional development in smaller colonies (DOC 52).

7 Colonial Policy, Economic Development and Welfare 1943–5

It has been seen that the summer of 1943 marks a watershed in the wartime history of metropolitan policy towards the colonial empire. Stanley's speech in July (DOC 21) signified the end of that fitful process of restating imperial goals begun in the dreary conditions of 1938–9 and hastened forward by the demands of war. The piecemeal definition of goals for colonial territories had played an important part in the evolution of Britain's publicly-stated war aims, contributing its mite to moral uplift, public order, and goodwill among the Allies. The Colonial Office, with its additional responsibility for mobilizing colonial resources, had found its hands strengthened. Stanley's confidence, however, did not spring simply from a sense of relief and achievement; it also reflected the growth of general concern with the future. Hasty improvisation and day-to-day preoccupation with survival had given way in many places to the routines of war. In the breathing-space thus provided, serious government thinking about reconstruction began early in 1943. The Labour Party published its views on post-war colonial policy in March. The military situation had by then definitely turned in the Allies' favour: plans for the invasion of France, 'Operation Overlord', began to be formed in August, and the prospect of Germany's defeat brightened with the Italian armistice on 7 September. In November, Churchill finally appointed to his Cabinet a minister for post-war reconstruction. The Colonial Office was also under pressure to do more than rest on its laurels.

Part of its task had of course been done. In making commitments to economic development and welfare, in its advocacy of 'partnership', and by reasserting the goal of self-government, Colonial Office officials had already indicated their programme for a future some way ahead of most domestic departments of state. They were also fairly clear as to their priorities. The promotion of political change during the war, examined in the previous section, was unsystematic and generally limited in extent, not just because it reflected colonial variety and the accidents of gubernatorial enthusiasm or local preoccupation, but because in Whitehall it was seen as of less immediate importance than progress in education, training, and economic development. Ultimately education and welfare schemes had to depend for finance on local colonial economic growth; without such progress, underpinned by financial self-reliance, genuine self-government would be impossible. In the later stages of the war, much of the Colonial Office's planning for the post-war world therefore centred on the promotion of economic growth and prosperity. It was supervised chiefly by Sydney Caine, who had been appointed Financial Adviser in 1942 and was responsible for development and welfare policy from April 1943.

Planning ahead inevitably involved reappraisal of the past. It was assumed that in the machinery of the 1940 Colonial Development and Welfare Act the Colonial Office had a useful means to hand, and Caine therefore started by reviewing its achievements. The 1940 Act had operated on the assumption that colonial governments would draw up their detailed projects for consideration by the Colonial Development and Welfare Advisory Committee; once refined and approved there, schemes were to be scrutinized further by the Colonial Office and then sent forward for Treasury sanction of the necessary expenditure. Caine's investigations showed that these arrangements had worked far from perfectly (DOC 24). For more than a year public criticisms had been levelled at the slow tempo of activity and the limited expenditure approved under the Act, and they were now shown to have been well-justified. The fault lay less with either delay and obstruction in Whitehall or Treasury reluctance to release money than with the limited number and inadequacy of schemes being put forward by colonial governments. Caine argued that although the Colonial Office had publicly met critics by appealing to wartime difficulties, such an excuse was at best a half-truth and would soon be unavailable. The real weaknesses were essentially structural and could only be remedied by a much greater centralization of initiative and control in Colonial Office hands.

Caine's memorandum has acquired a distinct status in recent secondary literature. It has been interpreted as evidence of a new confidence in the Colonial Office's approach to planning, and related to a transformation, born of wartime experience, of metropolitan officials' capacity to direct initiatives in colonial policy. It may be seen as marking the point where the preoccupation with remedial social welfare under pressure of West Indian events finally gave way to the long-term planning of the colonies' economic future. Arguably the road ran straight from Caine's cogitations to its terminus in the new Colonial Development and Welfare Act of March 1945, which reflected imperial appreciation of the colonial war-effort and a determination to use imperial resources more effectively in a brave new world. As a counter to the view that here historians can see the working-out of the idealism generated by war, it has been emphasized that those involved in the redefinition and practical acceptance of colonial development were also very sensitive to the problems for Britain of industrial survival in a world dominated by the USA.

These views are to be taken seriously, but it is also important to understand their limitations. In focusing on the novelty of changes during the war, the contemporary emphasis on planning, and the analytical breadth of official vision, historians also reveal their preferences and professional bias. In writing of the development of imperial policies and of metropolitan policy-making, it is important not to be concerned with change at the expense of continuity; one must not admire rationality only to forget the lack of officials' time for careful thought and their imperfect information; there is little to be gained from discerning disinterestedness or determination while failing to recognize narrower self-interest and inertia. Selected documents are especially dangerous in this respect: they are apt to be seen as connected pieces in a single pattern rather than as misshapen prominences in a confused landscape.

In fact the path from Caine's review to the 1945 Act was far from smooth. The memorandum appealed to others in the office either with less time to give to such broad questions or perhaps lacking its author's ability, but Caine himself also admitted its inadequacies. 'It is by no means as full a treatment as the subject deserves. It has too much in mind the purely economic side, although that is, I think really fundamental to the development of true Colonial independence, and its proposals for definite action are nebulous'.[14] Caine wanted help and discussion because of his own 'inadequate equipment for such constructive work'. The result of his plea was a slow movement in two different directions which owed much to those perennial problems of the Colonial Office – its need to rely on the activity of local administrations and its vulnerability among Whitehall's departments. In such circumstances continuity with the past was inevitably pronounced. It was important both to avoid any appearance of failing to appreciate colonial administrative efforts, and to convey to potential critics everywhere a sense of continuous direction, purpose, and achievement.

Colonial governments had, of course, been exhorted to consider the development prospects of their territories in order to take advantage of the 1940 Act. They were now encouraged to pursue this further and to consider the immediate post-war needs of their charges. Just as Colonial Office officials had tried in 1939 to estimate the impact of war, so they now began to consider the likely effects of peace (DOC 25). As a result, the questions of development, welfare, and reconstruction began to merge, covered by the belief that the imperial government would give effect to its public commitments by assisting in some way with funds. Administrative changes were also made inside the Colonial Office itself. Caine's fear that questions of development were in danger of being taken out of the office's hands was widely shared. The result was the establishment of a new body, the Colonial Economic Advisory Committee, to consider all such development questions as the Secretary of State might refer to it, especially questions of general policy. It had the appearance of being high-powered as well as influential, with a membership of prominent public figures as well as officials; it certainly overshadowed the existing Colonial Development and Welfare Advisory Committee as a possible source of constructive ideas.

Despite these initiatives, the extent to which Colonial Office thinking remained set in an earlier mould rapidly became clear. Although the Colonial Economic Advisory Committee produced a variety of reports, it was hampered by the vagueness of its brief and its limited powers of decision. It suffered from the inability to find a constructive role somewhere between imprecise discussion of generalities and painstaking scrutiny of minutiae. Its first secretary, the economist W. A. Lewis, resigned because it seemed incapable of discussing systematically most colonial economic problems. Other members argued that the need for capital and industrial development were so great that it was essential to give great scope to both foreign resources and to private enterprise. These difficulties and frustrations were made abundantly clear when Stanley met the Committee after its first year's activity (DOCs 30 and 31). His appointment of Stockdale, fresh from the West Indies, as Colonial Office Adviser and Chairman of the Committee did little to improve matters.

These difficulties of the Colonial Economic Advisory Committee and the enthusiasm with which the Colonial Office worked for a new act to replace the legislation of 1940 are closely connected. As in 1939–40 when the revival of trusteeship had offered the Colonial Office a new and vital role, so in 1944–5 the retention of control over development and welfare were regarded as crucial to the department's own future. Constitutional arguments were not the only reasons why committees and individuals remained no more than advisory to the Secretary of State. Where, too, Britain's standing as a colonial power remained at stake, official control was still essential. As they were to show in the parliamentary debates on the new act, both Conservative and Labour sympathizers thought the imperial government should retain a prominent role, and not risk position and reputation simply by giving wide scope to metropolitan private enterprise or relying extensively on foreign funds, especially those of the USA.

Stanley therefore argued his case for a new Colonial Development and Welfare Act much in the manner of his predecessor, MacDonald (DOC 27). Above all, the maintenance of administrative morale, the scotching of enemy propaganda, and Britain's reputation as a colonial power, were to be secured by the timely and dramatic gesture of greatly increased funds and a long time-scale. However, the sensitivity of the Treasury in early discussions to the case for honouring previous commitments and making good the shortfall in development expenditure was being rapidly overwhelmed by fears as to Britain's likely budgetary position at the war's end (DOC 28). The Chancellor's reluctance thus forced Stanley to develop his position before the Cabinet. This was done with noticeable differences of emphasis. The Secretary of State for the Colonies now stressed the political pressures for an extended programme, the 'considerable benefit' to Britain in economic terms, and the contribution which development would make to sustaining a strong and united empire–commonwealth as the key to Britain's influence in international affairs (DOC 29). These arguments were largely accepted, and a new bill was pushed through Parliament in spring 1945. It made £120m available over ten years from March 1946, a figure slightly above that proposed by the Treasury and distributable with much greater flexibility as to annual expenditures than was possible under the 1940 Act. Colonial Office staff now turned to consider the broad allotment of these funds between different territories, so that local administrations would know where they stood .

It would be wrong to deny the existence in the Cabinet, the Colonial Office, and even the Treasury, of a genuine desire to promote colonial well-being; but idealistic or generous impulses were circumscribed and sometimes ousted altogether by some very stern realities. These came into clearer focus in the last months of the war. Although officials had learned much from wartime experience, recent events had nevertheless raised the question whether the imperial government was capable of performing the task it had set itself. While the general intention of the new Colonial Development and Welfare Act was widely welcomed, many commentators saw in the arrangements endorsed by the Cabinet too much of the old Colonial Office Adam, unredeemed by evidence that his ability to inspire, co-ordinate, and provide the staff for, effective planning had been significantly enhanced.

Just as the question of the Colonial Office's capacity remained a live issue, so too did that of the fundamental purpose of development. As calculations of Britain's post-war indebtedness and productive capacity became more precise, so the tendency to look to colonial resources as a defence against insolvency and an important aid to reconstruction reasserted itself. Mobilization for war seemed likely to continue in the shape of management for peace, as patterns of thinking common between the wars rapidly revived. Late in 1944 the Colonial Office had already seen the need to accommodate itself to this trend. Six months later it felt the pressure far more acutely. At the Treasury in April 1945 J. M. Keynes completed his now-famous paper 'Overseas Financial Policy in Stage III', sketching out alternative financial strategies for the period following the defeat of Japan which was then thought to be as much as two years away. [15] It was subsequently circulated to other government departments. For the Colonial Office, its importance lay especially in its suggestion that large amounts of colonial sterling balances should be written off or appropriated in order to ease Britain's difficulties. Officials not only saw technical problems in such a plan; they were sensitive both to the serious political difficulties it would create in the colonies, and to the fundamental implications it had for the recently-revived strategy of development and welfare (DOCs 32 and 33).

Not only were developments in Britain's international relations, and great power deliberations about the post-war world, weakening the position of the Colonial Office at this time; so too were the state of the metropolitan economy and, as a general election approached, the concentration of party political debate on matters of domestic welfare. The restoration of peace, it seemed, threatened greater difficulties even than the outbreak of war for the implementation of a constructive colonial policy.

8 Britain's Post-war Reconstruction and Colonial Policy, 1945–51

For the Labour government which took office under Attlee late in July 1945, the economic consequences of the peace had to be faced far sooner than expected, for the end of the war suddenly arrived when Japan surrendered on 15 August 1945. American aid ceased almost immediately, on 21 August. Britain's borrowings totalled £3500m, much of them in the form of sterling balances whose owners, along with the USA, wanted rapid repayment to assist their own reconstruction. With Keynes estimating Britain's exports at £400m per annum as against her annual need for £1100m–£1200m of imports even to sustain wartime consumption levels (let alone press on with reconstruction), clearly Britain's credit was extremely fragile. Reconstruction would take time, and the accumulation of further debt was unavoidable before a favourable balance of payments and trade could be restored. The continuation, even the extension, of wartime controls and austerity seemed inescapable, but in turn raised serious political problems given popular expectations.

Full of electoral euphoria, the government hoped for the best and avoided planning for the worst. Although the need for immediate American financial assistance was recognized, and the terms of the $3750m loan negotiated at Washington between September and December 1945 were less favourable than expected, this was for the time being enough to sustain politicians' confidence. In the absence of good luck and far-reaching measures of practical support, however, it was insufficient for more than a short period to buoy up the British economy and fuel the recovery Britain desperately needed. After promising well in 1946, exports fell back, and slow demobilization exacerbated manpower shortages. Government economic planning was perfunctory and a great deal was left hopefully to private enterprise; the balance-of-payments deficit continued to grow as world commodity shortages brought rising prices and more expensive imports. Budgetary policy was aimed at avoiding deflation and unemployment, and at underpinning the first steps towards the 'welfare state'. The terrible winter of 1946–7, a fuel crisis, loss of exports, and rapid spending of the dollar loan, were followed by the complete collapse of confidence in sterling and a financial crisis in August 1947.

Striking changes followed. Autumn 1947 saw the reconstruction of the government. Assault on the problems of economic survival was led by Sir Stafford Cripps, first at the new Ministry of Economic Affairs, and then from the Treasury after he succeeded Dalton as Chancellor in November. Serious economic planning replaced reliance on nationalization and financial manipulation; wage and price controls together with rationing and stringent taxation were used to restrict domestic consumption while avoiding inflation, and planned production was linked to an export drive directed towards North American markets and dollar earnings. Cripps, however, was still unable to avoid the devaluation of sterling in September 1949. His policies were also assisted by the organization of the 'Marshall Aid' programme for European recovery, formally launched in April 1948. Reflecting genuine concern for Europe's difficulties, but also the desire to protect the USA's long-term economic interests, this expenditure contributed enormously to the revival of European production and world trade. Consequently, by mid-1950, confidence in sterling had been restored, Britain's debt problems were at least temporarily under control, and her trade had a healthy balance.

Metropolitan economic difficulties were without doubt an extremely important determinant of imperial and colonial policy between 1945 and 1951, influencing both metropolitan decisions on a wide range of issues and the circumstances facing officials in individual territories. However, precise assessments of their importance in particular cases, and effective generalizations, remain very difficult. At times financial pressures or fears of future costs encouraged the government to cut its losses and withdraw from exposed positions. At the beginning of 1947 the potential benefits of a presence in Greece no longer seemed to justify the expense, and withdrawal was agreed. In the absence of any visible solution to problems in Palestine, the costs incurred helped to concentrate British minds on the decision to renounce her mandate there. Even in India, despite the Labour government's renewed commitment to self-government, the Cabinet only moved very slowly until the winter of 1946–7 when ministers also faced the Viceroy's insistence that they should anticipate the breakdown of order there. Other expenditure, however, was evidently acceptable; no one seriously questioned the costs of reoccupying the South-east Asian colonies and Hong Kong. No government has ever found it easy to reduce significant engagements inherited from the past; only a few have found it possible. In the absence of that careful planning which might have produced accurate or convincing analysis of imperial expenditure, and amid the tangle of existing commitments to imperial mission, colonial self-government and development, material shortages and financial costs alone rarely provided conclusive arguments against empire.

Far from prompting decisive steps towards decolonization, economic crisis in the late 1940s often had the opposite effect; rather than relinquish responsibilities, imperial Britain turned to develop every tangible resource and a few others besides. Although late in 1945, as the appointment of George Hall showed, the Colonial Office was seen as of little immediate importance, it came under steadily-mounting pressure from the Treasury and other government departments to exploit colonial opportunities in the interests of earning dollars for the sterling area and easing Britain's own financial and supply situation. Hall's replacement by Arthur Creech Jones did nothing to halt a process which only intensified once Cripps took charge of economic affairs. Britain's inability in 1947 to face up to sterling-convertibility and a freer international trading system necessitated renewed attention to colonial empire.

On the question of the sterling balances, as Caine's comments indicated might happen (DOCs 32 and 33), the Colonial Office retreated: by February 1947, while still resisting outright cancellation, it suggested their conversion to interest-free loans together with measures to prevent their being drawn down. As world commodity prices rose, the UK began to benefit at the expense of colonial producers from whom it still often bought (as in wartime) at fixed prices on long-term contracts. Colonial Office concern at the extent of this further subsidy to Britain (DOC 42) cut no ice with members of the Cabinet, which continued to press hard for increased colonial primary production.

Demands of this kind neatly complemented the Colonial Office's own reluctance to encourage colonial industry (DOCs 30 and 31) and were at least partially in line with its own interest in economic development; but they also exposed the department's weaknesses. Even in 1946 Colonial Office officials were well aware both that the ability of colonial governments to devise development plans remained limited, and that the Office itself was virtually powerless in the face of the obstacles to metropolitan supply of colonial import requirements. The Colonial Economic Development Council was established in October 1946, in the hope that it would evolve as a strategic and influential planning body, in that respect replacing the Colonial Economic Advisory Committee; despite periodic reconstitution, it too never justified itself and was dissolved in November 1951. New machinery was matched with more money through further Colonial Development and Welfare Acts in 1949 and 1950, but colonial development and welfare funds remained substantially underspent. Of the £120m promised in 1945 only about £25m had been used by mid-1949.

Conscious of the slow progress on this front, the Colonial Office began to explore other alternatives. In the circumstances of 1947, however, its initiatives were hitched rapidly to the ambitions of other departments. Cripps' speech to the conference of African governors in November (DOC 44) illustrates the tendency to redefine colonial welfare and to integrate colonial development ever more closely with Britain's own economic planning. Treasury support for the establishment immediately afterwards of the Colonial Development Working Party, chaired by the government's Chief Planning Officer and including the representatives of many departments, showed how the necessity of invoking wider support could turn into a loss of Colonial Office influence and control. Not all colonial administrators, however, were necessarily dismayed by such shifts in Whitehall's balance of power (DOCs 43 and 46).

Criticisms of the post-war development and welfare record of the Colonial Office and colonial administrations were frequently unfair, ignoring, for example, supply priorities which stifled colonial private enterprise or Treasury limits imposed on colonial borrowing in London. Moreover, it would be quite wrong to suggest that nothing was being achieved. Colonies were exploiting their earning capacity; in both 1948 and 1949 they ran a trading surplus with the dollar area of about £50m. Development projects were slowly bearing fruit in a number of different fields. Nevertheless achievements matched neither the expectations generated by the rhetoric of 1944–5 nor new post-war hopes; they were also marginal in terms of Britain's total export performance. This resulted in Cabinet criticisms of the Colonial Office and growing scrutiny of its efforts by, first, the Cabinet Economic Policy Committee and later the Committee on Colonial Development. Practical answers to the 'failure' were also sought outside both the Colonial Office and the established Colonial Development and Welfare framework, in the Overseas Resources Development Act of February 1948. In order to draw on wider official expertise and on the entrepreneurial skills and capital of the private sector, the Act set up the Overseas Food Corporation and the Colonial Development Corporation, with borrowing powers of £50m and £100m respectively.

Creech Jones and many of his staff were alarmed at these changes, not simply for reasons of *amour-propre*. While afraid of the political effects in the colonies of slow progress with development programmes, they feared still more local reactions to the charge of metropolitan exploitation (DOC 51). Urban unrest and rural protest in many colonial territories at this time gave point to their worries. Simultaneously, however, almost any development was likely to be defended on grounds of the beneficial side-effects of metropolitan expenditure. By late 1948–9 there was mounting concern among Western allies with the need to promote colonial economic growth as an essential defence against the spread of communism. On the one hand this contributed to the declining significance of Colonial Office efforts as Labour's sympathies and British interest coalesced in active involvement with Commonwealth-wide schemes such as the Colombo Plan, launched in January 1950. On the other hand, this combination of metropolitan and international needs was irresistible. It contributed significantly to what might be interpreted as the Colonial Office's frantic willingness to support extremely ill-considered plans, most notably the East African groundnuts project (DOCs 53 and 54), in the hope of rescuing at least something of its earlier optimistic expectations.

By 1951 colonial economic fortunes had undoubtedly improved since 1945. It is, however, doubtful whether this owed much either to Colonial Development and Welfare schemes, to other sources of metropolitan investment, to a Labour government, or to imperial planning. There is a strong case for thinking that devaluation, reluctantly accepted by the Cabinet in September 1949, contributed far more to colonial welfare and prosperity by stimulating exports from the sterling area. This was reinforced by international pressures outside British control. In June 1950 the Korean War began. Although the Colonial Office had now to consider afresh the implications of wartime needs on colonial resources (DOC 60), and possible colonial contributions to the UK's rearmament, the rising prices for colonial commodities which it generated were of considerable benefit to both producers and colonial government revenues.

9 International Problems and Imperial Policies East of Suez, 1945–51

By 1945 the Empire was at full stretch. From the Mediterranean to the Pacific the British faced herculean tasks of security and rehabilitation. In addition to re-establishing control over lost territories they occupied Italian colonies in Africa, and Dutch and French empires in South–east Asia. In 1946–7 1 million Britons were still in the armed forces. Yet Britain could ill afford the expense; she was indebted not only to the USA but to her own dependencies, notably India and countries in the Middle East. Demobilization was popular; it also made economic sense to withdraw the legions of the conscript army to fight the war on want at home. Reviving the domestic economy was the first item on the agenda, particularly of a Labour government committed to both the generation and redistribution of wealth. Imperial retrenchment, it might be thought, was another priority of a party that set such store by world peace, self-determination, good relations with both the USA and USSR, and the democratic reconstruction of Europe. Those with their heads in the clouds believed that in the age of the 'common man' the empire would wither away; Attlee, with his feet on the ground, sought an escape from empire. As the Indian Raj entered its final phase, the Prime Minister suggested a general retreat (DOC 35). Just as possession of India had in the past been held to justify a host of territorial acquisitions, so now it seemed that the surrender of India might prompt a complete reorientation of British strategic thinking based instead on North America. As rocketing defence-estimates coincided with economic crises, obstructed industrial recovery, and jeopardized welfare programmes, it seemed only sensible to tailor commitments to capacity. In addition, continuing ventures in Greece, Indonesia, Palestine and Iran soured relations with America and Russia, while other Afro-Asian responsibilities blinded the British to the possibilities of any narrowly European future.

But if Labour was the heir to a 'little England' tradition or, to put it no higher, the bipartisan parsimony that assessed the value of empire as the sum of victories divided by taxation, Attlee's government was also in no mood to be profligate with the legacy of 'Greater Britain'. The decision to go ahead at once with Indian independence inspired the hopes of colonial nationalists far more immediately than it influenced metropolitan minds towards relaxing political controls elsewhere. Millstones in one light, in another colonies still shone like jewels. A radical reappraisal of imperial strategy, triggered off by the Prime Minister's paper pointing to the vulnerability of a maritime empire in an era of air power, was not pressed in the face of objections from the Chief of Staff and the Foreign Office (DOC 36). Oil, together with continuing traditional interests in Asia and the developing enthusiasm for Africa, confirmed the importance of the Middle East, and in asserting British paramountcy in the region Ernest Bevin swept into international relations along a red carpet worn almost threadbare since the days of Palmerston, Disraeli and Salisbury. With Attlee's blessing, Bevin was the master-builder of a foreign policy over-arching transfer of power in South Asia, conciliation of the Arab world, counter-insurgency in South–east Asia, and 'partnership' with Africa. His insistence on an independent world role for Britain won more plaudits from Churchill and Eden than from the MPs behind him; although they clashed constantly on domestic issues, Labour and Conservatives front benches agreed that without her empire Britain would become a pawn in American diplomacy and leave in her wake a vacuum which the Soviets were likely to fill. Empire and Commonwealth together provided not only hope of economic vitality in peace as previously in war but also the peacetime key to maintaining Britain's international influence.

The Labour government's commitment to what Herbert Morrison called 'the jolly old empire' reflected neither atavistic emotionalism nor slavish continuity. Bevin had a grasp of current affairs and a vision of a new world. Aware that colonies could be sources of weakness as well as strength, he preached the doctrines of delegation of power and non-interference and, in so doing, guided the official mind away from formal to informal empire. Whereas a century earlier such a preference had been a measure of Britain's world ascendancy, it was now a mark of her straitened circumstances. At the same time, just as he recognized that the USA was crucial to the security and economic recovery of Western Europe, so he hoped to draw America into the international defence of the Eastern Mediterranean, Middle East and South-east Asia where British influence had hitherto held sway. Neither approach, however, involved an acceptance of irreversible imperial decline or attempts to delay the inevitable. Indeed, it is important to guard against anticipating Dean Acheson's stricture on British myopia and listlessness in the aftermath of empire; Bevin, and later Eden too, calculated on winning time for Britain to recover her pre-war strength. To their chagrin the British were obliged to accept their immediate dependence upon the dollar at home and abroad, but they were also adamant 'that we are not subservient to the United States of America'. 'Constructive colonialism', 'partnership', and 'the transformation of Empire into Commonwealth' were means to appease residual American anti-imperialism, contain Afro-Asian nationalism, pre-empt communist penetration, and maintain world influence on the cheap. Attlee and the Commonwealth Relations Office took care to cultivate close links with Canada, Australia, New Zealand and South Africa, which were clearly sources of economic and strategic support for the UK, and they planned to lead the territories of the dependent empire eventually to self-government within the same association. Lyrical about Attlee's role in India, Bevin compared him with 'Durham who saved us in Canada' and 'Campbell Bannerman who created the Union of South Africa'.[16]

British foreign policy from August 1945 to March 1947 was marked in turn by fluidity, failure and frustration as the Grand Alliance collapsed and the Cold War commenced. Attempts to reach agreements with the USSR and prevent the partition of Europe proved abortive, and Anglo-Russian tension built up in Greece, Turkey and Iran. On the other hand, Bevin was consumed with anxiety lest America should withdraw into isolation and he strove to persuade her to accept a world role. Yet easy relations with the US were hampered not only by the terms of the American loan, but also by US commercial demands, the end of Anglo-American co-operation in atomic energy and the problem of Palestine.

Chaim Weizmann's confident prediction that the creation of a Jewish National home in Palestine would provide Britain with an imperial asset had not been fulfilled. Since the Balfour Declaration (1917), Britain had failed to resolve her conflicting pledges to Arab and Jew. Increased Jewish immigration in the 1930s had heightened difficulties in a sensitive area. Reduction of immigration, power-sharing and partition had been suggested in turn. In 1945 the White Paper of 1939, proposing Jewish autonomy within a larger federation, provided the point of departure for further consideration of issues intensified by revelations of the Nazi final solution, the plight of European Jews debarred by immigration quotas from entering the promised land, the terrorism of Jew and Arab, the strength of the Zionist lobby in the USA and support for Jews from Labour MPs and Winston Churchill. The administration of the Mandate was the responsibility of the Colonial Office but its strategic significance made it a matter for the Chiefs of Staff and the Foreign Office. Indeed, British policy towards Palestine was handled (some would say mishandled) by Bevin and, because the problem was 'poisoning' Anglo-American relations, it contaminated his global strategy for nearly three years.

British interests in the Middle East rested upon Arab co-operation; American goodwill necessitated a pro-Zionist policy; Arabs could not accept Jewish demands for increased immigration and the creation of a Jewish national state. The options of (i) a unitary self-governing state, (ii) partition, and (iii) a flexible scheme providing autonomy for Arab and Jewish provinces under central British trusteeship for a transitional period during which the country might develop towards either union or partition (DOC 41), were considered in turn. Impasse was reached on each count. Neither a negotiated nor an imposed settlement appeared feasible. Many believed that the British would achieve success with American support, but the Anglo-American Committee produced an impracticable report (April–May 1946). The Arab–Jewish Conference convened later in the year (September 1946) proved even less fruitful. As for unilateral action, a British Award could not be made without breaching obligations to one or other of the communities, and withdrawal was ruled out as an evasion not a solution to the local and international problems posed by Palestine. Not surprisingly in the bleak winter of early 1947 Attlee revived his proposal for a British retreat from the vulnerable soft under-belly of the Middle East. Though the argument favouring the centrality of the Middle East in British strategy again prevailed, the Cabinet now decided to refer the problem of Palestine to the United Nations in the hope that there would be found international support for the British scheme for a single bi-national state.

As it happened the United Nations found in favour of partition, in other words of the Zionist course, with the result that Bevin and Creech Jones jointly recommended to Cabinet a policy of neutrality (DOC 45). Since the United Nations plan lacked Arab support, the British government studiously avoided getting involved in its formulation and implementation. On 4 December 1947 the Cabinet laid down the principle that 'while His Majesty's Government should do nothing to obstruct the carrying out of the United Nations' decision, British troops and the British Administration should in no circumstances become involved in enforcing it or maintaining law and order while the United Nations Commission enforced it'. On 15 May 1948 the Mandate ended. No triumph this, as the *New Statesman* lamented:

> Forward, the Haganah!
> Forward, Arabia!
> *No Pax Britannica,*
> And war in Palestine![17]

Two days after Bevin had told the House of Commons that the issue of Palestine would be referred to the United Nations (18 February 1947), Attlee announced to the House the 'definite intention' of the government to transfer power 'to responsible Indian hands by a date not later than June 1948'. At the time this statement did not have the same jubilant ring which it later acquired. The Cabinet Mission plan of May–June 1946 – similar, despite its complexity, to the proposal for a bi-national Palestine – had been rejected, and the sub-continent was plunged into communal conflict. In Wavell's view a political solution seemed increasingly unlikely, and in such a deteriorating situation military training and caution contributed to his insistence on at least the contingency of a 'Breakdown Plan', a military operation to save British lives by organized withdrawal. By Christmas 1946, he had reached virtually the end of his resources, and had also lost the confidence of Labour leaders. In their view, in India more so than in Palestine, British prestige and interests were at stake, and the Cabinet remained adamant that a political settlement be found. Wavell's importunate tactics forced them to take new steps in this direction, and the publication of a deadline further concentrated minds.

While Bevin made clear his concern that a strong India be saved for Commonwealth defence, he was not a member of the crucial Cabinet India and Burma Committee. In so far as it was controlled by Britain, the transfer of power was directed by Attlee and Stafford Cripps, who dominated Pethick Lawrence (Secretary of State for India), and by Mountbatten who replaced Wavell in March and enjoyed in much greater measure than his predecessors the trust of his masters and of Indian politicians. The publication of a deadline concentrated minds; by 2 June Congress, League and the Raj had come to accept partition which, in its final form, was not to the liking of any party, and the date for departure was brought forward to midnight 14–15 August 1947. That the British succeeded here but not in Palestine can to some extent be explained by the fact that since 1942 Anglo-American differences over India had subsided.

In a sense it could be argued that retreat from India was no more and no less efficacious than retreat from Palestine. In each case the British protected British lives and avoided entanglement in local conflicts, yet in each case they were unable to prevent partition and communal bloodshed. From the imperial viewpoint, however, the results were vastly different. The shift from formal to informal empire in a spirit of partnership – the adjustment of the collaborative relationship – was more nearly achieved in South Asia than in the Middle East. Abdication of responsibility for Palestine heaped upon Britain the odium of Israel and American Jews while it soured the protracted Anglo-Egyptian negotiations over the Suez base and fuelled anti-imperialism in both Egypt and Iran where, in May 1951, Musaddiq nationalized the Anglo-Iranian Oil Company. With Morrison then at the

Foreign Office, Britain drifted towards war but was pulled back by Acheson and the American State Department. The Anglo-American coup that toppled Musaddiq and restored the Shah in 1953 confirmed that British overlordship in Iran had passed to the USA.

In Asia, by contrast, the Labour government outlined the framework of successor states and supervised the inheritance of the colonial legacy. Although they were disappointed by Burma's decision not to join the Commonwealth, and although they failed to win Indian participation in the imperial defence of the Indian Ocean, they 'saved for the Commonwealth' India, Pakistan and Ceylon. Attlee painstakingly persuaded both the Dominions and Asian nations of the value of a new, multiracial Commonwealth and amended its structure to allow inclusion of a republic (India). If the achievement of Indian independence was an inspiration to nationalists elsewhere, Nehru's steady emergence as a 'Commonwealth man' encouraged the British government to think of applying to other dependent territories the formula of 'eventual self-government within the Commonwealth'.

Withdrawal from a partitioned India brought the benefits of retrenchment combined not only with continued elements of dependence (arising, for example, from Indo-Pakistani disputes and sterling balances) but with American goodwill. Withdrawal from Palestine brought retrenchment in the knowledge that at least the United Nations or the USA would fill the gap. But in contemplating withdrawal from Greece, Britain was far less certain either of American support or of a successor-state compatible with her own Mediterranean interests. In March 1947, however, President Truman accepted responsibility for the defence of Greece, and in the strident language of Cold War ideology (the so-called Truman Doctrine) made the cause of the free world the cause of America. Using this theme, Bevin endeavoured to sustain Anglo-American co-operation without succumbing to American tutelage. In particular, while striving to iron out the crudities of the Truman Doctrine, he worked to convert this commitment into an enduring pledge to European recovery.

As his biographer has shown, Bevin seized upon Marshall's speech in June 1947 to take the initiative in devising a practical plan for the rehabilitation of western Europe.[18] Then, in January 1948, he launched the idea of 'Western Union'. In presenting his recommendations to Cabinet,in a paper significantly called 'The First Aim of British Foreign Policy', Bevin argued in favour of the creation of 'some form of union in Western Europe, whether of a formal or informal character, backed by the Americas and the Dominions' (DOC 48). Steering a course between British independence and Western consolidation, he sought to build up Western Europe as a bloc capable of withstanding Russian encroachments with US material help and British spiritual leadership but without Britain herself sinking to the status of either a European country or a satellite of the USA. With the resources of the Commonwealth and Colonial Empire behind them the British 'will show clearly that we are not subservient to the United States of America or to the Soviet Union'. As Attlee put it in parliament a few months later 'we are not solely a European Power but a member of a great Commonwealth and Empire'. Bevin played a pivotal role in working out a defence plan for Western Europe (Brussels Treaty 1948) which was broadened the following year to include the USA and Canada in the North Atlantic Treaty Organization.

By early 1950 the economic attractions of the colonies and their uses in the Cold War meant, as Oliver Franks (Britain's Ambassador in Washington and formerly Bevin's choice as chairman of the Committee on European Economic Cooperation) reported that 'anti-colonialism in the United States today is a traditional attitude rather than an active crusading force' (DOC 55). Nonetheless, Franks warned HMG of the dangers to Anglo-American solidarity in the United Nations posed by resurgent anti-imperialism and advocated a continuing public relations campaign in which prominence should be given to the potential for American investment in British colonies. During 1950, indeed, Foreign and Colonial Office representatives in Washington extablished good relations with the State Department on the handling of Colonial questions in the UN, and J. M. Martin reported to Sir Thomas Lloyd that this improvement was consolidated in

1951. What was important was not unanimity nor, indeed, congruent approaches since Americans 'look at these questions from a very different standpoint from ours and the causes of our differences are too deep-seated to be moved, at any rate in the immediate future'.[19] Rather Martin's optimism derived from changes in atmosphere and the dispersal of American 'misunderstanding, distrust and impatience'. The Chinese People's Republic, which the British government recognized (January 1950) but the US did not, was another potential source of Anglo-American divergence. Indeed, on this issue and on other cases of Asian self-determination the Labour government was rapidly overhauling the US administration in its bid to appear progressive. In a Cabinet Paper written in August 1950 shortly before he resigned, Bevin declared 'Since the end of the war, the policy of His Majesty's Government in South and South-east Asia has been to encourage the legitimate aspirations of the peoples of that area for independence . . . [O]ur support of nationalism in South and South-east Asia provides the best possible counter to communist subversion and penetration'.[20] Attlee and Bevin contrasted Britain's enlightened stance with the new American insensitivity to Asian wishes. Now that the Cold War had reached the Far East, the price of Anglo-American solidarity could be Anglo-Asian collaboration.

On 25 June 1950 North Korea invaded South Korea. Britain did not hesitate in condemning the North in the UN and in despatching land and air forces to the field. Her interests in Asia and her great power standing called for action despite the financial costs; here was an opportunity for the British Empire and Commonwealth to be seen as a third force in the world and a valuable ally to the USA. But the Labour government discovered that it was associated with an increasingly aggressive US policy. On 8 October MacArthur took the war into the North and on 26 November the Chinese entered the conflict, driving MacArthur's forces into retreat. British Cabinet members feared that President Truman would resort to the atomic bomb or at any rate retaliate in such a way as to provoke a Chinese invasion of Hong Kong and their southwards advance through Indo-China and towards Malaya. On 3 December Attlee flew to Washington. His trip can be seen as a triumph of 'third force' diplomacy; he pulled the world back from the brink of a wider war, he moderated American hawkishness (Truman dismissed MacArthur in April) and in January he presided at a Commonwealth Prime Ministers' Meeting which offered to mediate between America and China. On the other hand, the substance of American policy and particularly its hostility to China remained unaltered, and the British government found that the 'Special Relationship' trapped it in debilitating undertakings.

The escalation of war in Korea also threatened to divide Commonwealth members on the issue of alignment and non-alignment. Australia and New Zealand had increasingly sheltered under the American umbrella since the fall of Singapore in 1942, and on 1 September 1951 they and the US government concluded the Pacific Pact (ANZUS) which established a security council, albeit one which, to the embarrassment of the Foreign Office, Britain was not invited to join. Nehru, for his part, strongly opposed the formation of a Pacific Pact modelled on NATO since it would smack of Western imperialism and he withheld Indian troops from Korea. The non-alignment movement and regional pacts compounded the pluralism of the Commonwealth. Meanwhile the cost of defending colonies plagued the Ministry of Defence and the Treasury.

In the summer of 1950 the Cabinet committed the country to a defence expenditure of £3600m for 1951–4. Averaged over the years this sum represented a 50 per cent increase compared with spending in 1950–1. By January 1951 the amount for 1951–4 had risen to £4700m or nearly double the level envisaged before the outbreak of the Korean War. In the second half of 1951 the British economy suffered a record trade gap and current account deficit. These financial demands made grave inroads into the health and social security estimates, and in his budget of April 1951 Hugh Gaitskell introduced some charges into the health service. The demand for troops forced the government to rush through legislation in September extending National Service from eighteen months to two years despite the unpopularity and unproductiveness of such a measure. In addition to the war in Korea, Britain was engaged in building up a strategic reserve, preparing for imminent global conflict, pursuing an independent nuclear weapons programme, fighting insurgents in Malaya and maintaining a chain of garrisons throughout the empire. How could the colonies help?

In December 1950 Attlee as Prime Minister again took the initiative in asking the Minister of Defence to arrange for the Chiefs of Staff to examine whether or not Britain could now plan to place increasing reliance on Colonial manpower in her cold war effort (DOC 60). The Colonial Office felt that a clearer indication of government priorities was required, for if finance was the constraint it would be inadvisable to use colonial forces, whereas if manpower was the limiting factor then the colonies might well have a role to play provided that care was taken with the specific postings of particular colonial troops. Cohen (Africa division) and Paskin (South-east Asia and Far East) took into account the racial and political implications of the matter and agreed that it would be unwise to despatch African troops to Asian dependencies. The general conclusion was that 'under present conditions, the major contribution that Colonial Governments can make in the field of Commonwealth defence is to maintain security forces adequate to cope with any foreseeable internal disorder'.

The demands of imperial defence have been sure solvents of empires. After 1763 London had vainly attempted to shift the financial burden onto the shoulders of North American colonists; a century later, having learned their lesson in the Thirteen Colonies, the British chose to delegate the task of local defence in return for constitutional concessions. Those considerations which had begun seriously to limit the disposability of Indian forces for imperial purposes after 1918 were now by 1950 also affecting deployment of African resources. It had become an open question whether or not the military burdens of empire would speed up decolonization in the 1950s by alienating colonial nationalists still further and by overtaxing London's own ability to provide.

In early June 1950, a few weeks before the outbreak of the Korean War, the Secretaries of State for the Colonies and War (Griffiths and Strachey) visited Malaya to examine the campaign against the communist insurgents which had been waged since the declaration of the Emergency two years earlier. Malaya's rubber and tin won valuable dollars, especially with the boom in commodity prices during the

Korean War, but counter-insurgency cost Britain men and money. In order to wrest the initiative from the Chinese-dominated Malayan Communist Party it was essential to convince the majority of Malays, Chinese and Indians of that country that 'a non-Communist regime offered them greater opportunities for economic and social betterment than any Communist regime'. Preparations for self-determination were, at least for some, a part of this strategy. Malcolm MacDonald (Commissioner-General for South-east Asia 1948–55) explained to Griffiths and Strachey that the transition from colonial government to complete self-government should be abbreviated from 25 years, hitherto the generally-agreed though rarely-voiced estimate, to 15 years in response to 'factors over which we shall have little or no control'. The latter included the emergence of a new generation of Malayan leaders, the pressure of Asian and world opinion at the United Nations, and the advisability of retaining the support of those Malayan leaders who stayed loyal to the British during the Emergency (DOC 57). Did the Emergency accelerate or retard political advance? While the Cabinet accepted MacDonald's general reasoning, the precise effects of the insurrection upon Malayan decolonization are hard to assess; certainly the Labour government did not let the law and order problem panic it into 'premature withdrawal'.

In the context of South-east Asia as a whole, Bevin, briefed by MacDonald, had already tried to persuade Dean Acheson of the desirability of a Marshall Plan, rather than a NATO, for the region. Although the Americans were initially unresponsive, Bevin pursued the proposal and at a conference in Ceylon in January 1950 the Colombo Plan was launched, whereby the more prosperous countries in Asia or those with an interest in the region would join together to improve the standard of life of the peoples of South-east Asia. Bevin was gratified that the Colombo Plan was a practical expression of Western aid, of Commonwealth cohesion (for both India and Australia played major parts at the conference), and of the collaborative relationship which Britain was fostering with the new leaders of Asia. The Conservative government endorsed this policy in December 1951: 'Any patent weakening of United Kingdom initiative or support would reduce United Kingdom influence in the Commonwealth countries in particular, and in the area of South and South-East Asia in general'.[21] Similarly, in the specific case of Malaya, the Conservative government, while it pursued the insurgents more vigorously than its predecessors, continued the strategy of winning hearts and minds.

British diagnoses of the communist threat in South-east Asia in the late 1940s and early 1950s oscillated between complacency and the fear that the Malayan insurrection was part of an orchestrated plan by Moscow to undermine the West by knocking away its colonial props. Although the Foreign Office's survey of communism in Africa, conducted in co-operation with other government departments, concluded in August 1950 that the varied manifestations of nationalism and instability in that continent had not yet been exploited by international communism, the danger was there, notably in southern Africa (DOC 59). Constructive colonialism on the political as well as the social and economic fronts therefore seemed a wise precaution not only to British officials but also to increasing numbers in the USA.

10 Native Administration, Local Government, and Political Change in British Africa, 1945–51

Political changes introduced during the war in colonial territories were, as was noted above, generally of an *ad hoc* and unco-ordinated nature. However, late in 1945 and in the following spring, the Colonial Office began to think much more systematically about colonial political development, above all in Africa. That it should have done so is not wholly surprising. The bureaucratic momentum towards specialization in subject departments reinforced officials' sense of the untidiness of empire, the lack of information and co-ordination. The experiences of war had encouraged them to see in wider planning not only something virtuous and useful but almost the only means of maintaining a grip on reality when under great pressure. The rationalization of approaches to African politics was in part a logical response to the continuing influence of Lord Hailey, who had done so much to encourage pan-African thinking. It also flowed from the need to work out the implications of 'partnership' in the political sphere, and from the accumulating evidence of wartime which had reinforced earlier tendencies to question the appropriateness and efficiency especially of the African colonies' 'Native Authorities'.

'Bureaucratic momentum', however, is fragile and wayward, something only too easily transformed into 'ongoing inertia'. This might well have occurred under a Secretary of State like George Hall, for he had little interest in or knowledge of colonial affairs and was absorbed with Palestine. As it was, Hall's presence opened the way for officials with enthusiasm, some local knowledge, and a critical, constructive inclination, to take a lead. Much evidence points to the crucial part played in stimulating debate and shaping its conclusions by Andrew Cohen, first as member of the East

African department, and then, from February 1947, as Assistant Under-Secretary in charge of the Africa division. Debate followed from a long memorandum written, with Cohen's encouragement, by George Cartland (DOC 37). This confronted the question how successfully would the Native Authorities cope with the post-war world, to which the answer was 'not at all well'. Cartland endorsed Hailey's criticisms, stressing how they were inefficient and insufficiently representative of important articulate interest groups. The war had fully exposed these weaknesses, together with widespread corruption, by imposing excessive practical demands, by heightening political consciousness and criticism, and by demoralizing members of the colonial service on whom native authorities were very dependent. A review, and the establishment of new guidelines by Whitehall, were essential.

The review proceeded at several levels, inside the Colonial Office itself, in conversation with colonial service officials home on leave, and by sounding out governors. The latter had to be handled with particular care, with every opportunity being taken to deny any Colonial Office ambition either to 'bring to birth a declaration of policy composed of platitudes and idealistic generalisations' or to impose 'a blue-print of native administration'.[22] Personal contacts, such as Creech Jones' visit with Cohen to East Africa in summer 1946, were generally more productive of constructive exchanges than were despatches. Even so, considerable scepticism and resistance were encountered, as Cohen's survey in September 1946 shows (DOC 38). This did not alter officials' convictions that reform was necessary, but they recognized that consultation and persuasion would need to be prolonged. From this followed the careful organization of successive Colonial Office initiatives, notably the 'local government despatch' sent to African governors on 25 February 1947, the summer school in Cambridge during August at which African administrators discussed the implications of local government reform, and a conference of African governors at the Colonial Office in November 1947. Finally a conference of African official and unofficial representatives was called in September 1948.

This progression provokes important questions. Above

all, perhaps, there is the problem of placing this increasingly well-focused concern with political machinery within the wide range of Colonial Office activities at the time. Were attention to Native Administration and local government and the wish to link local low-level institutions with the Legislative and Executive Councils at the centre of colonial government, seen above all as crucial aids to the success of the economic development and welfare schemes? Or did these policies have an independent life and justification of their own? Was it the case, and was it recognised, for example, in the criticisms of the Colonial Office for being 'too political', that London valued political advance for its own sake, and intended to promote self-government rapidly, perhaps independently of progress on other fronts? There are questions too about the continuity of policy. Did the concentration on local government involve a significant new departure from the past? Is it to be linked to Labour's accession to power, or explained more specifically with reference to the influence of the Fabian Colonial Bureau and to Creech Jones' taking office? Why was it played down after 1948 when the emphasis of policy-makers seemed to shift in favour of constitution-making for whole colonies? Historians remain divided on these issues. Cut and dried answers are hard to come by in a situation where contemporary participants' views varied significantly, and where those who may have been clear in their own minds often had to deploy arguments with which they did not necessarily sympathize in order to win assent to courses of action they wanted adopted.

For public consumption, to impress colonial critics, and to win round colonial administrators, it was vital to emphasize the continuity of local government policy with the past. This view was refined in the African Studies Branch, newly established in the Colonial Office's Africa Division, in July 1947. 'In general the present Local Government theory defines, emphasises and generalises ideas which were immanent in the Conciliar and I.R. [Indirect Rule] traditions, but not fully clarified as essentials. The change is one of subtle emphasis, except on one or two points.'[23] It was asserted in the opening paragraph of the Local Government despatch, and was reflected in the Colonial Office's annual report for

1946–7. 'The Colonies in general were, at the beginning of the war already ripe for a big forward move in political, economic and social development.'[24] Such claims to continuity were encouraged by the constant need to refurbish Britain's reputation as a great colonial power and to avoid the appearance of giving way to criticism or external pressure; they reflect the Colonial Office's own need to assert itself and to establish its grip on policy. They also show how, consciously and unconsciously, history could be rewritten for official purposes.

That the local government policy had its instrumental or purely functional purpose is also undeniable. Evident in Cartland's memorandum, fresh as he was from the frustrations of a District Commissioner's posting, it is strong too in Pedler's reflections (DOC 39) on Cohen's stocktaking, and is to be found again in the Local Government despatch. With so much importance attached, as was suggested above, to the successful outcome of development policy, any impetus which could be imparted by sprucing up local administration to aid the large numbers of new recruits to the colonial service, was welcome. Local government would tap local talent, and encourage the enthusiastic involvement of many people with first-hand knowledge of colonial needs and problems.

The development of local government was also seen as a necessary means of political control. It was felt essential not to allow vociferous but unrepresentative minorities of educated Africans to concentrate political power in their hands as the result of their increasing incorporation as members of the legislative and executive councils. Now that the Membership system was being introduced to encourage political responsibility, so native administration reform was designed to link the councils with local government institutions, giving educated Africans roots among the people. It was felt this would contribute to effective representation and political stability, and probably moderate the pace of change. Low standards of public morality and widespread corruption might also be checked by greater popular involvement and accountability (DOCs 37 and 39).

As Parliamentary Under-Secretary in 1946, Creech Jones had watched the evolution of local government discussions, and, once in charge, was happy to support the policy of reform. From a metropolitan viewpoint there was something in it for everyone, idealistic decolonizers, paternalistic Fabians or simple do-gooders, imperialists anxious to hang on, and those with an eye primarily on tropical resources. The possibilities inherent in the abandonment of Indirect Rule for Local Government, and the inclination of the Colonial Office planners to be comprehensive, became clearer still as a result of the work of the committee set up in January 1947 to prepare agenda papers for the African governors' conference (DOC 40). Here, in the persons of Caine and Cohen, economic development and political reform were brought together and their implications for the future of British Africa explored. Unfortunately, these discussion papers and the Committee's final report in May 1947 are far too long for inclusion here. They looked forward to the inevitability of self-government, achieved under pressure of international and, increasingly, colonial opinion, reinforced by the wartime commitments of British political parties. However, there was little sense here of Britain being too impoverished for the task of colonial rule, or of her retreating in the face of nationalist hostility. 'Decolonization' was not mentioned; instead they planned in magisterial fashion the gradual devolution of self-government within the Commonwealth.

> It is clear that in Africa the period before self-government can be granted will be longer than in most other parts of the Colonial Empire. Prophesy as to the length of this period is idle, but it may be said that in the Gold Coast, the territory where Africans are most advanced politically, internal self-government is unlikely to be achieved in much less than a generation. In the other territories the process is likely to be considerably slower. During this period we shall be working against the background of an international opinion which disapproves of the state of dependence in colonial territories and is prepared if necessary to see efficient government and the ordered development of social and economic services sacrificed to the rapid grant of self-government in whatever form . . . At the same time we shall be faced with constantly increasing internal pressure for self-government on the part of the

> Africans, and political movements, with very different ideas from our own will certainly make it necessary for the constitutional programmes which we set ourselves to be radically revised from time to time. We must not be deterred by this factor from long-term planning, but the plans which we make must be flexible enough to have some chance of operating successfully not merely for the next five years, but with the adjustments which future circumstances will demand for twenty or thirty years or indeed longer.[25]

Economies would be developed, populations educated, cadres of administrators trained, nationalist enthusiasms encouraged and harnessed, all in peaceful evolutionary stages.

There is no doubt about the enthusiasm and radical clarity of these interlocking programmes for anticipating change and organizing the future. Equally strong is the sense they convey of unreality. If Palestine and India impinged on the deliberations of the Cohen–Caine committee, they did so only in the sense that members were resolved to avoid a repetition, however dignified: forewarned was forearmed. India's precipitate rush into independence and communal carnage in August seems neither to have deflected the Cambridge summer school members from their discussions of local government at Queens' College nor to have disturbed their relaxations on the playing fields of St John's.[26]

In the autumn, however, these balanced visions of the agenda committee were sharply challenged. The first onslaught came from hardened colonial servants, such as Richards and Mitchell, at the African governors' conference (DOC 43). These proceedings were less easily stage-managed than those of the summer school. Fundamental distinctions between East and West African conditions were constantly brought out. Proposals on education, training, and a host of development issues were widely endorsed, but there was little agreement, beyond some bald statements of principle, on either the pattern or the timing of constitutional change. Although the governors when in London found the reshaping of local government on more democratic, or at least more representative, lines broadly acceptable, developments on the ground reflected different, far less committed attitudes (DOC 47). Shaken up by the sterling crisis and cabinet reconstitution, metropolitan departments' new determination to revitalize the economy also put pressure on the Colonial Office's plans. Cripps' speech to the conference (DOC 44), unlike much in its proceedings, was enthusiastically received; a governor like Mitchell saw in it support for the local development to which he attached real importance. Such an alliance was likely to accentuate the Colonial Office's growing inability to control development policies, noticed above (DOC 46).

Unrest and riots in the Gold Coast in February–March 1948 completed the challenge, and were particularly worrying. They were not only unexpected but hit a colony which had seemed comparatively prosperous and was an important dollar-earner; the Gold Coast's progress in local government was regarded as especially promising, and the 1946 constitution was just getting into its stride. Colonial violence, now as in the 1930s, called into question Colonial Office assumptions and competence; it also threatened other imperial concerns – Britain's colonial record, progress in colonial development, the growth of colonial export earnings, metropolitan supply, and budgetary planning. It is not surprising that the Watson Commission of Enquiry into the disturbances was given a wide brief and asked to recommend action on anything it thought fit.[27]

The Commission confirmed what officials were already being forced to contemplate, that the restoration of stability and co-operation, of colonial 'collaboration', would involve economic and political concessions. Before its report was published decisions were taken which suggested a major change in Colonial Office strategy. On the economic front, where there was least room for manoeuvre, Creech Jones launched a general campaign of persuasion aimed at colonial producers everywhere (DOC 51). Politically, it was recognized that constitutional change in the Gold Coast would necessitate adjustments elsewhere and a shift in emphasis away from local government (DOCs 49 and 50). Once the report appeared in August 1948, officials proceeded with its detailed suggestions: the European Association of West African Merchants was dissolved, additional money was found for the cocoa-farmers, and the Coussey Committee was set up to devise a new constitution.

Some may see in these responses evidence of metropolitan panic, short-term reactions to a crisis, decisions taken without much thought for the future and influenced by events elsewhere, for example the developing emergency in Malaya. Others will emphasize how officials, taken slightly unawares, were nevertheless perfectly prepared after the discussions of the previous year simply to shorten the timescale on which Cohen's and Caine's plans would operate. Undoubtedly, however, they involved a swing by the Colonial Office away from the controlled plans of 1947 towards a preoccupation with political management through constitutional reform. Whether or not this entailed being blown off course, there were compensations: although other departments were anxious to shape development and welfare policies, the Colonial Office could confidently claim particular expertise in the sphere of colonial constitutional politics.

The Colonial Office also began to address itself again to the limits to which, even inside Africa, colonies could be treated alike. This did not mean that the general insistence on the indigenization of administration, expanding education, and local government reform, was forgotten. The idea that all political advance rested on colonies meeting certain criteria in such matters as size, security, financial and economic viability, was too deeply-rooted for that, and such policies were pushed forward wherever possible (DOC 58). It did, however, involve an acceptance that in some territories local conditions might necessitate peculiar policies and political arrangements. As a result, the Colonial Office, often in concert with the Commonwealth Relations Office, considered at length the constitutional futures of both particular types of colony and regional groupings.

It has already been mentioned that concern with the problems of Mediterranean defence raised questions, for example, about Cyprus and Gibraltar; these led to a three-year investigation into the future of the small islands and strategic bases with colonial status (DOC 52). Much of this work was purely exploratory rather than directly preparatory, and the principal concerns of most Cabinet members continued to set limits to both Colonial Office initiatives and metropolitan concessions to local demands in the field of constitutional reform. Political change and the promotion of self-government had to be reconciled with the supremely important goals of making Britain's economic ends meet, consolidating the Commonwealth as a third force in international affairs, and repairing the world-wide net of imperial and commonwealth defence. In these circumstances, superficially contradictory policies were inescapable. Where African producers were powerful and inhabited territories of little strategic importance, like the Gold Coast and Nigeria, the politics of 'partnership' seemed by 1951 to have resulted in great constitutional leaps forward as the British sought to retain the initiative (DOCs 49 and 50). In East Africa, the regional approach was finally abandoned in 1950 in favour of political advance on the basis of individual territories (DOC 62). In Kenya, however, the interpretation of 'partnership' hinged on the strength of the white community, which still seemed to offer firm guarantees of both prosperity and the colony's contribution to Indian Ocean defence. The pattern of colonial policy in Central Africa was largely dictated by the economic and strategic importance to Britain of Rhodesian mineral resources and the implications of the election victory in May 1948 of the Nationalist Party in South Africa. A conference of politicians from the three territories was held on the initiative of Roy Welensky, leader of the Unofficials in Northern Rhodesia's Legislative Council, in February 1949 at the Victoria Falls: this revived schemes for federation. Although in London ministers regarded much of the planning as 'extreme and impracticable' and political federation as 'not now a practical policy', they were forced to recognize that the Central African Council was becoming unworkable.[28] Southern Rhodesia's threatened withdrawal from the Council unless reform was forthcoming compelled the new Secretaries of State after the general election in February 1950 – Griffiths and Gordon Walker – and their officials to be more accommodating. Again a decisive role in developing Britain's policy was played by Cohen. As in 1946–7 so in 1949–51, this time in collaboration with G. H. Baxter who had responsibility for Southern Rhodesia at the Commonwealth Relations Office, Cohen mapped out the staged response by which successive conferences might devise a scheme of closer union ultimately acceptable to all parties (DOC 56). The Labour Cabinet followed on reluctantly, acutely aware of the political difficulties which any federal plans would involve, but also worried that failure to act would encourage Southern Rhodesia's alignment with South Africa (DOCs 61 and 63).

* * *

British imperial policy, distilled in the crucible of war and peace, was an alchemy of self-interest and altruism, the rhetoric and pragmatism of politicians and the drive and drift of civil servants, novel ideas and ingrained attitudes, metropolitan initiatives and peripheral reactions, a desire for uniformity balanced by a respect for colonial variety. In the development of that policy, however, there are few natural staging-points. The year 1951 marks no significant divide except in the most superficial of senses, that the Labour government was defeated at the General Election held in October and was replaced by a Conservative ministry under Churchill. Attlee's ministers, with varying degrees of initiative, had taken a host of major decisions, for the most part with Conservative concurrence. In South and South-east Asian affairs, on Palestine and Iraq, in approaches to Europe, to the USA, and to the Commonwealth, bipartisanship was very marked throughout the period 1945–51. Policy had also been moulded by the reorganization of the Colonial Office and the rebuffs it had suffered from other ministries. At the end of 1951, indeed, having been edged away from the centre of economic and international affairs, the Colonial Office had returned to what had always come naturally, namely, the political and constitutional aspects of colonial rule.

With office, there inevitably fell to the Conservatives an inheritance of unresolved problems in foreign policy, defence, and imperial management, not least in the Middle and Far East. It could be said too that question marks hung over the future of Central Africa, and of Malaya where the emergency was still under way. It remained unclear whether the latest attempts to promote colonial economic growth and welfare would meet more success than their forerunners. The substantial accord and the elements of uncertainty in politicians' minds were reflected by the incoming Conservative Secretary of State for the Colonies, Oliver Lyttelton, when, apart from dutiful swipes at Labour's colonial record, he expressed contentment with the essential principles of policy enunciated by his predecessors. The extent to which successive Conservative administrations from 1951 to 1964 either devised answers to their specific difficulties or had solutions thrust upon them will inform much of the commentary and selection of documents in the next volume.

Notes to Part I

PREFACE

1. A selection of documentary collections in order of publicatio
Arthur Berriedale Keith, *Selected Speeches and Documents c British Colonial Policy, 1763–1917*, 2 vols (London: 1918, 19: and rep. 1 vol. 1948) and *Speeches and Documents on the Britis Dominions 1918–1931* (London: 1932, 1938, 1948; Oxford: 196 1966, etc.); Robert McGregor Dawson, *The Development of D minion Status 1900–1936* (London, 1937); Vincent Harlow an Frederick Madden, *British Colonial Developments, 1774–183 select documents* (Oxford: 1953); N. Mansergh, *Documents an Speeches on British Commonwealth Affairs, 1931–52*, 2 vols, (O ford: 1953), and *Documents and Speeches on Commonwealth A fairs, 1952–1962* (Oxford: 1963); James Eayrs, *The Commonwealt and Suez: A Documentary Survey* (London: 1964); Colin W Newbury, *British Policy towards West Africa: Select Documents vol. 1, 1786–1874; vol. 2, 1875–1914* (Oxford: 1965 and 1971); A F. Madden, *Imperial Constitutional Documents 1765–1965: A Sup plement* (Oxford: 1966); N. Mansergh, *The Transfer of Powe 1942–7: Constitutional Relations between Britain and India*, 12 vol (HMSO, 1970–83); I. Mary Cumpston, *The Growth of the Britis Commonwealth, 1880–1932* (London: 1973); Bishwa Nath Pan dey, *The Indian Nationalist Movement, 1885–1947: Select Docu ments* (London: 1979); Hugh Tinker, *Burma: The Struggle fo Independence, 1944–48*, 2 vols (HMSO, 1983-4); Frederick Mad den with David Fieldhouse, *Select Documents on the Constitu tional History of the British Empire and Commonwealth, vol. 1, 'Th Empire of the Bretaignes', 1175–1688* (Westport, Connecticut an London: 1985).

INTRODUCTION

1. Kenneth O. Morgan, *Labour in Power, 1945–1951* (Oxford: 1984) p. 190.
2. C. Northcote Parkinson, *Parkinson's Law or the Pursuit of Progress* (London, 1961) pp. 18–19.
3. CO 825/35/55104/1942 (ff. 46–7) item 61.
4. Sir Arthur Dawe, minute, CO 859/19/7475/1939, cited in D. G. M. Rampersad, 'Colonial Economic Development and Social

Welfare: The Case of the British West Indian Colonies, 1929–1947', unpublished D.Phil. thesis, University of Oxford, 1979, p. 199.

5. The total for the whole empire approved under the 1940 Act by 31 March 1945 was £23 985 386, but of this only £5.7m. had actually been issued, Colonial 106, pp. 27–8, *PP*(1944–5) IX, 597 and Colonial 211, Table VIII, *PP*(1948–9) XXIX, 1.
6. A. J. P. Taylor to William Roger Louis, see Louis, *Imperialism at Bay 1941–1945* (Oxford: 1977) p. x.
7. Graham Spry, 'India as a Factor in Anglo-American Relations', July 1942, in N. Mansergh, *Transfer of Power*, vol. II, p. 472.
8. Gent to Sir George Gater, 17 June 1942, CO 825/35/55104/1942.
9. 'Draft Joint Declaration as Amended to meet Views of Dominions', 19 January 1943, WP(43)33 in CO 323/1858 pt.II/9057 B, item 40.
10. Ibid, item 137.
11. K. M. de Silva, *A History of Sri Lanka* (Delhi: 1981) p. 461.
12. CAB 98/41: CMB(44) First Meeting, 22 March 1944.
13. This report of 1940–2 was reproduced in Colonial Office Confidential Print in 1944 and was published in 1979 by Kraus Reprint with an introduction by A. H. M. Kirk-Greene and extra chapters on Southern Rhodesia, native policy, and the proposed amalgamation of the Rhodesias and Nyasaland.
14. Caine to Sir George Gater, 16 August 1943, CO 852/588/2.
15. 'Overseas Financial Policy in Stage III' [War Cabinet version circulated on 15 May] in *The Collected Writings of John Maynard Keynes, vol. XXIV, Activities 1944–46: The Transition to Peace* (ed. by Donald Moggridge) (London and New York: 1979) pp. 256–95.
16. Speech to the Bristol Festival of the Transport and General Workers Union, 30 March 1946, cited in Alan Bullock, *Ernest Bevin – Foreign Secretary, 1945–1951* (London: 1983) p. 234.
17. Cited in Wm. Roger Louis, *The British Empire in the Middle East 1945–1951* (Oxford: 1984) p. 531.
18. Bullock, *Ernest Bevin*, pp. 404 ff.
19. Martin to Lloyd, 22 October 1951, CO 537/7137.
20. 'Review of the International Situation in Asia in the Light of the Korean Conflict', CP(50)200, 30 August 1950 in CAB 129/41 and PREM 8/1171.
21. 'Colombo Plan. Note by the Secretary of State for Foreign Affairs, the Chancellor of the Exchequer, the Secretary of State for Commonwealth Relations and the Minister of State for Colonial Affairs', C(51)51, 20 December 1951, CAB 129/48.
22. Gater to Battershill/Mitchell/Hall/Richards, 22 May 1946, confidential, CO 847/35/47234/1/1947.

23. [R. E. Robinson] 'Development of Theories of Native Admin istration 1927–47', December 1947, CO 847/35/47234/7/1947.
24. Cmd. 7167, *The Colonial Empire (1939–47)*, July 1947, *PP* (1946–7 X, 403.
25. 'Constitutional Development in Africa', Conference of Africar Governors, 1947, paper AGC no. 2, pp. 2–3, CO 847/36/47238/1 Pt.1; and 'Report of the Committee on the Conference o African Governors', 22 May 1947, App. III, paras 2–3, CC 847/36/47238/1947.
26. African 1173. Confidential. Colonial Office Summer School o African Administration First Session August 18–28, 1947 a Queens' College Cambridge. African Local Government, CC 879/150. In his introduction as Chairman, Cohen noted, p. 5:

> The weather was brilliant; indeed we had an uninterrupted series of fine days. Anyone who knows Cambridge in Augus will realise what that meant. The river was much used and the Orchard at Grantchester served many teas to members of the School on Sunday. As a result of the arrangements made by Mr R. E. Robinson of the Colonial Office, we were able to play cricket on two afternoons. Those of us who have never graduated above village cricket had the privilege of batting and fielding on the stately and spacious John's ground, and, if we came from West Africa, of being bowled out by Mr Robinson himself.

27. *Report of the Commission of Enquiry into Disturbances in the Gol Coast, 1948,* Colonial no. 231.
28. Minutes by P. J. Noel-Baker, 24 January 1949, DO 35/3585, anc 11 July 1949, DO 35/3586.

Part II
Documents

DOCUMENT 1

West India Royal Commission: Extract from a Memorandum by the West India Department of the Colonial Office, 20 May 1938, CO 318/433/1

The view of the West India Department is that so far no case for any general commission has been made out. The idea is attractive politically, but it is felt that large-scale improvements in the West Indies could not be effected without very heavy further expenditure from United Kingdom funds, which present financial conditions would not be likely to permit. The appointment of such a Commission would therefore be likely to raise hopes doomed from the outset to disappointment: and the consequences in the long run might be most unfortunate.

DOCUMENT 2

West India Royal Commission: Minute by Sir John Campbell, 23 May 1938, CO 318/433/1

General

I am not acquainted with the day-to-day work of the Dept:. The following comments are based solely on such cases – usually important – as I have seen during the past eight years. It must be recollected that these, possibly, do not constitute a representative sample.

Broad case for a Royal Commission

Things are clearly, and as a matter of common knowledge, not going very well in the W. Indies. There have been fairly serious, and recurring, riots and unrest, over a wide area. Both sugar and cocoa are doing badly; there seems also little prospect of any near-future development. The probability would therefore seem to be that the underlying causes of this unrest are not likely, in the absence of some new policy steadfastly pursued for some time, to be removed? Unrest, possibly getting more and more serious, would therefore seem probable. Nor can the position in Palestine, I think, be excluded from consideration here; it is not improbable that the opinion may grow that there is something fundamentally wrong – something wider than the WI local problem. Whether that view be right or wrong, it is, one would think, likely to be put forward. The last R Comm: sat about forty years ago;[1] and this by itself would probably be considered – in the light of recent happenings – as a strong argument for a further authoritative general survey of the position.

Lastly, the broad position seems to be that more money must be found, if there is to be any substantial improvement in the near future. The main pivot of the thing is sugar; and nothing can be done with sugar in the absence of aid from the United Kingdom.

What one may call the normal arguments, available to the Dept: and the S/S [Secretary of State], are most unlikely to lead to anything material; but, if there were a considered recommendation from a R Comm: on the point, that would presumably carry great weight? My own view is that political and other pressure – principally the insistent pressure of the march of events – will in fact necessitate a review of the whole WI problem, on the broadest lines; and it seems to me that there is therefore a strong case for the appointment of a R Comm:.

Diagnosis of the main causes of the present situation

Subject to what has been said above under 'general', I would classify the main causes of the present situation somewhat as follows: –

(i) The marked conservatism of the general attitude in the W Indies. Traditionalism seems almost universal. There has been little real attempt to change policy, and practice, in a rapidly changing world. There are still many absentee landlords, I understand; there is still a marked 'plantation' attitude; an absence of energy and efficiency; a tendency to cling strongly to the belief that the former 'good times' are bound to recur; little effort to repay debt, or secure debt settlements more in consonance with the position as it stands today; – it strikes one as all early nineteenth-century mentality and practice.

(ii) The difficulties which the constitutional position creates as regards improvement of these fundamental conditons. The S/S[Secretary of State] has, in the majority of the territories, little real power; his advice has therefore to have regard to this.

(iii) The heavy cost of administration, relative to the revenue which can be made available. Many of the political units are, clearly, far too small for efficient administration on the present basis; there are some – hardly the size of a small provincial town in England – which are provided with the whole paraphernalia of a full-sized Government. While one recognizes the very great strength of the local feeling on this point, the financial and economic consequences are inescapable. Money, which should be available for development and social services, is necessarily spent on *personnel.*

(iv) The standard of administration, and of general efficiency, is low. Much of the work is undoubtedly badly done; the staffs are large, but very badly paid. The CDAC has been much impressed with this aspect of things: they have had many cases where it seemed to them that the administration had been markedly inefficient, and unsatisfactory.

(v) It all comes back to the root question of the economic possibilities of the territories. Apart from Trinidad – with its oil – they are primarily agricultural, with some subsidiary aid from forests, gums, minerals, and so on. One gets the impression that this position has never been squarely faced. Almost everyone seems to agree that, broadly, peasant settlement is essential; but the efforts in that direction have been spasmodic – and, I am afraid, badly thought out, and inefficient in actual operation. There is a heavy load of debt, contracted in much more prosperous times: the debt and credit problem still remains unsolved, though it has been approached here and there. The population is 'feckless': – easy going, little mindful of the future, largely lazy, basically primitive, but probably still, as in the past, potentially dangerous when things go seriously wrong. The general level of taxation seems to me high, considering the trade and production position broadly; in some areas, it is very high. I do not think that – apart from largely increased production, or a material rise in prices – any solution is likely to be found, generally, by tax increases; and increased taxation, in present circumstances, may I think be definitely ruled out – except perhaps in a few special areas. It would, in my view, be dangerous, and inadvisable in itself.

America

The USA is perhaps inclined to judge British colonial administration by the specimens which it sees of it in the territories on, or adjacent to, the American continent. While most Americans probably see little but the Bahamas, etc – the primarily tourist islands – Pan American airways are rapidly linking up all the British territories in the W Indies with the USA, directly or indirectly. One sees signs of a growing interest in the administration of these territories on the part of Americans, reflected in the American magazines. The W Indies are, to some considerable extent, the British show-window for the USA. I am afraid it is not a very striking exhibit. For the moment, the 'differentness', and the picturesque aspect, predominate; but criticism is already there; and it will I think grow. At any time, a Miss Mayo may arise for the W. Indies;[2] and, if the intention was to present a highly coloured picture, strongly critical of the British effort, material for that would not unfortunately be lacking, I think. There are many reasons why Americans should be interested in British colonial administration in the W Indian areas; and not a few why some of them should wish to paint a picture of that administration in as dark colours as possible. This consideration may not be without some importance in considering whether there should, or should not, be a R. Commission?

Notes

1. Under the chairmanship of Sir Henry Norman, it reported in 1897: see *Report of the West India Royal Commission*, C.8655, *PP*(1898)L.
2. Katherine Mayo was the author of *Mother India* (London and New York, 1927) and an American. The result of her inquiries into the state of India particularly in matters of health, the book presented readers with a dramatic picture of often appalling conditions; these she attributed above all to the nature of Indians themselves and to their own society, rather than to British rule. A vigorous public debate followed its appearance.

DOCUMENT 3

West India Royal Commission: Extract from Conclusions of a Cabinet Meeting held at 10 Downing Street, Wednesday 15 June 1938, CO 318/433/1

FOR SECRET RECORD IN DEPT 17/6/38.
SECRET. CABINET 28 (38)

8. The Secretary of State for the Colonies said that after careful consideration he had reached the decision that a Royal Commission ought to be appointed to examine the whole situation in the West Indies. He had been preparing a Memorandum for the Cabinet setting forth the reasons for and against a Royal Commission and asking permission to announce it within a week or two. Action had been precipitated, however, by an announcement that the question was to be raised in Parliament. Consequently, after discussion with the Prime Minister and the Chancellor of the Exchequer, he had found it necessary on the previous day to announce the intention of the Government to recommend a Royal Commission. He thought it necessary, however, to warn the Cabinet, that the Government would have to be ready to spend more money on the West Indies than at present. The Royal Commission was likely to report that the present position was rather discreditable, and its recommendations were almost certain to involve more expenditure. Some of this might perhaps be obtained from the West Indies themselves, as in some of the Islands there was the possibility of increased taxation. But part would have to be found from the Mother Country. It would be disastrous to send a Royal Commission and then reject its proposals purely on financial grounds. The Chancellor of the Exchequer had agreed that, notwithstanding this latter consideration, a Royal Commission was the proper course. The announcement had been well received in the House of Commons. In reply to a question, he said that a recent statement by Mr Lloyd George that the only telephone service in the Island was owned by an American Banana Company had been true a year ago but he thought it was probably not true today.

The Chancellor of the Exchequer agreed that, notwithstanding the probability that a Royal Commission would result in proposals involving increased expenditure, the course proposed by the Colonial Secretary was the right one. He hoped that the Royal Commission would ascertain why it was that Cuba could produce sugar profitably without any subsidy, whereas the British West Indian Islands were struggling in spite of a heavy preference. He would like to put on record that it would not be sufficient for the Royal Commission to recommend a larger subsidy for the Islands without full explanation.

The Lord President of the Council said that the United States of America provided an unlimited market for Cuban sugar, to which a large preference was granted.

The Secretary of State for the Colonies added that the best Sugar Companies in the West Indies were able to show a profit. Perhaps the Royal Commission would be able to show how that profit could be extended to other Companies.

The Chancellor of the Exchequer hoped that the Royal Commission would discover how efficiency could be achieved and the precise action that ought to be taken. It was not much use transmitting general recommendations to relatively inefficient administrations.

The Prime Minister recalled that the Royal Commission would be concerned not with Jamaica alone but with the whole West Indies. He had been into the question and it seemed to him that there was no short cut to the rehabilitation of the Islands. There were only a limited number of industries in the West Indies, and all were of an agricultural nature. The market for their products was limited, and, so far as sugar was concerned, was decreasing. It might be possible to make the sugar industry more efficient, but the probable consequence would be to increase unemployment, for example, by the adoption of labour-saving machinery. It might be necessary to take steps to enable the natives to obtain subsistence from the land without exporting the product of their labour. For that, more finance would be necessary, and he did not think that further expenditure could be avoided.

The Cabinet agreed –

> To approve the announcement made by the Secretary of State for the Colonies on the previous day in Parliament that a Royal Commission on the West Indies was to be appointed.

DOCUMENT 4

Outbreak of the Second World War: Circular Telegram from the Secretary of State for the Colonies to all Colonial Dependencies, except Palestine and Transjordan but including British North Borneo Company, 15 September 1939, CO 691/174/42154/1

IMMEDIATE
No. 54 Confidential

1. It must be appreciated that, as financial strain of prolonged war on Empire resources is likely to be great, all expenditure by government (and indeed by general public) should, as far as possible, be avoided which (a) involves use of foreign exchange . . . or (b) creates demand for unessential goods and so deflects men, material and shipping from war purposes. In this connection you will appreciate that it will be very desirable to replace imported goods of all kinds especially foodstuffs by local produce wherever possible.
2. Subject to the considerations at (a) and (b) above I should like to see the present activities of government continue on the scale at present approved or in contemplation in all cases where no serious difficulty is seen in financing them from local revenues. But in those Colonies where difficulty is already being experienced or is likely to be experienced in balancing the budget, or where the Colony is already in receipt of Treasury assistance, I should be glad of an indication as early as possible of the nature of the economies you would be forced to introduce were you to be called upon to carry on without Treasury assistance or Colonial Development Fund money for the period of the war.
3. I am anxious to see existing social services and development activities disturbed as little as possible, both because serious retrenchment and consequential curtailment of services at present juncture might have very unfortunate effect on Colonial peoples and also because on grounds of policy it is important to maintain our reputation for enlightened Colonial administration. In particular I am anxious to avoid any retrenchment of personnel.
4. The information asked for in paragraph 2 is required merely to assist me in my discussions with the Treasury and does not indicate any decision on the major questions of policy involved. In any event no retrenchment or curtailment of services should be undertaken pending further instructions.

DOCUMENT 5

Outbreak of the Second World War: Circular Telegram from the Secretary of State for the Colonies to all Colonies, 22 September 1939, CO 691/174/42154/1

No. 62 Confidential

My confidential circular telegram No. 54.

1. While it is very difficult to make any forecast of effects of war on Colonial budgets the following wholly tentative observations which developments may modify may be of use to you: –
   (a) Although experience in last war would seem to indicate that there will be a general rise in prices of all commodities, special action which is now being taken in this country and elsewhere to control prices and existence of large world supplies, actual, or potential, of many commodities may have result that prices of only a few Colonial commodities will rise considerably above their pre-war level. Moreover owing to rise in insurance, freights and other incidentals rise in prices in importing countries will not involve equivalent rise in prices received by producers. In some cases, however, quantities exported may increase substantially and in case of certain commodities where American consumption is dominant factor fall in value of sterling has already caused some increase in price.
   (b) Increase in total value of exports may not immediately result in increase in total value of imports. Restriction of imports from Canada and most foreign countries is as you know essential on exchange grounds. Normal flow of imports may well be restricted also by: –
      (i) Difficulties of shipping.
      (ii) Preoccupation of industry here and elsewhere with more essential war purposes.

   Whatever the value of exports falling off in volume of imports is therefore probable with consequent falling off of normal revenue and accumulation of funds locally.
   (c) A number of services in connection with war activities are likely to involve some fresh expenditure by almost all Colonial Governments.
2. Financial effort necessary to secure successful prosecution of war will entail unprecedented sacrifices by United Kingdom taxpayer. Continuance of assistance from United Kingdom Exchequer, whether directly or through Colonial Develop-

ment Fund, will in any event be difficult enough and difficulty would be increased if it could be shown that people of Colonial Empire were not already bearing their full share of the burden.

3. In these circumstances I consider that it is important to ensure that all classes make the maximum contribution to revenue which it is reasonable to ask having regard to their taxable capacity and I suggest that existing taxation should be reviewed with this end in view. Resolutions which have been received show how anxious the people of the Colonial Empire are to help in its defence and best psychological moment for securing consent to increase of taxation would seem to be in near future, possibly immediately after introduction of emergency budget in this country. No date has yet been fixed for this, but I will advise you when it is known.
4. While I appreciate that in many territories it would be inequitable and undesirable to increase the rates of direct taxation at present payable by the mass of the people, I am of opinion that the two following possibilities should be examined: –
   (a) That taxation paid by wealthier members of the community might be increased. Imposition of income tax or increase of it if it already exists would probably be the most scientific way of securing this and I hope that if it is at all practicable you will not be unduly deterred by administrative difficulties from imposing such taxation. Failing income tax some other form of direct taxation is I suggest indicated as being easiest means of ensuring that taxation is paid by those who can best bear its burden.
   (b) That on general grounds it is very desirable that some arrangement should be made to ensure that Governments obtain an adequate share of any excess profits accruing as the result of war. I suggest that whether or no prices are in fact already showing tendency to rise it will be desirable to pass legislation on the subject without delay. As regards profits from exports it may be found that only practicable method of achieving the object is some form of export duty based on the excess of war-time prices and quantities of over pre-war prices and quantities.
5. As regards local trade problem of excess profits will not arise if as I hope action is taken to prevent profiteering. If as may be the case (see paragraph 1 (b) above) there is a shortage of imports and an accumulation of funds locally, there will probably be a marked rise in margin between c.i.f. price of imports and their retail price as well as in the prices of local

produce. I have indeed already had indications from some Dependencies that this is occurring. Machinery to control internal prices of at any rate main articles whether imported or produced locally may therefore be required, as it was in most Dependencies in last war. Legislation is already in force in this country and in some dependencies and I suggest that where nothing has yet been done to meet the contingency early action will be desirable before any substantial rise actually takes place. United Kingdom control arrangements are so complicated that I doubt whether information as to those arrangements would be of value to you in dealing with the matter.

6. Please telegraph any comments you may have to offer on this telegram and in particular I should be glad to know before you are in any way committed by publication what action you would propose to take arising out of paragraph 4.

DOCUMENT 6

West India Royal Commission: Note by C. Carstairs,[1] 6 January 1940, CO 318/439/9

Arguments for and against the postponement of the publication of the West Indian Royal Commission Report until the end of the present war

I. *For*

This is briefly that the Report contains several passages which will provide material for hostile propaganda, which will take no account of other passages in the Report which give a less gloomy picture, or of ultimate proposals for Colonial Development.

II. *Against*

1. The West Indian Colonies have, for the last year or more been enjoying a comparative respite from industrial and other troubles, partly because it is widely known that the whole economic and social problem of the West Indies has been under consideration by the West Indies Royal Commission, and there is a general sense of expectancy pending the publication of the Report. This situation cannot be held indefinitely, and a more or less indefinite postponement of publication would almost certainly contribute to a gradual deterioration of the situation, and quite certainly give rise to the feeling that the Home Government, despite numerous expressions of concern in the past, have no intention of doing anything substantial to alleviate the lot of the West Indian.
2. Public opinion in this country and Parliament is awaiting the Report with interest. The Secretary of State is subject to periodic enquiries as to its progress, and statements have been made in the House of Commons which amount to a virtual undertaking to publish the Report. Its postponement would, therefore, come as a considerable surprise to interested opinion, and it would be difficult, if not impossible, to avoid giving rise to the suspicion that much worse criticisms of the Report than actually exist, and (as above) that the Government is not in earnest in dealing with Colonial problems.
3. The work of the Commission and the existence of the Report are well known abroad; a decision [not] to publish it will give rise to surmises as to its contents which could reach any height of extravagance without there being the possibility of an effective counter.
4. The proposal to publish a short version (on the pretext of

economising on paper) which would omit the offending passages, is open to the similar objection that much worse things would be thought to be withheld than are actually in the Report.

5. The attitude of the Commission must also be taken into consideration, especially that of Sir Walter Citrine.[2] He consented on the grounds of public interest to accept a very considerable mitigation of the severity of certain statements in the Report, and he would in all probability take serious (and effective) objection to postponing as casting doubt on his good faith and judgment in this matter. Other members, less wedded to the severer passages, might well object that postponement would by implication associate them with passages far more lurid than any in which they have in fact concurred.
6. The Secretary of State for Foreign Affairs may not be aware of the fact that the Report is not to be published in isolation, but together with a declaration of Government policy which will include the adoption of that recommendation by the Commission which is of best propaganda value, namely, the proposal to establish a fund of £1,000,000 a year from United Kingdom funds for Social Welfare Development. If, as may be assumed in the event of agreement by the Cabinet to the S. of S. wider proposals such a declaration of policy were made irrespective of the publication or otherwise of the Commission's Report, the Report would be published at a time when the declaration of policy would be no longer prominently in the public mind, with the result that the Government would have made the worst of both worlds by letting themselves into hostile criticism based on the Report without being able effectively to counter that by means of the development scheme.
7. There is finally the broad question of principle. Are considerations of pure wartime expediency (and debatable expediency) to over-ride the open and above board technique on which we publicly congratulate ourselves, and which is a part of the system of institutions and codes of behaviour for which we are professedly fighting?

Notes

1. Carstairs, Charles Young, b.1910; since 1 April 1939, Acting Principal Secretary, West Indian Department of the Colonial Office.
2. Citrine, Sir Walter McLennan, b.1887; General Secretary of the Trade Union Congress, 1926–46.

DOCUMENT 7

Colonial Development and Welfare Bill: Speech in the House of Commons by Malcolm MacDonald,[1] 21 May 1940, *Hansard Parliamentary Debates* (1939–40), vol. 361, cols 41–8, 50–1

I beg to move, 'That the Bill be now read a Second time'.

The heart of every Member in the House to-day is gripped by a deep anxiety, and throughout the nation that anxiety is felt, for so much of the most vigorous and best of our young manhood is at this moment exposed to mortal danger. In the fields of Belgium, in the air, and on the sea, they are engaged in defending, against a ruthless foe, our lives and our land and our liberties. There is no step that this House would hesitate to take to support their stubborn resolution, their glorious courage and their fighting skill, upon which, with the renowned martial qualities of our Allies, the future of civilisation depends. It is one of the awful features of the war that it releases almost universally forces of destruction. Material things, precious works of art, human lives and man's painfully achieved records of progress are all alike exposed to possible annihilation. The greater part of the time of hon. and peace-loving Members of this House is now also devoted to the stern business of destruction. The Prime Minister said that the policy of the Government is to wage war, and by far the greater part of those vast sums of money which we are asking the taxpayers to-day to contribute will be turned into weapons for discomfiting, defeating, destroying the enemy.

It is characteristic that whilst every ounce of our energy is thrown into that task, this House nevertheless finds time to turn and to offer substantial and indeed generous encouragement to Colonial development. In the midst of the ruin of so much, it is good to be engaged still upon certain works of construction. Moreover, there is another significance attaching to our proceedings this afternoon. At this critical hour let the world mark the passage of the Colonial Development and Welfare Bill through the British Parliament as a sign of our faith in ultimate victory. This nation will pass triumphantly through its present ordeal, however hard and grim and desperate the struggle may be. When the enemy is worsted and the war is finished, Britain will still exercise vast responsibilities for the government of Colonial peoples. In the meantime we must not default upon our Colonial obligations, we must not let slip the experienced skill of our guiding hand; we must still, even now, have a constant care to protect and to promote the well-being of our fellow subjects in the Empire overseas. In these sombre days our anxieties and our hopes are fully shared by the peoples of the Colonies. It seems to me that one of the most notable assurances that our cause is just is the fact that these distant peoples, alien to us in race, who are ruled by us, sprang instantly and spontaneously to our side at the moment of the declaration of war.

There are some 50 Colonial territories. Most of them are far removed from the scene of our European quarrels. They had no hand in the writing of that chapter in the story of international relations which closed so disastrously on 3rd September last. Many of them are comparatively small communities which, in those circumstances, might well have sought to excuse themselves from suffering the hazards and the dangers of modern war, but not a single one of them chose to take that course. On the contrary, every single Colonial territory has voluntarily associated itself with us, every one of them has asked in what way it could help best the Allied war effort, and they are contributing, by gifts of treasure, by the production of essential foodstuffs and raw materials, and by the eager raising of Colonial military units far in excess of anything that they did at a similar period in the last war. I think it is significant that these 60,000,000 people, scattered over 50 different territories, who are not yet free to govern themselves, who are governed by us, recognised instinctively from that experience that we are the true guardians of the liberties and the happiness of small peoples. Nevertheless, the proposals for assistance towards Colonial development which are contained in this Bill were not devised after war had begun. They are not a bribe or a reward for the Colonies' support in this supreme crisis. They were conceived long before the war. For many months before that the details of these proposals were already being worked out in the Colonial Office. They are a part of the normal peace-time development of our Colonial policy, and if we had not been engaged in war, the Government would still have been introducing this legislation in the present Session of Parliament.

The voters in this small democratic island have many large responsibilities, but they have none that is greater than their charge of the government of Colonial peoples. The problems of development and welfare in the Colonies are very different from those problems in this country. For instance, to take an extreme case, there are communities in parts of the Colonial Empire where life is as simple and ideas are as primitive as they were among our ancestors in this island some 2000 years ago. That is not typical. The Colonial Empire, of course, contains a great variety of peoples and of circumstances. There are countries within it where there are societies famed for culture and long-established civilisation. Nevertheless, it is true, generally speaking, that economic and social requirements in the Colonies are quite different, in many cases they are at a far, far earlier stage of development than they are in Western Europe, and it would be a profound error to suppose that economic and social standards which are established here and which are rightly considered as a minimum standard by our people in this country, can be translated at once, suddenly, to the many different peoples in the many different countries of the Colonial Empire. But what we do have to ensure is that the progress from their existing standards is steady, that it is suitable to the different climatic and other conditions in which they live, and that they have the actual means of making that progress at their disposal.

In the last generation there has been a great deal of wise government of the Colonies by experienced, sympathetic, understanding British administrators, aided to an ever-increasing degree by local executive officers and legislatures. The advance has been continuous. For example, the extension of the service of trained agricultural officers throughout the Colonial Empire has led to remarkable improvements in the methods of production and marketing of Colonial goods; the steady reinforcement of the Colonial medical service at every front in the Colonial Empire has resulted in an increasingly effective attack upon tropical and other Colonial diseases; and the slow expansion of the education service is gradually bringing enlightenment where sometimes only dark ignorance prevailed before. But in all this important process many Colonies have suffered from one handicap. The development of the resources and the services of a country is naturally an expensive business. It requires a considerable expenditure of money, it requires a certain reliable robustness of revenue, and the simple truth is that many of our Colonial territories have not had adequate means to achieve that object.

Of course that is not true of all of them. In some of the Colonies there are rich resources of material wealth. They are producers of gold, copper, tin, oil and rubber, and these countries are comparatively well off, having ample revenue to finance enlightened and progressive government. But that is not the situation in a majority of the Colonies. They are mostly and almost wholly agricultural countries, and though it may be that in the past the fruits of their soil were able to draw a goodly ransom from the markets of the world, that has not been the case during these latter years, when agricultural markets have been glutted and prices have often fallen to a disastrously low level. At present a majority of the Colonies cannot finance from their own energies and out of their own resources their own proper developments. They cannot undertake some of the engineering, irrigation and other works of capital development, they cannot afford to finance the agricultural and veterinary research, and they cannot afford to increase their service of agricultural officers, all of which are essential if the exploitation of their economic resources is to be realised to the full. Nor can the territories in some cases afford medical research, the building of clinics, hospitals and schools, and the steady increase of their health, educational and other technical officers necessary if the standard of their social services is to be what it should be.

Therefore the Government are introducing this legislation, because the British people who have assumed responsibilities for these Colonies in these circumstances must assume responsibility for providing the wherewithal for establishing these works. This principle has been partially recognised in the past. There is, for instance, the existing Colonial Development Act. That Act is a most valuable Measure which has been on the Statute Book for the last 10 years, but it is one which this Bill now seeks to supersede. Those who are familiar with the Debates of 1929 will remember that even then the primary purpose of our legislation was not to help colonial development for its own sake, but in order to stimulate that development mostly to bring additional work to idle hands in this country. It was devised as part of our scheme to solve our own unemployment problem.

In that respect, as in other respects, the Bill which we are discussing this afternoon breaks new ground. It establishes the duty of taxpayers in this country to contribute directly and for its own sake towards the development in the widest sense of the word of the colonial peoples for whose good government the taxpayers of this country are ultimately responsible. I should like to pay a tribute to one of my colleagues whose part in the achievement of this policy I have not noticed commented upon in the newspapers or elsewhere. It is very easy for a Colonial Secretary to devise a policy like this, and it is extremely easy for the Colonial Secretary to advance upon the Treasury and ask for several million pounds to be devoted out of the Revenue for this purpose, but it is not easy for the Chancellor of the Exchequer to grant that request. It is particularly difficult for him to do it in the middle of a great war, when many other urgent, irresistible and incalculable demands are being made upon his resources; but my Noble Friend who is being introduced this afternoon into another place, Viscount Simon, never demurred. He encouraged and supported these proposals as Chancellor of the Exchequer, and he accepted them, and I think that he, and his advisers in the Treasury who were equally sympathetic, deserve our praise for high statesmanship and vision.

This legislation proposes fresh departures in a number of directions from the points which have been reached by our existing Colonial Development Act. Briefly, I should like to mention the three most important of these. First, the moneys to be made available for colonial development are to be multiplied more than five-fold. Instead of a fund restricted to a maximum of £1,000,000 a year, this Bill would authorise expenditure on colonial research up to £500,000 a year, and expenditure on colonial development and welfare up to £5,000,000 a year. The provision with regard to research is to be made for an indefinite number of years, and the provision with regard to development and welfare is to be assured for the next ten years. These figures £500,000 and £5,000,000 are maximum figures so far as the present legislation is concerned. Even in more auspicious circumstances, and even if we were still in the blessed days of peace, it could not be supposed that we should arrive at once at that rate of expenditure. Time will be necessary for the careful working out and vetting of comprehensive well-balanced plans of development. Then time will be required for putting these plans into practice, and it will be some time after that before the many schemes involving development reach their maximum activity and costliness. Even in peace-time I think that that process of working up to the maximum of expenditure would perhaps take some two or three years, but in war-time, alas, other obstacles are likely to lie across the path. In some cases material which might be required for Colonial schemes will be being put to other more urgent uses, and in some cases labour which might be required for schemes of Colonial development will be engaged upon tasks which aim directly at the defeat of the enemy. I do not think that the maximum figures mentioned in this legislation are likely to be attained at any time during the war, but I can assure the House, and the great colonial audience outside this House, that we shall work towards these figures as far as and as fast as the exigencies of these unhappy times permit.

The second new departure to which I wish to draw attention is this. Under the existing Act it is not only the money but the object on which that money can be expended which is somewhat limited. For example, money out of the existing Colonial Development Fund had to be spent upon objects which were concerned with the material development of the Colonies, and under that definition some of the most important activities of colonial Governments were absolutely debarred from obtaining any assistance. For example, technical education might qualify, but as regards all the rest of educational activity, a Colonial Government could only appeal in vain for help from the Colonial Development Fund. In this legislation we are going to widen the whole field of works and activity which we can assist. Certainly the Government will attach particular importance to giving assistance to work of economic development, because these are the works which will increase most rapidly the material wealth of the colonies concerned. These are the works which will enable us to exploit to the maximum extent the natural resources of these territories, and these are the works therefore which will put a colony at the earliest possible moment in a position to finance out of its own resources the administration and social services which are required.

Dr Haden Guest (Islington North): To which works is the right hon. Gentleman referring?

Mr MacDonald: I was referring to all sorts of works, such as irrigation, agricultural development works, and similar works of economic development which will increase productivity. Our object under this legislation is to develop the Colonies so that as far as possible they become self-supporting units. But in the meantime their citizens must enjoy a proper standard of social services, and we shall count as qualifying for assistance under this Bill every part of the health and medical activities and every part of the educational activities of a colonial Government. In this legislation the word 'development' has not a narrow materialistic interpretation. It certainly covers the development of the material economic resources of a territory, but it also covers everything which ministers to the physical, mental or moral development of the colonial peoples of whom we are the trustees.

There is in the existing legislation a third cramping provision which we propose to abolish under this Bill. For the moment money out of the Colonial Development Fund can be contributed only towards the capital cost of works. We cannot contribute a penny towards the normal maintenance cost of those works. We can contribute towards the erection of a research station or a hospital or to the making of an improved transport system in a Colony, but we cannot contribute any money towards the running costs of those schemes once they have been created and established. Therefore, if a Colony could not afford out of its own revenue to maintain those hospitals, research stations or improved methods of transport, and so on, which it might have been given, those benefits to the Colony never came into being at all. It has been a rigid principle of Colonial policy up to date that every Colonial territory should be a self-supporting unit and that its citizens should have only those services which they themselves out of their own moneys could afford to maintain. That was a restriction which hit very hardly some of the smaller and poorer Colonies, and because of it they have had to do without services with which they really ought to have been supplied. Therefore, this legislation proposes to abolish that inability to make payments out of the Exchequer towards the maintenance cost of development work. If this Bill goes through Parliament we shall be able in future to contribute towards not only the initial costs of establishment but the running costs of any of those services which are needed in these days for the proper welfare of Colonial people.

* * *

In the midst of a struggle for our very lives the British Government are launching on new action which is worthy of the highest traditions of our Imperial policy. I will say no more than that. This is not a time for flowery oratory. This is not a time to celebrate in speech our great Imperial record. It is not a time for boasting. It is a time for that quiet inner confidence that in the struggle which now faces us we shall prevail and we shall survive, and that in the days of peace which our exertions shall regain for us it is our destiny to complete the great work for our Colonial peoples to which we set our hands long ago.

Note

1. MacDonald spoke as Minister of Health, having been moved from the Colonial Office a few days before when Churchill formed a new government on becoming Prime Minister, 9 May 1940.

DOCUMENT 8

The Atlantic Charter, 14 August 1941[1]

Joint Declaration by the President and the Prime Minister: 12 August, 1941

The President of the United States of America and the Prime Minister, Mr Churchill, representing His Majesty's Government in the United Kingdom, being met together, deem it right to make known certain common principles in the national policies of their respective countries on which they base their hopes for a better future for the world:

First, their countries seek no aggrandisement, territorial or other.

Second, they desire to see no territorial changes that do not accord with the freely expressed wishes of the peoples concerned.

Third, they respect the right of all peoples to choose the form of government under which they will live; and they wish to see sovereign rights and self-government restored to those who have been forcibly deprived of them.

Fourth, they will endeavour, with due respect for their existing obligations, to further the enjoyment by all States, great or small, victor or vanquished, of access, on equal terms, to the trade and to the raw materials of the world which are needed for their economic prosperity.

Fifth, they desire to bring about the fullest collaboration between all nations in the economic field, with the object of securing for all improved labour standards, economic advancement and social security.

Sixth, after the final destruction of Nazi tyranny, they hope to see established a peace which will afford to all nations the means of dwelling in safety within their own boundaries, and which will afford assurance that all the men in all the lands may live out their lives in freedom from fear and want.

Seventh, such a peace should enable all men to traverse the high seas and oceans without hindrance.

Eighth, they believe all of the nations of the world, for realistic as well as spiritual reasons, must come to the abandonment of the use of force. Since no future peace can be maintained if land, sea or air armaments continue to be employed by nations which threaten, or may threaten, aggression outside of their frontiers, they believe, pending the establishment of a wider and permanent system of general security, that the disarmament of such nations is essential. They will likewise aid and encourage all other practicable measures which will lighten for peace-loving peoples the crushing burden of armaments.

Note

1. The Declaration was widely publicized. This text is taken from Cmd. 6321, *PP* (1940–41) VIII, 591.

DOCUMENT 9

The Atlantic Charter: Extract from a Speech by the Prime Minister in the House of Commons, 9 September 1941. *Hansard Parliamentary Debates*, vol. 372, cols 67–9

The Prime Minister (Mr Churchill): Late in July I learned that the President of the United States would welcome a meeting with me in order to survey the entire world position in relation to the settled and common interests of our respective countries. As I was sure that Parliament would approve, I obtained His Majesty's permission to leave the country. I crossed the Atlantic Ocean in one of our latest battleships to meet the President at a convenient place. I was, as the House knows, accompanied by the First Sea Lord, the Chief of the Imperial General Staff, and the Vice-Chief of the Air Staff, together with the Permanent Secretary to the Foreign Office and others. We were, therefore, in a position to discuss with the President and with his technical advisers every question relating to the war and to the state of affairs after the war.

Important conclusions were reached on four main topics: First of all, on the Eight-Point Declaration of the broad principles and aims which guide and govern the actions of the British and United States Governments and peoples amid the many dangers by which they are beset in these times. Secondly, on measures to be taken to help Russia to resist the hideous onslaught which Hitler has made upon her. Thirdly, the policy to be pursued towards Japan in order, if possible, to put a stop to further encroachment in the Far East likely to endanger the safety or interests of Great Britain or the United States and thus, by timely action, prevent the spreading of the war to the Pacific Ocean. Fourthly, there was a large number of purely technical matters which were dealt with, and close personal relations were established between high naval, military and air authorities of both countries. I shall refer to some of these topics in the course of my statement.

I have, as the House knows, hitherto consistently deprecated the formulation of peace aims or war aims – however you put it – by His Majesty's Government, at this stage. I deprecate it at this time, when the end of the war is not in sight, when the conflict sways to and fro with alternating fortunes and when conditions and associations at the end of the war are unforeseeable. But a Joint Declaration by Great Britain and the

United States is an event of a totally different nature. Although the principles in the Declaration, and much of the language, have long been familiar to the British and American democracies, the fact that it is a united Declaration sets up a milestone or monument which needs only the stroke of victory to become a permanent part of the history of human progress. The purpose of the Joint Declaration signed by President Roosevelt and myself on 12th August, is stated in the Preamble to be:

> To make known certain common principles in the national policies of our respective countries on which they base their hopes for a better future for the world.

No words are needed to emphasise the future promise held out to the world by such a Joint Declaration by the United States and Great Britain. I need only draw attention, for instance, to the phrase in Paragraph 6, 'after the final destruction of the Nazi tyranny' to show the profound and vital character of the solemn agreement into which we have jointly entered. Questions have been asked, and will no doubt be asked, as to exactly what is implied by this or that point, and explanations have been invited. It is a wise rule that when two parties have agreed a statement one of them shall not, thereafter, without consultation with the other, seek to put special or strained interpretations upon this or that passage. I propose, therefore, to speak to-day only in an exclusive sense.

First, the Joint Declaration does not try to explain how the broad principles proclaimed by it are to be applied to each and every case, which will have to be dealt with when the war comes to an end. It would not be wise for us, at this moment, to be drawn into laborious discussions on how it is to fit all the manifold problems with which we shall be faced after the war. Secondly, the Joint Declaration does not qualify in any way the various statements of policy which have been made from time to time about the development of constitutional government in India, Burma or other parts of the British Empire. We are pledged by the Declaration of August, 1940, to help India to obtain free and equal partnership in the British Commonwealth with ourselves, subject, of course, to the fulfilment of obligations arising from our long connection with India and our responsibilities to its many creeds, races and interests. Burma also is covered by our considered policy of establishing Burmese self-government and by the measures already in progress. At the Atlantic meeting, we had in mind, primarily,the restoration of the sovereignty, self-government and national life of the States and nations of Europe now under the Nazi yoke, and the principles governing any alterations in the territorial boundaries which may have to be made. So that is quite a separate problem from the progressive evolution of self-governing institutions in the regions and peoples which owe allegiance to the British Crown. We have made declarations on these matters which are complete in themselves, free from a[m]biguity and related to the conditions and circumstances of territories and peoples affected. They will be found to be entirely in harmony with the high conception of freedom and justice which inspired the Joint Declaration.

DOCUMENT 10

The Colonies and the Impact of War: Confidential Code Telegram to Governors of African Dependencies from the Secretary of State for the Colonies, 21 March 1942, CO 822/111/46705

IMPORTANT
Unnumbered (A) 21st March

Addressed to the Governors of all the African Dependencies (except Somaliland) and to the British Resident Zanzibar. Governors of Kenya and Nigeria please furnish copies to Confgov. and Wagon respectively.[1]

1. Now that we have lost Malaya the main problem before our African Administrations, after defence, is to make good as far as the resources of their Territories allow the commodities formerly drawn from the Far East and to intensify all forms of local production which assist the war effort.
2. I shall give you every support in taking the action necessary to achieve these ends. Specific requests and instructions on certain production questions have already reached you and more may be expected. I am, in general, ready to approve and defend against criticism all sound and reasonable emergency measures required in the interests of production. I am doing everything possible here to deal expeditiously with the specific problems which have been put to me by individual Governors and by the Governors' Conferences. Any suggestions as to the particular points on which further help or information is needed will be welcome.
3. In the meantime, I propose to issue a brief personal message in general terms to African producers. The text of this message is given in my immediately following telegram. Provided that you see no objection I should be obliged if it could be published in . . . on the 26th March. It will be published here on that date.

Note

1. Confgov. and Wagon were the telegraphic codes for, respectively, the East African Governors' Conference with its secretariat in Nairobi, and the West African Governors' Conference secretariat at Lagos.

DOCUMENT 11

The Colonies and the Impact of War: Confidential Code Telegram to the Governors of African Dependencies from the Secretary of State for the Colonies, 21 March 1942, CO 822/111/46705

IMPORTANT

Unnumbered (B) 21st March

Addressed to the Governors of all the African Dependencies (except Somaliland) and to the British Resident Zanzibar.

Following is text of message referred to in paragraph 3 of my telegram Unnumbered (A) of 21st March. Begins.

Since I became Secretary of State for the Colonies I have been deeply impressed by the way in which the African Dependencies have helped forward the war effort.

Their contribution up to date is well-known and needs no words of praise from me. Some of the peoples in these Dependencies have already had the opportunity of fighting: and they have acquitted themselves against the enemy in Eastern Africa with great bravery and distinction. It may be that they will be called upon to fight again. If they are, they can be reckoned upon to show the same sterling and aggressive qualities.

In the meantime, we must take stock with a clear vision of the realities immediately before us. There has been a new turn in the kaleidoscope of war: and the demands upon Africa for the war effort have entered into a new phase. Many of the raw materials produced in the Far East are now denied to us: and we must look to Africa to make good these losses and to supplement our supplies on a bigger scale than in the past. There was, for the first two years of the war, an ample supply of many African products. Surpluses were being piled up: and some markets were being artificially supported. Many producers must have felt that they were not making the best contribution of which they were capable.

That stage is past. The demand for most African products has now a new urgency and new reality. The foodstuffs and minerals of the African Dependencies have become a vast armoury for the war effort. There is a new call to the producers in Africa to do their utmost to serve the needs of the United Nations.

Their efforts will receive all the support which it is within my power to give. To be effective the drive for production must be wisely planned and directed. There must, so far as is practicable in the varying and conflicting conditions of war, be clear and definite objectives for production. I shall set myself to give these directives and to furnish all help for carrying them through. Where there are obstacles in the way of the full production of the required commodities these obstacles must be surmounted: and I shall make it my business to see that they are.

CRANBORNE

DOCUMENT 12

The War Effort and Colonial Policy: Speech by the Under-Secretary of State for the Colonies (Harold Macmillan) in the House of Commons, 24 June 1942, *Hansard Parliamentary Debates* (1941–2) vol. 380, cols 2002–20

The Under-Secretary of State for the Colonies (Mr Harold Macmillan): An Under-Secretary in charge of the Estimates of his Department is always in an anxious and delicate situation. If I may suitably adapt a well-known phrase, like the legitimate wife throughout the ages he enjoys responsibility without power. My difficulties are, I think, increased rather than diminished by the fact that there has been no Debate on the Colonial Office since June, 1939. How short the interval in terms of months. How vast the valley that divides us from those years in terms of events. Since that Debate the impact of war has fallen upon the Colonial Empire, and I think the Committee will expect me to make some reference to the losses that we have sustained – cruel, but I dare aver, not mortal blows.

Meanwhile, I have fortified my memory by reading some of those Debates of former years, and I find that there is a kind of common form which it is expected that the Minister should follow. He has to tell the Committee that there are 55 territories, 60,000,000 people of different races, religions, civilisations, in different stages of development and so on. He describes the events of the year, singling out the more important developments, such as the foundation of a college, the building of a railway or the formation of a committee. He is always in the same dilemma. If he pitches his tale too high, he is accused of complacency; if he pitches it too low, he bores the Committee. After the Secretary of State has spoken, Members contribute in their divergent ways their meed of criticism or praise and my own memory of these Debates is that Members who stayed behind, usually stayed to contribute criticism. How different from those days are the vast and stirring events of three years of war. How puny seemed the problems then. How tremendous now.

I have said that we have had grievous losses of our territories. We have lost Hong Kong, the Straits Settlements, the Malay States, North Borneo, Sarawak, and now the march of war has taken in its devouring stride some of the smaller islands of the Pacific once renowned for beauty and for peace. Those places have been lost to us by military defeat. But it is not unnatural that, at the same time, such cruel disasters should have brought in their train criticisms of civil governments and of civilian populations. Who is to blame? Who is wrong? Whose head is to be put upon a charger? Those are the cries that naturally arise among people when things go wrong. But for my part I do not think the Committee will expect me to deal with those matters in detail. I do not think we should prejudge issues on which the evidence is still very lacking. We did not train the populations of the Far East for war. That is true. I wonder what would have been said had we done so. But do not let us forget that we brought to these territories peace, progress and prosperity, and at any rate, at this critical moment of the war, let us prefer to learn and apply the lessons, rather than to seek expiatory victims. What are these lessons? There are, of course, strategic and military lessons which do not come within my ambit. Then there is the task of the Colonial Office and the Colonial Governments themselves, which I can describe in a single sentence. It is the mobilisation of all the potential resources of the Colonial Empire, both of men and of materials, for purposes of war. Here, at any rate, I can assure the Committee there is no danger of complacency in my office in regard to that task. We know the tremendous size of our need and the character of the difficulties.

Let me first take materials. The loss of the Far Eastern possessions of the British Empire and of our Allies has meant an immediate loss of supply on an important scale. The present difficulties and dangers of the Indian Ocean threaten a potential loss of supply, or at any rate a serious interruption. We have lost 60 per cent of the tin production of the world, 90 per cent of the rubber production and a large proportion of wolfram, lead and other minerals. We have lost important sources of food supplies in sugar, tea, rice and oilseeds, and we are threatened with further interference with sources of supply. Therefore, we need to increase Colonial production for war purposes on an immense scale. We have to develop the mineral production. We have to push up the production of meat, hides, palm oil, groundnuts, and all the rest. Everywhere we must increase. In hardly any categories do we dare slow up. Indeed, what might be alleviation proves only too often to be additional burdens. Added to the burden of increasing the production of what we most need, we have also to buy production which we may not need and cannot ship but must purchase for the good life and prosperity of the local inhabitants. Examples of such production are the citrus in Palestine, cocoa in West Africa and bananas in some of the West Indian Colonies.

How can the Colonies best help? I think in three main ways. First, there is the stimulation of exports. We have agreed upon an export programme with our main customers, namely, the Ministry of Food, the Ministry of Supply and our American Allies. We have worked it out in detail. We have priorities arranged. Our supplies go to the United Kingdom, to the Middle East and to the United States, and in this programme we have the co-operation of our Belgian Allies and of the Free French. We employ a different technique for different purposes. As an example, we have set up the West African Produce Control Board to which I made some reference in answer to a Question to-day. This has been developed out of the original Cocoa Control Board. It will arrange a steady and consistent buying and price policy for West Africa. It will deal not only with cocoa but with oilseeds, groundnuts and other commodities. It will fix the appropriate prices at which shippers, acting as its agents, shall buy from African producers and the prices to be paid by agreement with our main customer, the Ministry of Food. As I have just said, it may be necessary, from time to time, to buy large quantities of produce which at the moment we cannot use or ship and to store it against further needs. The policy of the old Cocoa Board will thus be continued. As much cocoa as is required by the United Nations will be sold to them. The rest will be stored until it can be shipped. With regard to oil seeds of all kinds, the policy is to encourage production to the maximum, for we need all we can get.

I would like in passing to make some reference and pay a tribute to those engaged in the trade in West Africa. It has been a habit in the past to think that there is a necessary division of interest between the traders, the Government and the African people. I believe that to be altogether fallacious. I think all three can and should work together as partners in an enterprise which is for the benefit of West Africa generally. In all these new developments we have had every assistance from the merchants, who are now acting as agents for the Board and assisting its operations in every way.

Now I want to say a word about rubber. Output in Ceylon, already running at a high level, has been intensified. Steps have been taken to obtain the maximum possible production in East and West Africa. Neglected plantations are being revived. Abandoned areas of Ceara rubber, mainly situated in Tanganyika, are being exploited. Special officers are being appointed, and here we are able to get the assistance of some of the Malayan planters. All types of wild rubber both in East and

West Africa are being tapped. Prices are being fixed which we think sufficient to attract the maximum production. All territories are co-operating energetically in the drive for rubber, and I hope and believe that by all these energetic means we may help to fill the gap before the great production of synthetic rubber in the United States comes to help the joint war needs of the Allies.

Now as to minerals. Here we are the servants, and the Ministries of Supply and Aircraft Production are the masters. We minister to their needs, and what a list of these there is. Bauxite, wolfram, tin, graphite, copper, zinc, mica, manganese, chrome, iron ore, industrial diamonds. And what vast territories they cover. The Gold Coast, Sierra Leone, Nigeria, Northern Rhodesia, Ceylon, British Guiana, Cyprus – all these are helping in the world drive. The Committee will not expect me to give the figures of additional production, but I can assure them that the chief anxiety I have is not so much to increase by every means the productive power of the territories, but to secure the transport to convey it internally to the ports and from the ports and harbours when it has been obtained.

I have said that the first of the three main ways in which the Colonies can help is by stimulating increased production of all the things that we require. They can make their second main contribution by not importing. And the first item under this head with which I propose to deal is that of control of imports into the Colonies to stop unessentials. We had already instituted systems of import control, and we are now substituting for the old system of import licences what I would call the formation and formulation of a shipping programme for each territory. This, in fact, means the bulk purchase on Government account of such goods in order to make sure that they have the first claim on shipping space, using the import licensing system merely to control the import of innumerable small items of private need.

The second is to increase local food production. This is necessary not only in war, but was already being proceeded with before the war, for two main purposes – the improvement of the diet of the inhabitants of tropical areas, and the preservation and conservation of the soil by the substitution of mixed farming for the single export crop, which is so dangerous to soil fertility. The needs of war and, in many cases, the maintenance of large armies, have immensely stimulated these needs. Therefore, in West Africa we are concentrating chiefly upon rice, vegetables and dairy produce. Here the chief task of the Agricultural Departments is to give advice and guidance and to provide demonstration plots, seeds, etc., for the peasant farmer. In East Africa, we have both the white planter and the African peasant economy. We must help both. Here we are increasing wheat, maize, rye and other foodstuffs, as well as rice.

In the West Indies, where for so long agriculture has depended upon the production of a single export crop, sugar, and a large proportion of the people's requirements in the form of wheat, flour, meat, etc., has been imported, we are now trying to diversify agriculture both in large estates and in small holdings. Twenty-five per cent of the estate lands in Barbados and some other territories are being compulsorily turned over from sugar to food production. The same thing is going on in British Guiana, Jamaica, and elsewhere. Suitable steps on similar lines are being taken in Mauritius, Ceylon and Palestine. Even in the rocky and barren territory of Aden, the cultivation of vegetables, fruit, and other crops has been promoted by the Agricultural Officer on a considerable scale for the benefit of the garrison and people of that vital outpost. In a word, to-day the farmer is the best shipbuilder. Every ton of food that can be grown in a Colony saves a ship to bring it. Every ton of food that can be moved from one Colony to a neighbouring Colony saves shipping. Every ton of food grown in East Africa and moved to the armies of the Middle East saves the long haul round the Cape.

The third way in which we can help is by local manufacture and repair work. When the Eastern Group Conference was set up in Delhi in the autumn of 1940, Ceylon, Palestine and the East African Dependencies fell within the area with which it was concerned. They are making every possible effort to increase their resources for local manufacture, as are all the other Colonial territories. Our most important activities are, of course, centred in the Middle East, where the Middle Eastern Supply Centre is charged with looking after the supply and production of Cyprus, Palestine, and Aden. In Palestine, spare parts are being made and repairs carried out in the railway workshops and in other engineering shops for the Armies of the Middle East. Wherever possible, we have tried to stimulate production, and I may say, with some little personal knowledge of the difficulties, that we are finding the same difficulties as we have had in England and are trying to overcome them by the same enthusiasm and effort.

In order to help in the three ways I have explained – the increase of Colonial exports, the avoidance of the use of shipping, and the development of our engineering and repair work – we must have imports into the Colonies. We cannot increase our exports without having some increase in our imports, and those take two major forms. First, we must increase the imports of consumption goods. We must have more cotton piece goods for Africa if we are to have more production from Africa. Colonial peoples want things, not money. Englishmen must have fewer shirts in order that West Africans may have more cotton piece goods. That is the only way in which to get our additional production. We are getting a very good response when we go to the Board of Trade for our allocation.

But, secondly, we must import capital goods. If we get increased production, we have to move it, and we have got to increase the roads, the railways, the internal transport facilities, in nearly every territory. As the House knows, it is not easy in this time of war to buy locomotives and railway wagons off the peg. The capacity of the great engine and wagon-building firms is now allocated to other purposes. We have somehow or other, in the familiar way in which one can somehow drive along a difficult road, to get additional production, and by simplification, modifications of type, standardisation of pattern, obtain what we need. Here we get great support and assistance from the authorities, and the Ministry of Supply in particular. As regards roads, there is the great problem of building up our road transport, and it is not easy nowadays to get lorries. But I hope that somehow or other we shall scrounge them off somebody to the extent we need. There is, then, the humbler form of transport – the bicycle. Bicycles are badly needed in this country for munitions workers and other workers. But still more are wanted in the Colonies, where they are needed not only to take workers to and from their work, but also to take produce to the market. Many hon. Members, I know, have had the opportunity of visiting Nigeria and will have seen men on bicycles bringing in petrol tins their contribution of palm oil to the receiving centres. The bicycle is an important part of transport. Therefore, we have to fight with whoever allocates bicycles – the Board of Trade, I think – to get our fair share of bicycles.

As for external transport – harbours, cranes, the development of the movement out of the territories – there are, indeed, problems to be faced. Hon. Members will be aware of the criticism that comes particularly from casual visitors. I know of one harbour which is now moving in a single day an amount of exports equivalent to what normally in peace-time it moved in a month. We have further developments to make. Here we have to co-operate and work with the Admiralty and the Ministry of War Transport. All this means careful working out of import and export programmes. It means system, order, an immense degree of detailed control, combined with an enthusiastic and unrelenting pressure.

Mr Tinker (Leigh): Will the right hon. Gentleman tell me what he meant by capital goods?

Mr Macmillan: By consumption goods I meant cotton piece goods for daily consumption by the people. By capital goods I meant locomotives, wagons, and so on, for transport development. But apart from the claims of production, there are other very great claims upon the manpower of the Colonies. We have the Fighting Services, the Labour Corps, the Home Guards and irregular troops, Civil Defence and so on. Let me say something of the Fighting Services. The King's African Rifles, the Royal West African Frontier Force, and the Northern Rhodesia Regiment: their exploits in the East African campaigns which destroyed the Italian Empire are too well known to need further tribute from me. They were not subsidiaries, they were the main participants in those campaigns. These Regiments, like the British Army, have been multiplied many times over in strength since the outbreak of war. The Malta Regiment and the King's Own Malta Artillery have shared with the Imperial Garrison the proud distinction of this historic siege.

Perhaps I may be allowed here to pay once more my tribute to the people of Malta. What a shining example of all the qualities most needed in dark days they have shown. The Ceylon Defence Force, the Mauritius Territorial Force, the Cyprus Volunteer Force, and similar Forces in St. Helena, the Falkland Islands, Fiji and Tonga are all proud of their record, and with good reason. The West Indies have sent large numbers of recruits to the Royal Air Force, and to the skilled trades in the Army. In Palestine, Palestinians, both Jews and Arabs, are serving with His Majesty's Forces, in the Palestinian companies of the Buffs and the Royal Artillery, in the Royal Air Force and many other units. For the Labour Corps, large numbers have been recruited from West and East Africa as well as from other Colonies, and they are performing splendid service. Home Guards and Irregulars are being formed in many of our Colonies.

Earl Winterton (Horsham and Worthing): I am sorry to interrupt the thread of my right hon. Friend's discourse and I know that this is not a matter within the official competence of his Department, but can he mention the splendid war record of these indigenous inhabitants of Africa – the Southern Rhodesian African Regiment and the Basuto Labour Corps in Libya for example?

Mr Macmillan: I am very grateful to my right hon. Friend for his interruption if it has cleared up any possible doubt of gratitude on the part of the Government. I am merely dealing with the territories which fall within the province of my noble Friend. As

I was saying, Home Guards and Irregulars are being formed in many of our Colonies. We are starting where the need seems greatest and the danger most menacing. I welcome this method of associating our people directly with their own defence, and, should the necessity arise, they will develop the skill and resourcefulness of the Russian partisans. I think that I should say a word on Civil Defence. The new Permanent Under-Secretary of State at the Colonial Office is Sir George Gater, and what he does not know about Civil Defence is not worth knowing. We are relying on him, and I want to thank my old chief, the Minister of Home Security, for the help which he has given us in every possible way in obtaining the necessary materials we need. We are, therefore, trying with all the means in our power to meet the needs of the Army and of Defence in its broader sense. We have had to use for this purpose the same methods adapted as used in this country.

Naturally, [w]e have special problems in each territory which have to be taken into account. We have not hesitated to apply conscription to Europeans and local inhabitants where it seemed desirable to do so. But, of course, we are finding that, if we are to perform all these duties and provide the man-power necessary, we have to have a balanced system of organised man-power as we have developed it in England. Hon. Members will know that in this work we have had to take powers, some of which have been criticised in this House. Whether for military service or for production needs, the war is paramount, and we have to do distasteful things. We have to introduce, as we have in England, all kinds of measures foreign to our normal administration. I defend them unhesitatingly on the only ground on which they can be defended – the overwhelming, insatiable, devouring demands of war.

What is the machinery for all this effort? How can it be sustained, and how will it be achieved? First, there is the loyal spirit of the Colonial peoples. No machinery will be of any use without their acceptance of sacrifice, without their steady loyalty, and without their devotion to our cause. Without that, all these efforts would be in vain. I could tell the Committee of instance after instance, not only of gifts in money and kind, but also of pathetic, touching incidents of individuals desiring to help. These offers include, for instance, that of one chief and his three sons who proposed they should be dropped by parachute on Berlin to slay Hitler with bows and arrows, ambitious, but, alas, an impracticable plan.

Against this background of enthusiasm we have tried to build an efficient organisation in London and in the Colonies themselves. In London, the Colonial Office has been extended, particularly its Economic Department, and I should like to pay special tribute to the staff of this Department – we too have our 'boys in the back room'. Their task is immense. They are working day and night, and we have had to expand both personnel and accommodation. For our expansion in personnel, the Treasury helps us, and for our expansion in accommodation we help ourselves – the Ministry of Works and Buildings also help us with this. To house this new Department we have had our first territorial gain since the black days of war. The Colonial Office has occupied the old Scottish Office. This, indeed, is a portent. It is contrary to nature. It is like a small cloud no bigger than a man's hand, and I trust it is an augury of things to come. I should like also to felicitate the local Governments in the various Colonies, and the staffs of those Governments, many of whom have had to be released for service in the Army. Those left behind have had a greatly increased amount of work to do, often in unhealthy climates, with little or no opportunity for leave, and separated for years from their wives and children. One sometimes hears criticism – to my mind often mean and ungenerous criticism – of the Colonial Civil Service. From what I have been able to see in a few months, they have shown the greatest devotion during these difficult times, and have been working in the interests of the Colonies they serve. Under the stress of war, they have responded magnificently to the demands made upon them.

Now let me turn to organisation. In East Africa we have the East African Governors' Conference, comprising the Governors of Kenya, Uganda, and Tanganyika and the British Resident, Zanzibar, together with the Governors of Northern Rhodesia and Nyasaland. The G.O.C.-in-Chief East Africa attends its meetings. The Chairman is the Governor of Kenya. The Conference Secretariat, which is in permanent session at Nairobi, is, in fact, the focus where the common East African war effort is now co-ordinated. It conducts the affairs of the East African War Supplies Board and the Civil Supplies Board. Each Dependency has its own supply organisation, and these attempt to co-ordinate inter-territorially what each can give and what each needs, and the Supply Boards exercise a general control over the despatch of East African produce to the Middle East.

Then we have the West African Governors' Conference. This is presided over by the Governor of Nigeria, and here again the potential resources and the needs of the four territories are co-ordinated. This Conference, which has responded ably to the calls made under the new stress of war, is now being reinforced, as the Committee knows, by a Cabinet Minister resident in West Africa. A statement has already been made describing in detail Lord Swinton's directive and functions. I should like to add my tribute to his patriotism in undertaking this task, and to say how fortunate we are to have secured for this position a man of his wide experience and long record of public service. The West African Governors' Conference has attached to it already a Supply Centre covering the four territories. It has a Secretariat which maintains liaison with West African merchants and the Ministries interested in African problems. We are now to have a Regional Shipping Control Committee in Lagos, under the chairmanship of an officer of the Ministry of War Transport. The Supply Centre operates through local boards in each of the four Colonies, with a view to increasing the production upon which our hopes are set. In Palestine, the Supply Centre operates under the Middle Eastern Supply Centre, and the Governments of Palestine, Cyprus and Aden keep in close touch with the Middle East Supply Centre on all economic matters.

Mobilisation of the potential resources of the Colonial Empire, both of men and materials, for the purposes of war, as I said at the beginning, is our task. I have tried to describe – at too great length, I fear, but the subject is a very great one – what we are doing to achieve it. If hon. Members can suggest new ways, new means, new ideas, my noble Friend and I will accept them with readiness and gratitude. The problems that we have to face are new ones. In their solution we may well make mistakes. We may tread on many toes, and we shall certainly break eggs to make our omelette. We have not unlimited time to plan and think and study. We must act. Our task reminds me of the old story of the town council and the bridge. The town council after long discussion decided to build a bridge and passed the following resolution: 'Resolved, that we shall build the bridge. Resolved, that the materials of the old bridge shall be used in the new bridge. Resolved, that the old bridge shall remain while the new bridge is being built.' I say the same of ours. Some task!

I feel that I must, after my attempt to describe our short-term needs, say something of the future. In the midst of the hurly burly of war it is refreshing and stimulating to lift one's eyes occasionally to a further horizon. It is not for me to put forward a new Imperial policy. I can only give the Committee a few impressions formed in a very short tenure of office, with little respite from other pressing and urgent duties. The conception of Empire has had many different forms and has passed through many different stages. There have been the early explorers, dating from the Phoenicians in ancient times to the French,

Dutch, English and Portuguese adventurers of the Renaissance. The explorer and the trader, sometimes alas the slave trader, have gone hand in hand. Then the phase has changed. The missionary – never let us forget what we owe to the missionary – the trader and settler, and then the chartered company under the genius of men like Rhodes and Goldie, have been the pioneers. In this phase the chartered company performed the rudimentary functions of government. What Mary Kingsley called the legitimate trader takes the place of the slave trader, and a new era begins. Time passes. The responsibilities of government, ever growing, can no longer be sustained by chartered companies. Government assumes them, and the functions of the Government and the trader separate. Perhaps the last great man to give dynamic conception to this new Imperial theme was Joseph Chamberlain. It was he who put before the country the conception of developing this great inheritance. By degrees this conception of development has become one of development in the paramount interests of the people of the many widely differing territories which go to make up the whole.

This view, the product of the strong strain of idealism and humanitarianism running through British thought, has been expressed in practical form in the policy of the British Government. It is accepted and endorsed by public opinion. In the meantime, following the setting-up of law and order in the Colonies, the opening-up of communications, internal and external, the discovery and development of new raw materials, trade and commerce, it comes about that all these divergent interests which grow up in the Colonies have to be reconciled. The indigenous population, alongside them the administrator, the missionary, the trader, the planter, the settler and the immigrant population from other territories, all these varying elements must be welded together into a coherent whole. All must form members of a single body, material and spiritual. The Empires of the past have died because they could not change with the times. They were rigid. They conformed to a fixed pattern. By contrast our Empire has had the great quality of adaptation. By that it lives.

There is, however, a frequently expressed theory that the Colonies, when they have grown to full stature, will drop off like ripe fruit. It is based upon an analogy which, to my mind, is quite fallacious and has done great harm. It is the common analogy between nations and families. It is said that children necessarily grow up, wish to start upon their own, and therefore separate themselves from their parents. But this is a false comparison. Among men, parents necessarily age, wither, decay and die by the mere efflux of time. The sons look forward necessarily to stepping into their fathers' responsibilities. But this is not true of nations. There is no need for them to decay, and therefore the relationships between a mother country and other countries may not be the short ties of a generation but may be of a lasting character. It is true that nations themselves may decline. Perhaps before the war some pessimists might have said that of our country. Who can say it now? Is this country growing old like a stag-headed oak? Does the sap run stagnant now? Are there no young shoots left? If any man takes so petulant and depressing a view, I will tell him the remedy. Let him seek, if he is so fortunate as to be admitted to it, the finest company in all the world, the boys in blue with wings on their breasts. The war has shown us certain inescapable facts, of which we will learn the lesson. Self-government without security means nothing. Independence without defence is vain. The future of the world is in larger organisations and not in breaking up into a large number of small countries. It is in the light of these events that we should think of our future relationship with the Colonies as a permanent and not a transitory thing.

The governing principle of the Colonial Empire should, therefore, be the principle of partnership between the various elements composing it. Out of partnership come understanding and friendship. Within the fabric of the Commonwealth lies the future of the Colonial territories. According to different needs and different conditions there will be the greatest divergence of local responsibility, but, however far these may be developed, there are broad Imperial problems which only admit of corporate resolution. Trade, currency and monetary questions, defence, transport by sea, land and air – all these are Imperial questions. Capital development itself, on which the future of the territories depends, must be thought of as a whole.

Mr Maxton (Glasgow, Bridgeton): Is the right hon. Gentleman now enunciating a settled Government policy, and is the policy of the future which he is enunciating the Government's interpretation of the appropriate Clause in the Atlantic Charter?

Mr Macmillan: I am enunciating a conception of policy which is based upon the impressions that I have formed after a comparatively short tenure of office. In general terms it has the support of my noble Friend, with whom I have consulted before making it.

Dr Haden Guest (Islington, North): The right hon. Gentleman used the word 'partnership,' but the present relation between the Colonies and the Mother Country is not one of partnership. It is subordination, and the Colonies have not equality of

government economically or politically. Does the right hon. Gentleman mean equal partnership?
Mr Macmillan: That was the conception I was trying to develop.
Dr Guest: But it is a new policy and not the policy of the Government?
Mr Macmillan: Not at all. Perhaps in the hon. Gentleman's own relations there have been junior and senior partners. What I was trying to convey was that this was an organisation that should not be broken up but should continue in a spirit of partnership.
Dr Guest: Is it real partnership or just another form of words to delude people?
Mr Macmillan: Perhaps the hon. Gentleman will develop that theme when he speaks and allow me to develop my theme. The Colonies depend upon capital development. Before the passing of the Colonial Development and Welfare Act there was too much tendency to think of each Colony as a separate financial proposition instead of thinking of the show as a whole. Some Colonies are poor and some rich. The estate must be considered as a whole. We want no depressed areas in the Colonial Empire. A start has been made in the West Indies with the appointment of Sir Frank Stockdale as Comptroller of Development and Welfare. This was one of the most fruitful results of Lord Moyne's Commission. Many proposals are being already carried out, even in war. Here another sort of co-operation in the field of advice and research is being brought about by our close relations with our Allies the United States in the Anglo-American Caribbean Conference.

What more can we do at this stage of the war? I think there are two things we can do. We can make changes or prepare for changes in the organisation of the Colonial Service with two chief aims. First, we should seek increasing opportunities for the people of the Colonies to fill posts in the public service of their own countries. The organisation of the Civil Services, and, more than that, the whole structure of the educational system in the Colonies must be so devised that the peoples will be able to acquire the qualifications for service and the desire to serve. That is our first aim. But however much development there may be in this direction, the Colonies will still need help from outside. Few of them have or are likely to have for some time so large a reservoir of highly qualified expert technicians in administration, in science, in agriculture, in mining and so on to be able to supply all their own needs. Therefore, our second aim is to have a mobile force of such experts at the command of the Secretary of State to be posted wherever in the Colonial Empire they are most needed at a particular time. Of course, we have this to some extent now, but it is hampered by purely financial considerations. The mobility of the Colonial Civil Service is strained by these considerations because the poorer Colonies may need the best men but may not be in a position to pay the salaries for their services. Therefore, the unification of the Colonial Service which has been going on gradually since 1930 is now to be taken a step further. The last Secretary of State, Lord Moyne, had initiated a plan to achieve this purpose. The present Secretary of State is working out these proposals in consultation with the Colonial Governors. We shall then come to the House with a request for the necessary financial provision, and I hope that we shall be generously met.

There is a second thing we can do. Our development policy must be thought of as a coherent whole and not in single compartments. The Secretary of State has the advantage of a number of advisory committees on a number of technical subjects. We have recently added to these the Colonial Labour Advisory Committee. I am much indebted to the Trades Union Congress for helping me to get two such good members as Mr J. Hallsworth and Mr A. Dalgleish, both of whom have considerable knowledge of international labour problems; and to the British Employers' Confederation for finding us Sir John Forbes Watson and Mr C. W. Murray. We have also the advantage of Sir Frederick Leggett, the Chief Industrial Commissioner of the Ministry of Labour. The healthy development of trade unionism on sound lines is one of the most urgent needs of many of the Colonies. During the last few months experienced trade unionists have gone from this country as colonial labour officers. Six men have been appointed to British Guiana, Trinidad, Nigeria, the Gold Coast, Sierra Leone and Palestine. With the help of the Minister of Labour we have now seconded for service in the Colonial Labour service 12 of his experienced officers.

In addition to the technical Advisory Committee, we have Lord Hailey's unique gifts at our service. Post-war problems of all kinds affecting the territories are his daily task. With the help of eminent scientists he will advise on the organisation of research work over the whole field, and he has £500,000 a year to do it with. In addition, we must direct research not merely to nutrition, education and so on, but also to practical economic ends. I think it was Lord Swinton who stated once that sometimes there was not sufficient contact between the officers engaged on the spot in connection with forestry, agriculture, minerals and so on and the actual users of the products. Therefore, the practical application of science to industry is a form of specialised research which will be pursued and the slogan of it will be 'the application of scientific research to market needs.' That is the best way in which we can help to promote ultimately the increased prosperity of the peoples in the Colonies.

Most important of all, we have the Colonial Development and Welfare Act. In the long run the standard of living and the expenditure on social services in the Colonies will depend on the economic prosperity of those Colonies. This means for the moment one thing. It means the promotion of long-term capital investment. The problem is too big for private investment alone. We need large-scale public investment on public needs. This should be accompanied by private investment publicly guided as well as by ordinary private investment as an adjunct and ancillary. The recent history of Palestine shows what can be done by capital investment on an ambitious scale. At present the only immediate return from investment in many Colonies has been the mineral resources. If the Colonies, and especially Africa, are to be raised to play their proper part in the world, we must have long-term capital investment which will not be expected to be profitable for the first years or even generations. The Colonial Development and Welfare Act gives us the instrument for long-term planning. Unless the plans are prepared now, they will not be ready for the period after the war. There is a long delay between the preparation of a plan and its execution. Schemes have to be drawn up, blue prints have to be made, and before the contracts are placed there is a great interval. We want, therefore, to prepare now our list of plans and of priorities, so that we can, probably competing in a very crowded post-war market for capital development all over the world, be ready to put forward on behalf of all the Colonies our demand for a fair share of reconstruction work.

It is to this Act and the machinery accompanying it rather than to any new body that we should perhaps look for assistance. This Act will help to preserve continuity of policy. In administering it the Secretary of State for the time being will no doubt wish to fortify himself with advice from experts, and in choosing advisers he will be in a position to balance the claims of ripe experience and age with the claims of youth and enterprise. He will not look only to retired pro-consuls; the machinery must have room for young, active and even untried men. In this field, in fact, it will be already filling the place for which it has been suggested that a Colonial Council should be created. Nor must we neglect among our investments the development of local products, local markets and secondary industries. I should like in passing to mention the experiments at Achimota College. The ancient handicrafts of

West Africa are being revived and the potter and the weaver re-established. These efforts are expected to do two things – to meet war needs and to make a contribution to post-war economy. At the same time we have to work out, in conformity with plans now being discussed in many quarters, how we can fit our commodity control systems into whatever become the world systems after the war. At any rate, in the West African Products Control Board, made for war, though I am not making a statement of policy, I think we have an instrument the value of which will not be lost.

The Colonies are poor. Why are they poor? Because of capitalist exploitation, or because of insufficient capital? Because they are too much governed, or too little governed? Because we interfere too much, or too little? Because there are too many white planters and settlers, or too few? Because there are too many European traders, or not enough? No. They are poor because they are just beginning. They are four or five centuries behind. Our job is to move them, to hustle them, across this great interval of time as rapidly as we can.

Mr Riley (Dewsbury): In some cases we have had these countries under our control for three centuries already.

Mr Macmillan: I had mainly in mind Africa itself, many parts of which were not opened to human discovery until two generations ago, and I say that their real trouble is that they are, as it were, in the Middle Ages. To bridge this great gulf we must hold out to them the hand of friendship, of comradeship and of faith. We can devise new systems of government, new mechanisms of administration – that is necessary; but we shall not do the job by these means alone. We shall do it only in the way that all big jobs are done, by vigour, decision, imagination, ruthless and overriding zeal.

'The lot is fallen unto me in a fair ground: yea, I have a goodly heritage.'

DOCUMENT 13

Far Eastern Policy: Minute by Lord Cranborne, 14 July 1942, CO 825/35/55104/1942

I have read Mr Gent's and Mr MacDougall's note on Far Eastern Policy,[1] and should like to have a discussion on it. It contains most interesting and far-reaching proposals. But I must confess I do not feel altogether happy about them. They involve considerable concessions by us, without any *quid pro quo* by the other Pacific Powers. This will only be regarded by China and the United States as a confession of failure on our part, without any reflection on them, whereas it is in fact the United States who have above all brought about the present situation in the Far East by their refusal to shoulder their responsibilities and co-operate with other nations in restraining Japan in the years before this war. Moreover, were we to accept such a post-war settlement as this in respect of our Far Eastern territories, it would be difficult, if not impossible, for the Dutch to refuse to do the same, and they would certainly, from what Dr Van Mook said to me,[2] regard us as having let them down, if not actually betrayed them.

It seems to me that what we have first to decide is where, if anywhere, we have failed. Is it in the administration of our territories or merely in their defence? It may well be said that our administration has not been perfect, that it was too rigid, that it did not show itself capable of adapting itself to the conditions of war, that it was too much concerned with material improvements and too little inspired by a high spiritual outlook, and so on. But, taken by and large, our record of administration is not one of which we need be ashamed. We created Singapore and Hong Kong, two of the greatest ports in the Pacific, out of nothing. We made of Malaya one of the richest and most vital producing areas of the world. We brought to her peoples law and order, happiness and prosperity. These are no mean achievements. Where we did fail was in giving them protection from Japan, and this criticism may equally be levelled against the Dutch and the Americans. I suggest that, in considering the future of the Far East, it is on this defence aspect that the Allied Powers – and the Institute of Pacific Relations – should concentrate. The Allied Pacific nations must aim at building up in the Pacific an effective system of mutual defence. This will no doubt involve considerable concessions by all concerned. There may have to be international ports, where all members of the peace system have equal rights. As a consequence, these ports may well have to be managed, both as to their defence and administration, by international bodies. We should, I feel, be prepared to agree to Singapore and Hong Kong coming under such a regime. But it must be on a basis of reciprocity. Concessions which we make at Singapore and Hong Kong, the Americans should also make at Manila and Honolulu, the Dutch in their ports, and the Chinese at certain selected places.

Hong Kong, no doubt, is in a slightly different category from Malaya and our other Pacific territories. It forms almost part of the mainland of China. It may be that we may have to agree to a resumption of Chinese sovereignty there. But this should surely form part of the general deal, and be conceded in return for facilities given to us and other Pacific nations in treaty ports in China. I agree strongly with Sir G. Gater that we should not decide now to lower our flag there after the war. To put it on no higher plane, that would be to surrender one of our main bargaining counters before the negotiation begins.

Nor do I much like the idea of multilateral agreements between the local Rulers in Malaya and the United Nations. The Malayan States will never be strong enough to stand on their own feet in the modern world. They must come in to some great power's sphere of influence. If they have treaties with several nations, they will only play off one against another and become a source of friction. We are the obvious people to keep an eye on them. It may well be, of course, that the Chinese and Americans, and possibly the Australians, will want some international cartel to control and supervise the production of Malayan rubber and tin, and that we may think it wise to agree to this. But we should, I feel, maintain political control of these areas.

In conclusion, I think it is most important that we should not allow ourselves to be manoeuvred into the position of having been alone responsible for what has happened in the Far East. In fact, I feel that the responsibility of the United States is far heavier than ours. If they had been willing to collaborate with the League of Nations in the early days of the China incident, all that has happened since might, and probably would, have been averted. In fact, they hung back not only till it was too late to save the situation, but until they were actually attacked. By all means, let us shoulder our share of the blame. But do not let us shoulder theirs too.

C. 14.7.42.

Notes

1. On 30 June G. E. Gent and D. M. MacDougall of the Hong Kong service talked with Foreign Office officials; differences between the two Departments on the question of Hong Kong and Malaya emerged and each side agreed to draft a note on Britain's future policy towards the Far East.
2. Dr H. J. van Mook was Minister for Colonies in the Netherlands Government in Exile and Lt.-Governor of the provisional government of the Netherlands East Indies 1942–8.

DOCUMENT 14

A Public Declaration on Colonial Policy: Minute by Harold Macmillan, 1 September 1942, CO 323/1848/7322

Sir George Gater

I have read this file very patiently. I do not think the P. M. can have realised the true nakedness of the land when he made the statement of September 9th, 1941 – especially the last two sentences. The declarations are not complete in themselves, nor are they free from ambiguity. They are scrappy, obscure and jejeune.

I observe from reading the War Cabinet minutes of September 4th, and the memorandum submitted by the Council Secretary dated September 3rd, that no such phrases were ever suggested. Also a perusal of the correspondence between Lord Moyne and Mr Amery shows how careful they were not to put forward such a sweeping claim. The P. M. must have written the declaration more or less on his own.

I must confess that if I had had the time (or the inclination) to research into all this, I would have toned down the reply to Mr Creech Jones of July 1st, 1942, from a warm to a frigid – or at least a tepid – welcome of his plans for a white paper.

What then are we now to do?

1. We *cannot* publish the white paper; that would really be most dangerous and foolish.
2. How can we get out of it? I think only by personal appeal to Creech Jones.

I should like to be authorised by the Secretary of State to see him – if possible *after* he has received the flattering invitation of S. of S. to help us in another sphere. I should explain to him

(a) That merely to republish declarations of the past, without reference to the future development of policy, would be very unwise from the point of view of British and Colonial opinion .

(b) That to publish our intentions and plans, even if fully formulated by H. M. G. would be unwise from the point of view of U. S. A., and other allied opinions. This for two reasons.

(i) It would seem rather bad manners, in view of the meeting of the Pacific Relations Committee and other formal or informal discussions which may now be proceeding or may be carried on.[1]

(ii) It would be very bad tactics, because we should be disclosing our hand prematurely, before a Peace Conference.

Therefore, I should ask him to let the matter drop.

If any other member put down a question, I should have to try the same tactics.

I am sorry that all this work has been caused. It will not be altogether in vain, because it has revealed a serious weakness in our recording machinery. We have no complete list of our pledges and commitments. In private life, this leads inevitably to bankruptcy.

HM 1/9/42

Note

1. A reference to the forthcoming conference of the Institute of Pacific Relations, held at Mont Tremblant, Quebec, 4–14 December 1942.

DOCUMENT 15

A Public Declaration on Colonial Policy: Minute by Lord Cranborne, 4 September 1942, CO 323/1848/7322

I agree that the White Paper will not do. Declarations on Colonial Policy seem to have been mainly conspicuous by their absence, and, where any have been made, they are vague in the extreme. On the other hand, our situation is not a happy one. The Americans are asking that the Atlantic Charter should be applied to Colonial territories. Parliament has asked that we should produce a Colonial Charter, as an addition to the Atlantic Charter. We have resisted both these demands on the grounds that our Colonial policy has been made abundantly clear by a series of declarations, to use the Prime Minister's words, 'complete in themselves, free from ambiguity, and related to the conditions and circumstances of the people and territories affected'. Now it turns out there are no such declarations. We might have rectified this situation by reverting to the idea of a Colonial Charter, difficult though this would be to draft. But Lord Halifax has unfortunately broached the subject prematurely in a conversation with Mr Hull, and Mr Hull has turned it down. What are we now to do? It looks as if we may be driven to a further consideration of the joint Anglo-American declaration envisaged by Mr Hull himself. This too wld seem to be the best way of dealing with Mr Creech Jones. Mr Macmillan's suggested approach to him is most ingenious. But it has, I am afraid, this weakness. How can we say to him that it is unwise to publish past declarations and pledges without reference to the future developments of policy, when the Prime Mnister has said, in effect, that there is no need for declarations on future policy; our position has already been made clear in past declarations? If, on the other hand, some Joint Declaration were produced, we could then say quite reasonably to Mr Creech Jones and other enquirers that we had now got a new definition of policy towards backward peoples, adhered to jointly by Great Britain and United States, and that it would be misunderstood by American public opinion if, subsequent to that, we published a unilateral collection of government statements of an earlier date.

I cannot say that I am enamoured of the idea of a joint Anglo-American declaration. What Mr Hull said to Lord

Halifax in private conversation may have been all right; but the document which eventually emerges from the State Dept. is likely to be very different, and almost certainly far more embarrassing. We are, however, in an embarrassing situation anyway, and that may be the best way out of it, especially as it seems probable that Mr Hull will press his proposal strongly.

At any rate, I see no reason to say anything to Mr Creech Jones now. He is unlikely to raise the matter next week. and Parliament then fortunately adjourns again for another fortnight. In that time, the Hull proposal can be further explored.

C. 4.9.42.

DOCUMENT 16

Far Eastern Policy: Extract from the Minutes of a Meeting by G. E. Gent, 11 September 1942, CO 825/35/55104/1942

Secret

The memorandum was further discussed yesterday at a meeting of the following Ministers

Mr Attlee
Lord Cranborne
Mr Eden
Mr Amery

who were accompanied by officials from their respective Departments.[1]

Mr Attlee said that the memorandum was based on the idea that the Far East was to be treated as a separate problem from that of Colonial territories in other parts of the world, but could there not in general be said to be a single Colonial problem having much the same general characteristics everywhere?

Mr Eden said that the special feature of the Far East was that, besides the British, there was a group of the leading countries in the United Nations which was intimately concerned with the territories in the Far East, the United States, China, Holland and to some extent Russia; whereas they had no such interest for instance, in Africa.

Mr Amery said that he was not happy about the proposal in the memorandum that we should give up Hong Kong. In his view we should approach the whole subject from the standpoint that we are giving up nothing, and particularly he stressed the overriding importance of strategic considerations;if it were proposed that we should give up any territory we should first be quite sure that it would not be a strategic loss to us, but what we might give up would be counter-balanced by gaining something of no less strategic value.

Mr Eden stressed that our aim was to secure collective defence in the Far East and particularly to ensure that the United States committed themselves to play their part in a United Nations defence system. His idea was that each country would be responsible for maintaining the defence of their own territories but would share in a general collective undertaking and in reciprocal facilities for each other's forces in the bases etc. in the several territories.

He said that there were three objects before us: (1) Guidance for the British Delegation at the Pacific Relations Conference. (2) The education of opinion here and in America. (3) The question of Mr Cordell Hull's suggestion for a joint Anglo-U.S. declaration about the future of Colonial territories as a kind of appendix to the Atlantic Charter.

Mr Amery repeated his warning as to the importance of judging the future requirements of our policy in the Far East according to the dictates of strategy. What the future value of Hong Kong might be could not at present be accurately judged. Possibly its cession to China might be considered in exchange for such a place as Hainan on the ground that the latter would be more useful to us from the strategic point of view.

Lord Cranborne explained that there was nothing in the memorandum to commit the British Government to surrendering any British territories, and especially it envisaged that any settlement between the United Nations should not be merely one-sided as far as we were concerned, but that all would contribute to the general advantage.

Mr Attlee explained that there was an important political aspect about all this, and that in the view of the Labour Party the British electors would not be content to go on bearing a financial burden in respect of Colonies for which the advantage mainly accrued to a capitalist group. The maintenance of national sovereignty over Colonies required the maintenance of national armaments; and in respect both of armaments and sovereignty over backward peoples the political views which he shared were in favour of the substitution of an international system of responsibility and control. National sovereignty and national armaments had shown poor results and would inevitably lead to renewed war in due course. A new conception of international collaboration and responsibility and a pooling of the burden, including the financial burden, of armaments was required.

Lord Cranborne said that he did not accept that our record in the Colonies, and particularly in Malaya and Hong Kong, was a poor one. Not only we but also the Dutch in the Netherlands East Indies and the Americans in the Philippines had rendered great service, and effectively established great reforms in our respective territories to the great advantage of the native peoples. We have all fallen down in one respect, namely, defence, and as far as the British were concerned we might be said to have less blame for this than the Americans *vis à vis* Japanese aggression.

Mr Eden said that our principal object must be to establish a system in the Pacific region in which the United States will not only consent to participate but will be definitely anxious to participate. Clearly the mere restoration of the *status quo* with all concerned clinging rigidly to their pre-war rights and policies would not attract the Americans to incur any obligations for the future defence of such an arrangement. There must be an agreed system of administration, standards, responsibilities, and mutual obligations which would be sealed by a willingness of all concerned to contract to defend, and it would be important from our point of view that the Dominion Governments should be at every stage at one with us in formulating British policy in this region.

Lord Cranborne explained that his idea of the Pacific Regional Council proposed in the paper was that it should comprise representatives of the great Pacific powers and the Dominions. The Council would be responsible for stipulating a certain set of principles to which the local governments would conform. But the sovereign authority in each territory would rest with the power or country concerned and not with an international body.

Note

1. This was the paper on British Far Eastern Policy on which the Colonial Office had been working since early July.

DOCUMENT 17

A Public Declaration of Colonial Policy: The Viceroy to Secretary of State for India, 2 January 1943, CO 323/1858/9057B

SECRET DECYPHER OF TELEGRAM
IMMEDIATE
12. S.C.

Personal. Your personal telegrams of December 13th Nos. 21405 and 21406. Colonial policy. I have read them with the greatest interest, and am grateful for the opportunity of commenting on them. They are matters on which I have thought it better not to bring in my Government, and comment which follows represents my personal view. I have seen Dorman Smith's comments in his (? telegram) of December 17th No. 944 as affecting Burma, and I am sending him copy of my present telegram.[1]

2. My own general feeling is as follows: I agree that we must take account of misunderstandings, jealousies and prejudices on the part of the United States of America, and that it would not be wise to leave our colonial record merely (? to) (? speak) for itself. We must (? therefore) be prepared to cultivate it both by indirect propaganda and to some extent by endeavouring to establish a common front with the United States of America in regard to it. I would myself see very great advantage in indirect propaganda if that could be arranged (value of speeches such as Cranborne's recent speech in the Lords is very great from that point of view),[2] though I think it essential to avoid adopting an apologetic attitude and equally essential to avoid allowing United States of America to come in on field of which they have no experience (save in the Philippines) for which they have no responsibility, and from entry into which they may stand to gain very substantial political and commercial advantages.

3. I feel, next, that we must take account of entirely mistaken feeling existing in United States of America (compare Richard Law's recent report of his visit there)[3] that whether in India, the Colonies, or elsewhere in the Empire we are merely anxious to hand over, and that we regard ourselves as past our best, and exhausted by our existing responsibilities. Nothing is further from the case, though where we are dealing with highly developed and wealthy countries with substantial reserves of manpower, and great commercial

assets, such as India, which might be capable of standing on their own feet with some assistance from us, it has been and still (? omission) our policy to place responsibility on the shoulders of those countries. But Great Britain is going to be pretty tightly squeezed after the war with loss of export markets, liquidation of foreign investments, and the like, and the importance to our trade of colonial empire is clear. The war breeds strange superstitions but I am not myself able to share the confidence of those who appear to think by some act of faith or financial legerdemain it will prove possible after the war to sustain standards of living in United Kingdom from sources other than the annual harvest of our national wealth. My very strong disposition therefore would be to give nothing to any foreign power in colonial or imperial field that we can possibly hold on to. (?consistently), that is, with the maintenance of our general relations with the United States of America.

4. So far as the Mother country is concerned we have got at once to watch her interests in relation even to Dominions. Smuts' recent speech on colonial question,[4] while I have the most profound respect for his character disinterestedness and record, is consistent with the view that we should shed our interest in our very valuable colony, which we alone have built up, and which we alone (with some help from the Dominion) are at the moment responsible for defending, to the nearest Dominion. I am quite conscious that South Africa has always had ambitions to absorb as much of pre 1900 British Empire in that (? continent) as she can. But structure of her polity has above it much that must remain brittle until her internal synthesis is completed. Nor will she even be capable either financially or in terms of manpower of carrying defence and other obligations to such areas by herself. Those obligations will fall back on us substantially, and so long as that is so, we must remain in my judgment senior partner in those areas and watch the interests of the Mother country as much against the Dominions where a clash of interest comes as pre-occupation of Foreign Powers such as United States of America.

5. I examine next to what extent (?by) compromising with United States of America (who are the only people who matter for the present purpose) we shall buy off ill-feeling, misunderstanding and prejudice in that country. With great respect, I do not myself believe, subject to your better judgment, and that of the Cabinet, that we shall do anything of the sort. The (?Middle) West has a high opinion of the

capacity of the United States of America. So have the United States of America as a whole. The element in that country which has any real understanding of European or major colonial problems is very small: the element which is jealous of, and prejudiced against Great Britain is very large. It is too easy for a great industrial country which contains its own granary and meat and milk producing areas as well as an extensive range of natural resources to condemn the colonial system out of which our Dominions have grown. Good relations with State Department, the White House, or President of the day (such as the present President) to whom our debt is incalculable are important. But it is fair to point out that we are not dealing with a dynasty or with an autocratic ruler. Electoral changes may render completely out of tune a policy which we have made great sacrifices to support in the hope that it would suit us on a long view. I suggest that we ought to be extremely cautious in tying ourselves up in certain areas of colonial and foreign policy. Nor can I feel confident that United States of America will not return to isolation at, or shortly after, the end of the war, while I am familiar with, though I do not accept, the argument that in certain circumstances it would necessarily be to our complete disadvantage that they should do so.

6. (?I agree) that the question of (?defence) is relevant to propositions contained in my preceding paragraphs for to the extent that we might regard ourselves as incapable of defending certain areas and might have to call in, in normal conditions, the help of any other great Power, we should to that extent give that Power a claim to come in. So far however as major operations of a world character are concerned, we shall no doubt always have to consider position as regards first class points such as Singapore in terms of support we can secure from our Allies at the time as part of a common defence policy. Other areas may in a major conflict assume abnormal temporary importance such as to necessitate general Allied control, or substantial Allied assistance, for the period of emergency. But in the ordinary course I would have hoped that Great Britain would be able to man and equip the Colonies adequately from her own resources. And I would suggest that there is much to be said against giving anything substantial, in terms of a right to foreign countries to butt in, in return for undertakings of interest in our colonial defence which either may never have to be implemented, or which course of events would oblige our

allies of the time to give us anyhow, whether there are previous understandings or not. I think we can claim too that conditions in which we are fighting at the moment are completely abnormal, and that arrangements such as those for Lease-Lend on the one side, assuming a satisfactorily decisive victory, and for the making available, with impact involved on our sovereign rights, of naval bases etc., to United States of America in the West Indies (?etc.) on the other, are wholly special in character.

7. Finally in the economic and commercial field, the American objective in the post-war period is likely to be free trade for all. That is a proposition which can be argued both ways. But people likely to benefit most by it are the Americans. It would be contested with extreme vigour so far as India is concerned, and it would not necessarily be at all to our advantage or to the advantage of colonial territories under our control. But it is only to be expected that the urge of big business (and to some extent of State Department, as representing United States of America feeling) will be strongly in the direction of reducing as far as possible trade slump, and immense unemployment, that in United States of America as in other countries of the world will follow conclusion of the war and demobilisation of armies. We have already had ample evidence of American anxiety to dig in on air routes, to establish an exclusive claim in such matters as building of transport aircraft, etc. I do not blame them for that, but we are entitled to take account of it betimes, and look after ourselves.
8. On the (?specific) proposals put to the Dominion Prime Ministers, in general I would comment that while accepting advantage of trying to remove the misunderstandings etc., I see in certain circumstances some danger in general declarations of this type. The Atlantic Charter, great as its advantages and importance have been, has in it the seeds of severe controversy in the Indian field. Any general declaration that we may make in the colonial field ought, I would urge, [to] be most carefully worded. Once it is on paper we are tied to it. And while we may have agreed to it with our friends, our friends may not be in Office in another couple of years, and we must in its wording protect ourselves, and our successors against any construction in excess of the maximum we ourselves had in mind in concluding the Declaration.
9. I would comment secondly that Peace Treaty ought not to be a post mortem on British Empire attended by relatives and

debtors. We have borne a major burden of this war, and we must be prepared as I see it to fight our corner at Peace Treaty and elsewhere (?and still) surrender nothing that we can possibly hold on to. That is a further argument for care in the working (*sic*) of any Declaration such as the present.

10. Subject to the above, I agree that there would be some advantage in a joint declaration. Strictly. and (? it may be) it is vital that it should be specifically laid down that each (? parent) state should have the unquestioned right to administer its own territories without interference from other partners in the general Colonial Board. I also agree that it is of extreme importance that India should be excluded from the purview of these proposals ((? our own) interests apart extreme offence would be given in this country by any suggestion of interference either by Americans or Chinese in its internal affairs). Nor could we accept, given the (omission) divisions in this country and substantial delay which may yet elapse before full self government or Dominion Status can be attained that she should be recognised as entitled to speak as a Parent State (I am uneasy on that point as statement by Hull quoted in your 21406 that general statement would make it plain that attainment of freedom involved not only mutual responsibility of 'Parent States' but 'of those who aspired to it', and I think point ought to be most carefully watched).
11. As regards misconceptions about British Colonial policy, I would strongly advocate that we should try to deal with these by indirect rather than by direct methods. Latter have far too much appearance of acceptance on our part of validity of criticisms levelled against us, a (? validity) which I do not myself accept.
12. I am shy about welcoming *sans phrase* American interest in British Colonial Empire. (Paragraph No. 5 of telegram to the Dominions). Proposition unless qualified may have more read into it by the United States of America than will suit us. Americans have neither a Colonial Empire nor experience of one. We have both, and on a large scale. I agree in that connection that it is of great importance to make it clear that no arrangement that could be come to would be merely an Anglo-American (? control), and that any such arrangement would be the equal concern of all powers with overseas possessions. We need to bear in mind possible reactions of that position on Africa (West Africa and Sudan) so far as France and German, or any other great power which in the

remoter future, in which we shall be bound to by this declaration, may establish a position in these areas. And I should be wary of paying too high a price for a hypothetical American undertaking to take a share in defence of areas which hitherto we have held with exceedingly light forces, and the fate of which will always in practice be likely to [be] subordinated to the policy of Great Powers.

13. As for line of declaration suggested in penultimate paragraph of telegram to Dominion Prime Ministers I have touched above on possible violent conflict between United States of America and Imperial and Indian interests in tariff and economic field in post war period. I would urge most strongly that it is a point of potential importance. On a further important point I note that it is suggested that Colonial policy is to be 'in the best interests of peoples concerned and of the world as a whole'. I would urge that we should not tie ourselves to so broad a proposition. For we may take it that the United States of America will regard themselves as likely to be best judges of what the 'Best interests' are. In the event of any (? general) pooling of Colonial interests such as is now under consideration, I would leave judgment of that matter with senior partner in worst (*sic* ? each) area. Thus Americans would be senior partners as regards Philippines, and we as regards the West Indies and those African territories in which our interests predominate over those of any other country. The same is true of the Sudan though it is not of course a Colony.

14. I have not attempted to do more in this telegram than comment generally, for co-ordination of views of the Dominion Prime Ministers and my own must be done in London. But the issue is of very great importance, and I should be grateful if I could continue to be kept in touch with it. If there is any aspect of this matter on which you would like me to comment further, please telegraph.

Notes

1. Dorman-Smith, Col. Rt Hon.Sir Reginald Hugh, b.1899; Governor of Burma 1941–6.
2. Debate on Colonial Policy, 3 December 1942, *Hansard Parliamentary Debates* (1942–3) vol. 125, cols 401–16.
3. Law, Richard Kidston, b.1901; MP (U and C) 1931–54; Parliamentary Under-Secretary of State (1941–3) and Minister of State (1943–5) at the Foreign Office.

4. In response to British consultation with the Dominions, Smuts, as Prime Minister of the Union of South Africa, had begun to develop publicly his views on the decentralization of London's control of her colonies and its concentration in local regional centres. For his views as expressed to Americans late in 1942, see 'The Future of the Colonies', *Times* 24 December 1942, p.4e; and Louis, *Imperialism at Bay*, pp. 209, 219, 338 and *passim*.

DOCUMENT 18

A Public Declaration of Colonial Policy: Secretary of State for the Colonies to Deputy Prime Minister (Attlee), 14 January 1943, CO 323/1858/9057B

SECRET AND PERSONAL

I have just seen the Canadian reply to our latest approach on the Colonial Declaration. Paras 2 and 3 seem to raise rather an embarrassing issue. The truth, I suppose, is that we do not think the Atlantic Charter at present applicable in its entirety to Colonial territories, or at any rate to primitive Colonial territories. There is, for instance, the principle of self-determination, which finds a prominent place in the Charter. Can it possibly be said that the African Colonies are fit for the application of this principle? Or the West Indies? Or the Pacific Islands? It is queer that such intelligent men as Norman Robertson and Hume Wrong do not see this.[1] At any rate, I wonder whether it ought not be explained to the Dominions Governments. Otherwise, we shall merely look shifty, and they will tend to take the American view as opposed to ours. The Atlantic Charter was originally intended, as I understand it, to be concerned primarily with the European countries at present overrun by Hitler. They are adult nations, capable of deciding their own fate. No doubt, the time may come when even the most backward of our Colonies [will] also become adult nations. But at present they are children and must be treated as such. Ought we not to say so, so as to avoid further misunderstanding? I should very much like to know what you think about this.

Yours ever,
(Sgd) Cranborne

I am sending a copy of this letter to Anthony Eden and Oliver Stanley.

Note

1. Robertson, Norman Alexander, b. 1904; Canadian Under-Secretary of State for External Affairs, Ottawa, 1941–6. Wrong, Humphrey Hume, b.1894; Canadian Assistant Under-Secretary of State for External Affairs, Ottawa, 1942–4.

DOCUMENT 19

'Notes on Future Policy in Central Africa', Colonial Office Memorandum by G. F. Seel, April 1943, CO 795/122 Pt I/45104

SECRET.

Notes on Future Policy in Central Africa

1. The Royal Commission in paragraph 477 of its Report expressed the belief that Southern Rhodesia, Northern Rhodesia and Nyasaland would become more and more closely interdependent in all their activities, and that identity of interests would lead them sooner or later to political unity.[1] It recommended that H.M.G. should take an early opportunity of stating its acceptance of this principle. But paragraph 480 went on to say that before amalgamation could be contemplated as a practical and salutary development, there should be a greater degree of certainty that the Southern Rhodesia policy of 'parallel development', modified as time might show to be necessary, would in the long run prove to be in the best interests of the natives.

   This view, which is the kernel of the Commission's recommendations, was arrived at in spite of divergent opinions, as intimated in the separate notes attached to the Report, as to the urgency of amalgamation and the respective merits of native policy and development as practised in the different territories.
2. Although the outbreak of war made it impossible for H.M.G. to give this large question the consideration which is essential before far-reaching decisions can be taken, an opportunity presented itself in 1940 for Lord Hailey, who was visiting other African territories to study the systems of native administration, to extend his journey to Southern Rhodesia with a view to advising whether there were such divergences between its native policy and that of Northern Rhodesia and Nyasaland as to present an obstacle to amalgamation. The Report which he submitted affirmed that there were real divergences of native policy and that it was not possible to assume that longer experience of the operation of the systems followed would show that they had been reduced; the contrary was indeed equally likely to be the case. He was therefore forced to advise that the divergence in native policies appeared to remain a factor which, though not necessarily conclusive against amalgamation, must be taken into account.

3. Lord Hailey's Report has not been published and it was stated in Parliament in February, 1942, that it was impossible for H.M.G. and for Parliament to give the necessary consideration to the amalgamation issue at the moment, and it had therefore been agreed with the Government of Southern Rhodesia that publication should be deferred until such consideration became practicable.
4. Amalgamation is hardly a live issue in Nyasaland either amongst Europeans or Africans. As far as Africans are concerned, it is indeed unpopular throughout the Territories. In Northern Rhodesia it is a factor which has to be taken into account at every turn in the political situation, because the elected members continue to press their demand for a majority in the Legislative Council, and the definite rejection of this demand would probably lead to an immediate revival of a demand for outright amalgamation with Southern Rhodesia. For the time being the position is held because the elected members have been admitted to participation in the War Committee of the Executive Council, which in effect is a kind of War Cabinet, and has a considerable influence in determining general policy in the territory. In Southern Rhodesia, Sir Godfrey Huggins and his Cabinet appear to be observing a kind of truce in regard to amalgamation. This is confirmed by a statement made recently in Nairobi by Sir Godfrey Huggins in which he explained that a gentlemen's agreement existed between Southern Rhodesia and the Dominions Office by which both agreed not to discuss controversial issues during war-time.[2] He added that when the war was finished the question of the future of Rhodesia would require settlement. But warnings have been received both from the Governor of Southern Rhodesia and from Lord Harlech that the Southern Rhodesia Government are beginning to feel that, so far from co-operation between the three territories being encouraged, they are in fact tending to drift apart;[3] and there is in particular disappointment over the restrictions which it has been thought necessary to place on the use of the Inter-territorial Conference Secretariat as a channel of co-operation, so as to avoid any implication that developments in the direction of closer association are being countenanced while His Majesty's Government has assured Parliament that it has reached no decision about amalgamation. The difficulties regarding labour recruitment in Nyasaland for Southern Rhodesia, due primarily to the prior demands in

manpower of the East African and Middle East Commands, are also a continuing source of friction.

5. Meanwhile, free expression has been given in this country and in the United States and elsewhere to the idea that the settlement of the world after the war should include full provision for the common people (by which is usually meant the indigenous majority) of all 'colonial territories' to order their own affairs to the fullest possible extent. This has almost certainly reinforced that body of opinion on both sides of the Atlantic which would endorse the hesitation felt by the Royal Commission in urging immediate amalgamation, if this means subjecting Africans in Northern Rhodesia and Nyasaland to all the implications of the Southern Rhodesia native policy. Indeed, the authors of the American pamphlet 'Africa and the Atlantic Charter'[4] have cited the second article of that Charter as ruling out the amalgamation of these territories.

   ERRATUM
   Paragraph 5. Last line. Delete 'the amalgamation of these territories' and substitute:— 'plans of this kind without more clearly defined guarantees than have yet been proposed as to the protection of native rights.'

6. On the other hand, the experience of the war in matters such as war production and supply and the maintenance of Empire land and air communications in Africa have confirmed and emphasised the Royal Commission's view that these three territories would become increasingly interdependent. Moreover, the idea is becoming more prevalent that the partition of homogen[e]ous areas into small political divisions is inconvenient and retards both security and development; and there is an increasing acceptance of the views that groups of colonies should, wherever possible, be 'regionalised'.

   There have been several instances in the last few years of Northern Rhodesia's dependence upon the good offices of Southern Rhodesia for the solution of temporary difficulties of supply, and it will not have gone unnoticed in the latter territory that it was the Southern Rhodesia Armoured Car Regiment which was called in in October, 1942, to provide the necessary background of military force while the detention of certain persons in the copperbelt was effected.

7. It will therefore be surprising if the pointers to increased interdependence are not more numerous and convincing after the war than when the Royal Commission made its

examination. The real question may well be whether it is practicable to achieve and maintain the desired rate of development in the northern territories, so remote of access from the outside world, without the active co-operation of the European community in Southern Rhodesia. Insistence upon the fuller long-range opportunities theoretically available to Africans under the native policy of His Majesty's Government may involve a retardation to some extent of material advancement such as might be expected from a properly controlled extension of colonial enterprise from across the Zambesi. In this connection it should not be forgotten that the Royal Commission remarked that Southern Rhodesia along her own course had progressed furthest in the provision of certain social and development services.

8. There is another factor to be weighed in approaching this question of amalgamation, which for obvious reasons is not discussed extensively in the Royal Commission's Report. Is the integration of Northern Rhodesia and Nyasaland with Southern Rhodesia likely or not to result in their being absorbed, together with their southern neighbour, in the Union of South Africa? In many quarters in Southern Rhodesia amalgamation is advocated as affording a means of fortifying the position against northward encroachment by the Union, and no doubt the large and at present probably more influential majority in Southern Rhodesia are anxious to avoid encirclement. On the other hand, infiltration from the Transvaal in such areas as the Fort Victoria district is persistent, though not so far sufficient to disturb the balance, and as a rule the Dutch South African is more prolific than the ordinary British type of settler,[5] so that the balance of population may conceivably at some future date alter in favour of the former. Politicians in Southern Rhodesia hope that after the war schemes for the settlement of British ex-servicemen and their families will counteract any such tendency; as against this we have Lord Harlech's opinion that Southern Rhodesia, which already has some 60,000 Europeans, is incapable of supporting more than 100,000 white people; and if it becomes a question of marginal existence for Europeans, there is no doubt that it is the Afrikaans-speaking Dutchman rather than the Briton who will win in such a contest. It would be useful if the views of Lord Harlech could be obtained on this question whether Southern Rhodesia's ultimate future lies in absorption into, or co-operation as an independent neighbour of, the Union of South Africa.

9. If the Union should succeed in absorbing Southern Rhodesia, the resulting state would probably achieve so dominating a position in the sub-continent as to overshadow Northern Rhodesia and Nyasaland whatever efforts might be made to prevent this. In that case the present discussions as to the merits of the respective native policies would become largely academic. But there are by no means sufficient grounds for regarding such a development as inevitable, and it is worth while considering, on the basis that Southern Rhodesia will maintain its independent position, whether the difficulties as regards native policy are really incapable of solution.
10. The divergences which the Royal Commission and Lord Hailey noted are to a very large extent ideological. When the report was first published, the Governor of Nyasaland (Sir Donald Mackenzie Kennedy) saw no great difficulty in securing some agreement on native policy such as would effectively preserve the essential aims of the United Kingdom Government. The Governor of Northern Rhodesia (Sir J. Maybin) thought that there was 'at least sufficient hope of obtaining agreement to justify the attempt'.

It would be idle to expect any solution which involved the abandonment by Southern Rhodesia of its present native policy as embodied in the Conciliation Acts,[6] as part of a bargain from which she obtained in return amalgamation with the northern territories. But it is equally necessary, if any realistic basis is to be found for considering this question, to face the issue whether H.M.G. would or could in the last resort enforce any greatly dissimilar policy in such places as the Copperbelt where there is a considerable non-native population standing in the same economic relation to Africans. In this respect the following passage from a note written in the Department in 1939 still appears not to be inapposite.

> It must be said at once that if . . . it is sought to exact concessions from Southern Rhodesia which would affect European 'paramountcy' in the settled areas, agreement is most unlikely. In that case little will be left but to try to induce Mr Huggins to co-operate in some such way as is suggested in the Commission's Report, in the unification of departmental services and joint planning for the future . . . Since acceptance of 'the principle of amalgamation' will be out of the question, it seems doubtful whether Mr Huggins could count on political support in Southern Rhodesia for such a course.

If, on the other hand, H.M.G. do not seek to impose upon Southern Rhodesia a policy which in all probability they could not enforce in the settled parts of Northern Rhodesia, there seems a fair chance that a policy could be agreed upon which would ensure freedom for native development over most of the combined area . . . It is, however, probably inescapable that any agreed policy must involve admitting that in certain areas, where native competition threatens European labour, measures will be taken to safeguard that labour. Time alone will show whether such measures could be permanently effective, but any attempt to exclude them rigorously at this stage may well result in retarding the general development of the whole area, confirm European opinion in the view that its political future is being prejudiced for the sake of the natives, and immensely complicate the task of H.M.G. in administering Northern Rhodesia itself.

11. It is perhaps not always realised how dangerous it is from the point of view of intra-Imperial relations, to harp on the excellence of the United Kingdom principles of policy in relation to Africans, and make their acceptance a condition precedent to adjustments which suggest themselves on economic, defence and other grounds, when communities such as Southern Rhodesia are in a position to look over the fence and see for themselves how far the claim to pre-eminence in theory is unsubstantiated by actual performance. It would also be unwise not to recognise that, while opinion in Southern Rhodesia (and especially among the Labour Party there) will be adamant upon any question affecting the immediate economic position of the white workers and their families, there is a body of opinion in the Colony which though small at present is of growing influence, and which is beginning to show a sense of responsibility towards the huge African majority and its future. Before, therefore, amalgamation is rejected or (probably worse still) again shelved indefinitely, on the ground that there is no prospect of compatibility in this matter of native policy, it would seem no more than prudent to consider carefully whether there is no hope of obtaining agreement on the basis of some formula which would preserve the position of Africans in Northern Rhodesia and Nyasaland and possibly even afford some better long-term prospect than can at present be descried for Africans in Southern Rhodesia itself.

12. If we approach the question in this way, the first step must obviously be to try and discover some formula of native

policy over the whole area to which opinion, both in this country and in Southern Rhodesia, could be expected to subscribe. Any such formula must permit of variations in detailed application to different parts of the area. The following is suggested purely as a basis for consideration: –

(a) Acceptance of the general principle that in African countries, as and when Africans become qualified to take part in public affairs, provision should be made for them to do so on a representative basis, the nature of such representation to be worked out in each country in the light of experience. (Paragraph 491 (3) of the Royal Commission's Report shows one way in which this question might be approached).

(b) Agreement as to the need for progressive education of Africans in public affairs through local native institutions and other organs of local self-government. So far as Northern Rhodesia and Nyasaland are concerned, the objective in this should be in rural areas, complete local self-government subject to laws enacted by the central legislature and applicable to the whole territory, and in urban areas, including the Copperbelt, provision for natives to be represented on local government bodies and eventually to take part themselves in those bodies.

(c) The progressive admission of properly qualified Africans to local and central government services in all grades, at any rate in Nyasaland and Northern Rhodesia.

(d) Education for natives to be without restriction of degree or quality except where it might be justifiable in the general interest, e.g., to regulate the supply of individuals with a particular training to the demand for such individuals. Facilities sufficient both in quality and quantity to be provided to equip Africans, both male and female, to participate in all social services, and ultimately in the local administration and control of such services.

(e) Acceptance and affirmation of the present native land policy in Nyasaland and Northern Rhodesia.

(f) Natives to be effectively free to work either as producers or wage-earners within their own territory or outside, subject to satisfactory conditions of employment and rates of wages. The general principle to be observed is that nothing should be done which would prejudice the existing opportunities for the employment of Africans in any skilled or unskilled occupation or the prospects of extending such opportunities in the future, subject to safeguards for European workers in specified areas. Compulsory labour to be prohibited except where still permissible under tribal custom and not contrary to the International Convention.

(g) Natives to be allowed to grow such crops and to keep such stock as may be most profitable to them and to take up industrial and commercial occupations, subject only to regulations, e.g., for safeguarding against disease such as apply generally to all persons without racial distinction.

13. If there is any prospect of agreement on some general statement of native policy in this area, the next question is, what political system can be suggested for the combined territories. It would be unprofitable to discuss this question in detail in advance of knowledge of the general reactions of the Southern Rhodesia Government to the kind of approach suggested in these notes, and the Royal Commission themselves did not feel able to do more than indicate (in paragraph 491) some 'broad propositions' which should receive recognition in the constitution of an amalgamated territory.

It is, however, very doubtful whether the immediate creation of a unitary state would be either feasible or advisable. It would, in effect, mean the extension to the whole area of the almost complete self-government which Southern Rhodesia enjoys today. The prospects of Parliament agreeing to this on the strength of a compromise on native policy, which would obviously require to be tested by time, are remote. Moreover, there are the very real doubts which the Royal Commission felt as to whether the European population in the combined territories is as yet adequate to shoulder the full responsibilities entailed. (Report, paragraph 482).

The possibility of some federal arrangement on the lines which have been suggested for East Africa, with a central authority to whom executive and legislative powers would be reserved in respect of certain specified subjects, is complicated by the fact that Southern Rhodesia already has a full Parliamentary system. It must be assumed that she would not be willing to surrender any part of the authority of her Parliament to any interterritorial authority. Some other plan must, therefore, be looked for which would be regarded by Southern Rhodesia as a positive step forward, while preserving for the northern territories a period within which African development with assistance from the Imperial Government can be extended.

14. In the separate note which they appended to the Report, Lord Bledisloe and Mr Ashley Cooper said that they would welcome the appointment at no distant date of a single Governor for all three territories, or, alternatively, the constitution of the Governor of Southern Rhodesia as High Commissioner for the (unified) northern territories. It is suggested that some solution along the lines of the second alternative should be explored. The outlines of such a solution might be: –

    (a) The Governor of Southern Rhodesia to become High Commissioner for Northern Rhodesia and Nyasaland, which would continue to be administered as at present under separate Governors. To amalgamate the two northern territories at this stage would tend to create an authority whose status and responsibility would be such as to make the interposition of a High Commissioner between him and His Majesty's Government difficult to work in practice.

    (b) The present system of government in Southern Rhodesia would remain undisturbed, and the administration of Northern Rhodesia and Nyasaland would be conducted on the same general lines as hitherto. It would, however, probably be necessary to admit the principle of an unofficial majority in the Legislature, at any rate in Northern Rhodesia, but this should be done in the first instance by increasing the number of nominated representatives of natives. This would become less objectionable if, simultaneously, an unofficial majority was being adopted in Kenya as part of closer union proposals in eastern Africa.

    (c) Barotseland should be placed under direct administration by a separate Commissioner, responsible to the Governor of Northern Rhodesia.

    (d) As an alternative to a council with legislative functions for the combined territories, which seems appropriate in eastern Africa, there should be an inter-territorial council on the lines proposed by the Royal Commission in paragraph 495 of its Report, with no legislative or executive powers, but with the object of promoting co-ordination between Government services in the several territories and framing plans for development.

    Associated with this council there might be a Development Commission to assist in the formulation of development and welfare schemes and advise on the allocation to Northern Rhodesia and Nyasaland of monies from the Colonial Development and Welfare Vote. It would probably be a great inducement to Southern Rhodesia to accept any such general scheme as is here outlined, if she participated by appointing a member of this Development Commission. His Majesty's Government should also be represented on this Commission, perhaps by nominating the Chairman. The Northern Territories share of its expenses could be provided from the Colonial Development and Welfare Act.

(e) In the course of the interterritorial council's work, as the unification of particular departmental services between the territories appeared feasible, this should be effected with proper safeguards for the position of individual civil servants in the northern territories. If the Colonial Service re-organisation now in prospect materialises, there seems no reason why Southern Rhodesia should not to some extent participate in this scheme and employ officers of the new unified service in positions where qualified local men are not available (though the strong prejudice against frequent transfers would have to be taken into account).

(f) At the end of a specified period of years, the position should be reviewed to see whether any further organic change in the direction of closer integration of the three Territories was desirable. Until that time it is assumed that the present position as regards the reservation of assent to certain classes of legislation in Southern Rhodesia would remain (though it would probably be politic to avoid making express reference to this in any settlement). The general control of His Majesty's Government in the Northern Territories would continue, being exercised through the High Commissioner and the Governors.

15. The above suggestions are only indicated in barest outline, and much detailed consideration would obviously be necessary before a workable scheme could be presented. In any case, they hinge on at least two cardinal assumptions; that agreement on a statement of native policy is possible, and that a very wide latitude is given to the High Commissioner and the Governors in the detailed administration of the northern territories, subject only to the control of the Secretary of State on broad issues of policy.

Notes

1. *Rhodesia-Nyasaland Royal Commission Report*, Cmd 5949, *PP* (1938–9) XV.
2. Marginal minute on original: 'This is only based on a press report, we are trying to confirm it'.
3. William George Arthur Ormsby-Gore, 4th Baron Harlech, b.1885, was High Commissioner for the UK in the Union of South Africa, and High Commissioner for Basutoland, Bechuanaland, and Swaziland, 1941–4.
4. *The Atlantic Charter and Africa from an American Standpoint: A Study by the Committee on Africa, the War, and Peace Aims* (New York, 1942) pp. 33–4.
5. Marginal minute on original: '& much more political. cf the position of Natal in the Union'.
6. Conciliation Acts: Southern Rhodesia's labour legislation, as embodied in successive Industrial Conciliation Acts, was designed to protect especially the position of skilled white labour. The position of Africans under the 1934 Act described in the Bledisloe Report (Cmd 5949, pp. 174–5) was essentially unchanged when the Secretaries for Native Affairs in the three territories described current practice in 1951: 'In Southern Rhodesia no legal provision exists for the recognition of African trade unions. It is not that any law in Southern Rhodesia specifically bans African trade unions, but simply that the Industrial Conciliation Act, under which European trade unions are recognised, excludes Africans from the definition of "an employee"; and thus does not make provision for the registration of trade unions of African employees'. Cmd 8235 *Central African Territories: Comparative Survey of Native Policy*, *PP* (1950-51) XXVI, para 73.

DOCUMENT 20

Note by Lord Hailey on 'Draft Declaration by the United Nations on National Independence' by H. C. Hull, 5 May 1943, 4O 323/1858 / 9057B

There are difficulties both of substance and of form. The major difficulty of substance is the announcement of the decision to establish some form of international control over the 'areas released from political ties with nations formerly responsible for them'. Mr Hull may be thinking primarily of Korea, Eritrea or Libya, but there are some at least among the United Nations which will see here evidence of an intention to withdraw other areas also from the 'ties' which have bound them to colonial Powers. Nor, indeed, do I think that such an intention has been entirely absent from Mr Cordell Hull's mind. It would be dangerous for us to agree to any declaration in the proposed form until we had some clearer indication on this point. It is one thing to propose international control for the ex-Italian areas; it is another to contemplate it for British, French or Dutch areas recovered from the Japanese. It must be realized also that in its present shape the declaration is bi-lateral; but it purports to be a declaration of policy by the United Nations, and must, therefore, be agreed by other colonial Powers than the U.K. and the U.S.A.

The second difficulty of substance lies in the attempt to insist on fixing dates upon which the colonial peoples shall be accorded the status of 'full independence within a system of general security'. I have some doubt whether the President himself would insist on this; he has spoken rather about the necessity for a period of 'graded education' than about the need for 'liberation'. It will be noticed, however, that the prescription is qualified by the insertion of the words 'at the earliest practicable moment'. It is possible that the U.S.A. might accept here some alternative phrase – such as 'to create conditions which will make it possible to declare in advance the date at which the various colonial peoples shall' etc.

On the point of form, the chief difficulty seems to lie in the insistent repetition of the term 'independence'. Americans will, however, argue that Article 3 of the Atlantic Charter can have no other implication; and it would be hazardous for us to argue at this stage that it can have any other meaning. To endeavour to substitute the term 'self-government' would lead to questions which we should ourselves find it difficult to answer. We have made a strong point of the fact that in the case of India, Dominion status implies a potential status of complete autonomy. But much has been said also about the possibility that some of the colonies at all events shall attain Dominion status. Does it then mean something different in their case? To imply that there is a distinction between self-government and independence suggests a refinement which will be viewed with a great deal of suspicion in the U.S.A.

One has to admit at the same time that the use of the word 'independence' may create an awkward reaction in some of the colonies. We might perhaps endeavour to meet the difficulty by substituting in regard to the colonies the phrase 'the exercise of the right to choose the form of government under which they shall live'– the term used in the Atlantic Charter.

At first sight there is some attraction in the suggestion that we should make a 'unilateral' declaration of our own. But I believe that we should only fall back on this in the last resort. It will not get us out of all our difficulties. If it is to carry any weight in the U.S.A. it will have to satisfy the criteria which American opinion applies in such a case. It must carry all the appearance of implementing the Atlantic Charter. Americans feel that we are already repenting of having committed ourselves to it; and whatever they may feel about some of its articles themselves, it would be asking too much of them to expect that they will forego the opportunity of making us 'toe the line' in regard to Article 3. Again, a declaration by us must lead off with those resounding statements of principle on which America insists – for to Americans a declaration of this nature is rather of the nature of an advertisement of the character of the party making it than a guarantee of performance. In short, it will be almost as difficult to frame a 'unilateral' declaration that would carry weight with Americans, or which would not be scrutinized with suspicion by them, as it would be to agree a form of declaration with them.

If, therefore, we are to have a 'unilateral' declaration, it should probably take a somewhat different form to the present draft, and be directed only to making our position clear to the people of the colonies. The question of Regional Councils or Commissions would then have to be taken up separately with the U.S.A. and with other Powers concerned.

Hailey 5/5/43

DOCUMENT 21

Colonial Affairs: Extracts from a speech by the Secretary of State for the Colonies (Oliver Stanley) in the House of Commons, 13 July 1943. *Hansard Parliamentary Debates*, vol. 391, cols 48–52, 55, 57–9, 62–4, 66–9.

The central purpose of our Colonial administration has often been proclaimed. It has been called the doctrine of trusteeship, although I think some of us feel now that that word 'trustee' is rather too static in its connotation and that we should prefer to combine with the status of trustee the position also of partner. But we are pledged to guide Colonial people along the road to self-government within the framework of the British Empire. We are pledged to build up their social and economic institutions, and we are pledged to develop their natural resources. Those objects have often been proclaimed, and for me to proclaim them again to-day would be one more speech in a world where speeches now are rather at a discount and it is more deeds that count. What I propose, therefore, to do is not to expound the theory of Colonial administration nor to clothe these general principles in second-hand eloquence, but to give some account of the progress that we have made in the past and to outline some of the practical steps that we hope to take in the future.

It is the tendency, both here and abroad, for those who criticise, or indeed for those who are interested in Colonial administration, to concentrate on political evolution, and it is by our success in that field, success in advancing these Colonial territories towards self-government, that critics are apt to test both our sincerity and our efficiency. I do not mind being judged by that test if those who use it are aware of and understand the full content of the approach to self-government. But it is dangerous if that test is to be too narrowly interpreted, for hon. Members will all agree that, if self-government is to succeed it has to have solid, social and economic foundations, and although without them spectacular political advances may draw for the authors the plaudits of the superficial, they will bring to those whom it is designed to benefit nothing but disaster. It is no part of our policy to confer political advances which are unjustified by circumstances, or to grant self-government to those who are not yet trained in its use, but if we are to be true to our pledge, if we really mean as soon as practicable to develop self-government in these territories, it is up to us to see that circumstances as soon as possible justify political advances and to ensure that as quickly as possible people are trained and equipped for eventual self-government. Therefore, to my mind, the real test of the sincerity and success of our Colonial policy is two-fold. It is not only the actual political advances that we make, but it is also, and I think more important, the steps that we are taking, economic and social as well as political, to prepare the people for further and future responsibilities. So I shall not speak at great length on the political advances already made, although in the last year, even in war-time, with all the difficulties that that brings, the advance has been substantial.

In Jamaica we have given them the promise of a new Constitution, which is now being worked out in detail. That Constitution was largely suggested by the people of Jamaica themselves, and I believe, from every report that I have seen from that island, they welcome a real opportunity of showing their capacity for administering their own affairs. I hope that when that Constitution is in operation they will make the fullest use of the opportunities that it gives and that by the wide use of those opportunities, despite the many obvious difficulties and problems which face them, their success will lead, when the Constitution comes to be reviewed as it is to be after a period of five years, to still further advances.

In Ceylon a promise of full internal self-government under the Crown, in all matters of internal civil administration, to be brought into force as soon as practicable after the war, has been made, and the Board of Ministers have been invited to formulate their own schemes for the carrying-out of that pledge. That promise was given by the Government in all sincerity. It was explained that during the war there was no opportunity for the detailed discussion which in a matter of this complexity and magnitude must take place, but it is our real desire that as soon as possible after the war this promise can be implemented. The length of time that that will take must depend very much upon the progress which Ministers themselves can make in preparing a constitutional scheme.

In Malta a promise of a similar character has also been given, a promise which the Government were glad to give and which the House was glad to hear. There was a period before the war when Malta enjoyed internal self-government. Hon. Members will recollect the circumstances which led to its withdrawal. Italian influence, Italian propaganda, and I am afraid in some cases Italian money, wrecked that particular period of self-government, but in an island which now has nothing for the Italians but hatred and contempt all of us can look forward after the war to the experiment which was not a success before meeting with full success.

There runs through all these three major constitutional developments during the last few months a similar line of approach. In all cases the Government, who are finally responsible, have laid down the field of advance, but in all cases the people of the Colonies themselves have been asked to suggest the constitutional machinery which they desire and which they, after all, are the people who are going to work. I very much hope that that method of approach, which I think has been successful in these cases, will form the normal method for constitutional advance in the future. Those examples, Jamaica, Ceylon and Malta, are the outstanding instances of political development in the last few months, but almost all over the Colonial Empire continual small changes, additional members here, lowering the franchise there, are all tending towards the same goal of eventual internal self-government.

Mr Maxton (Glasgow, Bridgeton): Can my right hon. Friend say whether his right hon. Friends the Dominions Secretary and the Secretary of State for India are following the same general principle? In the matters of Newfoundland and India they do not seem to be moving along the same lines as the Colonial Office.

Colonel Stanley: On the contrary, with regard to India I should have thought that it was following exactly these lines. The essence of the Cripps Declaration was to lay down the area and to ask the Indians themselves to suggest the method. I should not like to speak for my right hon. Friend the Secretary of State for the Dominions; he is very capable of speaking for himself.

Mr Maxton: My right hon. and gallant Friend said that the Colonial Office was following the same policy as the India Office, but as far as I know the Colonial Office are not throwing into gaol the people they are asking to make a Constitution.

The Chairman: I do not think we can go further into that matter.

Colonel Stanley: I am sorry, Major Milner, that you have prevented the pursuance of this interesting red herring.

I have given three outstanding examples, but there are many other cases all over the Colonial Empire of continuous political advance. For instance, in West Africa there has recently been an addition of a number of unofficial members of the Executive Council – two in the Gold Coast, two in Sierra Leone and three in Nigeria. All of these gentlemen, with one exception, are Africans. In British Guiana, following the recommendation of the Royal Commission, the Legislative Council has been completely reconstituted, with the result that the elected unofficial members are now in a decisive majority. So much, therefore, for what, even under the stress of war, we have actually accomplished in the political field during the past few months.

Let me turn to what I consider is even more important, and that is what we are going to do to prepare the Colonies, however backward some of them may appear to be at present, for political responsibility in the future. I want to develop two main themes – educational advance and economic development – because I regard these two as the twin pillars upon which any sound scheme of political responsibility must be based. Let me deal first with educational advance. I want to include under that heading many subjects which would have made the educational formalist of the 19th century wince. I do not mean by education just the literary education which was his dream, nor the classrooms, the books and the teachers which were his tools. I do not even mean the 20th century equivalent of 'the three R's'. The education I have in mind goes far beyond the classroom walls, far beyond the teacher's voice. It cannot only be found in books. It cannot be learnt by heart. It does not end with schooldays. Sometimes it does not even begin until schooldays are over. The sort of education that we want as a basis for political development is education by life for life. It must, of course, include the more formal kind of literary education, and therefore I shall deal with higher and elementary education in the Colonies. I want, too, to deal with subjects which I consider just as important – education through local government, education through community effort, such as trade unions and co-operatives, and education through actual practice in administration.

* * *

There is one area in particular which does need now detailed investigation, and that is the area of British West Africa. It presents a number of difficulties. First, there are several existing centres of education of different standards and doing different work. Then the various Dependencies in the area are widely separated from one another. There are great contrasts not only between the Dependencies themselves, in their economic, social and political development, but within each Dependency between development on the coast and development inland; and, finally, the war, although it has not directly taken place upon their soil, has had a great and lasting impact upon their conditions. At the same time that we have this Commission inquiring into the general problem of the relations of the universities, I am setting up a Commission of Inquiry into higher education in

British West Africa, and I am glad to say that my right hon. and gallant Friend the Member for Kelvingrove (Lieut.-Colonel Elliot) has accepted an invitation to be Chairman of that Commission. Hon. Members will, I am sure, feel that this is a great act of gallantry on the part of one who, so recently, had what was really a miraculous escape from death and has since been undergoing a painful convalescence. Needless to say, among the invitations to serve upon this Commission I have extended invitations to three African representatives, who will give, not only invaluable but indeed indispensable service in a work of this kind, and, of course, the work of the Commission will necessitate a visit to West Africa, probable at some time in the Spring of next year.

* * *

Now I pass to the question of primary education. I agree with my hon. and gallant Friend the Member for Wycombe (Sir A. Knox) that it is just as important for the future of the Colonies as the question of higher education. In higher education, you are dealing with the training of the leaders, but what is just as essential in a democracy is the training of the led, because the success of self-government does not depend only on the capacity of the leaders to lead, but also on the ability of the community to respond. It is not only the political field that is affected. The spread of elementary education through the Colonies is really a necessity, for everything we are trying to do, every social improvement, every economic development, in some measure demands an increase of knowledge among the people. Every new health measure, every improvement of agricultural methods, new co-operative machinery for production and distribution, the establishment of secondary industries – all these are going to make increasing demands upon the people, and they will be able to respond only if they have had some educational opportunities. No one who surveys elementary education in the Colonial Empire as a whole can pretend to be satisfied with the present position. Great efforts have been made in the past, first by the Churches – and let us pay a tribute to the real work which has been done by missions of various denominations in the various parts of the Empire – and more recently great efforts have been made by the Government, and, of course, the scope and the content of elementary education throughout the Colonial Empire are continually increasing. But yet in many Colonies we see, first, a mass of illiteracy among adults and, secondly, an all too small percentage of present-day school population, giving, therefore, little hope on present lines of reducing that mass of adult illiteracy. I believe that if we are to get full advantage from the various reforms which we propose in the Colonial Empire, that position has to be altered radically and it has to be altered urgently.

The size of this problem is so great that we can only hope to solve it within any reasonable period of time if we can evolve a new technique, and the whole question of the drive upon mass illiteracy is now being considered by my Advisory Committee on Education. I hope shortly to receive their report, and I do not want to anticipate its contents, but there are certain points which will, I think, strike hon. Members as they strike me. The first is that in this particular technique we have much to learn from experiments already carried out, and successfully carried out, in other countries, in Russia and in China, for instance. The second is that we shall have to make the fullest use of new methods which invention and industrial development have placed at our disposal in the past few years, the cinema, broadcasting and above all the film strip, new teaching techniques which were not available 20 or 30 years ago.

The third, and to me the most important, is this: I believe that the only road to success is through the enthusiasm of the peoples concerned. This effort to deal with mass illiteracy has to be not a Government but a community effort, an effort in which all are interested and in which all play their part. I do not believe that the reforms can be carried through in any reasonable time by an educational bureaucracy, however large or however efficient. They can only really be carried through by the enthusiasm of the people with the help of the educationists. When I receive that report I shall ask all Governors to take it into account in framing the educational plans which they are now engaged upon. One thing is certain, that however we approach this problem, whatever new technique we can devise, it will call for the expenditure of large sums of money, and for that expenditure we shall have to, and shall be able to, have recourse to money provided under the Colonial Development and Welfare Act.

Let me turn to education through local government. I do not believe there is any better training for the art of government than participation in local administration. Our own history shows that our constitutional government, developed here in Westminster, has owed a very great deal to our experiences in local administration, and I wonder how many Members there are in this Chamber who received their first lessons in the political arts in the administration of their local councils. It is very unfortunate, with regard to Colonial development in the past, that too little attention has been paid by popular imagination, either here or in the Colonies, to the development of local government. There always tends to be overemphasis on advance at the centre, as if that was the be-all and end-all of progress, and equally therefore a tendency to overlook the opportunities which local government gives. I regard the extension of local government as one of the quickest and certainly the surest methods of making certain of the extension of central government. We are doing all we can to extend this local self-government, and if I can give only a few examples it is by no means an exhaustive list of the advances made.

* * *

Finally, let me pass to the Colonial Service and the possibilities for training in self-government offered by the Colonial Office itself. There are in the Colonial Empire 250,000 public servants of all kinds. The vast majority of them are of Colonial birth and service in their own home country. I do not know that people realise how small is the proportion of Europeans recruited either in this country or, to an increasing extent, in the Dominions. Out of 250,000 there are only between 5,000 and 6,000 so recruited. There are two lines of development which after the war have to be followed. The first is to stimulate and to encourage the staffing of the Colonial public services by the people of the Colonies themselves. I think this progressive association with the day-to-day administration of government in the Colonies is as genuine an advance towards self-government as any spectacular development in the political field. Of course , it is no good just saying that we will encourage this in theory. What it means in practice is that we should afford to the people of the Colonies the necessary training which will enable them to take on these jobs, and that, of course, links in with the importance of higher education.

Secondly, we have to recognise that in the Colonies as a whole we shall continue to need a substantial number of European Civil servants. There is no inconsistency between saying that we want to increase the proportion of jobs in the Civil Service in the Colonies held by the inhabitants of the Colonies themselves and saying that we shall continue to need Colonial servants from this country or from the Dominions. The developments which we have in hand are going to demand not merely skilled technicians of every kind, but there will inevitably be many additional posts, as the whole economic, health and educational field opens up. Many of the posts will be filled from the Colonies, but in other cases there will be a need for the special qualifications which can be obtained only from outside. I am reviewing the whole future organisation of the Colonial Service. It needs detailed preparation, but this preparation is well advanced, and I hope before long to be able to lay concrete proposals on this subject before this House.

Well, so much for the educational advance side of our two-fold problem. I now want to turn for a short time to the question of economic development. Our objective in the Colonial Empire must be to make the Colonies self-supporting. By 'self-supporting' I do not mean self-contained. I do not mean a narrow autarchy. I mean Colonies which are able to support an adequate and sound economic basis which will meet the needs of Government and peoples and which will give a reasonable standard of life. It is pretty clear that unless we succeed in doing this any talk about self-government is really humbug. There cannot be any real self-government if you are financially dependant. Political responsibility goes ill with financial dependence. I do think that in this branch of activity the Colonial Development and Welfare Act has given a new opportunity which none of my predecessors ever really possessed. I wonder whether we quite realise what a tremendous change was brought over the whole Colonial scene by the passage of that Act – and I must say what an Act of faith the passage of that Act was, in the summer of 1940, just after Dunkirk, and at the time of greatest peril for this country and this Empire. By passing that Act we have driven a breach into the old, rigid system of Colonial financial self-sufficiency. It is a system which meant that a poor Colony, because it was poor, was unable to start those reforms and developments which alone held out any promise of increasing its permanent wealth. It is on that line that we have to look at expenditure under the Colonial Development and Welfare Act and not as something which is merely a perpetual subvention to local budgets. There is no future on that line.

* * *

Now, on the question of secondary industries, we all agree that all over the Colonial Empire it is agricultural production which is going to be predominant, but we also agree that in many Colonies it will not be possible for them ever to reach or to maintain any reasonable standard without some increase in their present scale of industrialisation. That growth must be reasonable. I cannot think of anything more fatal to the economics of the Colonies than a rash, mushroom, industrialist growth, fostered by high protective tariffs unrelated either to local products or local markets.

The kind of development I have in mind in secondary industries falls into two classes; first, industries for the processing of the natural products, whether for home consumption or for export or, for export, carrying them one further stage before they leave the country. Secondly, there is a class of simple manufactures which does not call for the import of large quantities of raw materials and where the local market will be adequate to absorb the full production of a unit of efficient size. Of course, during the war we can only foster the setting-up of secondary industries which have a bearing upon the war needs and the war effort. But certain local industries which we are encouraging by providing machinery, particularly in East Africa, although they have as their primary purpose the meeting of a war need, will fall into one or other of those broad categories. I recognise that in the early stages it will no doubt be necessary for industries of this kind to have from the local Government some moderate protection, whether by tariffs or by other means, but I frankly feel that any industry which cannot start except with excessive aid from the Government had better not start at all, because an unnatural industry of that kind will in the long run only damage the Colonial economy.

There are two questions which are bound to arise when we deal with this expansion of secondary industries in the Colonial Empire. The first is the effect it will have on our own industries at home. My own belief is that a wise expansion of secondary industries in the Colonies will not re-act adversely upon our export trade as a whole and will in the long run prove beneficial. After the war our main industrial asset will be our industrial skill, and the only classes of goods in which we shall be able to compete on terms of equality will be those which require skill for their manufacture. To enable us to compete in the Colonial territories in the cheapest classes of goods would need preferential treatment so great as to question our position as trustees for the territories. Consequently, if it were given, it would defeat its own end, because where the margin is so small, as unfortunately it is to-day in many of our Colonies, this raising of the cost of living would simply dry up the demand. The more the Colonies are able themselves to supply their own cheaper necessities, the more will be available from the surplus for overseas purchase and the more will be available to buy the better class of goods which need skill in their manufacture, and in which, therefore, the export industries of this country will be able to compete on fair terms.

The second question is, What place is there for private enterprise in this post-war Colonial industrial development?

Dr Haden Guest (Islington, North): Will the right hon. and gallant Gentleman tell us what these secondary industries in East Africa are? It is a very important new development, which may have very great effects.

Colonel Stanley: I will give the hon. Member the complete list when I reply, if he will ask me. One of the most important is the manufacture of sulphuric acid. I have not got the list by me, but there are half-a-dozen small industries, the names of which I will give him. I was about to touch upon the part to be played by private capital in post-war Colonial development. This is a subject fraught with great danger, and to deal with it at great length might be to involve myself in that political controversy which all of us are anxious to avoid – at any rate on weekdays. But I can, I think, say without any danger of controversy that if private capital has any place in our economy here after the war, it will certainly have a place in the economy of the Colonies. As I see it, the financial resources of the Colonial Governments and the financial assistance which His Majesty's Government are to give under the Colonial Development and Welfare Act, will be fully needed for basic developments and social advances, and I think we shall need and be glad of, the assistance of private capital. Under proper control – and everybody agrees that in Colonial territories it should be under proper control – I think it could be of great benefit to the Colonial territories [AN HON MEMBER: 'Question.'] There is no hope, and I hold out no hope, to the 'Get-rich-quick' type of industrial *entrepreneur*. Their time is past in the Colonial Empire. The Colonies have passed the stage of economic development in which a man, though he had to look for great risks, also looked for great profits. What I hope is to give a chance to the efficient producer with reasonable security to get a reasonable return. I believe – although some hon. Members opposite may laugh at the idea – that after the war there will be found a number of industrialists who will have a real desire, apart from the profit motive, to assist in this task of Imperial development. [*Interruption.*] Well, miracles do happen.

Sir Richard Acland (Barnstaple): Is the right hon. and gallant Gentleman relying on a miracle of there being some industrialists who want to promote African welfare rather than dividends? Suppose the miracle does not come off. What then?

Colonel Stanley: No, I never rely on miracles. That is one of the reasons why I never try to start a new political party. I did try to make it plain that the whole resources of Colonial Governments and His Majesty's Government would already be committed to the full in various developments, and that we needed as much as we could get of assistance from private capital.

The final question I wish to deal with is the question of some kind of economic advisory board or committee, whatever it may be. One thing is certain, that after the war economics will play a far greater part than before in Colonial administration, both in the Colonies and in Whitehall. Members of this Committee who realise that have, in the past, put forward many suggestions for some new form of machinery. Among these has been that of a central development board. I think that has two disadvantages. The first is a practical one, the difficulty of planning these things at the centre. I believe that when you come down from broad principles there is only one place where your new road, your new reservoir or your new drainage scheme can be planned, that is, on the spot, by the people who know the conditions. The second disadvantage is even more important. I think those who advocate this kind of central planning are apt to forget that the Colonies are growing up, and that you will find there to-day a vivid and instructed interest in their own affairs which you would not have found 20 years ago. They will expect to have a say in their own development, and will not be content to have their plans handed out to them from Whitehall, however competent and respected is the body which hands them out. The detailed planning will have to be done on the spot.

But what Colonial administrations will want, and what they will expect to get from me, is guidance on general principles, on broad lines, and it is on those broad questions that I shall want advice for myself. I have at the Colonial Office a number of advisory committees, dealing with education, agriculture, research and social services, composed of men of great technical qualifications and knowledge of the subject, who in their various branches give me invaluable help. But there is none on economics, which is perhaps the most important of all. That I believe to be a definite gap. It is not easy, when people are already so engaged on matters perhaps more closely and immediately connected with the war, but I hope shortly to be able to complete the setting-up of an Advisory Committee on Economics to deal with broad policy on general lines.

Mr Riley (Dewsbury): There is an Economic Adviser now with Sir Frank Stockdale in connection with his administration in the West Indies. Is not this Economic Adviser now at work there?

Colonel Stanley: Yes, I think I announced that in the Caribbean Debate. He did go rather after everybody else, but he has been there for a year now.

Mr Maxton: Surely the Empire Marketing Board covered this ground and had a number of distinguished economists working on it. If I remember rightly, the right hon. and gallant Gentleman was one of those who disposed of that organisation.

Colonel Stanley: No, I think the hon. Member is wrong on both points. The Empire Marketing Board had a much more limited field than I anticipate this body will have, and at the unfortunate decease of the Empire Marketing Board I was not in a position of such responsibility, I am afraid, as to have any share in it.

I am afraid I owe the Committee a double apology. One is for my sins of commission, because despite all my efforts at compression I have trespassed over long on its time and patience. The other is for my sins of omission. In a survey such as this, necessarily broad which I have tried as far as possible to relate to a central theme, obviously I have had to omit all reference to many important problems and many interesting developments. Each individual Colony has its particular difficulties, its particular problems and its particular conditions. I have obviously been unable to refer to them. I should, however, like the Committee and particularly the Colonies to know that it is not because I ignore their existence, not because I do not realise their importance and not that I am not striving to find their solution. I hope, and I think it is a hope shared by many Members of this Committee, that we shall be enabled sometime in the future to repeat the experiment which was such a success in the case of the West Indies, to debate the problems and difficulties of one particular area at a time.

It only remains for me to say that anybody who occupies my position now in time of war must suffer from a slight feeling of impatience. There is so much to do and so much we are prevented from doing by the shortages which are inevitable in war-time – the shortage of expert advice, the shortage of labour and, above all, the shortages of material. Therefore, this time, which we should so much like to be a time of action, has essentially to be a time of preparation when we make up our minds where we are going and how we are going there, so that as soon as we can start, as soon as peace gives the signal, we can get rapidly under way. Meanwhile, I have no inclination to apologise for the British Colonial Empire. In the past, as even our critics must admit, we have brought to millions of people security for life and property and an even-handed justice which they have never known before. Now it is our responsibility and pride to help those millions along the road to a full, happy and prosperous share in the world of the future.

DOCUMENT 22

'Constitutional Development in West Africa', Colonial Office Memorandum by O. G. R. Williams, June or July 1943, CO 554/132/33727[1]

CONSTITUTIONAL DEVELOPMENT IN WEST AFRICA

These notes are based very largely on the four confidential reports by Lord Hailey to the Secretary of State on Native Administration and African Political Development.

References to these reports are indicated as follows:-

The Report on Nigeria	= A
The Report on the Gold Coast	= B
The Report on Sierra Leone	= C
General Report on Native Administration and African Political Development	= D

The numbers following the reference letters are of paragraphs of the respective reports.

Lord Hailey's reports are not easy to summarise satisfactorily as they deal with a very complex problem and his recommendations, where he makes any definitely, are necessarily couched in cautious and qualified terms.

A good idea, however, of his general attitude and conclusions may be gathered from the following passages from his General Report on Native Administration and African Political Development.

D.149 'There are forces both at home and in the dependencies which will exert increasing pressure for the extension of political institutions making for self government, and for the fuller association of Africans in them. The strength of this pressure is likely to be largely enhanced as the result of the war. Unless we have a clear view of the constitutional form in which self government is to be expressed, the answer to this pressure will be ill-coordinated, and may lead to the adoption of measures which we may afterwards wish to recall'.

D.175 'But there are already advanced sections in some dependencies which look for the satisfaction of African ambitions in the wide extension of native representation in the Legislative Councils and the concession of an unofficial majority in them. They are, in effect, unable to read the future in any other terms than the expansion of Parliamentary institutions of the normal type'.

D.135 'Practical considerations demand that the Africans' participation in the political institutions of Government and in the central responsibilities of the administration must be developed *pari passu* with the progress of the native authorities in the sphere of local government. Participation in such activities, otherwise than through the native authorities would not, as has sometimes been urged, prejudice the position of the latter. Given a clear recognition that their position is to be that of agencies of local government, it will be obvious that they have an expanding field of action within which their traditional authority should be unimpaired, and should indeed in some cases be enhanced'.

D.139 'It is in our readiness to admit Africans to such posts (i.e. posts in the Administrative Service) that they will see the test of the sincerity of our declared policy of opening to them the road to self-government. That indeed is a view that is constantly taken by newspapers in West Africa'.

D.140 'If a territory can only attain cohesion through the presence of an alien bureaucracy, then it is clearly better that it should continue to remain under external control rather than attempt to manage its own affairs'.

An admirable summary of his general conclusions is contained in the concluding paragraph of Lord Hailey's general report:

D.188 'Measures for improving the physical and social conditions of the people must now have a claim on our attention which should take precedence of other considerations. It is no disparagement of those whose chief interest lies in furthering political advance, to say that the satisfactions of the ambitions of what is still a small minority of Africans can be no substitute for the expenditure of the protracted effort and the considerable financial sacrifice which may be needed to meet the more elemental needs of the great majority of the people. But the two conceptions are fortunately not mutually exclusive; the situation only demands that we should not allow our pursuit of political ideals to detract from the attention which must be given to the pre-eminent needs of social advance. In the political sphere, the most important of our immediate problems is to interest Africans in measures designed to further social and economic developments, and to secure their full co-operation in them. The solution suggested in this Memorandum is, on the one side, a resolute development

> of local institutions, combined with progressive admission of Africans to all branches of the government services, and on the other, a policy of caution in political matters which, while leaving an opening for advanced opinion to play its part, would keep the substance of power in the hands of the official government, until experience has shown us under what constitutional forms the dependencies can move most securely towards the final stage of responsible government'.

The suggestions with regard to constitutional policy tentatively put forward in these notes make two assumptions:

(1) That it is agreed to be most important that political advance should proceed as far as possible parallel with economic and social development and should, as far as possible, be made to be dependent on that development. Social development is intended to include (a) advance in primary, secondary and higher education and (b) progressive measures for the training and employment of Africans in posts at present held largely or wholly by Europeans. It is not unlikely that considerable pressure will be brought to bear upon HMG to make substantial political concessions in advance and quite independently of any such material or social development. To make such concessions, however, might have most deplorable results, particularly in West Africa where there is such an enormous gulf between the small group of politically-minded Africans with varying degrees of European culture living for the most part in towns and the vast bulk of African cultivators living under tribal conditions, even though those tribal conditions are themselves becoming more and more deeply affected by direct or indirect European influences.

The difference between these two sections of the community is far greater than that between urban and agricultural workers in this country or between the most highly educated class of people in this country and the rest of the community either urban or rural.

Indeed in West Africa the differences might be more truly expressed as one of kind rather than of degree.

D.187-8 (In this connection see Lord Hailey's General Memorandum 187 and 188, especially the latter).

The difficulty of the task in present circumstances must be realised. In Lord Hailey's words (General Memorandum paragraph 162)

'It is indeed doubtful whether we are justified in attempting to plan the political future of these populations when we have still so much to learn about their reaction to the new environment which circumstances are creating for them and when we have as yet made so few experiments in placing the African in situations where he must exercise initiative and final responsibility. At the best we can for the moment only indicate certain lines of advance which existing circumstances make possible to us.'

(2) The second assumption is that when considering what to do in West Africa, no regard need be had to possible reactions in East Africa. It would be very difficult, if not impossible to defend any policy which resulted in retarding the political development of West Africa merely because such development would not be in line with what, for quite other considerations, was regarded as the policy to be followed in East Africa.

For the purpose of discussion a very rough tentative plan of political development is sketched in the appendix to these notes. As regards the earlier stages they are largely based upon Lord Hailey's recommendations or suggestions, the only important variation being that some suggestions are made for further development of Legislative Councils which Lord Hailey would prefer to see kept as they are until some success has been attained in the development of the Regional Councils which he recommends. The difference is merely a matter of degree and not of principle but I think it will be probably found expedient to make some concessions in the sphere of the Legislative Council while the other changes are in progress and not wait until they have themselves reached a later stage, provided that those changes are not such as to seriously embarrass the Government in its future plans.

It is very important that the educated politically-minded Africans who, although few at present, will be steadily growing in numbers with the advance of education, should not be antagonised by a misunderstanding of the intentions of His Majesty's Government. It is important therefore to be as definite as possible in stating those intentions and also to explain frankly that it is at present impossible to be definite about the later stages of the programme. Lord Hailey's views as to the importance during what must necessarily be an experimental period of avoiding irrevocable commitments and preserving room for as much elasticity as possible seem to me to be eminently sound but the success with which they can be put over will depend a good deal upon the confidence which we succeed in inspiring in the minds of educated Africans. If our plan should contemplate no development at all in the Legislative Councils during the earlier stages we should be running the risk of arousing opposition to the whole of our schemes for constitutional advance. The problem is to devise such development in the Legislative Councils as will not compromise our general plan.

It will be noticed that the tentative plan in the appendix contains no reference to Executive Councils. This is because there does not appear to be any room for development in that sphere until stage 5 of the plan has been reached. It seems probable that if H.M.G. had been in a position to point to a plan of constitutional development on some such lines as is sketched in the appendix, it would have been found possible to avoid the premature introduction of unofficial members into Executive Councils. This subject has been forced upon us in West Africa by precedents elsewhere and considerations of immediate political expediency in West Africa itself. It is indeed a good illustration of the need for a plan to avoid further concessions which might prove to be more embarrassing.

It should perhaps be stated that the tentative plan in the appendix is intentionally made very general in character and takes no account of the obvious fact that the form of the problem as presented in the different West African Dependencies will call for considerable modifications in the attempted solution as between one Dependency and another; for example the problem of the Gold Coast is differentiated from that in Nigeria in many ways, not least perhaps by the fact of the entirely different character of the Native Administrations in Nigeria and in the Gold Coast Colony and Ashanti.

APPENDIX

Tentative plan for constitutional development

References to Hailey.

The plan has been divided for convenience into stages but it will be appreciated that these stages will not be reached simultaneously in all four Colonies, that they tend to merge into one another and to overlap so that in some places two stages might be developing at the same time, and above all that there can be no question of finding a uniform solution for all four Colonies.

Stage 1

B. 148. (a) *Municipal Councils.* Increased African representation on existing Municipal Councils, in some cases by elected members, in others by nominated.

C. 15. D. 117. 158. Aim would be African-elected majorities on the councils based on an increasingly liberal franchise and also more liberal qualifications for membership.

Parallel with the above developments, an increasing degree of responsibility to be developed upon Municipalities.

While the above developments are going on, new Municipal Councils would be formed as opportunity offered in suitable areas at present not enjoying any Municipal rights.

A. 16. 43. 96. B. 127. 139. D. 39–65. 109. 133–5. 163. (b) *Gradual modernisation of Native Authorities.* This will involve the introduction of younger and better-educated members in an increasing proportion and the gradual replacement of authoritarian regimes, where they exist, by forms of authority reflecting more fully and actively the will of the community. This will of course need very careful handling of conservative minded authorities like the Northern Nigeria Emirs, who may need a good deal of persuasion before they accept any changes.

A. 97. B. 167–9. D. 166. (c) *Parallel with (a) and (b) the development of Regional or Group Councils.* These would, in the first instance, be purely advisory, would mainly consist of Africans and, so far as possible, would be drawn from, or otherwise linked closely with, the various Native Authorities within the region.

Broadly speaking, the Regional Councils would cover agricultural areas, including any other areas which for special reasons could not be treated as Municipalities.

B. 170.
(c.f. A. 97.)

(d) *Development of African representation in Legislative Council.* This could be done in two ways, (1) in the case of elected members, by broadening the franchise and by substituting where practicable election for nomination as regards existing membership, and (2) by the addition to the council of further African nominated members to represent more adequately various African interests or sections of the community. Special measures to be taken on lines advocated by

A. 91.

Sir B. Bourdillon, to enable the African members to play a more active and effective part.

It should be emphasised here that the aim of this development is not the substitution, under existing constitutional forms, of an African majority, but a council more fully representative of the various African interests involved in the complex makeup of the community.

At the same time it may be necessary to reconsider the representation on the council of interests other than African, e.g. those of the European merchants and mining companies. There is also the special and difficult case of the Syrians.

Stage 2

(a) *Municipal Councils.* The widening of the franchise and the progressive elimination from Municipal Councils of all elements except those of an elective character.

The gradual increase in the scope and responsibility of the Council's functions.

The gradual contraction of the Governor's overriding powers.

D. 166–7.
D. 180.

(b) *Regional Councils.* The gradual devolution upon the Regional Councils of functions other than advisory. These would include, in the first place, minor legislative or rule-making powers, the scope of which could be extended in the light of experience, and if the experiment should be successful might enable a good deal of legislation at present passing through Legislative Council to be devolved upon Regional Councils. (One of the problems will, of course, be to do this without introducing tiresome variations of detail as between one region and another; and also to differentiate satisfactorily the functions of the Regional Councils from those of Native Authorities which will not necessarily be constituent parts of such Councils.)

B. 171.
A. 92. (Bourdillon)
D. 168.

(c) *Legislative Council.* The gradual transformation of African representation on Legislative Councils (except in the case of municipal areas) by the substitution of representatives of Regional Councils (either elected or nominated in some way acceptable to local opinion) for representatives of various African interests or communities on the present basis.

Stage 3

Regional Councils. The gradual transfer of certain more important legislative powers from the Central Legislature to Regional Councils.

B. 171.
D. 168.

This is obviously a matter which will call for very careful handling. The choice of subjects to be transferred and the nature of the safeguards under which the new powers are to be exercised will present difficult problems and may take a long time to work out satisfactorily.

Stage 4

D. 176–179.

Legislative Councils. The introduction of African unofficial majorities, whether partly or wholly elected.

It is very questionable whether there should be any stage 4. Experience elsewhere suggests that unofficial majorities do not afford an education in self-government but merely a training in irresponsible opposition to Government. Paramount powers would have to be reserved to the Governor to ensure that irresponsible majorities did not wreck the administration and the exercise of these powers would be a frequent source of violent controversy both locally and in this country.

Stage 5

Towards self-government.

1. With the progress of education should go the progressive Africanisation of the higher posts of the Colonial administrations.
2. These factors are bound to lead to an increasingly impatient demand for self-government.

It is obvious that it would be very unwise to attempt to foreshadow now the form which self-government is likely to take in West Africa, or the method by which it is to be acquired. It is suggested, therefore, that all that can be said about stage 4 [stage 5?] at the present time is that any further developments in the direction of self-government should be preceded by conferences of all the African interests involved with representatives of the British Government. Whether these Conferences should take place in Africa or in this country is a matter which would have to be considered nearer the time. There are arguments in favour of either procedure.

Such Conferences would afford an opportunity to make clear to the Africans what is involved in self-government, i.e. its responsibilities as well as its privileges. No country can be really self-governing if it has to depend on some external authority for financial grant-in-aid or is unable to maintain law and order within its own boundaries. In a place like West Africa, it would be obviously absurd to think of all the existing Colonial units as being equally fit for self-government. The conferring of self-government upon a 'Federation' of all four territories is a possible conception but great practical difficulties are involved.

So long as His Majesty's Government in the United Kingdom remain ultimately responsible for what goes on in West Africa, there would have to be certain rigidly reserved powers and subjects.

3. African opinion, unless it profits to a surprising extent by its probationary training during the first three stages, is likely to press for the fulfilment of its aspirations in ways which would be unlikely to be in the true interests of African communities. Parallel with the constitutional development tentatively outlined above, there would of course be, it is to be hoped, a considerable material improvement in the conditions of life for the bulk of the community and a progressively widespread increase in education.

4. A good many years (perhaps a good many generations though it would be impolitic to say so openly) must elapse before the possibilities of stages 1, 2 and 3 have all been at all fully exploited, but while this process is going on there will presumably be an insistent demand for quickening the pace and for the handing over to the African communities of some degree of responsibility for their own affairs. This would be a natural and healthy development but it will raise problems of great difficulty.

Note

1. In this document paragraph sub-headings not emphasised in the original have been printed in italics for the convenience of readers.

DOCUMENT 23

'Constitutional Development in West Africa': Note of a Meeting held on 29 July 1943, CO 554/132/33727

NOTE OF A MEETING HELD IN THE SECRETARY OF STATE'S ROOM ON 29th JULY

Present:

Secretary of State
Lord Hailey
Sir George Gater
Sir Arthur Dawe
Mr Palmer[1]
Mr Cohen
Mr Varvill[2]

The Secretary of State referred to the paper prepared by Mr Williams on constitutional development in West Africa[3], which he thought provided an admirable basis for long-term planning. The paper was based on Lord Hailey's Memorandum on Native Administration and African Political Development and the Secretary of State said that he would be very interested to hear Lord Hailey's views on the proposal. *Lord Hailey* said that he was in general agreement with the proposals, which, he observed went further than his own suggestions. He had two main points which he wished to make.

In the first place he referred to the difficulty of getting the educated West Africans to understand that H.M.G. sincerely intended in the long run to grant a real measure of political responsibility. These people were inclined to distrust the reality of our intentions and it was most important not to antagonize them by anything that was said about future progress in the development of political responsibility in West Africa. Lord Hailey thought that an opportunity should be taken of obtaining recognition of an abiding character for the steps which were to be taken. He mentioned the statement of 1917 about self-government in India. *The Secretary of State* asked whether that had convinced politically-minded Indians. *Lord Hailey* said that the trouble had been that Indians had felt that we had not moved fast enough since. *Sir George Gater* asked whether Lord Hailey meant that the statement should be general or should relate to West Africa alone. *Lord Hailey* said that it might form part of a statement on general policy. *Sir Arthur Dawe* said that the intention behind the memorandum had been that the issue could be confined to West Africa and that a statement of H.M.G.'s intentions covering West Africa might be made. Sir Hubert Stevenson[4] had suggested something of the kind in his recent discussion with the Secretary of State.

Lord Hailey said that what he had in mind was a full-dress statement by H.M. Government which would bring Parliament in. The reason why he was so anxious for such a statement was that the steps which could actually be taken to grant further responsibility to West Africa were necessarily slow and tentative. In order to carry West Africans with us it would he felt be most helpful if the affirmation of Parliament could be obtained for the ultimate aim of responsible self-government. *The Secretary of State* said that the difficulty was that the only practicable course to take in Parliament would be to obtain a resolution by the House of Commons supporting the policy which H.M.G. proposed to carry out. Any statement covering the grant of political responsibility in West Africa must necessarily look forward a long way into the future and be in very general terms. Parliament would not be likely to accept anything but concrete proposals affecting the immediate or near future. The Secretary of State also suggested that white papers on African policy had not always been successful in their effects in the past. He would therefore prefer that any announcement which were made should take the form of the publication of a despatch to the West African Governors setting out the policy to be adopted.

Turning to his second point, *Lord Hailey* asked whether we were going effectively far enough in creating the beginnings of self-government in West Africa. What the memorandum proposed to do was to develop representative institutions, to encourage the development of local government to the maximum possible extent and to increase the numbers of Africans in the Administration. All this was excellent, but he wondered whether we should not go further and bring the unofficials into the Government itself. He suggested that the conception of the Governor-in-Council should be made into a reality as a beginning of the development of self-government. At present the Executive Council of the Governor in the West African territories was advisory and not really executive. What he suggested was that unofficials, who would mainly be Africans, should be made into heads of groups of departments and should sit as such in the Executive Council. They would not of course be ministers but if and when the stage of full Parliamentary government was reached they could be turned into ministers. What Lord Hailey felt that we ought to avoid was the extension of Parliamentary responsibility by enlarging the powers of the legislature before we had the basis on which to build such responsibility. We did not want to bind ourselves to the development of normal political institutions and then to have to think again as we had had to do in India. The proposal which he had just made would have the advantage of associating Africans more closely in the Government and enabling them to learn how to govern without committing us immediately to any line of political development.

Lord Hailey thought that such a step which might be taken immediately, would not involve too violent a departure at the top and that it would be combined with building up from below by the development of local government. Reliance on the development of local government alone would be very disappointing to educated West Africans. Lord Hailey thought that if nothing were done on this line they would very soon begin to resent the fact that their representatives were in a purely advisory capacity on the Executive and Legislative Councils.

The Secretary of State asked whether it might not be difficult to find people with sufficient capacity actually to play an effective part in the running of departments or groups of departments. The scheme could hardly work if the men appointed were merely token heads of departments who contributed nothing and indeed were handicapps [sic]. It was pointed out also that it would be important to consider the attitude of the European officers in the Service to such appointments. *Lord Hailey* thought that it would be found that such heads of departments would in fact contribute something to the work of the departments under them. They would of course require to be properly handled, but this had not proved impossible in India. Lord Hailey quite agreed that the standard of development was more advanced in India than in West Africa but he did not think that this should prove a fatal obstacle. He pointed out that all important measures would have to come before the Executive Council. In India it had been found very rare for completely impossible proposals to be put forward by Indian Ministers.

In answer to a question, Lord Hailey said that he would have no hesitation in suggesting that an Emir or other Chief should be appointed to one of the posts he had in mind if a suitable man could be found. *The Secretary of State* asked whether it would be easy to find someone who would command support throughout the territory in Nigeria, but *Lord Hailey* thought that this difficulty need not be regarded as too serious. The idea of a single man representing Nigeria as a whole as opposed to a particular part of it or a particular tribe or group of tribes admittedly did not exist at present, but would inevitably grow up.

The Secretary of State said that he felt serious doubt about the appointment of puppet heads of departments and that he would prefer that as a first step Africans should be attached to departments or groups of departments as advisers, such appointments carrying with them automatically a seat on the Executive Council. If this arrangement was a success, it might be possible to proceed later to the actual granting to such unofficials of responsibility for departments or groups of departments. *Lord Hailey* agreed that it might be advisable to proceed gradually as the Secretary of State suggested. The important point was that there was an enormous gulf to be bridged between the present state of affairs and any form of political responsibility. What was wanted was education in responsibility. At present educated Africans had no responsibility except in a few cases where they held senior official posts. If no steps were taken, the leading educated Africans would develop into a chartered opposition and suddenly administrative responsibility would be thrust upon them without their being ready to assume it. His suggestion was designed to avoid this situation. *The Secretary of State* said that it was important that Africans should learn to defend unpopular measures to their own people. He thanked Lord Hailey for the suggestions which he had made and said that it would be necessary to consult the Governors on the ideas put forward in the memorandum and also on any suggestion for bringing Africans more closely into the administrative machine in an advisory capacity.

The Secretary of State then referred to paragraph (b) in stage 1 of the tentative plan for constitutional development put forward in the memorandum. He asked how the gradual modernisation of Native Authorities could be achieved. *Lord Hailey* said that this was being worked out gradually in the Gold Coast by a natural process. In Nigeria educated Africans were being brought onto the Councils of Native Authorities, and it was desirable to encourage this to the maximum possible extent. In other parts of Africa the same process was taking place. The difficult area would be the Northern Provinces of Nigeria where educated men had practically no place in the working of the Native Authorities and where the Youth Movement had no hold. *The Secretary of State* asked how educated Africans were brought into the Native Authority machine in Western Nigeria. *Lord Hailey* said that one of the principal methods was by bringing in representatives of the Town Councils who were usually elected. Public opinion was itself insisting that Native Authorities should take educated men on to their Councils. In

Eastern Nigeria there was no serious difficulty as the Native Authorities were small and had developed little and in many cases themselves welcomed the assistance of educated men. The object to be aimed at was the conversion of Native Authorities into local Government bodies with members elected by the people. At present in most cases members of Councils were chosen by the Native Authority himself.

Notes

1. Palmer, Harold, b.1895; since 30 June 1942, Principal Secretary, Eastern Department of the Colonial Office.
2. Varvill, Michael Hugh, b.1909; seconded from the Colonial Service in Nigeria to the Colonial Office, 1943–7.
3. Document 22, above.
4. Stevenson, Sir Hubert Craddock, b.1888; Governor and Commander-in-Chief, Sierra Leone 1941–8.

DOCUMENT 24

Colonial Development: Extract from a Colonial Office Memorandum by S. Caine, 12 August 1943, CO 852/588/2

. . . There is a general uneasiness about the slow tempo of action under the Colonial Development and Welfare Act. We have an alibi, becoming a little worn with use, in war conditions; but I am increasingly dubious whether things will be very much better after the war without radical changes in the present procedure.

2. I am not thinking in this of the kind of changes we have lately had under consideration, that is, speeding up the machinery for examining schemes or making vague grants for unspecified purposes to Colonial Governments. The first might save a few weeks in dealing with applications; the second would save Colonial officials some labour in preparing applications. Neither would ensure that more schemes are prepared in the first place. A few weeks earlier or later in the grant of approval will rarely make or mar an important scheme; and a Colonial Government is unlikely to pigeonhole a scheme in which it really believes because it dislikes the procedure necessary to get assistance. By all means let us 'streamline' the procedure if possible, but something more fundamental is needed to secure any spectacular change.
3. Quite simply the trouble as I see it is that not enough schemes are produced in the first place. There is not enough thinking, above all not enough original and coherent thinking, about the possibilities of development. Machinery for that kind of thinking for the Colonies is virtually non-existent.
4. This has been recognised from the start of the new development policy in 1940 and underlies the proposal urged upon Colonial Governments for the formation of Development Committees as well as the establishment of the Stockdale organisation. For reasons to be explained, I doubt if either of these projects – certainly not the first – goes far enough to provide the answer.
5. The concepts which underlay the 1929 Act are still, I think, at the bottom of our present ideas. They envisaged a flow of applications from Colonial Governments, an Advisory Committee to "screen" them, and the Colonial Office passively doling out the money. It was assumed that the schemes

put up would normally be projects already in existence; it was revealing that one of the questions in the standard application form asked why the scheme had not previously been put into operation, the idea being apparently that Colonial pigeon-holes were full up of complete but deferred projects. We have advanced a little on that conception but not very far. It is now recognised that Colonial Governments will have to think up new schemes as well as look in the pigeon-holes; but they are given no help in doing so (except partially in the West Indies). The Advisory Committee, which might have grown into an originating body, has almost disappeared even as a screening organ; and the Colonial Office retains its purely passive function.

6. As regards the passivity of the Colonial Office, there seem to be three parts the Office could play in this matter; that of waiting for schemes to be submitted and then passing judgment on them – essentially a negative role; that of stimulating Colonial Governments to put up schemes by giving guidance, suggestions and advice; and that of itself framing schemes. So far, over much the greater part of the field, the first has been the role chosen for the Colonial Office. Very little guidance or suggestion of a practical kind has been given to help Colonial Governments in inventing or working out schemes; and the occasional tentative moves towards such action which are made within the Office always seem to come up against one insuperable obstacle or another. A very few schemes under the Act have actually been framed in the Office, but they have been either of a research character arising out of investigations started in the United Kingdom (e.g. Jamaica food yeast) or deal with matters such as central recruitment and training which have necessarily to be handled here.

7. In making this criticism I do not ignore the very valid objections which exist to any policy of 'prodding' Colonial administrations too energetically while they are in their present overworked state. But I cannot help feeling on the one hand that these objections sometimes cover a more fundamental reluctance to take the initiative out of local hands; and on the other that it is going to be a poor excuse before Parliament and the country to say that, because the instrument we have chosen proves, at least temporarily, to be ineffective, we have thrown our hands in rather than try to find another one. When we have excused the slowness of action in wartime by referring to lack of material and personnel, we have always managed to say, or to imply, that

at any rate the time is being made use of to prepare plans, both broadly and in detail. This is only sporadically true; a few Governments have prepared plans of some comprehensiveness, but I doubt whether any have nearly approached the ideal of completeness. Many, so far as we are aware, have done hardly anything. When the war is over, we shall be asked where our plans are, and the answer is likely to be somewhat embarrassing.

8. We have to face to-day a new concept of the place the State must take in planning. There is much nonsense talked which suggests that no development can take place unless it is planned by Governments. Nothing is more demonstrably untrue for the Colonial Empire, where tremendous developments have been produced by the planning of private enterprise. Given the same conditions, I believe private initiative could do much more. But all the signs are that the conditions are not going to be the same. State regulation will be imposed by 'priority' requirements, by wide-spreading international economic agreements and by the difficulties of securing private finance even if it is not desired for internal reasons. The point about finance is especially important. In the past much money for development was found through the activities of private individuals who might be called economic prospectors. In the future, conditions of taxation and control of capital markets are likely to prevent the private investor risking his money in Colonial ventures, and the State will have to find a far bigger proportion. If it is going to do that effectively and intelligently, it must develop machinery for doing the economic prospecting which was formerly done by large numbers of private persons acting on their own account.

9. My main thesis is that it is wrong to expect this work to be done by that maid-of-all-work the 'Colonial Government'. It is a job needing specialised qualities different from those of ordinary administration and needing continuous thought, not odd half-hours snatched from a busy day of current work. It is instructive to look at other people's experience in this. Russia, which takes planning seriously, has an entirely separate Planning Commission as one of its major Government Departments. We may also draw some guidance from the Tennessee Valley Authority. It is hard to get any description of that body which is not couched in terms of adoration or revilement, but two things do seem to emerge. First, it is concerned with what I have described elsewhere as outline planning — providing basic services, not settling who

is to produce what; and second, it was necessary to set up a body independent of the existing authorities, who no doubt have their time filled with their own jobs, in order to conceive and carry out the major projects which were believed to be necessary.

10. In suggesting that the planning of new development is work which ought not to be expected of the ordinary machinery of Colonial Governments, I do not by any means mean that Colonial administrators are never capable of conceiving and carrying out large programmes of development. There are many obvious examples to the contrary, including the large and wise use which individual Colonies have made of the Colonial Development Act 1929 and the New Act of 1940. It is, however, in a sense a lucky accident if a Colony has a Governor and a department capable of work of this kind, and I am not sure that it would be right, even if it were possible, to choose our senior officials primarily with an eye to development work. They have many equally important functions of current administration to perform, and in most cases discharging those functions is a quite adequate task for the energies of one man. I think our own experience inside the Office emphasises the difficulty of trying to frame large constructive proposals in the intervals of dealing with the multitudinous details of current business. In all this, I am thinking mainly of development of an economic character or new capital developments of the character of social improvements, e.g. slum clearing, extensive re-planning of urban areas, etc., and not of the mere extension of welfare services, education, health, and so on. I hope the educationalists and medical men will forgive me if I suggest that the latter consist primarily of the multiplication of processes and facilities which are essentially already familiar to us and do not involve new constructive planning of the same character as major economic developments of improvement work.

11. A further feature of the problem is that we cannot really expect to find in every small Colonial Administration all the qualities, experience and knowledge necessary for the initiation of really new development. A number of individual dependencies are no more than large districts, and it is no more reasonable to expect all the ideas which are necessary to flow from the Government of British Honduras or the Gambia than it would be to expect them all to emerge from the mind of the District Officer in charge of a comparable area in Nigeria.

12. I think that there is in fact no dispute in the Office that the machinery of Colonial Administration needs supplementing to carry out the task of planning development. The unanswered question is how that supplementation can best be effected. No doubt some addition of a special development staff in the larger Secretariats would be useful, but I am very doubtful whether that would go anything like far enough. The further step which has been much in our minds is that of setting up special organisations on regional bases with the function of advising and prompting Colonial Administrations in development work. The model of such organisations at present is Sir Frank Stockdale's team in the West Indies. There can be no question but that the creation of that organisation has effected a considerable improvement in that area, but I am not sure whether even that goes far enough. Sir Frank Stockdale's work is still a good deal handicapped and slowed up because essentially he is merely acting as a projection of the Colonial Office in the examination of schemes initiated locally. He can and does go further and suggests schemes to Colonial Governments which he thinks they ought to put up, but he has not himself the staff to work out such schemes in detail and is still dependent on Colonial Governments to submit an actual proposal. It is clear from the figures that this is one of the major causes of delay.
13. We have considered the institution of similar organisations on a regional basis elsewhere, and progress has been made in theory towards such an establishment in West Africa on a somewhat tentative and provisional basis. I am sure that the idea needs to be developed, but it is to be borne in mind that there will still remain various Colonies which cannot conveniently be fitted into any regional organisation. There are also sometimes political implications in a regional organisation attached to such an organ as a Governors' Conference which may impede the growth of the necessary development organisation.
14. I think we are in danger, too, of assuming that if we can get adequate regional organisations set up, that will largely be the end of the matter. I do not believe that those organisations can function adequately without a considerable strengthening at the centre as well. As regards the territories which do not fit conveniently into a regional organisation, it is difficult to see how they can get adequate assistance in the planning and execution of their development except

from a central organisation. From both these points of view, I think a strong organisation in or attached to the Colonial Office, with considerably more powers or at any rate habit of initiation than exists at present, is really essential if the prospects of rapid development held out by innumerable Ministerial statements are to be realised.

15. It is interesting in this connection to look at the example which is being given to us by the Colonial Research Committee.[1] That Committee has with great emphasis repudiated the idea of confining itself to the merely negative or censorial function of passing judgment on schemes devised by other people and submitted to it. It has taken its function to be the systematic examination of the whole field of Colonial research and the initiation of schemes wherever they are necessary to remedy deficiencies. The Committee is taking the various departments of research individually, and is trying to stir up the responsible authorities to elaborate proposals for extension of the work, and is itself making practical suggestions. The Committee is, in fact, making a real effort to deal comprehensively with its own admittedly limited but still large and important section of the whole development field, and, properly supported, it should be able to make effective the revolution in Colonial research which was foreshadowed by the 1940 Act.

16. There is, I think, very strong reason for thinking that something similar is required to cover the field of economic development and what I have described as major social improvements. This is perhaps getting dangerously near the idea of a Colonial Development Board. That idea has admittedly very many dangers, but the fact that it is so frequently put forward does represent a very definite uneasiness as to the adequacy of the present machinery. It is no doubt necessary to avoid creating a new organ of Government which would duplicate or challenge the general authority of the Colonial Office, but there is clearly a widespread feeling that either by modification of the existing organs of Colonial Administration or by the creation of something new, machinery should be created which should be capable of much greater initiatory activity than is at present shown by the old machinery.

17. Another suggestion which has been made for meeting this basic need is that of the creation not of a semi-political Colonial Development Board but of a body bearing a commercial form although not intended to be operated in a

commercial spirit, e.g. the Imperial Development Authority advocated in a recent book entitled *Wealth for Welfare* by H. W. Foster and E. F. Bacon, which has received a conditional blessing from the *Economist*.[2] The general concept of the authority set out in this book seems altogether too grandiose, and the detailed proposals are in many cases half-baked, but there are none the less many attractions about a body which can act with the comparative freedom of a commercial concern. Another way of expressing the gap in the present organisation on the side of the economic development is that we need a service of economic prospecting; i.e., we need to be able to send freely and promptly experts of every kind to particular Colonies to report on particular possibilities of developments, their work being caried out in the same spirit as that of a mining prospector. At present, it needs a portentously heavy machinery to get started any investigation of that kind, but an independently operated authority or company could sent [sic] out investigators with as little formality as a big commercial enterprise sends out a representative to explore the possibilities of a new market.

18. The device of a company clothed in commercial form but in fact working as the agent of Government may have other advantages in the carrying out of particular works of development, e.g., on the lines of that rather mystic body, the T.V.A. without involving all the political implications of direct action by the administration in its own name. It is possible that we could learn a good deal from the methods of the Government inspired companies of the Belgian Congo.

19. There are certain common factors in all these possible lines of development, i.e., greater activity and initiative by the Colonial Office itself; or the establishment of a Colonial Development Board, or the creation of a Government-controlled company or companies. These are: the establishment at the centre of a habit of initiative in investigation, having the power to send out technical investigators without having to make a formal scheme on every occasion, the practice of dealing where appropriate, direct with Colonial interests concerned, and, of course, implicit in the whole, the grant of much greater discretion by the Treasury. It may be noted, as a type of the kind of thing which ought to be done on a much larger scale, that we have in fact been operating on something like these principles in the particular case of Jamaica food yeast, where we are now proceeding through an ad hoc Government controlled company and

have in fact run the whole thing from the Office with only a more or less courtesy consultation with the Government of Jamaica.

20. Admittedly one of the main difficulties of any change in method involving greater activity at the centre is that it must infringe the sphere of responsibility of Colonial Governments. I think we are perhaps too nervous of that. I cannot avoid the feeling that sometimes when we speak of avoiding offence to the susceptibility of local opinion nothing more is really involved than the susceptibility of the official group. There is real danger that the privilege of Colonial officials to have the sole right to deal with matters of development may be as great an obstacle as the privileges of private property are sometimes alleged to be.

21. I have not ventured at this stage to set out precisely suggestions for adoption. The basic things we should aim at are the development of strong regional organisations for development of areas which are suitable for organisation in that way, with, however, strong central organisation for general supervision and assistance, and particularly with a much greater development of initiatory power at the centre. Whether that can best be done by the development of ordinary administrative machinery of the familiar civil service type, or by boldly experimenting with new forms such as special development authorities cast in a commercial mould, is a matter for further examination.

S.C. 12.8.43.

Notes

1. The Colonial Research Committee was appointed in June 1942 to advise the Secretary of State for the Colonies on the expenditure of the sums provided for research under the Colonial Development and Welfare Act 1940. Its chairman was Lord Hailey.
2. Editors' italics. Caine is referring to H. W. Foster and E. V. Bacon, *Wealth for Welfare* (London, 1943).

DOCUMENT 25

Wartime Economic Planning: Confidential Circular Despatch to Governors from the Secretary of State for the Colonies, 28 April 1944, CO 852/588/2

Sir,

All Colonial Governments have already devoted considerable thought to the planning of the future social and economic development of their territories and several Governments have prepared comprehensive plans in detail. Consideration has also been given in the Colonial Office to the general character of such planning, bearing in mind particularly but by no means exclusively, projects for assistance under the Colonial Development and Welfare Act. A memorandum on the subject has been drawn up which it is hoped will be of assistance in the work of planning, including the revision and extension of the plans already drawn up by Colonial Governments.

2. It has also been thought that it would be of assistance to Colonial Governments to have before them certain views which have been formed on the effects of war-time changes on Colonial economic structure and organisation and a second memorandum has been prepared on these subjects. I thought it desirable to refer these two memoranda to the Colonial Economic Advisory Committee, which has expressed its agreement with them; and I now have the honour to transmit the enclosed copies for your consideration.

3. Of the general points made in the first memorandum, I wish to draw special attention to four:-

(i) First, development plans ought not to be simply a list of such desirable new works as happen to attract attention but the result of a truly comprehensive examination of what is needed for the fullest development of the basic resources (material and human), services and organisation of the territory;

(ii) Secondly, without belittling the need for welfare expenditure, the basic objective of sound development in any dependency must be the improvement of productive and earning power (in which health and education services may well play an important part) and not simply additions to income at the United Kingdom taxpayers' expense; the ultimate objective being to place the dependency in a position to support itself adequately without external assistance;[1]

(iii) Thirdly, there is need everywhere for both public and private enterprise and the acceptance of a continued necessity for a wider range of governmental activity must not obscure the important part which private initiative, both local and external must play in the future as in the past;

(iv) Fourthly, development must be a joint enterprise undertaken together by the United Kingdom and the Colonies themselves and, while His Majesty's Governments are prepared to contribute much more generously than in the past and over a period of years, it is expected that Colonies which have resources of their own available (including hitherto untapped resources of taxable capacity) will contribute their fair share to the joint enterprise.

4. There are similarly certain outstanding points in the second memorandum, on the effects of war-time changes, i.e.:-

(i) There will be a transition period after the cessation of hostilities, possibly of some years, in which many of the war-time controls and other special economic arrangements will be retained while being gradually relaxed;

(ii) During this period certain Colonial industries will be faced with special problems of adjustment (to which further reference is made below), but it is not thought probable that there will be any general failure of the demand for Colonial produce in the transition period;

(iii) It is not at present possible to predict with any confidence how far the various special marketing arrangements built up during the war for individual Colonial products will become permanent. An endeavour will certainly be made to apply the lessons learned, for instance in the management of the West African Produce Control Board, but it must not be assumed that any measures will be practicable to organise trade permanently on the basis of fixed prices for the Colonial producer;

(iv) Colonial producers may be intimately affected by wider plans in regard to international economic organisation and policy which are now the subject of tentative discussion and of which I shall take care to inform Colonial Governments as soon as plans are sufficiently crystallised.

5. [2]As regards the special problems of adjustment in the transitional period, I have already addressed you on one particular question, that of demobilisation, but it may be desirable here to add some comment as regards possible difficulties with particular industries. It will of course be realised that it is impossible to predict with any accuracy and the absence of mention of any probable difficulty in any individual industry must not be taken as any indication of assurance for continued demand for its produce. There does not in general appear to be any reason to fear acute difficulties with the staple products of East Africa, although the special war-time demand for rubber will disappear when Far Eastern rubber production is again available and the specially intense demand for locally produced foodstuffs will no doubt also decline.
6. Certain particular problems arising in connection with the planning of particular aspects, e.g., the promotion of secondary industries and the active participation of Government in other forms of economic enterprise, are being further examined by the Colonial Economic Advisory Committee and I should address you further as occasion may arise in the light of any reports or recommendations which the Committee may make on such matters.
7. [3]I am sending a similar despatch to the Governors of the other East African Dependencies and a copy is also being sent to the Chief Secretary of the Governors' Conference.

I have the honour to be, Sir,
Your most obedient, humble servant,
Oliver Stanley.

Notes

1. To the Gambia, to paragraph 3(ii) was added: 'this does not of course exclude the possibility of more generous assistance to territories which for special reasons are unlikely ever to achieve an economic development sufficient to maintain an adequate standard of welfare.'
2. Paragraph 5 was altered as follows:
   - to Gibraltar and N. Rhodesia, omitted entirely and despatch dated 19 April;
   - to Cyprus, Malta, Falkland Islands, Nyasaland, Trans-Jordan, Aden, Fiji, Western Pacific, Mauritius, Seychelles, St Helena, first two sentences only included;
   - to the West African Colonies,

for its produce at the present rate. It is possible that in the transition period, the demand for minerals from West Africa will decline, in some cases seriously. Bauxite in the Gold Coast is an obvious example. When Far Eastern rubber production again becomes available, it must also be assumed that the demand for rubber from West Africa, at any rate at anything approaching present prices, will disappear. The demand for oil-seeds and vegetable oils and for cocoa is, on the other hand, likely to be reasonably well maintained and certain industries which have suffered from the war, e.g., gold mining and export of bananas, may hope to recover their pre-war position.

- to the West Indian Colonies,

for its produce at the present rate. Among West Indian products, there will no doubt be a substantial decline in the demand for bauxite from British Guiana, at any rate in the period immediately after the war, and there may possibly be a decline in the demand for sea island cotton, but most other products should meet with a satisfactory demand in the transition period and it will no doubt be hoped that certain trades which have been interrupted, particularly the export trade in bananas, will be resumed. In the case of sugar, it is conceivable that conditions of general over-supply will be re-established within a few years after the end of the war but in any event it is most unlikely that any actual restriction of Colonial sugar output during the transition period will be contemplated.

3. The wording of this paragraph varied according to the circumstances of the Governor being addressed. The version printed here was sent to East African Governors.

DOCUMENT 26

Draft Directives for Further Planning in South-east Asia: War Cabinet Paper, 18 May 1944, CAB 66/50

SECRET.
W.P. (44) 258.
18*th May*, 1944.

WAR CABINET.

POLICY IN REGARD TO MALAYA AND BORNEO.

REPORT OF THE COMMITTEE.

WE were appointed by the War Cabinet at its meeting on the 6th January (W.M. (44) 2nd Conclusions) to consider the question of the constitutional policies to be followed in Malaya and in the British territories in Borneo on their liberation, and to recommend a directive on which the authorities responsible for planning the Civil Administration of these territories after liberation can work.

The composition of the Committee was as follows:—

The Lord President of the Council (*Chairman*).
The Secretary of State for Dominion Affairs.
The Secretary of State for India.
The Secretary of State for the Colonies.
The Secretary of State for War.
The Attorney-General.
The Parliamentary Under-Secretary of State for Foreign Affairs.

2. *Malaya*.—A directive on the probable lines of future policy is indispensable for those who have the duty of planning the Civil Affairs policies and as a basis for the directive to be issued in due course on these matters to the Supreme Allied Commander, S.E.A.C.; and, on the understanding that no publicity is given to the policies contained therein, we are in agreement on the terms of the directive for this purpose, which form Appendix I to this report.

3. *Borneo*.—The four British territories concerned (North Borneo, Sarawak, Labuan and Brunei) are at present in a

United States sphere of command, the S.W. Pacific. His Majesty's Government are entitled, under the terms of the Charter of the Combined Civil Affairs Committee, to provide the American Commander with directives on Civil Affairs policies in these British territories, and a directive on Civil Affairs will need to be framed at the appropriate time for issue to him. But it is not our function to examine the form in which any such directive for that purpose will need to be framed. We have concerned ourselves only with a directive on which the British planning staff should work. For this limited purpose we have agreed upon a directive in the terms of Appendix II to this report.

4. It will be noted that the Borneo directive proposes the acquisition by His Majesty's Government from the British North Borneo (Chartered) Company of its sovereign and administrative rights in North Borneo. We are of opinion that confidential discussion for this purpose should be opened with the Court of Directors of the Chartered Company, though we recognise that in the present uncertain position as to the value of the Chartered Company's assets in the Far East it would be premature to reach any agreement on the financial terms on which such a settlement could be reached.

5. In the case of the Borneo directive, as in that of the Malayan, there is no question of any publicity being given to the policies beyond the confidential discussions which will be involved with the Chartered Company and the Rajah of Sarawak.

6. To sum up, we accordingly recommend, with the proviso that no publicity for these policies is involved, that the Secretary of State for the Colonies be authorised—

(*a*) To issue the directive at Appendix I to the authorities responsible for planning for the Civil Administration of Malaya on liberation;
(*b*) To issue the directive at Appendix II to the British officials at present planning for Civil Administration in British Borneo after liberation;
(*c*) To open confidential discussions with the Court of Directors of the British North Borneo (Chartered) Company with a view to coming to an understanding (without at this stage any financial commitment) as to the conditions on which the administration of North Borneo would be transferred from the Company's responsibility and control to that of His Majesty's Government; and
(*d*) To open confidential discussions with the Rajah of Sarawak, who is at present residing in this country, with a view

to the preparation of a new Agreement on the lines proposed in paragraph 3 (*c*) of Appendix II attached.

(On behalf of the Committee),

(Signed) C. R. ATTLEE.

Offices of the War Cabinet, S.W. 1,
18*th May*, 1944.

APPENDIX I.

DRAFT DIRECTIVE ON POLICY IN MALAYA.

1. The restoration of the pre-war constitutional and administrative system will be undesirable in the interests of efficiency and security and of our declared purpose of promoting self-government in Colonial territories. The first of these interests requires a closer union of the territories comprising the relatively small area of the Malay Peninsula; and the second requires that self-government should not merely develop towards a system of autocratic rule by the Malay Rulers but should provide for a growing participation in the Government by the people of all the communities in Malaya, subject to a special recognition of the political, economic and social interests of the Malay race.

2. On general grounds, and more particularly in order that His Majesty's Government may be in a better position to ensure the development of the country on the lines indicated above, it is necessary that the old position in which His Majesty had no jurisdiction in the Malay States should be remedied and that it should be possible to legislate for those States under the Foreign Jurisdiction Act.[1] Immediately on the reoccupation of Malaya, direct authority will be exercised by the Military Commander, who will carry with him sufficient authority to enable him to exercise such direct powers and control over the territory as will be necessary during the period of military administration. This military authority will, however, not enable His Majesty to legislate for the Malay States under the Foreign Jurisdiction Act and, moreover, the jurisdiction of the Military Commander will not persist when the military administration gives way to a permanent civil administration.

3. In considering the proper way to achieve these objects, it is

necessary, on the one hand, to make certain basic assumptions and, on the other hand, to be prepared to meet a situation when the liberation of Malaya has been effected, on which those assumptions may be found to be wrong or incomplete and in consequence the prepared plans may have to be varied. The future position and status of the Malay Rulers in particular cannot finally be judged before liberation when it will be possible to assess not only their individual records but also and especially the attitude of the people of Malaya to the advantages or otherwise of maintaining the Sultanates as institutions in the several States. For the present we have no reason for any other assumption than that the Sultanates as an institution will continue to enjoy the loyalty and traditional respect of the Malays.

4. On that assumption, it is considered that the proper way to achieve our purpose will be to make fresh treaties with the Rulers under which such jurisdiction would be ceded to His Majesty as would enable him to legislate for the States under the Foreign Jurisdiction Act. A fresh Treaty with each Ruler should for this single purpose be concluded on behalf of His Majesty as soon as feasible after reoccupation. The actual signatory of such Treaties on behalf of His Majesty would appropriately be the G.O.C., but the negotiations would be carried on under instructions from the Secretary of State for the Colonies by Civil Affairs Officers or special representatives of His Majesty's Government, subject always to the proviso that the actual time for opening negotiations with the Rulers must be governed by Military exigencies and left to the discretion of the Military Commander.

5. The acquisition of this Jurisdiction by His Majesty will enable an Order-in-Council to be made to provide for the future central and local government of the country. This jurisdiction will render unnecessary any further dependence on Treaties with Rulers in any future revision of the constitutional arrangements.

6. The new constitutional arrangements for Malaya should provide for the special treatment of the port and Island of Singapore, in the early stages at any rate, in view of its distinctive characteristics in the Malayan picture.

7. The rest of the peninsula, including the British Settlements of Penang and Malacca, should be constituted a Malayan Union. For the Malayan Union a constitution should be devised which would provide for a single united authority representing the States and the Settlements, subject to the jurisdiction of His Majesty under statutory powers. At the head of the Union Government would be a Governor with an Executive and a

Legislative Council. The seat of this Government would conveniently be in or near Kuala Lumpur.

8. The co-ordination and direction of the policies of Government in the Malayan Union and Singapore will be secured by the appointment of a "Governor-General" at Singapore, with the power of control over the local Authorities in Malaya and Borneo.

9. Co-operation in all administrative matters requisite between Singapore and the Union will be ensured by particular agreements for joint consultation and action.

10. On the assumption explained in paragraph 3 it will be no part of the policy of His Majesty's Government that the Malay Rulers should lose their personal position in their State territories. Indeed, it will be the intention, that, by the association of their territories in the Union, the Rulers will have opportunities to take part in wider activities than hitherto for the general advantage of the country as a whole, and may thereby enhance their sphere of influence and prestige in Malaya.

APPENDIX II.

DRAFT DIRECTIVE ON POLICY—BORNEO.

(North Borneo, Labuan, Brunei and Sarawak.)

1. The restoration of the pre-war constitutional and administrative systems in the four territories will be undesirable in the interests of security and of our declared purpose of promoting social, economic and political progress in Colonial territories. These purposes require—

(*a*) The direct assumption by His Majesty's Government of responsibility for administration in North Borneo.
(*b*) The integration of Labuan with North Borneo.
(*c*) The cession to His Majesty of full jurisdiction in Brunei and Sarawak.

The purpose of political progress requires also that self-government in Brunei and Sarawak should not merely develop towards systems of autocratic rule but should provide for a growing participation in the Government by people of all communities in each territory.

2. On general grounds, and more particularly in order that His

Majesty's Government may be in a better position to ensure the development of the country on the lines indicated above, it is necessary that the old position in which His Majesty had not full jurisdiction in these territories, with the exception of Labuan, should be remedied and that it should be possible to legislate for them all by Order-in-Council. Immediately on the reoccupation of these territories, direct authority will be exercised by the Military Commander, who will carry with him sufficient authority to enable him to exercise such direct powers and control over the territories as will be necessary during the period of military administration. This military authority, even if it fell to be exercised by a British Commander, would, however, not enable His Majesty to legislate for the three States, North Borneo, Brunei and Sarawak, by Order-in-Council, and, in any case, the jurisdiction of the Military Commander would not persist when the military administration gave way to a permanent civil administration.

3. It is considered that the most effective way to achieve our purposes will be:—

(*a*) To acquire from the British North Borneo (Chartered) Company the sovereign and administrative rights which they possess and have hitherto exercised; and thereafter to provide for the future government of the territory on its liberation by an Administration under the direct authority of His Majesty's Government.

(*b*) To incorporate the present Settlement of Labuan in the new Administration for North Borneo.

(*c*) To conclude new treaties with the Sultan of Brunei and the Rajah of Sarawak at the earliest opportunity which will accord to His Majesty such jurisdiction in their States as will enable His Majesty to legislate for these territories under the Foreign Jurisdiction Act to the fullest extent. In the case of Sarawak, the new treaty should also secure the acceptance by the Rajah of a resident British Adviser whose advice must be sought and acted upon in all substantial matters of policy and administration. (The present treaty with Brunei already provides for a resident British Adviser.)

3. The territories in Borneo are still comparatively undeveloped and they have few racial or other affinities. At this stage, therefore, the basis for closer union between them hardly exists. Community of policy and of administrative action can, however, be assured from the outset under the direction of the Governor-General at Singapore, whose appointment is recommended and

the promotion of closer union should be a continuing matter of our policy.

Note

1. The Foreign Jurisdiction Act of 1890 empowered the Crown to exercise jurisdiction within a foreign country as if it had acquired that jurisdiction by conquest or the cession of territory. Theoretically interpreted as jurisdiction over British subjects alone, in practice the provisions of the Act were brought to bear upon the indigenous peoples as well, and, with the passage of time and the accumulation of precedent, the more comprehensive application of the FJA achieved a kind of validity. Up to 1945 Britain recognised the Malay Rulers as sovereign within their own states; with the conclusion of the MacMichael Treaties in 1945–6 the Crown gained sufficient authority to apply to the Malay states the FJA upon which rested the Orders in Council establishing the Malayan Union in 1946. Some opponents of the Malayan Union claimed that this extension of the FJA to the Malay states was illegal, but the irony was that the Malay Rulers could not contest it or the new treaties in English Courts without themselves submitting to English litigation and thereby abandoning their pretensions of sovereignty. See J. de V. Allen, A. J. Stockwell, L. R. Wright (eds) *A Collection of Treaties and Other Documents affecting the States of Malaysia, 1761–1963* (London, Rome, New York: 1981) vol. I, pp. 1–15, 117–22.

DOCUMENT 27

Colonial Development and Welfare. Secretary of State for the Colonies to Chancellor of the Exchequer, 21 September 1944, CO 852/588/11

My dear Chancellor,
I think you must have been expecting that I should in due course be coming forward with proposals to extend and increase the provision for Colonial development under the 1940 Colonial Development and Welfare Act. I gave Kingsley Wood[1] notice of that probable necessity last year and, with Treasury agreement obtained at the official level, I have several times stated in the House that I should not hesitate to ask you for more money as soon as I thought the time had come.

I believe that the time when we must take action in this sense is now upon us. The end of the fighting in Europe will, I am convinced, be the psychological moment at which to announce our intention to make fully adequate provision for the assistance from His Majesty's Government which will be necessary for a dynamic programme of Colonial development. It is the moment at which to demonstrate our faith and our ability to make proper use of our wide Colonial possessions. It is also the moment when the minds of administrators in the Colonies will be turning even more definitely towards planning for the future, and when a clear call from here will give them faith in the permanence and adequacy of our policy. I have been worried by recent reports both from the West Indies and West Africa that there is today more cynicism than faith. Finally, it is the moment at which to kill the enemy propaganda lie that the policy announced in 1940 was forced on us by our critical situation and that we never mean to implement it. Nothing would better confirm faith in our sincerity than that at the height of our success we should confirm and amplify this policy which was first announced in the depth of our disasters.

Conversations have already taken place between some of my people and yours, so that I think I can spare you a good deal of detail. The main facts are that, although we have never so far been able to spend anything like the sums envisaged under the 1940 Act, the various Colonies have now reached a fairly advanced stage in the preparation of plans for future expenditure, and it is quite certain that within a few years after the end of hostilities, the sums required are likely substantially to exceed the £5,000,000 per annum at present provided for. Things have progressed furthest in the West Indies, because there we set up a planning organisation at a very early stage, and the West Indies are already pressing against the total of a million and a quarter per annum which was tentatively allocated to them and which of course represented a share of the total much larger than would have been allotted on a population basis. West Indian experience is therefore a good sample of what is likely to happen elsewhere as soon as planning machinery really gets going. In addition, we have to take account of the fact that our Far Eastern territories, which before the war were expected to need only negligible help, will be a good deal poorer than they were before the war. Although direct rehabilitation costs will of course be dealt with separately, they are likely to be applicants for assistance under the Colonial Development and Welfare Act for new developments, especially in the comparatively under-developed areas of Borneo, for which we shall have a new responsibility.

I have, therefore, two practical requests to put to you. First, I think it is essential, in order to give a secure basis for planning, to extend the period of the Act. This is in any case natural, since the real commencement of its operations has been deferred by five years of war. I should propose, on the assumption that amending legislation would be passed some time in 1945, that the period of the Act should be extended to 31st March, 1956, and that 1946/47 should be the first financial year under the new arrangements.

Secondly, I want to ask for an increase in the limit of annual provision as laid down in the Act. This has been discussed between our officials, and I understand that you have already accepted in principle the necessity for some increase. The proposal which your people have made is that we should simply double both the development and the research provision, which would then stand at £10,000,000 and £1,000,000 per annum respectively. They are reluctant to propose any larger annual figure because they feel, and I very much sympathise with their feeling, that we are unlikely to attain even these figures in the early years, and may therefore be embarrassed in the future if too high a target is set. On the other hand I cannot regard the figure of £10,000,000 as adequate for the later years of the decade now in question. I could consider a figure of that order if it were possible to devise any arrangement by which under-spendings in the early years could be carried forward to the later years. I believe, however, that any arrangement of that kind, e.g. by the creation of a self-contained fund, is viewed with great objection in the Treasury.

I should therefore be very greatly obliged if you would consider the alternative of increasing the annual limit by stages over the ten year period. My detailed suggestion is that the new Act should provide for a maximum of £10,000,000 per annum for the first three years, i.e. up to 1948/49, a maximum of £15,000,000 for the next four years, i.e. up to 1952/53, and a maximum of £20,000,000 for the last two years, i.e. up to 1955/56. I should be prepared to agree that these figures should include the necessary provision for research and for certain other new grants to the Colonies, in particular for the development of higher education, which we have previously contemplated would have to be found outside the Colonial Development and Welfare Vote. Broadly, the cash difference between the Treasury suggestion and my present proposals is that the latter contemplate an average of £15,000,000 per annum over the ten years, while the former would involve £10,000,000 for development plus £1,000,000 for research plus possibly another million for higher education and other purposes, i.e. a total of £12,000,000 per annum. Grants in aid of ordinary administration and special grants which were in existence before 1940 and have not been absorbed under the Development Vote would of course continue to be provided outside the Act on the ordinary Colonial and Middle Eastern Services Vote, as would any special assistance required for the occupied territories in the Far East after their liberation.

I very much hope that you will be able to agree to this modified proposal. It seems to me that it has the merits from your point of view of avoiding a large increase in the burden on the Exchequer in the early post-war years when our budgetary difficulties are likely to be greatest. It is worth bearing in mind also that a part of the assistance given towards development is in loan form and comes back in due course to the Exchequer, and I should [hope] that out of the increased provision now contemplated, a larger proportion than heretofore would be in loan form. It is also a mitigation of the apparent burden placed on this country that, unless all our expenditure on development proves fruitless, it will result in a real increase in Colonial production, which should strengthen our general financial position either by offering increased supplies of goods for which we shall not need to provide non-sterling currency, or by increasing our sale to foreign countries and particularly hard currency countries.

I make no pretence, however, that this is going to be a profitable transaction on a purely financial calculation. The over-riding reason why I feel that these proposals are essential is the necessity to justify our position as a Colonial Power.

It may well be that it will take a little time to get all the details settled, but I very much hope that we shall be sufficiently in agreement to make it possible for a statement of the intention of His Majesty's Government to propose fresh provision for Colonial development to be included in the King's Speech at the opening of the next Session of Parliament.

Needless to say, I am at your disposal for any discussion you would like.

Yours sincerely,
Oliver Stanley

Note

1. Wood, Rt.Hon. Sir Kingsley, b.1881; MP, and Chancellor of the Exchequer May 1940–September 1943; d. 21 September 1943.

DOCUMENT 28

Colonial Development and Welfare: Chancellor of the Exchequer to Secretary of State for the Colonies, 25 October 1944, CO 852/588/11

My dear Oliver,

I have your letter of the 21st September in which you put forward various proposals for extending and increasing the provision for Colonial development under the Colonial Development and Welfare Act, 1940.

This is, as you say, a matter which has already been the subject of preliminary discussion by officers of our two Departments, as a result of which I intimated that I would be willing to consider favourably a proposal for extending the period for development and welfare grants to 10 years from some current date and, at the same time, the doubling of the limits in the 1940 Act, i.e. there should be provision for expenditure of up to £10 million a year for development and welfare schemes and £1 million a year for research.

You, however, now ask for a further progressive increase in the annual limit, and suggest that for the financial years 1946–48 inclusive it should be £10 million, and then for 1949–52 inclusive £15 million, and finally for 1953–55 inclusive £20 million.

I have considered your proposal very carefully and I feel bound to say that I do not like at all the idea of a rising rate, and indeed it seems to me it would be very hard to justify in present circumstances. Our assistance to the Colonies is an external and not an internal payment and none of the compensatory benefits to which increased internal expenditure gives rise would accrue to us. Thus any increase in assistance under the Colonial Development and Welfare Act is, in fact an addition to the adverse balance of payments which we have got to correct.

I recognise the desirability of making some substantial gesture to justify ourselves before world opinion as a great Colonial power and also to reassure the Colonies themselves as to our intentions. Thus I am able to agree to doubling of the limits in the 1940 Act, and the extension of the period of the Act so that you may have a 10 year run with the increased limits from 1st April, 1946.

This in itself, involves a substantial sum and besides it, there will be special liabilities which will make heavy demands. Malta and Palestine are, I understand, already at various stages of consideration and besides them, there is the at present wholly unknown problem of the Far Eastern Colonies. I feel that our problem of oversea payments is likely to be one of increasing difficulties and that it would be unwise to undertake a commitment involving an increasing scale of assistance.

After all £11 million per annum is not a trifling figure for the taxpayers of this country to meet after the war for a purely external payment and I feel that the Colonies should be content with this.

Yours ever,
John Anderson.

DOCUMENT 29

Colonial Development and Welfare: Cabinet Memorandum by the Secretary of State for the Colonies, 15 November 1944, CO 852/588/11

SECRET.

W.P.(44) 643.
15*th November*, 1944.

WAR CABINET.

FUTURE PROVISION FOR COLONIAL DEVELOPMENT AND WELFARE.

MEMORANDUM BY THE SECRETARY OF STATE FOR THE COLONIES

1. The next few years may well determine the future course of the Colonial Empire. The participation of the Colonies in the war and the gratitude felt by this country for their efforts have increased our awareness of past deficiencies in our administration. Perhaps more than ever before the public to-day are interested in the Colonies and anxious for their development. On the other hand, hundreds of thousands of the natives of the Colonies, in one branch or another of the Armed Services, have been enjoying a standard of living to which they have never been accustomed before, have travelled thousands of miles from their native villages, and will return with a desire for some of the improved conditions which they have seen and experienced elsewhere.

2. Realisation of these new conditions was given expression in 1940 by a new Colonial Development and Welfare Act, which provided for spending up to a maximum of £5 million a year for ten years on development and welfare, with an additional £500,000 a year for research. This Act, passed at the time of our gravest danger, was a magnificent gesture, but I am afraid, for reasons outside our control, it has remained little but a gesture. Shortages of technical staff, of materials and of man-power have largely prevented the translation of this legislative permission into reality. In fact, the estimated total of expenditure up to the end of the current financial year is only £3,790,000 against the £20 million which the Act would have permitted. Although this short-fall was due to no lack of sincerity or drive but entirely due

to physical limitations, it has undoubtedly produced in many of the Colonies and even within the Colonial Service a cynical belief that the gesture was never meant to be more than a gesture.

3. In these circumstances I believe the time has come when it is necessary for us to declare our intentions for the future. Since 1940 we have been able to do a considerable amount of planning; and indeed things are now speeding up to such an extent that in 1945–46 expenditure is expected to be at least £4 million.

4. At my request Colonial Governments have been preparing outline plans of the developments which will be necessary to provide basic economic and social services—communications, water and irrigation schemes, health, education and so on—on the minimum essential scale. I have received such outline plans from a number of Colonies, including several of the larger African territories, and, of course, from the West Indies, where the Comptroller of Development and Welfare has been working for over 3 years. I can, therefore, estimate much better than in 1940 how much money will be required, after allowing fully for what can be found from local resources of taxation and from public loans and making a realistic assessment of how much work local Public Works Departments can undertake and local supplies of labour can execute. As a single example I will quote an estimated minimum requirement in Nigeria of £27 million in 10 years.

5. On the basis of the information in the preceding paragraph my proposals, which, in my judgment, represent the minimum needs of the Colonial Empire over the next few years, if our frequently declared policies are to be implemented, are as follows: —

(i) that the Act should be extended for a further ten years as from 1946;
(ii) that the annual sum should be increased. My proposal is that for the three years 1946–47 to 1948–49 the provision should be £10 million per annum; for the next four years, 1949–50 to 1952–53, £15 million; and for the last three, 1953–54 to 1955–56, £20 million. These would be over-all sums and would include provision for research and certain additional schemes such as higher education which I otherwise should have had to bring forward outside the scope of the present Act.

I have deliberately adopted the policy of increasing the annual figures as time goes on. Experience has shown that planning and preparation for Colonial development is bound to take time, that, as in rearmament, the actual expenditure increases by stages, and that it is only in the later years that full provision is needed.

6. I have discussed these proposals with the Chancellor of the Exchequer. He agrees that the Act should be extended for another ten-year period, and he agrees also that some substantial increase in the financial provision is necessary. He finds himself, however, unable to commit himself to anything further than a provision for the ten-year period of £10 million a year for development and £1 million for research. As I understand it, he does not base his alternative proposal on any criticism of my estimates of what the Colonial Empire will require but solely on the financial exigencies of this country.

7. I am afraid I am unable to accept the Chancellor's proposal. He has, if I may say so, treated me with great fairness, and it is in full agreement with him that I bring this matter to the War Cabinet. He feels, as I do, that the War Cabinet should have before them both the needs of the Colonial Empire, which I shall stress, and the difficulties of national finance, which he must emphasise.

8. Although the differences in money between my proposals and the counter proposals of the Chancellor are small in comparison with the national finances, they are to my mind fundamental when applied to Colonial development. From the over-all plans which I have so far received from Colonies, I am convinced that whereas under my proposal (with some pruning), it will be possible to undertake a practicable but far from extravagant scheme of development, with the Chancellor's figures planned development over a period of ten years would be impossible and in practice we should have to be content with a collection of individual projects instead of integrated plans, a practice which has been properly criticised in the past and which cannot give the best returns from the money. I have had, too, some opportunities of judging the psychology of Colonial peoples and Colonial administrations, and I am convinced that anything short of my plan would fail to meet their natural expectations and aspirations.

9. I am not pretending that the assistance to the Colonies which I propose will not impose some burden upon this country. I do, however, feel that the Colonial Empire means so much to us that we should be prepared to assume some burden for its

future. If we are unable or unwilling to do so, are we justified in retaining, or shall we be able to retain, a Colonial Empire? The burden, however, is infinitesimal compared to the gigantic sums in which we are and shall be dealing. Nor is the apparent burden wholly real. If these sums are wisely spent, and the plans devoted to increasing the real productive power of the Colonies, there will in the long run accrue considerable benefit to us, either in the form of increased exports to us of commodities which otherwise we should have to obtain from hard currency countries, or in the form of increased exports from the Colonies as part of the sterling area to the hard currency countries outside.

10. But I am not basing my argument on material gains to ourselves, important as I think these may be. My feeling is that in the years to come, without the Commonwealth and Empire, this country will play a small rôle in world affairs, and that here we have an opportunity which may never recur, at a cost which is not extravagant, of setting the Colonial Empire on lines of development which will keep it in close and loyal contact with us. To say now in 1945 that with these great stakes at issue we shall not be able to afford £15 million in 1949, or £20 million in 1953, is a confession of our national impotence in the future. I take a less pessimistic view of our national future and it is for that reason that I ask the War Cabinet to approve the proposals which I put forward in paragraph 5.

O. S.

Colonial Office,
15*th November*, 1944.

DOCUMENT 30

Colonial Development: Colonial Economic Advisory Committee Questionnaire with Colonial Office Response, n.d. (autumn) 1944, CO 852/588/2

C.E.A.C. (44) 46

ANSWERS TO MEMORANDUM FROM THE ECONOMIC ADVISORY COMMITTEE

Question	Answer
1. Is the Committee to assume that in those Colonies at present organised primarily on the basis of native institutions, economic policies must be compatible with the maintenance of the general structure of such institutions subject to gradual transformation over a period of generations, and should not require or be likely to provoke their rapid remodelling within a period of a few years?	Yes; but it is important to remember that the speed of social change will not be determined solely by official policy but will be importantly affected by the many economic and social forces to which the communities in question are now being subjected and especially by desires and aspirations which may show themselves among the members of those communities themselves.
2. Can the Committee assume that the Secretary of State would be willing to contemplate the use of an expanded agricultural service and of considerable resources of capital and administration, to develop, in areas where physical conditions make it appropriate, by methods of education, persuasion, and financial inducements, the growth of agricultural sys-	Yes.

tems based upon larger farming units and using modern methods of cultivation – in co-operative farms or other suitable types of collective unit?

3. Can the Committee assume that it would be possible for the Secretary of State to pursue an industrial policy primarily directed towards the creation of a limited number of planned and balanced industrial centres situated in the main regions of the Colonial Empire (the West Indies, West Africa, and East Africa, for example) rather than towards the grant of equal facilities for the encouragement of factories in every Colony?

   No. The development of manufacturing industries is likely to be mainly determined by the practical advantages which particular areas and places may present for such development, but official policy must allow quite as much weight to the desirability of developing a balanced and diversified economy in each individual territory as to any advantages of convenience in the concentration of development in selected areas.

4. If the answer to the third question is in the affirmative then the Committee would like to know whether the Secretary of State would think it practicable and wise to bring into existence new instruments for both planning and execution – including, in particular, the sending of teams of industrial experts to promote the growth of such centres of industry in the main regions of the Colonial Empire and the creation of Public or semi-Public Corporations for the promotion of investment and enterprise,

   In view of the answer to question 3, this question does not strictly arise. The Secretary of State would, however, favour the creation of new instruments for the planning and execution of industrial development including separate Departments of Industry and Commerce and Development Corporations acting on a semi-commercial basis with Government finance. The executive powers with which such new instruments might be endowed would have to be determined, subject to the advice or direction of the and whether such new instruments could be given executive powers independent, within appropriately defined limits, of existing Colonial Governments.

Secretary of State, by the Colonial Government or Governments concerned, and could not arise independently of those Governments.

5. Finally, it has been suggested to the Committee that the savings of the United Kingdom may prove insufficient to meet all the demands for capital that will be forthcoming from the United Kingdom and from other places, and cannot therefore be adequate to provide all the money that is required for rapid economic development in the Colonies on private and public account. Should the Committee assume that any capital which may be forthcoming from foreign sources to assist in Colonial development must be in the form of private investment in commercial enterprises, or is it reasonable to suppose that, at some suitable time in the future, His Majesty's Government would be willing to approach foreign governments or any international investment fund that may come into existence with a view to raising loans, upon its own guarantee or otherwise, for Colonial development?

It should be assumed that investment of foreign capital will be in the form of private investment and commercial enterprise, i.e. predominantly investment of an equity character, and that H. M. G. will not approach any foreign countries or any international investment fund which may be established, specifically for loans for Colonial development.

DOCUMENT 31

Colonial Development: Extract from the Minutes of a Meeting of the Colonial Economic Advisory Committee, 19 December 1944, CO 852/588/2

Colonial Economic Advisory Committee

Minutes of the 9th meeting held at 2.30 p.m. on Tuesday, 19th December, 1944, in the Duke of Devonshire's Room at the Colonial Office, Downing Street, S.W.1.

Present: The Secretary of State for the Colonies

The Duke of Devonshire (Chairman)
Mr Clauson (Vice Chairman)

Sir Bernard Bourdillon
Mr Dalgleish
Mr Durbin
Sir William Goodenough
Lord Hailey
Mr Hallsworth
Sir John Hay
Sir Hubert Henderson
Sir Harold Howitt
Mr McLean
Professor Plant
Professor Robbins

Sir George Gater
Sir Alfred Beit
Mr Caine
Sir Clifford Figg[1]

Mr Sweaney (Acting Secretary)
Miss Orde Browne

[The meeting began with an address by the Secretary of State in which he outlined proposals for the new Colonial Development and Welfare Act. He announced the appointment of Sir Frank Stockdale as Colonial Office Adviser on Colonial Development, and his intention to ask Stockdale also to take over as chairman of the Economic Advisory Committee:

first of all because the proposals for economic development in all Colonial plans would have to be co-ordinated and secondly because he did want in all these plans to emphasise the particular importance of economic development as distinct from welfare . . . the whole object of the Colonial Development and Welfare Act . . . was that at the end of [its] period . . . the Colonies' own resources would have increased sufficiently for them to maintain a decent standard of life . . . Nothing could be worse than to give Colonial peoples the impression that the Colonial Development and Welfare Act was a permanent subsidy to their social services which the taxpayer of this country would undertake to pay without thought either of return, or indeed of supervision.

The Secretary of State referred briefly to the Committee's procedure and to its recent achievements, stressing the value of its advice on particular issues and current administrative questions, and welcoming its reports on wider problems, notably the development of manufacturing industry and mining policy. He then invited suggestions and criticisms relating to the Committee's work.]

(Paper *C.E.A.C. (44) 46* containing the Secretary of State's answers to the questions addressed to him was circulated at the meeting.)

Sir John Hay asked whether problems relating to the territories now occupied by the enemy were excluded from the discussions of the Committee or had not advanced to a stage when the Committee could properly advise on them.

Colonel Stanley did not think that they had yet advanced to a stage when the Committee could advise on them. At present they could only be tackled by ad hoc committees and there was of course the question of military security.

Mr Durbin said that speaking for himself, as the member of the Committee who had been least satisfied with the work of the year, he would say frankly what was in his mind. He thought members had been extremely happy in discussing these problems with one another and in the courtesy and co-operation they had received from the official Advisers, but at the same time he felt that on the second category of questions mentioned by the Secretary of State the progress of the Committee had been disappointing. He had found the making of a programme and the consideration of the important fundamental matters of raising the standard of living of the Colonial peoples very difficult for two reasons. In the first place because of the enormous scale of the problem. The more generous sums that were contemplated by the Government under the new Act would add up to an extremely small sum of money – a large sum for the tax-payers to contribute, but a very small fund out of which to stimulate and finance the economic development of 60 million people.

Colonel Stanley said that the Colonial Development and Welfare Vote was not the only source of funds for Colonial Development. Many Governments had built up very considerable capital balances during the war.

Mr Durbin thought that these would not amount to even double the sums contemplated under the new Act. The view of many students of the problem was that we should need something like £1,000 million a year in this country for the development of 40 million people who were already at a far higher standard of living than was usual in the Colonies. It was difficult to see what practical policy could be pursued in view of the immensity of the problem and the expenditure required. Although he had not studied the Secretary of State's answers yet with the care they required, they seemed to suggest that the scale of development on the industrial side would be very small. He understood that the suggestion of concentration was rejected on political grounds.

The second difficulty had been to discover any administrative or economic or industrial machinery whereby any policy could be carried out. The Committee had seen a brief survey of the existing machinery and the simple conclusion was that unless people could be found on a very large scale no policy of industrial development could be carried out in the Colonies. Because of these two difficulties he found it very difficult to see how any substantial rise in the standard of living of any of the large groups of primitive people would result during the next 15 years from the deliberations of the Committee or the policy of the Government.

Colonel Stanley agreed that the capital resources of Colonial Governments would not amount to more than double the sums contemplated under the new Act, but he still lived in a world where £120 million was a substantial sum. He had not got the figures, but while these resources were not enormous they were substantial compared with any expenditure which had ever previously taken place in the Colonies.

Mr Hallsworth thought it would be useful if the Committee could have some idea of the extent of these resources.

Lord Hailey pointed out that capital resources should be understood not only as reserves in hand but as loan raising capacity.

Mr Caine said that the capital sums in the hands of Colonial

Governments at the end of the war might be expected to run into tens of millions. Moreover the figures of the annual expenditure by Colonial Governments on capital goods, public works, etc. amounted to many millions before the war and this expenditure was still continuing. Altogether the suggestion of doubling the £120 millions from the Colonies' own resources was not far out. The Committee could be given figures of the actual balances.

Mr Durbin said that even with £240 million he could see no substantial hope for the development of such a large body of people. He thought borrowing from foreign governments and selecting limited areas of development was the only hope.

Colonel Stanley thought that one difficulty about limited areas of development was that if, for instance, it was decided to develop one part of Nigeria as the industrial area for West Africa, it was almost the German 'herrenvolk' idea – one concentrated in one part of Nigeria all the opportunities offered by industrial development and relegated the rest to an agricultural population. It might offer economic advantages but it would also have very great social disadvantages.

Mr Durbin said that the alternative of spending considerable sums of money upon piecemeal improvements, which nowhere added up to a living and fruitful industrial system, was a waste of money.

Lord Hailey said it should not be assumed that the only way of improvement was by rapid industrialisation, although he agreed that industrialisation had its place in general development. But the improvement of agricultural conditions was very important and the expenditure required there, although considerable, was not so large as might be involved in large industrial development. He would look to see a very considerable increase in agricultural production as a result of the expenditure of this money. The improvement of communications was one of the first ways of stimulating agricultural development; the improvement of agricultural services and of irrigation were others. Industrial development must begin with small scale enterprise. until industrial aptitudes were more developed, with markets largely provided by the growth of agricultural production and the greater consuming capacity of the people. He did not think, therefore, that the money which ought to be spent by Government in supporting and stimulating such industrial development would necessarily be a very large sum. Looking at the opportunities, the staff available and kind of aptitudes of the people we had to reckon with he thought that in ten years we could make a very considerable advance with £240 million. But we could make very little advance on the industrial side and perhaps on other sides also unless we had an economic staff in the Colonies acquainted, not only with industrial conditions, but with commerce. This staff must have its statistical side also.

Colonel Stanley hoped that Mr Durbin did not feel that the limitation on the actual sums at the disposal of Governments, which he (Mr Durbin) regarded as too low, but which still left a fairly substantial amount, would prevent the Committee from doing a great deal of very useful work in the economic development of the Colonies. Did the Committee feel that there were any other handicaps in the way of its work?

Sir Bernard Bourdillon asked whether anything was being done in the Colonies to overhaul the staff position. He felt that in a Colony the size of Nigeria the present Secretariat machinery was not really suitable for modern conditions.

Colonel Stanley said that he did not want to get involved in questions of increases in the Secretariat. He understood Sir Bernard's point, but it was easier to criticise the present arrangements than to devise a solution.

Sir Bernard Bourdillon said that it was a mistake to establish a new set-up beside the old; the old must be incorporated into the new.

Sir Harold Howitt said that on the question of finance, it seemed almost impracticable to ask for assistance from some other country; it was as good as admitting that we controlled too large a portion of the earth and had better give up some. He thought the sums of money which had been mentioned could in time produce very useful effects.

Mr Dalgleish said that when a sum was mentioned as being the likely cost of, say, a bridge, it did not mean that that was the outside edge of the sum required. For instance he understood that something over £1 million was to be spent in Nigeria on 42,000 miles of road. That would be nothing like the sum ultimately required for that road if it was to be any use. There would have to be hotels, fuelling stations, small spare part industries, etc. along it.

Colonel Stanley agreed that just building a road without developing water supplies, agriculture, etc. was really a waste of money. There was quite a lot of money among the Africans in Nigeria now and he hoped that as a result of building the road the Africans would start hotels, fuelling stations, etc.

Sir John Hay said that that showed one could not measure expenditure on Colonial Development merely by the capital sums mentioned.

Sir Bernard Bourdillon agreed. The £120 million was not all that was available to start industry in the Colonies. There would also be equity capital from this country and elsewhere.

Colonel Stanley agreed. He did not regard the £120 million as the only or even the largest source of Colonial investment. All he meant in his answer to question 5 was that he did not believe in an approach to foreign Governments, because he could not imagine that money being lent without strings being attached to it and he did not believe that Colonial peoples would welcome an industrial development which tied them perpetually by financial strings to the United States of America.

Lord Hailey thought that what we wanted was so to stimulate private enterprise, including local enterprise, that the development of industry would come from the resources of the country itself. He believed that would be much healthier than any attempt to borrow large sums of money from outside.

Mr. Durbin asked whether, supposing it was the case that we could not dispose of sufficient resources to develop the 60 million people for whom we were responsible, we should exclude the help of richer people.

Colonel Stanley said that he did not rule out equity investment. But he did not believe that it was possible to spend in the next few years enormous sums (compared to the fairly substantial figures proposed) without dislocating the whole social life of the Colonies, which would be disastrous to them.

Sir Hubert Henderson said that the investment Mr Durbin would like to see would be borrowing from abroad and was only sound on the scale he contemplated if it was likely to open up sources of foreign exchange; otherwise it would reflect on our position as guarantor. The picture Mr Durbin presented of concentrated industrial development in one place was not the way industrial development ever had proceeded. He could imagine that there might be places where it would be desirable as an experiment but he did not think the Colonial Empire was well adapted for it. He agreed that we should assist the development of industries in the Colonies. But the lines on which these industries should develop were clearly marked – certain processing and other secondary industries that fitted in naturally with local conditions. To create in the void an entirely new set-up of inter-dependent industries was a highly speculative undertaking especially as it was proposed to do it with borrowed money from outside. The £1,000 million a year for 40 million people in the United Kingdom, which Mr Durbin set against £12 million a year for 60 million people in the Colonies, was a computation of the total amount of British savings: it did not comprise merely money voted by Parliament, but included such little sums as a man might spend, say, in putting up a cottage. The greater part of it would never come into the capital market, but consisted of the trifling little sums of individuals. That was the way in which the greater part of investment everywhere must be done. He would be horrified to think that the greater part of the £120 million was to be used to develop factories; he thought most of it would be used to create public utilities.

Lord Hailey asked whether the funds to be provided under the new Colonial Development and Welfare Act could be used as a support for borrowing by Colonial Governments and whether the loans in question would have to be short-term loans limited to the duration of the Act.

Colonel Stanley said that a scheme could be made by which the loan charges of a Colonial Government would be met for a certain period under the Act. But it could not extend beyond the period of the Act.

Mr Caine said that there had been cases in the past in which a Colonial Government had felt that after a period of five years or so it would be able to meet the charges but that it could not do so to begin with and an arrangement had been made for the charges to be met under the Act for that period.

Lord Hailey said that if the Fund could be used as a basis for guarantee it would make very much more capital available. Referring to Colonel Stanley's invitation to members to make suggestions for the work of the Committee, he asked whether they could consider certain major questions of policy, such as the future tariff regimes of the Colonies, or whether it would have to be considered outside as a question of politics. It affected all questions of borrowing from abroad and influenced private investors.

Colonel Stanley said that these questions must obviously also be considered outside, but speaking for himself he would welcome the consideration by the Committee of any of them, including the tariff question mentioned by Lord Hailey. But there was always the proviso that, because these questions were bound up with wider questions which, though not beyond the knowledge, were beyond the official cognisance of the Committee, decisions might have to be taken which either anticipated the recommendations of the Committee or were adverse to them. Provided that was fully understood, he would welcome for his own guidance any advice of the Committee on these problems.

It was clear, said Colonel Stanley, that there were very considerable fundamental differences between certain members of the Committee. He did not see why that should prevent a lot of very valuable work being done. If they could not agree they could agree to disagree. They could take the middle view, and on that basis, even if it was not what they would like, see what they could do to help. No doubt when the Committee had studied the answers to their questions they would be putting up another paper to him. With regard to procedure, he would be very grateful for any suggestions for improvements; otherwise he thought the Committee could continue as before.

Sir Hubert Henderson felt that the discussions of the Committee seemed to be either on very general issues, such as those raised in the report on Mineral Policy, when a lot of time was spent in essentially abstract discussions on such questions as state socialism versus private enterprise which might as well apply to Europe as to the Colonies and were discussed without any reference to the concrete problems of the Colonies; or at the other extreme the Committee discussed ad hoc questions such as cotton marketing in Uganda, a detailed question that most members did not know very much about. They never seemed to get to grips with the actual concrete problems of development and policy which lay ahead of all the Colonies.

Colonel Stanley thought this was partly because he had not yet got the Colonial plans from which these problems would emerge and all he could refer to the Committee at the moment were the particular questions which were thrown up, and [to] which he referred not so much in order to decide whether to set up a cotton mill somewhere, but because he was afraid of taking a step with a cotton mill or a cement factory which would prejudice development as a whole. However, when the programmes under the new Act came in and Sir Frank Stockdale was asking the advice of the Committee, they would get away both from abstract considerations and from small detail.

Mr Dalgleish asked whether the first part of Colonel Stanley's answer explained why, when recommendations had been made by the Committee, it was not unusual for the Governor of the Colony concerned to be consulted to find out what the implications of a particular recommendation were. For example, in the case of the Malta cement industry, the Governor had been asked for his views.

Colonel Stanley said that he must ask the opinion of the Governor of a Colony, who bore the responsibility, under him, in that Colony. However convinced he was of the rightness of the advice of the Committee he could only advise the Governor; he could not impose a course of action on the Governor without giving him an opportunity to state his views. Governors were usually glad to receive advice, but they must be in a position to say 'this has this particular reaction in my Colony.' It had to be remembered that the Colonies contained a very large number of human beings, some of whom were getting fairly well forward and were not very easy. We were getting less and less to the position where we could impose upon them economic solutions, however right we might think them in pure economics; we had to carry them with us and that was the job of the Governors.

Colonel Stanley regretted that he had now to leave the meeting owing to another engagement. He thanked the Committee very much for a most useful discussion.

Lord Hailey expressed the gratitude of all members to Colonel Stanley not only for giving them an opportunity to hear his views, but for actually discussing them with the Committee.

Colonel Stanley and **Sir George Gater** then left the meeting.

[. . . .]

4. *Other business*

It was agreed that the Secretary of State's answers to the questions of the Committee should be brought up at the next meeting[.]

The Committee then adjourned leaving the date of the next meeting open.

Note

1. *Devonshire*, 10th Duke of, Edward William Spencer Cavendish, b. 1895; Parliamentary Under-Secretary of State for the Colonies, 1943–45.
   Dalgleish, A., of the Transport and General Workers Union, was a member of the Colonial Office Labour Advisory Committee and, in 1948, of the Watson Commission on Gold Coast affairs.
   Durbin, Evan Frank Mottram, b.1906; Senior Lecturer in Economics, London School of Economics; 1940, Economic Section, War Cabinet (temp.); 1942, Personal Assistant to the Prime Minister (temp.); MP (Lab.) 1945–8.
   Goodenough, Sir William Macnamara, b.1899; Director of Barclay's Bank, 1929–51, and Member of Council of Foreign Bondholders.
   Hallsworth, Joseph, b. 1884; Secretary-General, National Union of Distributive and Allied Workers, 1916–49; Member TUC General Council, 1926–47; Member Central Price Regulation Committee, 1939–47.
   Hay, Sir John George, b. 1883; businessman, with South-east Asian interests especially in rubber, palm oil, and banking.
   Henderson, Sir Hubert Douglas, b. 1890; Member West India Royal

Commission, 1938–9; Economic Adviser, HM Treasury, 1939–44; Professor of Political Economy, Oxford, 1945–51.
Howitt, Sir Harold Gibson, b. 1886; Member of Council of Institute of Chartered Accountants 1932–68, of Agricultural Marketing Facilities Committee 1943–66, of the Air Council 1939–46; Chairman and Deputy-Chairman of BOAC, 1943–8; member of many other boards and committees.
McLean, John; Chairman, Overseas Committee of the Association of British Chambers of Commerce, with wide experience of merchant trade.
Plant, Professor Arnold, b. 1898; Professor of Commerce, London School of Economics, 1930–65; civil servant, Ministry of Production, 1942–5.
Robbins, Professor Lionel Charles, b. 1898; Professor of Economics, London School of Economics, 1929–61; Director, Economic Section of Offices of the War Cabinet, 1941–5.
Beit, Sir Alfred, b. 1903; Trustee of the Beit Trust; MP (U) 1931–45.
Figg, Sir Clifford, b. 1890; Deputy-Chairman International Tea Committee, 1933–47; Business Adviser to the Secretary of State for the Colonies, 1939–45.

For Secretary of State (Stanley), Bourdillon, Hailey, Gater, Caine and Clauson, see Biographical Notes.

DOCUMENT 32

Post-war Financial Policy and the Colonies: Minute by S. Caine, 9 June 1945, CO 537/1378

Secretary of State.
TOP SECRET
This is a most interesting memorandum,[1] well worth reading for its entertainment value quite apart from its very great importance in substance. After a vivid analysis of war-time financial history and the position in which we are now placed Lord Keynes turns to an examination of future policies.

He describes two obvious alternatives. The first is to refuse any financial aid from America and in effect to withdraw into a more or less closed economy conducting our foreign trade on a rigidly bilateral basis and hoping to associate at least a certain number of our present sterling area associates with us, in such a new organisation of economic relations. It would involve continuation of perhaps even closer control than has been enforced during the war and submission to even more drastic rationing and restriction of consumption than we are now suffering. Incidentally, and of interest to us departmentally, Lord Keynes suggests that one of the sacrifices necessary for such a policy would be the Colonial Development Programme.

This alternative Lord Keynes calls Starvation Corner; it might alternatively be called the Russian Model.

The other obvious alternative which Lord Keynes names Temptation is the easy acceptance of large loans from America on terms as to interest etc. which would be superficially generous but would in fact burden us with a debt charge probably greater than the total reparation charge which anybody hopes to get out of Germany.

Lord Keynes suggests that we should try and avoid both these alternative evils and try a third plan. The basis of his plan is not so much to accept the fact of our present difficulties as inevitable and seek what assistance we can to get out of them as to argue that it is quite inequitable that we alone of the victorious powers should end the war with a burden of indebtedness to our own Allies and associates (whom he suggests might appropriately be described as our mercenaries) and that what is needed is a re-distribution of the costs of the war. He suggests a number of detailed adjustments by which this could be achieved, e.g. U.S. would refund to us as a sort of retrospective Lend Lease operation our expenditure in the States before Lend Lease came into operation and would also make credits available on easy terms. The Sterling Area countries would be asked to make contributions calculated primarily with reference to the sterling balance they have built up, but varied in accordance with individual circumstances.

The basic idea of a redistribution of the costs of the war is very attractive but as a Department we are not concerned with the likelihood of its proving acceptable to the other countries. Our concern is in the Colonial share of the contribution which is proposed from Sterling Area countries.

At first sight the proposals are startling. Sterling balances to the extent of £35,000,000 in the case of Palestine, and £85,000,000 in the case of other countries outside the Far East are to be 'cancelled' and another part from the sterling balances are to be 'funded'. This means in effect making a free gift of the sums of money in question to H.M.G.

As I say, these proposals are startling but I suggest that we ought not to take up a completely non-possumus attitude. If a general settlement on anything like the lines suggested by Lord Keynes could be achieved it would be a tremendous advantage both to the U.K. and to the Colonies themselves, and if some participation in such a scheme by the Colonies is necessary for its success I do not think we should refuse absolutely to consider what part we can play.

The contribution actually asked from the Colonies however seems to me impossible. The sterling balances held on Colonial account are only to a small extent owned by Colonial Governments. I analysed them in a recent letter to Sir Wilfrid Eady[2] and I think you will find it interesting to read both that letter and subsequent correspondence with Lord Keynes. If Colonial sterling balances were to be 'cancelled' to anything like the extent proposed, Colonial Governments would first have to acquire them by some process of taxation (except to the extent that they could meet demands simply by surrendering their own surpluses). The only process of taxation which one can envisage which would meet the need would be some sort of capital levy, the technical administration of which would be extremely difficult.

A substantial part of the Colonial sterling balances is represented by currency reserves. Lord Keynes of course recognises this and is clearly prepared to raid those reserves and reduce them below their present statutory or customary level of 100% or more of the circulation. We have in fact been turning over the possibility of establishing a fiduciary portion in the case of Colonial currencies but hitherto we have contemplated that any money so released from the currency reserves would be applied to Colonial development. It would however be technically possible to devote such money to gifts to H.M.G. At a guess the money which might be made so available on any reasonably safe principle of fiduciary issue might be of the order of £25,000,000 to £30,000,000. There are many sorts of possible variants to such an arrangement e.g. instead of handing the money over absolutely to H.M.G. it could be treated as an interest-free loan to be called upon for repayment only if all the other currency reserves were used up.

Lord Keynes would clearly be prepared to increase the sums which can be released from currency reserves by depreciation of the currencies. This has been suggested in one or two quarters in the case of Palestine but hitherto the idea has been strongly disfavoured by the Bank of England and the Treasury. I have always thought that it might be inevitable for Palestine if there is no other way of getting price levels adjusted but I think it would be most undesirable in any other case.

As regards the rest of the so-called Colonial sterling balances, a number of considerations emerge from the detailed analysis in my letters to Sir Wilfrid Eady which I think indicate that it is nothing like as simple as Lord Keynes suggests to write any of them off. There is for instance mixed-up in this figure of Colonial balances a considerable element of temporary business reserves as to which it is very often a matter of chance whether they are held in deposit with a local Bank or in a deposit in London. The cash reserves of a local Sugar Company for instance will be held in a local Bank and would be reflected in the holdings of that Bank in London whereas the cash reserves of a Sugar Company domiciled in London would not appear in the figures at all.

I do not think, therefore, that we could agree to anything like the full programme suggested by Lord Keynes as regards the Colonies. In any case it would look extraordinarily odd to be promising a sum of £120,000,000 for Colonial Development and simultaneously to be contemplating a cash surrender of precisely the same amount. I do suggest, however, that we should not refuse to examine lesser possibilities, e.g. some manipulation of the currency reserves as suggested above or possibly some settlement of outstanding issues about distribution of Colonial defence expenditure less generous to the Colonies than we had hitherto hoped for.

More generally, I myself am rather doubtful about the whole basis of dealing with sterling area countries by exacting contributions in relation to their sterling balances. It is true that these balances represent an apparent profit made out of the war, but they are undoubtedly influenced to some extent by the degree to which the country concerned has been going without things during the war. That is, if one country has enjoyed a large income but has managed to spend it by not restricting its imports as it ought to have done, it will have smaller sterling balances, whereas another which has been virtuous and restricted its consumption on goods during the war will have built up larger balances and will now be called upon for a larger contribution.

Finally, it will, no doubt, be urged on behalf of the Colonies that they are in the position of special wards of the U.K., and therefore ought not to be called upon for the same order of contribution as more independent countries. None the less, as already indicated, I suggest that if anything like Lord Keynes' scheme is to be examined in detail we should not refuse to consider what participation can be offered on behalf of the Colonies, although it must inevitably be very much smaller than Lord Keynes' figures suggest.

You will find it of incidental interest to read paragraph 8 and certain other references to our prospects of regaining an adequate level of exports. We in this Department have recently been increasingly concerned about the attitude of mind of British exporters which makes almost credible Lord Keynes' paradox that exuberant inexperience is the only recipe for success. It is perhaps a criticism which could be made of the general scope of his memorandum that, apart from these incidental references, he devotes insufficient attention to the very fundamental necessity of increasing our productive efficiency if our world position is to be maintained.

SC *June 9th, 1945*

Notes

1. The memorandum under consideration is Lord Keynes' paper 'Overseas Financial Policy in Stage III', War Cabinet Paper W.P. (45) 301, dated 15 May 1945. For a published version, see Introduction note 15.
2. Eady, Sir Crawfurd Wilfrid Griffin, b. 1890; Joint Second Secretary to the Treasury, 1942–52.

DOCUMENT 33

Post-war Financial Policy and the Colonies: Minute by S. Caine, 15 June 1945, CO 537/1378

The Secretary of State discussed with me yesterday. He felt very definitely that there could be no possibility of accepting anything approaching Lord Keynes' full proposals as applied to the Colonies. To do so would have a disastrous political effect even if there were any possibility of in fact finding means to surrender such large sums of sterling now standing to Colonial credit. He agreed, however, that it might be politic to express willingness to consider whether, as part of some much wider scheme, some much smaller and possibly only nominal contribution could be made on Colonial account. This might be merely a technical adjustment in the position of the currency reserves as suggested in my minute.[1] It would, of course, be difficulties [*sic*] in any such attempt to convey the impression that the Colonies were playing their part, since the more we emphasise that to the world at large the more it will appear that we are taking away from the Colonies. It would be rather difficult to devise such an adjustment as could be represented e.g. to the Dominions, as a real contribution to the problem while explaining to the Colonies themselves that it [*sic*] fact it cost them nothing.

No immediate action is required. We can wait for the matter to be pursued further in the Cabinet or otherwise. Meanwhile, Sir George Gater and Sir Gerard Clauson will no doubt be interested to see. Mr J. B. Williams should also see and would perhaps arrange for these papers to be registered Top Secret.[2]

SC *June 15th, 1945*

Notes

1. Document 32.
2. Williams, John Basil: since 1 March 1943, Assistant Secretary in the Colonial Office.

DOCUMENT 34

'Federation of West Indies', Colonial Office Memorandum by P. Rogers, n.d.,[1] CO 318/466/2

FEDERATION OF WEST INDIES

1. *Colonel Stanley's despatch.*
In a despatch of the 14th March, 1945, Colonel Stanley, then Secretary of State for the Colonies, put forward certain proposals in respect of the federation of the West Indies. That despatch followed prior semi-official consultation with the Governors of the Colonies concerned.

Colonel Stanley's despatch began by reaffirming the basic aim of British policy as that of quickening the progress of all Colonial peoples towards the ultimate goal of self-government. It pointed out that under modern conditions, however, there were serious difficulties in the way of very small units maintaining full and complete independence in all aspects of government and suggested that the immediate purpose of developing self-governing institutions in the individual British Caribbean Colonies should keep in view the larger project of their political federation as the aim to which policy should be directed. The Secretary of State recognised that existing differences between the Colonies in the area would make it impracticable to set up immediately a federal organisation and that in any case movements towards political unity must come from within. The aim was, however, in the Secretary of State's view the development of federation in the Caribbean at such time as the balance of opinion in the various Colonies was in favour of a change and when the development of communications made it administratively practicable. The ultimate aim of any federation which might be established would be full internal self-government within the British Commonwealth. It would be important that such federation should have the requisite financial stability and be able to carry on its administration without recurrent financial assistance from outside.

The Secretary of State then went on to refer to the developments which had taken place in joint West Indian services, etc. and to the desirability of a lead being given by His Majesty's Government in favour of the aim of federation. He therefore asked that the despatch should be published and an early opportunity taken to debate the issue in Colonial Legislatures. If all the Legislatures were to declare themselves in favour of the aim of federation, the next step would be to consider means whereby proposals could be drawn up for such closer association between West Indian Colonies as might prove immediately feasible. One possibility would be a conference of West Indian delegates to consider the formulation of such proposals.

2. *West Indian feeling.*

Replies to that despatch are not yet complete but it seems likely that they will present the following general picture.

The Bahamas is opposed to participation in any Caribbean federation. The debate on the issue in the House of Assembly was poorly attended and the vote against it was unanimous, while there was very little support for the proposal in any section of public opinion.

The Legislative Councils of British Guiana and British Honduras have passed resolutions declaring their readiness to enter into discussion with the other Caribbean Colonies in any conference which may be called. The course of the debates in both Colonies, however, and general opinion there, showed a general doubt as to the advantages of either Colony entering into any federation. In the case of British Honduras, the history of previous attachment to Jamaica in the nineteenth century has made opinion suspicious that any federal organisation would in practice merely mean a reversion to its old subordination to Jamaica. British Guiana, for its part, rightly considers that many of its problems are distinct from those of the West Indies and is anxious lest the setting-up of a federal organisation should mean that its own peculiar problems would be ignored.

The West Indian Colonies proper, however, have all welcomed, or rather are all likely to welcome the aim of federation and several of them have proposed the setting up of local committees to further that end. They are all likely to declare themselves ready to enter upon discussions for the furtherance of closer association. Apart, however, from difficulties which will clearly arise when discussion of the aim gets down to discussion of means, there is (as has been revealed by the course of the debates and public discussion of the issue) likely to be opposition from two main quarters to federation, apart from the peculiar position of Jamaica where Bustamente may well feel that his personal position is threatened by proposals for a federal organisation. On the one hand there is likely to be opposition from the older and more conservative groups, particularly among white commercial interests, on the ground that they are doubtful about the financial implications of federation and, in the case of the richer Colonies such as

Trinidad, that this would mean that they would be bearing the burdens of the smaller and poorer Colonies. On the other hand there is likely to be opposition from certain of the left wing groups on the ground that the setting up of a federation might delay the advance of individual Colonies towards self-government.

Difficulties may also arise from the East Indian communities in Trinidad and British Guiana, especially in the latter where the East Indians are the largest single community and where some of their political leaders look to the future of the Colony as belonging to an independent India rather than to a future of closer association with the British West Indies.

It must moreover be emphasized that there are genuine political and social differences between the Colonies which may make it difficult to bring about any close association for some time. There are differences of history, e.g. the length of time that some of the Colonies have been British (Barbados has been British throughout its history since it became a British Colony in 1627 whereas Trinidad only formally became a British Colony in 1814 and has had no history of near self-government such as is possessed by Barbados, Jamaica and British Guiana). These historical differences have left their mark on the political and social make-up of the Colonies, even today. There are moreover astonishing differences in social conditions throughout the area, and even in so small a group as the Windward Islands where, for example, Grenada exhibits practically no colour feeling, whereas in St. Lucia, with its French tradition and semi-French white groups there is surprisingly enough, not only colour feeling but even a social colour bar in certain quarters.

Nevertheless, there is a great deal of support, particularly among the younger and more left-wing groups in favour of federation, as has been demonstrated by such meetings as the Labour Conference held at the end of last year in Barbados, and there are signs of a growth of common West Indian feeling. The acceptance of a single University for the whole area is only one sign among many that there is a growing appreciation that each individual Colony is not sufficient unto itself but must play a part in the context of the British West Indies as a whole. In my view, there is now a balance of opinion in favour of the aim of federation, at any rate in the West Indies proper.

3. *Administrative difficulties* in the way of federation must also be borne in mind. To make even a rapid tour of the whole area, travelling by plane between the Colonies, takes not less

than four or five months. In many cases communications between individual Colonies are slower and more difficult than between those Colonies and the United Kingdom, owing to the direction of trade, and although air services are clearly vital in increasing and developing inter-communication they cannot entirely take the place of regular communication in the ordinary course of trade and at a cost within the means of, at any rate, the middle grades of society. The distances between the Colonies cannot be ignored. It is, for example, roughly a thousand miles between Jamaica and Trinidad or, to use the useful technique adopted by the Irvine Committee on Higher Education, if a map of the West Indies were superimposed on one of Europe it would show British Honduras over Great Britain, British Guiana over Turkey and Barbados just north of the Crimea. The difficulties with which a federal staff would have to deal in such an area and the effect of distance on the nature of their work are sufficiently obvious.

4. *The need for federation.*

Nevertheless, it is clear that there is need for closer association and for the development of a federal organisation. Politically and socially it is essential that the Colonies should lose their present extreme parochialism, and administratively it is important that highly skilled staff should be available which are beyond the means of any single Colony to provide from its own resources. This has already to some extent been achieved through such organisations as that of the Comptroller and more is envisaged in such forms as the Director-General of Civil Aviation for the West Indies, a West Indian Telecommunications organisation and so forth, but more remains to be done. It is possible moreover that there might be certain financial and economic advantages in federation, though this is more doubtful.

Most important of all, however, is the fact that it is clearly impossible in the modern world for most of the present Colonies in the area to reach full self-government on their own, e.g. it is ludicrous to think of, say, Barbados or British Honduras, with their populations of 200,000 and 60,000 respectively, standing on their own feet in international discussions. The great pressure of Pan-Americanism against British Colonies within the area must also be reckoned with, though it is a factor to which West Indian opinion is astonishingly blind and even opinion in British Guiana takes practically no account of it.

5. *Procedure.*

In view of the general picture of West Indian conditions given in the first part of this memorandum it is a matter of real difficulty to decide just how far it is politically and administratively possible to put forward practicable proposals for a federal organisation and also what is the best method of proceeding. It is, I think, clear that we shall have to count the Bahamas out for the time being since, apart from the fact that their problems are in many ways distinct from those of the Caribbean proper, it is at present politically impossible to dragoon them into any federation and their political problems must for the time being be dealt with separately. It is, however, important that as far as possible British Guiana and British Honduras should be brought into the discussions on federation and the proposals which follow relate to those two Colonies and to the West Indian Colonies proper.

Colonel Stanley's despatch of the 14th March, 1945, envisaged that if the Colonies concerned were to declare themselves in favour of the aim of federation, there should be called a conference of West Indian delegates to consider the formulation of the proposals for closer association. The next task (once Colonies' replies are complete), is therefore, to convene such a conference, to decide where it should be held and how it should be composed.

Although in many ways there would be considerable convenience in holding the conference in London, my own view is that if only on grounds of sentiment it would be best that it should be held in the West Indies, perhaps in one of the smaller Colonies or in Barbados, to avoid a feeling of domination by local sentiment in either Jamaica or Trinidad. It is also important in my view that the delegates should be West Indians (debates in many of the Legislative Councils showed strong opinion in favour of this) and also, I feel, desirable that they should be unofficials. Moreover it is essential that there should be a feeling that the delegates are in no way puppets of Government and my own suggestion is that there should be two delegates from each Colony (or in the case of the Windward Islands, group of Colonies,) who should be elected by the elected members of the Legislature. It would, of course, be open to them to take advisers if they were desired in any Colony. The Chairmanship of the Conference would be a matter of no little difficulty. There is something to be said for allowing the conference to elect its own chairman but on balance I am inclined to the view that it might be more effective to have someone a little outside politics in the area as a chairman, and I suggest that the Comptroller would be the best person for this very difficult job.

Clearly, however, the conference could not hope to meet with any success without anything before it as a basis of discussion and the following part of this memorandum attempts to consider both what forms of federal organisation might be practicable in the West Indies and how these might best be put to the conference as a basis for their consideration.

6. *Proposals for a federal organisation.*
Two extreme courses are theoretically possible. One is to attempt no form of central organisation but merely to continue for the present on existing lines and encourage the development of central institutions such as the Comptroller, the Director General of Civil Aviation, 'unified' West Indian Services, a West Indian Council of Agriculture, etc. and participation in the Caribbean Conference system. That to my mind would be unacceptable both to us and to West Indian opinion on grounds which, I hope, are clear from the preceding part of this memorandum.

The other extreme course is to attempt to set up a single Colony for the whole area with a single Legislature and a single administrative machine. That too, seems to me at present politically and administratively impracticable for the reasons which have already been given.

We are, therefore, I suggest left with a choice between one of the two main courses proposed below, although these main lines of approach are, of course, susceptible of almost infinite variation.

The first and least ambitious course would be to set up a British West Indian Conference system with a permanent secretariat and a permanent chairman, something on the lines of the present Caribbean Conference system. This would at least have some value as a focus of British West Indian sentiment, would enable more attention to be devoted to common problems, particularly through the secretariat and permanent chairman, and would have the great advantage of providing a basis for further advance whenever this proved practicable. In my view, however, such a Conference would not provide a sufficient political focus for the area, nor would it sufficiently facilitate the participation of the West Indies as a unit in international matters. There would be some danger of the conference becoming merely a debating society and also of it tending to duplicate the work of the Caribbean Conference. In short, administratively its value would be small, and politically, its effect likely to be depressing rather than stimulating. We may be forced to accept this, nevertheless, in the last resort, and it might, I suggest, form one of the alternatives to be put before the conference of delegates as a basis for consideration. I suggest, however, that we should aim at the rather more ambitious proposal which follows. This is a proposal which in my view we should put before the conference of delegates as the course of action which His Majesty's Government in the United Kingdom are disposed to favour, while making it clear that the decision of the conference is for the delegates themselves and that the proposal is put forward to facilitate their discussion. The proposal would be the immediate setting up of a Federal Government with separate Colony Legislatures. The Federal Government might be on the Australian model, i.e. its functions and powers would be restricted to a certain number of definite subjects, leaving the remainder to Colonial Legislatures, though with provision for the addition of subjects to the Federal administration with the concurrence of the constituent Colonial Governments. The Federal Government might be constituted on the following lines:–

(i) An office of High Commissioner with a central Secretariat primarily devoted to planning duties, i.e. an expansion of the work already done to some extent by the Comptroller's organisation, which might be taken over, together with separate Departments for subjects which would come under the authority of the Federal Legislature.

(ii) A Federal Legislature of two chambers, one of which would be a Senate elected on a territorial basis by existing Legislatures, including nominated and official members and the Upper Houses in existing two-chamber Legislatures, and the other a Lower House or House of Representatives directly elected on a basis of universal adult suffrage.

(iii) An Executive Council on the present Jamaica model in which the High Commissioner would have the same reserve powers as are possessed at present by the Governor of Jamaica. On the one hand it is clear that West Indian opinion would not accept anything less liberal than the provisions of the present Jamaica constitution, and on the other hand it is suggested that in the initial stages of the federation it might be unwise to go further and set up a ministerial system proper, though this would have to be foreshadowed as a development within a set period of say five or ten years. The question of reserve powers is a difficult one which is dealt with in more detail below.

(iv) There might also be advisory committees of the Legislature dealing with matters which are the concern of that Legislature, and embryo ministers on the Jamaica model.

(v) The subjects to be dealt with would probably be primarily for the constituent conference to decide but should include, at any rate, defence, a common customs tariff, common income tax, common West Indian Services (i.e. Administrative, Medical, Legal, including Judicial, and Police) inter-Colony shipping and aviation, telecommunications and broadcasting, and planning functions including surveys, statistics and research (which perhaps, however, would hardly come within the scope of the Federal Legislature itself). As previously suggested, there might be provision for the addition of subjects at a later stage, with the concurrence of the constituent Colonies.

(vi) Individual Colonial Legislatures could continue as at present and might be modified as thought desirable individually from time to time, though in Barbados there would have to be provision to enable effect to be given to the decisions of the Federal Legislature, including the use of reserve powers by the High Commissioner.

(vii) *Finance*. It would clearly be desirable, as stated in the despatch of the 14th March, 1945, that the federation should be financially independent but this might raise difficulties in the initial stages owing to the number of present grant-in-aid Colonies which would be included. It is suggested that for the first ten years only there might be a Treasury grant-in-aid without Treasury control on the lines at present proposed for the closer union of the Leeward and Windward Islands, i.e. a grant-in-aid calculated according to that which would have been paid if the individual Colonies had continued as separate entities. (This would of course have to be put to the Treasury for their concurrence).

7. *Reserve Powers.*

This question will undoubtedly be one of the more difficult ones politically. It seems to me inevitable that at the outset there should be provision for the use of reserve powers by His Majesty's Government in the United Kingdom under the Federal organisation, but West Indian opinion would not be likely to accept anything going further than the Jamaica provision by which the Governor (or in the case of the Federal Government, the High Commissioner) can ignore the advice of his Executive Council in matters affecting public order, public faith and good government, etc. but can only overrule the views of the Legislature with the concurrence of his Executive Council, and then again only in matters affecting public order, public faith and good government, etc.

There would, moreover, be a difficult issue in respect of the use of reserve powers in the constituent Colonies. The greatest difficulty would be in Barbados where there are at present no reserve powers. It seems to me essential, however, that there should be provision for these if the Colony joined the federation, since one constituent government could hardly possess greater powers than the federal government itself, while moreover it would obviously be essential that decisions of the Federal Government should be capable of implementation throughout the area. This would, no doubt, be bitterly opposed in Barbados but it seems to be inescapable. There is, moreover, the issue of what the method of procedure should be for the use of reserve powers in the other constituent Colonies in matters outside the scope of the Federal Government, i.e. should the decision be that of the Governor himself subject to the concurrence of the Secretary of State, as it is at present, or should the submission be through the Governor himself to the High Commissioner and be for the latter's decision, subject to the Secretary of State's approval. This course seems cumbrous; there is however already provision for Governors to act on their own responsibility in cases of emergency and that power would presumably remain. That being so, it would in my view be most desirable that all matters affecting the use of the reserve powers on individual Colonies should come through the High Commissioner, who should act again with the advice of his Executive Council, though he need not be bound by it except where votes of the Federal Legislature were in question. The alternative of having dealings direct in such matters between individual Governors and the Secretary of State would seem to me to falsify the whole aim of setting up a Federal Government, and militate against the closer union of the constituent Colonies.

8. *Correspondence.*

The issue would also arise of whether correspondence on matters which were the concern of a constituent Colony Government and not of the Federal Government should be direct between Governor and the Secretary of State or should be through the High Commissioner. In practice it seems to me inevitable that at the outset, until the federation possesses powers of full internal self-government, correspondence should be direct between individual Governors and the Secretary of State, since it would be far too cumbrous to have everything going through the federal machine. Copies of all correspondence should, however, I suggest go automatically to the High Commissioner's office and he should be entitled to express views on any matter as he wished. There could also, I suggest, be provision for certain functions and powers of the Secretary of State to be transferred gradually to the High Commissioner and the Federal Government until the ultimate stage of full internal, self-government was reached.

9. It is suggested that a memorandum putting the above proposals should be drafted and sent to Governors semi-officially with a covering letter explaining our views and reasons for putting forward this line of approach, and asking for Governors' views on the substance and wording of the memorandum.

P. ROGERS

Note

1. Although this memorandum is undated, it was clearly prepared by Rogers in February 1946. A slightly different version (including an additional section to 6 (vii) on the division of financial responsibility between the federal government and the constituent colonial governments) was circulated within the Colonial Office but not to the governors as Rogers had suggested (para. 9). The paper became the basis for further Colonial Office discussions, notably the meeting attended by, amongst others, Creech Jones, Stockdale, Caine, J. B. Williams and Rogers on 2 September, when it was agreed to plan a 'conference on general federation' for the following autumn. On 14 February 1947, local opinion having been tested, Creech Jones wrote to West Indian governors formally proposing such a gathering.

DOCUMENT 35

Future of the Italian Colonies. Memorandum by the Prime Minister, 2 March 1946, CAB 131/2

TOP SECRET

D.O. (46) 27.
(*Also C.O.S.* (46) 54 (O).)
2nd March, 1946.

CABINET

Defence Committee.

FUTURE OF THE ITALIAN COLONIES

MEMORANDUM BY THE PRIME MINISTER AND MINISTER OF DEFENCE.

IN C.O.S. (46)43(O) it is laid down that strategy demands that there should be no potentially hostile Power flanking our sea or air communications through the Mediterranean and the Red Sea. The assumption, which is in my view based on a strategy formulated in the past, is that this line of communications is vital to the interests of the British Commonwealth and Empire and that it is possible under modern conditions of warfare to render it secure. In my opinion neither of these propositions is self-evident. The following points seem to me to be relevant:—

1. It is to be observed that the British Empire was built up in the era of sea power. The maintenance of such widely scattered territories was only possible because of the dominant position of the British Fleet. Our strength at sea and the position of Malta and Gibraltar gave us the command of the Mediterranean, while our control of Egypt through our political influence secured the Suez Canal. Thus from 1870 to the present war we had the convenience of this short route to the East.

2. It was in my view demonstrated during the late war that the naval and air arms are interdependent. Fleets in open waters have had to be provided with carrier-borne aircraft both for offence and defence. Fleets in narrow waters were only able to operate under the protection of shore-based aircraft. For a time when we were unable to provide this in the

Mediterranean we had to revert to the use of the Cape route.

3. Accordingly to make sure of being able to use the Mediterranean route in wartime we must be able to deny either side of the Straits of Gibraltar to the enemy. We must be strong enough in North Africa to prevent a Power in control of Italy from closing the narrows south of Sardinia and Sicily. We must have strong enough Air Forces in North Africa to beat off attack from the European Peninsulas and adjacent islands. Therefore in the Western parts of the Mediterranean we must be sure of a strong and friendly France and Italy and a Neutral, if not a friendly, Spain. In the Eastern parts we require friendly Powers in Greece and in the Levant. We have also to continue by agreement with its Government to use Egypt as a base and have forces strong enough to prevent attack coming down through the Levant either by land or air against the Canal Zone. If the assumption is made, which I think is necessary, that we should be unable to put forces in Europe strong enough to defend from attack by the strongest Continental Power the countries bordering on the North of the Mediterranean, it would appear that our hold must be very precarious.

4. The advent of air power means that instead, as in the era of navalism, of being able to maintain the route by the possession of Malta and Gibraltar and by a friendly attitude on the part of Egypt, we must now provide very large air forces in North Africa, large military forces in Egypt and Palestine and also large sums of money for the deficit areas, such as Cyrenaica and Libya, if we wish to occupy them as air force bases.

5. In the Red Sea, where formerly we had only to maintain Aden, we have now to keep on good terms with Ibn Saud, and also apparently to occupy Eritrea and Somaliland, which are also deficit areas.

6. I consider that we cannot afford to provide the great sums of money for the large forces involved on the chance of being able to use the Mediterranean route in time of war. I think that it is, at best, only a chance. In the last war if Spain had given Hitler air facilities we could not, I think, have kept the Straits of Gibraltar open. Equally, if Hitler had put another four Divisions in North Africa at the time of El Alamein, it is doubtful if we could have held the Canal. To bank on the friendship and strength of Spain or Italy and on the ability of Turkey and the Levant States to form a basis of resistance from attack from the North, seems to me a gamble.

7. But, assuming that the odds are reasonably favourable, is it clear that the benefits which we should have to purchase at so great a cost are worth while? Presumably, the strategic communications which it is suggested we must preserve are those with India, but the position of India is changing. It is not certain whether she will remain within the Commonwealth. She will increasingly have to depend upon her own Armies for her defence. It would appear doubtful if the time saved by the use of the Mediterranean route for the purpose presumably of reinforcing India is worth the cost. It may be suggested that we are specially interested in the oil of South Persia and Iraq, but I suggest that we are not in a position to defend this area from a determined land attack from the North. Our communications with the East Indies and Australasia could be maintained by the use of the Cape route, or, even in the latter case, through the Panamá Canal if we have a close understanding with the United States.

8. The argument that we must have control of the Mediterranean route is a two-edged weapon. If Russia desires to be able to unite her Fleets, as she did in the Russo-Japanese war, she may claim that the Baltic and the Suez Canal are as important to her as the latter is to us. She may claim to occupy Bornholm, just as we hold Malta, and to dominate politically Denmark, just as we do Egypt. She may claim not only the control of the Dardanelles, but passage through the Suez Canal in order to keep sea connection between her Black Sea, Baltic ports and Vladivostok. In the changed conditions of the world and in the modern conditions of three dimensional warfare, it is, I think, necessary to review with an open mind strategic conceptions which we have held for many years. In the present era we must consider very carefully how to make the most of our limited resources. We must not, for sentimental reasons based on the past, give hostages to fortune. It may be we shall have to consider the British Isles as an easterly extension of a strategic era [*sic*] the centre of which is the American Continent rather than as a Power looking eastwards through the Mediterranean to India and the East. I have not taken into consideration here any results that may flow from the development of Atomic warfare.

I should like the Chiefs of Staff to consider the arguments put forward here and to let the Defence Committee have an appreciation of the strategic position of the British Commonwealth in the light of our resources and of modern conditions of warfare.

C. R. A.

DOCUMENT 36

Future of the Italian Colonies. Memorandum by the Secretary of State for Foreign Affairs, 13 March 1946, CAB 131/2

ANNEX

Memorandum by the Secretary of State for Foreign Affairs[1]

I have been giving considerable attention to the whole problem of defence in the Mediterranean, Middle East and the Indian Ocean. The first comment I should like to make is on the Prime Minister's paper (D.O.(46) 27). Looked at purely from the point of view of communications, it is quite true that if the Mediterranean in time of war is given up, then so far as our communications with the other parts of the Commonwealth and Empire are concerned, they could, as indeed they were in the last war, be maintained. On the other hand, a very great political issue is involved which affects us more from the peace-time point of view. Our presence in the Mediterranean serves a purpose other than a military purpose which is vital to our position as a Great Power. The Mediterranean is the area through which we bring influence to bear on Southern Europe, the soft under-belly of France, Italy, Yugoslavia, Greece and Turkey. Without our physical presence in the Mediterranean, we should cut little ice with those States which would fall, like Eastern Europe, under the totalitarian yoke. We should also lose our position in the Middle East (including Iraq oil, now one of our greatest economic assets), even if we could afford to let Egypt go.

2. If we move out of the Mediterranean, Russia will move in, and the Mediterranean countries, from the point of view of commerce and trade, economy and democracy, will be finished. We have a chance of holding Italy in the Western civilisation, and although Yugoslavia is really under Russian control at the moment, the position there is very uneasy and one wonders how long as a Mediterranean people Yugoslavia will put up with Russian control. There is also the question of Greece. It is essential from our point of view that Greece remains with us politically. Without forces and bases of defence in the Mediterranean from Gibraltar to the East it will be impossible to maintain a foreign policy in Southern Europe on a democratic basis.

3. There also arises the problem of Spain. Franco and his regime are a passing phase and I am not without hope that within the next year there will be a great change in Spain. But if we sacrificed the Mediterranean, then there is no doubt that the Iberian Peninsula would be completely lost to us. Therefore from a political point of view it is essential to maintain the Mediterranean as a trade route and as a trade area, to utilise both, and to maintain the principles of Western civilisation in that area.
4. The other problem which arises is our position in Egypt where we have vital interests. If we gave the impression to the Egyptians that we were unable or unwilling to maintain our position in the Mediterranean, they would have no inducement to meet the requirements for defence which I wish to put forward in the negotiations for the revision of the Anglo-Egyptian Treaty.[2]
5. There is in addition the question of whether we shall be compelled to develop within the United Nations Organisation a 'Western Zone'. At present there are two realities in Europe, the 'Eastern Bloc' created and dominated by Russia, and the 'Mediterranean Zone' controlled by Great Britain. We talk a lot about a 'Western Group', but shall we be able to bring it into existence or maintain it once we abandon our position as the Mediterranean Power? I doubt it. We are entitled to construct a 'Western Zone' if we can. It would be in keeping with the Charter. It has been denounced by Russia as a 'Western Bloc' directed against her, but we are entitled to build up good neighbours and a defensive area from Scandinavia to France and thus construct a 'Western Zone'. If this country showed signs of leaving the Mediterranean and of giving up any idea of maintaining a 'Western Zone', the Russians, as I have said, would enter the Mediterranean and they would inevitably be challenged by the Americans who would have to come in and try to take the place which we had abandoned. This situation would produce a collision between the great conflicting powers, on whom we, having forfeited our position, should lack the power to bring conciliatory influence.
6. The other point which influences me in the European scene is that we are the last bastion of social democracy. It may be said that this now represents our way of life as against the red tooth and claw of American capitalism and the Communist dictatorship of Soviet Russia. Any weakening of our position in the Mediterranean area will, in my

view, lead to the end of social democracy there and submit us to a pressure which would make our position untenable. The alternative proposals I will now proceed to develop are therefore inspired not by any idea of weakening our position in the Mediterranean but rather of strengthening it.

7. Turning now to the general defence position, the outstanding point which gives me very great concern is that our centre of communication and command is in another country's territory (Egypt). What I am anxious to achieve, in order to prevent pressure being placed on His Majesty's Government from time to time, is that the whole heart and centre of command shall be on British territory. Therefore, I am strongly in favour of the Mombasa proposal and the more I study the map the more I am convinced that the right position for the central Imperial command-post lies in East Africa. In the first place I feel convinced that we can thereby defend our Middle East position. Secondly, it strengthens our position with South Africa, for East Africa is the one area which is troubling General Smuts the whole time.

8. But the third and equally important point is that the Cabinet Mission to India will have to consider how to defend the Indian Ocean. East Africa is important as a key position for the defence of that area as well.

9. The advantage from the Foreign Office point of view of such a scheme of defence is this. When we open negotiations with Egypt our policy should be that we want communications and the heart of things to be on our own territory. Egypt may well then beg us to stay. It is only because she thinks there is no alternative that she is taking her present attitude. It would be far easier for us were we able to withdraw our forces and to secure bases and facilities which in time of trouble would be kept on a care and maintenance basis and would be ready for use at any moment. The second point is that we have sooner or later to open negotiations with Egypt and France on the future of the Canal. It is a far better position to be asked to defend the Canal than to have to ask others for privileges.

10. I therefore feel that this move would strengthen us with India, South Africa and the African Continent and in addition put us in a better position with the Middle East.

11. Another very important point is that once we are on our own territory, I am convinced that the partnership policy which I have been trying to foster will have a better chance of development.

12. It has been suggested that the headquarters could be moved to Palestine. But Palestine is in an uncertain political position, and if we spend millions of pounds there we might in ten years have to move, or our presence there might become a source of international dispute. On the other hand, if the Jews discover that we are no longer so dependent on Palestine for our own strategic purposes, it will be easier for us to settle the Palestinian problem and thus consider establishing bases and obtaining facilities there on a larger basis. Then there is Transjordan. We are negotiating a treaty with that territory and although Transjordan is, I understand, not so well adapted as a military base, facilities could be obtained under the new treaty which would be of equal advantage.[3]

13. There is also the question of Cyprus. Could we devise a plan of strategical defence which would mean that Cyprus would no longer be useful to us strategically? This matter will become acute. Russia is already demanding a base in the Dodecanese. If at the same time we were to develop Cyprus as a strategic base, that would add strength to the Russian demand for a base in the Aegaean. Unless, therefore, there was a paramount strategic reason to the contrary, I would like consideration to be given to the abandonment of Cyprus as a military base, and the demilitarisation of the island. I recognise that there would be difficulties from the Colonial aspect but I am discussing the question purely from the international aspect of difficulties with Russia and other countries. On the other hand, if Cyprus is to be maintained for strategic reasons, then our whole policy towards Cyprus will have to be reviewed, for we have starved the Cypriots, treated them very badly, and must mend our ways if it is necessary for the British Empire to develop the island as a strategic base.

14. Turning to West Africa, I have always been in favour of strategic and economic communications for the development of a great port on the West African coast at Lagos, and it will be remembered that in the war I suggested that Italian prisoners and [of?] war labour should be used for purposes of developing a road right across Africa. This would open up a great expanse of territory for trade and commerce generally. In my view the opening of such a route would be of great strategic value, and if in war the Canal was closed, as it was in the last war, this communication line would be of great value to us. Further, such a project would

be helpful in connexion with the uranium deposits in the Congo.

15. I am anxious that an early decision on this particular proposal should be arrived at. I hope the Chancellor will see the importance of spending in the future British money on British soil, keeping it within the sterling group and prevent the building up of any further sterling balances for defence in Egypt. Although a great capital outlay may be needed to accomplish this now, I feel it ought to be begun at once. In my view it will modernise the whole character of our defence as well as our trade and bring into the British orbit economically and commercially a great area which is by no means fully developed yet.

13th MARCH, 1946 (Initialled) E.B.

Notes

1. This Memorandum was circulated, with a covering note D. O. (46)40, to members of the Cabinet Defence Committee, and was discussed on 18 March together with Document 35.
2. The Anglo–Egyptian Treaty of 1936. For the negotiations, see Louis, *British Empire in the Middle East*, especially Chap. 6.
3. The Treaty with Transjordan was signed on 22 March 1946. The details are discussed in Louis, *British Empire in the Middle East* 354–6.

DOCUMENT 37

Native Administration Policy: Colonial Office Memorandum by G. B. Cartland, n.d.,[1] CO 847/25/47234

CONFIDENTIAL

Memorandum on factors affecting Native Administration policy.
(Memorandum by Mr Cartland)

Even before the present war the certainty that Native Administration, as it had been practised, was the philosopher's stone of Colonial administration was being questioned not least by those responsible for its operation and guidance. Educated Africans and others of the de-tribalised and rising middle classes have always been in a greater or less degree suspicious of the policy. They have contended that it was an expedient of the European administrator to divert the natural political aspirations of the African. Although some of the new middle classes have found their place in the scheme of Native Administration, many have not; and there is little doubt that this opinion is still current. Generally departmental officers have been highly critical of Native Administrations as instruments of policy on the grounds of their inefficiency. Even Administrative Officers have experienced a sense of frustration in their dealings with them. These views suggest the conclusion (1) that the basis of Native Administrations is not broad enough; (2) that the Native Administrations are not sufficiently efficient to rise to the duties imposed upon them; and (3) that the general policy requires review with a view to reinforcement and re-direction.

2. Apart from the natural evolution of the Native Administrations during the war two new factors emerge.

(1) Native Administrations as at present constituted may find it difficult to satisfy the more critical demands of the returning African troops, experienced as they will be, whether literate or illiterate, in the affairs of the world.

(2) The new policy of development on which we are now embarking will make increasing demands on the machinery of the Native Administrations and impose upon it a greater strain than in pre-war years. It is essential that real political development should keep pace with the material and social development which is planned, both in order to satisfy the widening political horizon of the new classes including the returned soldiers, and in order to play an effective part in the execution and

administration of the new development policy. It is no longer sufficient for the Native Administration to be a mere expedient to provide the Central Government with cheap local agents to carry out the details of its day to day administration but it is necessary that it should become an active partner in, and an essential instrument of, the development policy.

3. The time, therefore, appears to be ripe to take stock of the present state of Native Administration; to review the policy in the light of progress already made and of the needs of the future; and, if necessary, to restate the policy giving it such new direction or emphasis as may be considered necessary. In addition other steps may be required to infuse new life into it.
4. It is most fortunate that we have a comprehensive and authoritative account of the state of Native Administration in Lord Hailey's confidential Report of 1940–42. A number of changes have taken place in different territories since that date, such as the introduction of the Native Authorities Ordinance in the Gold Coast Colony and the development of Provincial Councils in Central Africa. But, apart from these local developments, the broad picture described by Lord Hailey and the conclusions drawn in his first chapter on general principles remain substantially unchanged. I am not aware that any Secretary of State has ever issued an official statement of policy on the subject of Native Administration although a number of such documents have been drawn up locally and the general policy has been described in various unofficial works. In his Report Lord Hailey has drawn attention to a number of points requiring attention and to at least one point upon which it will be desirable to have a statement of policy. This point concerns the position of the Native Administration vis a vis the Central Government and raises the question whether the Central Government should ultimately be formed of a federation of Native Administrations or whether the Central Government should continue in its present form with the Native Administrations acting as its local agencies. In other words the time has come to decide in broad terms the ultimate goal of the policy.
5. It seems clear, therefore, that there is a case for an authoritative statement of policy. This would of course have to be in general terms, as the local application of the policy of Native Administration differs very widely from territory to territory. If such a statement of policy were to be issued it

might be worth while taking the opportunity to rename this system of Government and to describe it as local Government or African local Government. The advantages of this change would be (1) to eliminate the word "native", which, although it has not been widely criticised in this particular use, is generally objectionable in some parts of Africa; (2) to distinguish the new phase of the policy from the old by the new name which might help to overcome existing prejudices; and (3) to indicate the proper and intended sphere of this form of Government.

6. Since such a statement could only indicate policy in the broadest terms, the success of its local application, and in fact the actual form which it will take locally, will depend very largely on the men who are responsible for putting it into operation. The general territorial policy of any Colonial Government will, of course, be formulated by the Governor and his advisers, but the details will have to be settled at the provincial and district level owing to the wide differences of local circumstances and the tribal organisations existing within each particular territory. The working out of the policy and its execution, therefore, rests almost entirely upon the Provincial and District Administrations within the very broad terms of the general policy. They are responsible for formulating and applying the local policy and a very heavy responsibility rests upon them. The first requisite, therefore, for a successful local Government policy is that the district commissioners should be of the highest moral and intellectual calibre with a very definite vocation and faith in their work and its objects. Added to this is required inspiring, enthusiastic, capable and far-seeing leadership on the part of the Provincial Commissioners who must set the course.

7. In this connection it is rather disturbing to find that many District Officers suffer from a sense of frustration. This is no doubt due to a variety of circumstances, many of which are connected with war-time conditions. During the war the attention of officers has been increasingly absorbed in matters unconnected with their real work of developing Native Administrations and dealing with general native problems. In addition, long tours, overwork and increasingly difficult general conditions, a rising cost of living and a variety of war-time personal problems have made the work of the Colonial Service more difficult and have sapped both its energy and enthusiasm for tackling big problems. To some extent this sense of frustration was growing even before the

war. It was as though the great impetus which the Lugard school gave to Colonial administration was slowing down and losing direction in the general aimlessness and drift of the thirties. This feeling was due in part to the pre-occupation of the Service with an increasing burden of petty routine duties which were felt to be keeping them from their real work. But the problem went much deeper than this. The results of the policy of Native Administration were not always heartening and progress was slow. Progress in fact seemed to depend on the individual officer and ground was often lost if a firm and energetic hand was withdrawn. The machinery often could not hold its own, let alone progress, without continued pressure and has suffered greatly from lack of continuity of staff and policy. Much hard work by individual officers must have been lost by failure to follow it up for one reason or another. The policy itself was in some places not felt to be keeping pace with the times and, in the absence of any local statement or directive, was not very clearly defined except in unofficial writings. There was in fact a growing consciousness of an absence of leadership. This feeling has developed during the war and is very disturbing as, at no earlier date, was strong leadership more necessary. The problems are bigger and more pressing than ever before. There is a vast development problem to be tackled in a post-war setting of most complicated political and economic conditions. The morale of the Service has suffered and the recruits of the last five years have shown little sense of vocation. This is scarcely their fault. They joined the service when it was strained and at a low ebb. They have had no training and have little understanding of the history and policy of our Colonial administration. They have had little opportunity or encouragement to make amends by study even where books are available. This should, of course, correct itself to some extent when the probationers course is re-started but there still remains the problem of the present state of the Service which will influence the attitude of the new recruits.

8. In attempting to launch a revised policy of Native Administration the state of the Service is a factor which must be taken into very close consideration. Much could be done to improve the existing position by inspiring in the district staff a feeling that there is a conscious overall policy, and that the local application of that policy is being carefully planned by enlightened Provincial Commissioners, ready to give the district staff an enthusiastic and sympathetic lead. There are

indications that, in some territories at least, the present service has lost confidence in some of its Provincial Commissioners. This of course, raises the question of the selection for these posts of enthusiastic and energetic officers endowed with both knowledge and vision to take the lead in implementing the new policy.

9. There are several ways in which new stimulus might be given to the work and policy of the service. Colonial Governments might make more adequate library facilities available for use by the District and Provincial Commissioners, so as to enable the officers to inform themselves on what is being done elsewhere, and on the general trend of thought in connection with local Government in Africa. They should also have access to works on local Government elsewhere, including this country. This provision of library facilities is a matter which should be taken up on a more general plane, as it applies to other aspects of Colonial policy with equal force.

10. It would also be well worth considering introducing an official Journal for circulation to all administrative officers and others concerned. The Journal would provide a medium for informing the Service on what was happening in African Affairs generally in all territories. Through the Journal experience gained in dealing with particular problems locally could be widely circulated. New legislation would be reported. Book notices would enable local libraries to be kept up to date. The scope of the Journal could usefully be extended to deal with matters affecting land, native law and the native courts. It would be essentially the professional Journal of the Administrative Service.

11. A further point with regard to personnel is the necessity of enabling District Officers to travel widely in their districts in order to visit and supervise outlying Native Authorities. This again is a matter of wider concern and is of pressing importance in regard to matters other than the development of Native Administration. To make touring possible it is essential that the amount of routine work performed by District Commissioners should be cut down either by relieving them of such work or by increasing and improving the quality of their clerical assistants. Lord Hailey has suggested the development of an intermediate African Administrative Service. This has certainly been given some consideration on the West Coast, but nothing has so far been done about it. The advent of the Development Officer or the District Assistant, as he is called in some territories, may go some way towards

meeting this problem although these appointments were designed primarily to meet the additional work which will arise out of the development programmes. There are many duties of a purely war-time and temporary nature which have been imposed on District Commissioners and which should be considerably reduced in the coming months and years; but even their disappearance will not solve the problem. Excessive routine and office work was becoming increasingly acute in pre-war years, and received mention in Lord Hailey's African Survey. If we wish to give the policy of Native Administration a maximum chance of success there is no doubt that this question of the District Commissioner's work must be given serious attention. Apart from this there are many duties which engage the District Commissioner's attention, which are not worthy of his education and training or the expense to the Government of his salary and incidental expenses. This is a matter which it may be necessary to bring some pressure on governments to tackle.

12. A step which could be taken to pool experience and to infuse new enthusiasm both into the Administration and into the local Governments would be the development of regular conferences. The practice of holding conferences of Provincial Commissioners, Conferences of District Commissioners within the provinces and Conferences of the Native Administration staff and dignitaries, followed in some territories should be extended.

13. As far as the administrative officers are concerned I think that a great deal could be done to maintain their interest and enthusiasm and keep their minds flexible by arranging regional conferences in East, West and Central Africa; and also by arranging visits to other territories to see how common problems are being tackled there. I consider that the administrative staff works far too much in watertight compartments and that we should take advantage of the unified service to ensure that promising officers have an opportunity of seeing how problems of administration are tackled in other countries. This might be done either by short visits or by secondment on an exchange basis for a period of two or three years. There is, I know, the argument that it is difficult to use an administrative officer in districts of a territory with which he is not familiar on account of differences of languages and customs. But against this must be set the advantage of bringing different and wider experience to bear on the local problems and I am quite certain that exchanges of officers and visits of officers would have a very healthy effect

both on the Service itself and on the effectiveness of the work it performs.

14. Lord Hailey has suggested in his Report that the Secretary of Native Affairs and his office should be responsible for keeping policy up to date and for correlating and co-ordinating Native Administration policy and work inside the territory. There is no doubt that a great deal of benefit could be derived from the proper functioning of the Secretary of Native Affairs and his staff. This Office has, however, not been so generally successful as might have been wished and, in some territories at least, it has now been abandoned. There is no doubt that where the post is filled by an energetic and enthusiastic officer with both knowledge and vision it could be of extreme value in the application of a new local Government policy and its future merits serious consideration.
15. In many parts of Africa the Native Administration has achieved little and is little more than a rather inefficient school for giving local dignitaries and their clerks some rudimentary training in administrative work. If the policy of Native Administration is justified then the Native Authorities must be transformed into reasonably efficient organs of local Government, which must fulfil some useful local functions now while their personnel is gaining experience. It is useless to expect the machine to function satisfactorily unless there is a reasonably efficient local Government service. The pay and conditions of local service must be made sufficiently attractive to obtain a good type of recruit. They must be given systematic preliminary and refresher training. The remuneration and training of Chiefs or other Heads of the local Government bodies must be adequate to maintain their prestige and influence both among their traditional followers and among the new middle classes.
16. In this connection there is one other matter which should be considered. The standard of African public morality is low. There is a growing tale of leading Africans from the public service, the professions, native administration service and other positions of trust who have been convicted of various forms of dishonesty or betrayal of trust. Many people think that those caught are but a tithe of those guilty of this sort of conduct. What is even more distressing than individual lapses is the marked lack of public conscience in these matters exemplified by public subscriptions to finance appeals from convictions for dishonesty. In the case of a recent subscription of this sort I believe that the convicted benefici-

ary found it necessary to sue the Secretary and organiser of the fund for a portion of the proceeds which he had misappropriated. As a further example the Havers Report on the cost of litigation on the Gold Coast does not reveal the local African bar in too good a light.[2] There is no need to elaborate on the subjects of unprofessional conduct and an irresponsible press. This is a problem to which we cannot afford to be blind and its solution is probably the most difficult of all the problems raised in this memorandum. The question of moral standards might be regarded as the particular concern of the Missions and the educationists and they have undoubtedly done their best. But if African participation in local or central government is to be successful the Colonial governments must face this problem squarely. The question of what is to be done is extremely difficult. It is suggested that the problem should be closely examined, possibly by a committee, and a first step might be to obtain reports on the subject from psychologists or sociologists who are studying in Africa, with a view to determining whether anything can be done to raise the moral standards of the new African society. This is, of course, a matter which would require the most tactful and confidential handling in all stages.

17. I have not dealt in this memorandum with the details of the policy which should be laid down for African local Government but rather with some of the factors which will condition the success of the policy should an attempt be made to revise and to re-launch it.

Notes

1. The memorandum is undated, but was written early in 1946.
2. [C. R. Havers, Recorder of Chichester 1939–51, Chairman]. *Report of a Commission of Inquiry into Expenses incurred by Litigants in the Courts of the Gold Coast and Indebtedness caused thereby* (1945).

DOCUMENT 38

'Native Administration Policy', Memorandum by A. B. Cohen, 28 September 1946, CO 847/35/47234/1/1947

NATIVE ADMINISTRATION POLICY

In May Mr Cartland and I were instructed by Sir George Gater, following discussions with Lord Hailey, to undertake preliminary enquiries of certain officers of the East African Governments with regard to the necessity for a review of native administration policy. We have had lengthy discussions with Mr Wyn Harris, a Provincial Commissioner in Kenya; Mr Gayer, head of the new Public Relations and Social Welfare Department in Uganda; and Mr Hudson, Secretary for Native Affairs in Northern Rhodesia. In addition I discussed the matter with Mr Kennedy, Secretary for African Affairs in Uganda, and with one or two other officers in East Africa.

2. Broadly speaking, the main points on which we were consulting these various officers were:—

(1) Whether closer and more continuous contact between the Colonial Office and African Governments was required on questions of native administration policy, and whether closer contact and consultation between African Governments themselves was also required, with fuller interchange of information;

(2) Whether the machinery for dealing with native administration policy requires strengthening both in the African Territories and in the Colonial Office;

(3) Whether steps require to be taken to give further assistance to officers in the field in the execution of policy with regard to native administration;

(4) Whether there should be a general stocktaking with a view to the possibility of the preparation of a statement on the present objectives of policy in regard to native administration.

3. There was general agreement on the part of all whom we consulted as to the necessity for action on points (1), (2) and (3). The nature of the action proposed will be discussed below. Generally speaking, the officers concerned welcomed our approach to them on these matters. There was less unanimity with regard to (4). Mr Hudson was in favour of the preparation of a statement which he thought would do much good to the Service. Mr Gayer was inclined to be in favour.

Mr Wyn Harris was more doubtful. It must be emphasised that these officers were speaking purely personally.

4. The approach made to certain Governors by letter on this subject has not produced such encouraging results. Sir E. Richards has sent a reply which, while of considerable interest, in effect says that everything required is already being done in Nyasaland, and that no general review is necessary.[1] Sir William Battershill is opposed to any formal enquiry into the policy of native administration and is particularly anxious that no publicity should be given to any study of the subject which may be undertaken. Sir Philip Mitchell, while in favour of periodical study of different aspects of native administration in each territory, so as to keep other Governments and the Colonial Office and Parliament fully informed of what is going on and to stimulate examination of the subject on the spot, is not in favour of a stocktaking with too wide a canvas. Sir John Hall has sent no letter, and I have not discussed the subject with him, but I do not believe that his reaction to the letter sent to him was favourable.[2] The West African Governors who have been consulted, while raising no objection to informal discussions by the Colonial Office with their officers, are sceptical of the results of any general examination of policy.
5. I do not think that these reactions should be regarded in too depressing a light. When I discussed the matter with Sir William Battershill, I discovered that he had not fully understood the purpose of our enquiry and that, while he was opposed to a formal or public enquiry into native administration policy, yet he fully accepted that the working of native administration required examination and would be very willing, when the staff situation permitted, to arrange for such an examination in Tanganyika by ordinary administrative methods. I think that the replies to the letters sent show that it would have been better either to have confined these letters to a simple request that the Governors should agree to informal discussions with their officers or to have explained at much greater length what was in fact in our minds. Moreover in the case of the West African Governors, who had no document at all in front of them, it is perhaps hardly surprising that they do not appear to have fully grasped our intentions.
6. While I was in East Africa I had two long discussions on the subject with Sir William Battershill, and one with Sir Philip Mitchell. The results were encouraging. Sir Philip Mitchell is probably better qualified to advise on the subject than almost anyone serving in Africa. As an ex-Secretary for Native

Affairs, who assisted Sir Donald Cameron in the preparation of his famous memoranda on Native Administration, he has a great experience of the whole subject, and that experience extends to all the East African Territories. I found that Sir Philip Mitchell expressed views similar to those which we had put forward in the course of discussion here and that encouraged me greatly to believe that there was something in the views which we had separately formed. He is very much in favour of a greater degree of interchange of information and visits between African Governments. He believes in the building-up, under the Secretary for Native Affairs or the equivalent in each Territory, of Sections of the Central government Machine qualified to deal with the technical aspects of native administration policy. He said that he now thought that he had been wrong in having the Secretaryship of Native Affairs in Tanganyika abolished ten years ago. He believes that some reorganisation in the Colonial Office is required so that general policy on native administration may more effectively be kept under review. He thinks that, if such a reorganisation could be carried out, it might be possible for some general statement on the objections [*sic*] of policy to be produced in two or three years' time. He would welcome the holding of a conference with officers from the African Governments to discuss questions of native administration policy. Sir William Battershill's approach to the subject is that of one who has not previously served in Africa, but it has been borne in upon him that the so-called system of 'indirect rule' is not in fact in operation in many areas of Tanganyika. He is anxious for the full facts of the present situation of native administration in Tanganyika to be assembled by his officers, with a view to reassessing the requirements of policy.

7. Generally speaking I am confirmed in my feeling that it is necessary for the Colonial Office to make its views felt in this matter. Much constructive work on native administration is at present being initiated or carried into effect in the three East African Territories; but there is little knowledge in each of them of what is being done in the other two. A great deal of what is being done has never been communicated to the Colonial Office and, in certain quarters there is a large degree of ignorance of the Colonial Office attitude to these questions. It has indeed been said recently in connection with the discussion of this subject that the Colonial Office, in what it does, is moved wholly by political rather than practical considerations. The extent to which we concern ourselves with the problems of administrative officers in the field is not

appreciated, and there appear to be strong grounds for the Colonial Office to make it generally understood that it is deeply exercised about the whole problem of native administration and anxious to find every possible means of helping officers in this field in their task of carrying policy into execution.

8. The question therefore is what action should be taken and I deal with this in the succeeding paragraphs, taking points listed in paragraph (2) above one by one.

(1) Closer contact between the Colonial Office and African Governments and between African Governments themselves on native administration policy.

There is general agreement that closer contact should be secured. With the resumption of administrative reports, much more general information will be available, but this in itself is not sufficient. A large number of printed and typed reports are prepared by all Governments and many of these could with advantage be circulated to other Governments and to the Colonial Office for information. The interchange of visits between territories should be encouraged. The Land and Law Panels of the Colonial Office are already organising the interchange of information on these matters. This should also be organised for the political and local Government side of native administration. The necessity for closer contact and for the interchange of information should form the subject of part of a circular despatch to Governments. This point could be elaborated, but sufficient has been said to show what is intended.

(2) Improvement of machinery of African Governments for dealing with native administration policy.

There is general agreement on the East African side that a section of the central machinery of Governments, under the Secretary for Native Affairs or the equivalent, should be built up with a view to keeping native administration policy under continuous review and advising on its development. This should include officers specialising in African land tenure, African law, and in certain cases also social welfare and co-operation, etc. Such a group already exists in Kenya, although it is not yet in full operation. It is being built up satisfactorily in Northern Rhodesia and in Uganda. In Tanganyika Sir William Battershill proposes to have a Secretary for

African Administration and Local Government as part of his reorganised central machine of government. In Nyasaland similar machinery on a smaller scale will be required, but the opportunity for embarking on its establishment will probably not come for another year. It is desirable that the importance of this machinery should also be emphasised in a despatch to the east and Central African Governments. Whether something similar should be said to the West African Governments is a matter for the West African Department to consider.

(3) Machinery at the Colonial Office to deal with native administration policy.

Proposals for putting the Colonial Office in a better position to keep general policy with regard to native administration under continuous review were made in section (5) of my memorandum of the 3rd April.[3] The weakness of our present machinery is that native administration questions are dealt with in the Colonial Office by each of the Principals dealing with the various African territories. There is no single officer with special knowledge of the problems in all territories. The heads of the two African departments provide a coordinating link on each side and until recently the head of the African Division provided a link between East and West Africa. With the separation of the two African departments into two separate Divisions of the office, this final link has now been broken. But in any case we have never had effective machinery for keeping policy under review or for judging proposals from one territory in the light of the experience of another. We are thus not in a position to carry out our essential function of comparison and co-ordination.

I suggest that the first requirement is to arrange for a single Principal to deal with all work relating to native administration in East and West Africa, including African law and African land tenure, reporting to the Head of the West or East African Department as the case may be. This officer would be Secretary of the Land and Law Panels. The change could be made fairly easily and would place the Colonial Office in a much better position to perform its proper co-ordinating function. The officer concerned should be provided with a Research Assistant to carry out factual studies in particular subjects as and when required.

In addition I should like, as a suggestion to be carried into effect at greater leisure, to renew the proposal made in my memorandum of the 3rd April that an Adviser on African Local Government should be appointed in the office. His function would be to keep a general view of the development of native administration policies in East and West Africa. He would visit the territories frequently, would keep in close touch with officers on leave, and would study all the available written material on the subject. I would emphasise again that the suggested appointment is not intended to lead to a greater degree of centralisation in Whitehall. On the contrary, by keeping the Secretary of State more continuously informed of what was going on all the time in the Territories, the appointment should make it possible to achieve a greater degree of decentralisation. In any case the purpose of the appointment would be primarily so that the study and recording of development in native administration could be properly organised both here and in Africa. There would thus be no question of derogating from the powers of Governors to deal with the actual problems of administration.

I have always envisaged that such an adviser would be a retired officer from the African Service. But Sir Philip Mitchell, who is in favour of the appointment of an adviser on these lines, suggests that it should be someone from outside, possibly from one of the Universities in this country. He emphasises that it is important that such an officer should have a scholarly mind, and he believes that someone with a University background could make a great contribution to the over-all study of the whole subject.

(4) Assistance for Administrative Officers in the field.

This point is dealt with at length in paragraph 6 of my memorandum of the 3rd April and I need not go into detail here.[4] Action seems to be required particularly in relation to freeing officers in the field from routine duties in order to enable them to concentrate on the real work of native administration and in keeping officers better informed of the reasons for Government policy and of developments in other territories. All these points should, I suggest, be dealt with in a despatch to African governments and in particular emphasis should be laid on the necessity of providing each District Office with a competent Office Manager, and, on the information side, on the importance of informing all officers fully of the actions of Government and of arranging the interchange of visits between different territories, the holding of District Commissioners' Conferences and sending officers to courses, etc. in this country. The important question of establishing a periodical Colonial Office bulletin is being taken up separately.

(5) The question of a general stocktaking on native administration policy with a view to the possibility of preparing a statement on the present objectives of policy.

Whether or not a statement of the objectives of policy is required, it is clear that most Governors are doubtful about the value of such a statement. Governors are nervous of anything like a blueprint of policy, which was of course not at all what was intended. Nevertheless it is evident that Governors will need a good deal more convincing before they would welcome such a statement and we ought, I think, to move cautiously in the matter. At the same time I believe that there are strong grounds for further consultation with officers of the African Governments both on native administration policy itself and on the machinery for forming it and carrying it into effect. I do not think that we shall get much further with individual consultation and I should be in favour of arranging a Conference with Secretaries for Native Affairs and others sometime next year. Sir Philip Mitchell suggested to me that this might take the form of a summer school at one of the Universities, an idea which he put forward before the war. I think that this is an excellent suggestion, and the summer school procedure would have the advantage of keeping the discussion informal, but at the same time providing an opportunity for getting down to the real problems with the various Secretaries for Native Affairs. The Conference should also be attended by other officers on leave, both senior and junior, although they would not necessarily attend all the sessions, alternative programmes being provided for them. Another advantage of having a summer school would be that if, after consultation, the Governors wished to limit the Conference merely to an exchange of ideas, with no attempt to produce any conclusions, a summer school could still usefully be held, although its value would be reduced. In other words the procedure would be highly flexible. I should envisage that the summer school would last for about 10 days and that about 40 people would attend it. Sir Philip Mitchell said that he would be quite prepared to send over one or two of his senior officers specially to attend it. I need not deal here with the agenda for such a summer school, since that could be worked out at leisure if the general proposal were approved. I have made some enquiries of Sir Ralph Furse[5] as to the possibility of securing a college at Oxford or Cambridge about July if the idea were approved and he thinks that this might well be possible. He has promised to make further enquiries without involving any commitment. Colonial Governments would have to agree to meet most of the expenses.

(6) *Summary*.

The proposals in the above note are as follows:—

1. A circular despatch to East and Central and, if desired, West African Governments should be prepared dealing with the following points:—
   (a) The necessity for closer contact and exchange of information between the Colonial Office and African Governments and between African Governments themselves on native administration policy.
   (b) The improvement of the machinery of African Governments for dealing with native administration policy.
   (c) Methods of assisting administrative officers in the field in the execution of native administration policy.

   The Department are preparing the first draft of such a despatch for consideration.
2. Consideration should be given to the improvement of the machinery of the African Division of the Colonial Office in relation to native administration policy. In particular one Principal should deal with native administration questions affecting both East and West Africa. A Research Assistant should be appointed with a view to carrying out studies on particular subjects. Consideration should also be given to the possibility of appointing an Adviser on African Local Government to the staff of the Colonial Office.
3. Arrangements should be made for the holding of a summer school on native administration at one of the universities next summer. African Governments should be invited to send their Secretaries for Native Affairs to this summer school and also certain other suitable officers who might be on leave at the time.

A. B. Cohen 28/9/46

Notes

1. Richards, Sir Edmund Charles, b.1889; Governor and Commander-in Chief Nyasaland, 1942–8.
2. Hall, Sir John Hathorn, b.1894: Governor and Commander-in-Chief Uganda, 1944–51.
3. 'Native Administration Policy. Notes for Further Discussion', memorandum by Cohen, 3 April 1946, CO 847/35/47234/1/1947, following document 37, above.
4. Ibid.
5. Furse, Sir Ralph, b.1887; Assistant Private Secretary to Secretary of State for the Colonies 1910–14, 1919–31, and Director of Recruitment to the Colonial Service, 1931–48.

DOCUMENT 39

Native Administration Policy: Minute by F. J. Pedler, 1 November 1946, CO 847/35/47234/1/1947

1. I am most grateful to you for giving me an opportunity of saying what I feel on this question,[1] for in my view the initiative which Mr Cohen has taken is one of the most important and valuable things which has happened recently in this Office.
2. Africa is now the core of our colonial position; the only continental space from which we can still hope to draw reserves of economic and military strength. Our position there depends fundamentally on our standing with Africans in the mass. And this depend[s] on whether we make a success of African *local* government.
3. Happily, for about forty years we have avoided fighting Africans, and during this time we have, by means of our administrative policy (native authorities, local native councils, and so forth) built up a most valuable goodwill between ourselves and the mass of primitive Africans.
4. This goodwill is now imperilled. The racial conflict deliberately fomented by Azikiwe in Nigeria,[2] and the messianic fervour with which he is regarded by many Nigerians, raise a serious danger that we may come to blows with Africans in Nigeria. If this should happen it would immediately embitter our relations with Africans throughout the continent. While Nigeria appears at present to be the danger point, there are delicate situations in other places.
5. Since Africans first entered the executive council of the Gold Coast in 1942, the handing over of important positions in the central governments to the small minority of literate Africans has gone ahead very quickly. They are on executive councils in the West, in legislative councils in the East, in the Administrative Service in Nigeria and the Gold Coast; they have a majority in the Gold Coast legislature and may shortly expect a majority in the Nigerian legislature.
6. The pace of these changes testifies to the sincerity of our policy of granting self-government as soon as possible. But these changes represent concessions to a class of literate Africans who are a small minority. If this small minority were soundly based on the conscious, informed support of the illiterate mass, all would be well. But it isn't. I am not suggesting that the literates ought not to have their places in

councils and so forth, but we need to call in the African masses to keep the balance. The illiterate masses can only take a positive part in government through the development of vigorous local authorities of suitable form and function.

7. Mr Cohen says that officers in the field complain that the interest of the Colonial Office is 'too political'. There is no doubt that the impression has spread widely among Government officers and among Africans that the native authority policy is being allowed to fall into the background and that the future lies with central institutions and the literate African. This has had a depressing effect on the Administrative Service, who can raise much enthusiasm for local authorities, but from most of whom the central authority is remote.
8. What is wanted now is a vigorous policy of African local government which will progressively democratise the present forms and bring literates and illiterates together, in balanced and studied proportions, for the management of local finances and services. Failing this, we shall find the masses apt to follow the leadership of demagogues who want to turn us right out very quickly. The position and prestige of such persons has been much enhanced by our policy of the last four years.
9. I range myself with Mr Cohen in advising that the objectives of policy should be stated. Indeed, without a definition of objectives, the rest is useless. All the emphasis on methods, exchange of information, etc., is futile if it is not clear to what end all this is intended.
10. My own view, for what it is worth, is that His Majesty's Government should give the fullest support to any measures which will enable the common people in any locality to participate in the management of their own affairs, and that the contrary claims of tribal chiefs, African politicians, centralised departments and financial purists should not be allowed to stand in the way unless there are very special reasons why they should.
11. Now, there is a tremendous field of 'technique' in all this. Although Government is an art which cannot be learned from lectures, books, or circular despatches, it has, like other arts, a technique which needs to be studied and taught. How and when to persuade a chief to commit political euthanaesia: how to arrange for illiterates to register votes: how to convert tribal customs such as the Ibibio 'good son' into a balanced representation of literates and illiterates: how to reconcile the claims of the native courts and the 'European' courts: how to separate the judiciary from the

executive functions in native authorities: how to solve the language problem in native courts: how to establish native institutions in multi-tribal urban communities: what dangers you incur if you leave the women out of account: how a local authority may be made to grow out of a single successful service such as a cattle insurance scheme or a lorry park: and so on. All these problems have been solved successfully, and most of them in other places have been unwisely and unsuccessfully handled. The job of knowing all this and seeing that the information gets passed around is a full time job for an officer enjoying at least the status of a full adviser. I should have thought that it deserved the whole-time attention of an Assistant Under-Secretary of State.

12. I strongly support Mr Cohen's proposals in his paragraph 8(6) with the provisos (a) that the 'summer school' should be made an important function and should be used to test out thoroughly the reaction to a strong lead on the question of policy on the lines suggested above; and (b) that an Adviser or preferably an Assistant Under Secretary of State should be provided to devote his whole time to questions of African Local Government.

F. J. Pedler
1st November, 1946.

Notes

1. Pedler's minute was written in response to Cohen's memorandum, (Document 38).
2. Azikiwe, Benjamin Nnamdi, b.1904; editor-in-chief of the *West African Pilot* since 1937; President of the National Council of Nigeria and the Cameroons, 1946; Vice-President of the Nigerian National Democratic Party, and elected to the Nigerian Legislative Council, 1947–51.

DOCUMENT 40

Colonial Policy in Africa: Directive to the Agenda Committee for the Conference of African Governors, February 1947, CO 847/36/47238/1 Pt I/1947

CONFIDENTIAL DIRECTIVE TO COMMITTEE.

1. In view of the large body of opinion in this country, in Africa and internationally which holds that more rapid political, economic and social development is required in the African Territories, the Secretary of State has decided to hold in London during 1948 a Conference of official and non-official representatives from these Territories to discuss the problems involved. The Secretary of State has also decided that, in preparation for this Conference, there should be a Conference of Governors and Governors designate of the African Territories in November, 1947, also in London.
2. The Secretary of State has set up a Colonial Office Committee to formulate detailed proposals as to the matters to be placed on the Agenda of the Governors' Conference and subsequently on that of the 1948 Conference insofar as the discussions with the Governors indicate that this would be appropriate; to advise on the preparation of particular papers to be placed before the Conferences; and, where appropriate, to submit draft recommendations on the issues to be raised.
3. While the Colonial Office Committee will be primarily concerned with the problems of African development in framing its recommendations it will have to take into account the possible application of these in relation to Territories outside Africa.
4. In formulating its recommendations, the Committee is asked to pay particular attention to the following points:

   (a) The possibility of giving unofficial members of Legislative Councils a closer association with the executive work of Government;

   (b) Means of developing more effective machinery for African local government;

   (c) Means of securing the more efficient organisation of the economy of the Territories, so as to enable their natural resources to be developed more rapidly;

   (d) Means of securing the more rapid and effective development of the social services, with special reference to education and medical services;

(e) Means of improving the machinery of government, and in particular of securing a greater degree of devolution of responsibility to the Governments and Legislative Councils.

This list of subjects is not intended to be exclusive.

5. The membership of the Committee will be as follows:—

Mr S. Caine (Chairman)
Mr A. B. Cohen
Mr L. N. Helsby (Treasury)[1]
Mr K. E. Robinson[2]
Mr P Rogers
Mr J. B. Williams
Mr C. [G.] B. Cartland (Secretary)

6. Until it is possible to announce the decisions mentioned in paragraph (1), the contents of this directive should be regarded as confidential.

Notes

1. Helsby, Laurence Norman, b.1908; Lecturer in Economics 1931–45, Assistant Secretary at the Treasury, 1946–7; Personal Private Secretary to the Prime Minister, 1947–50.
2. Robinson, Kenneth Ernest, b.1914; Assistant Secretary and Head of the Department of Economic Intelligence and Planning, Colonial Office.

DOCUMENT 41

Palestine: Joint Memorandum by the Secretary of State for Foreign Affairs and the Secretary of State for the Colonies, 6 February 1947, CAB 129/16

TOP SECRET

C.P. (47) 49
6th February, 1947.

CABINET

PALESTINE

Joint Memorandum by the Secretary of State for Foreign Affairs and the Secretary of State for the Colonies

Under the authority given to us by the Cabinet on 22nd January (C.M. (47) 11th Conclusions, Minute 2) we have spent the last ten days in exploring, in conversations with representatives of the Arabs and the Jews, the possibility of finding some settlement of the Palestine problem which might be broadly acceptable to all parties. These conversations have confirmed our fear that there is no prospect of finding such a settlement.

2. *The Arabs* have again put forward the plan which they presented at Lancaster House in the autumn – that Palestine should be given early independence as a unitary State with a permanent Arab majority. They have, however, indicated that they would be ready to discuss modifications of their political proposals *if* they were first given a firm assurance that –

(a) we were prepared to exclude the possibility of Partition as a solution; and

(b) we agreed that there should be no further Jewish immigration into Palestine.

3. We are satisfied that there is no possibility of moving the Arab Delegations from the first of these conditions. They are implacably opposed to the creation of a Jewish State in any part of Palestine, and they will go to any lengths to prevent it. Delegates representing the younger generation of Arabs have stated their sincere conviction that their contemporaries would

take up arms to resist the imposition of Partition. Whatever doubts there may have been on this point in the past, we must now take it, as one of the facts of the situation, that Partition would be resisted by the Arabs of Palestine with the support of the Governments and peoples of all the Arab States.

4. On the second condition, about Jewish immigration, there is a possibility of some compromise. The point on which the Arabs will insist to the last is that they must have some satisfactory assurance that it will not be possible for the Jews, by continuing immigration, to secure a majority in Palestine. For this purpose, however, it is not essential to provide, as the Arabs are now demanding, that there shall be no further Jewish immigration at all. Other safeguards less drastic than this could secure the Arab objective of ensuring that the Jewish community shall not, by immigration, obtain an absolute majority in Palestine. Provided that satisfactory assurances could be given on that point, we should not despair of securing some agreement on immigration.

5. *The Jews* still interpret the Balfour Declaration and the Mandate as implying a promise that a Jewish State will be established in the whole of Palestine. Their first suggestion was that we should rescind the White Paper of 1939 and continue to hold the Mandate on a basis which would enable them to build the foundations of that State by unrestricted immigration and economic expansion. We made it clear that His Majesty's Government were not prepared to maintain in Palestine a purely tutelary administration under the protection of which such a Jewish policy could be carried out. The issue we presented to the Jewish representatives was the need to find some practical means of initiating in Palestine self-government evolving towards independence.

The Jewish representatives then indicated that, while still maintaining the justice of their full claim, they would be prepared to consider as a compromise proposals for the creation of "a viable Jewish State in an adequate area of Palestine". They would not themselves propose a plan of Partition, but expressed willingness to consider such a proposal coming from His Majesty's Government.

6. The essential point of principle for the Jews is the creation of a sovereign Jewish State. And the essential point of principle for the Arabs is to resist to the last the establishment of Jewish sovereignty in any part of Palestine. These, for both sides, are matters of principle on which there is no room for compromise. There is, therefore, no hope of negotiating an agreed settlement.

7. In these circumstances we have tried to find a solution which, even though it may not be acceptable to the two communities in

Palestine, is one which we could conscientiously recommend and defend to public opinion in this country and to the United Nations.

8. We have been reluctantly forced to the conclusion that such a solution cannot be found along the lines of Partition. Partition has certain intrinsic weaknesses. Wherever the frontiers were drawn, large Arab minorities would be left within the Jewish State. The area left to the Arabs could not be economically self-supporting and even if it could be attached to Transjordan, the standard of services which it now enjoys could not be maintained. The location of Jewish settlements is such that the Jewish State would have to include the major economic assets of the Arab community. Thus, any scheme of Partition which would satisfy the Jews would be demonstrably unfair to the Arabs.

Apart from the merits, we must also consider the consequences of advocating Partition. If we did so, we should have to face the resolute hostility of the Arab world. Even if we were prepared to accept the consequences of this hostility, it is by no means certain that we could count on the support of the Jews. They have not been willing to put before us any detailed plan of Partition; but, from the general statements which they have made, it is clear that they would expect to obtain under Partition a very substantial area of Palestine. It is therefore most unlikely that they would support any Partition plan which His Majesty's Government would feel justified in putting forward.

Furthermore, the existing Mandate gives us no authority to move in the direction of creating an independent Jewish State, whether under Partition or otherwise. For any solution along these lines it would be necessary for us to obtain the prior assent of the United Nations. We should have little chance of securing the necessary two-thirds majority in support of any scheme of Partition. For a scheme which was not endorsed by the Jews it is even doubtful whether we could rely on the full support of the United States. The views expressed on behalf of the State Department in recent telegrams leave us with the impression that the United States Government will to the end remain an uncertain and unreliable factor in this problem.

9. In these circumstances we seek the authority of the Cabinet to put before the Arabs and the Jews the alternative plan outlined in the Appendix to this memorandum.[1]

This has as its primary object the development of self-government in Palestine, with the aim of enabling the country to achieve its independence after a short transition period under Trusteeship. It provides for a substantial measure of local autonomy in Arab and Jewish areas; and enables Arabs and Jews to collaborate together at the centre. It contains special safeguards for the "human rights" of the two communities. It provides for the admission of 100,000 Jewish immigrants over the next two years and for continuing immigration thereafter by agreement between the two communities or, failing that, by arbitration under the United Nations. Thus, it should go some way towards allaying Arab fears of unrestricted Jewish immigration, while avoiding the extreme course of denying to the Jews any further immigration without Arab consent.

10. This plan incorporates many features taken from the Provincial Autonomy scheme and from the proposals put forward by the Arab Delegations.[2] It will not, of course, meet the Jewish claim to sovereignty; but it does make reasonable provision for Jewish immigration and economic development. It should meet the views of a large number of moderate Jews throughout the world who do not support the more extreme claims of Zionism.

It is consistent with the principles of the Mandate; but it adds, what has hitherto been lacking, a practical promise of evolution towards independence by building up from the bottom political institutions rooted in the lives of the people.

The initial steps in such a policy could be taken at once under the existing Mandate; and if we concluded that it was possible to do so, we could avoid the practical difficulties which would arise in the country if there were a long interval between the announcement of a new policy and its initiation after approval by the United Nations. At the same time, the plan is fully consistent with the Charter of the United Nations, and provides for regularising the position by the negotiation of a Trusteeship Agreement. These features would cause the United States Government to hesitate before opposing the plan.

11. We recognise that these proposals offer no guarantee for the preservation of our military position in Palestine after the five-year period of Trusteeship. On the other hand we do not think that either of the alternatives open to us would be more advantageous from a strategic point of view. If we had to refer the problem of Palestine to the United Nations without ourselves making any recommendation as to its solution, we could have no guarantee that British troops would be able to remain in the country even for so long as five years. And Partition, far from conferring any strategic advantages on us, might not only involve us in a heavy military liability in Palestine, but might also weaken our strategic position in the Middle East as a whole. At a time when it is one of our main pre-occupations to reduce our

overseas military expenditure and to avoid any further slowing down in the planned rate of demobilisation, we should find it difficult to justify the great military risks involved in a policy of Partition.

From a purely military point of view, the most satisfactory solution would no doubt be for His Majesty's Government to continue to administer Palestine under the existing Mandate without applying for a Trusteeship Agreement. We are convinced, however, that the maintenance of British administration without reference to the United Nations would be so strongly challenged that we should soon find our position untenable.

12. We therefore ask for authority to put to the Arabs and the Jews the scheme outlined in the Appendix to this memorandum on the understanding that, if agreement were reached on this basis, we should proceed to give effect to it.

If, as is more likely, we find that no agreement can be reached, we shall report to the Cabinet whether in our judgment this solution is likely to meet with any substantial measure of acquiescence from even one of the two communities in Palestine; and shall invite the Cabinet to decide whether His Majesty's Government would be justified in bringing it into operation on their own authority pending the negotiation of a Trusteeship Agreement.

If we are unable to report any such prospect of acquiescence, we believe that the only course then open to His Majesty's Government will be to submit the problem to the United Nations, explaining the efforts we have made to find a solution but making no positive recommendation.

E. B.
A. C-J.

Notes

1. The four-page appendix has not been reproduced. The plan referred to for a bi-national state was rejected by both sides, with the result that Bevin announced on 18 February in the House of Commons that Britain would refer the problem to the United Nations Organization.
2. The Provincial Autonomy Scheme had been put forward by the Colonial Office in January 1946, as a means to bridge the gap, for example, between the Foreign Office desire for a unitary state and the Colonial Office preference for partition. It envisaged the division of Palestine into separate Jewish and Arab provinces under a central government as trustee, and allowed for a prolonged period of Colonial Office administration during which Arab economic and social conditions might be improved and common political institutions fostered.

DOCUMENT 42

'Prices of Colonial Export Products', Draft of a Memorandum by the Secretary of State for the Colonies for presentation to the Cabinet, March 1947,[1] CO 852/989/3

I attach a Note regarding the prices paid by this country for bulk purchases of Colonial export crops. I invite the careful attention of my colleagues to this Note, for it deals with a question which has recently become of primary importance in the discharge of our moral responsibility for the welfare of the dependent Colonies.

2. Though the Note is I fear long, the point at issue is simple. There are a number of cases in which Colonial producers are today receiving from H.M.G. for their products very substantially less than current market prices, and there are others in which they are being compulsorily denied access to the most favourable markets.

3. This is a legacy of arrangements which had every justification in war-time. Now their only justification is the financial advantage to the United Kingdom. I know full well how important it is that our overseas payments should be kept as low as they possibly can be, but I cannot believe that this justifies a course which is contrary to our declared policy in regard both to Colonial and to commercial matters and contrary also to the policy which has long been pursued by the Labour Party.

4. In my view, there are the strongest objections to a policy whereby Colonial producers are compelled either by political or economic pressure to sell to the United Kingdom at prices substantially below those ruling in the open market or being charged to foreign buyers. The guiding consideration in fixing bulk purchases of Colonial products should be the current world market value of the commodity, as nearly as it can be estimated in the absence of fully operating commercial markets. We should not attempt by means of Colonial export licensing or other controls to force to this country exports of a particular product, save only where such an arrangement is made under an agreed international allocation scheme. I recognise the danger of balance of payments difficulties arising out of the payment of higher prices for Colonial produce but consider that those difficulties can best be dealt with by separate arrangements dealing with the broader question of the utilisation of the sterling balances held on Colonial account.

5. I believe that international opinion will regard the policy we pursue in this matter as a crucial test of the sincerity of our oft-proclaimed principles of Colonial trusteeship. I believe also that, if we even appear to be abusing our political sovereignty to secure at the expense of Colonial producers a financial advantage to ourselves, we shall irretrievably damage our relations with the dependent Empire and teach its peoples to think that they can get fair treatment only by establishing complete political independence.
6. I invite the Cabinet to endorse the principles set out in paragraphs [25 and 26] of the Note.[2]

A.C.J.
March, 1947.

Notes

1. Neither this memorandum nor the Note to which it refers went before the Cabinet, owing, first, to persistent opposition from the Ministry of Food and the Treasury to any suggestion of higher prices for producers, and, second, to Creech Jones's wish to promote other issues at Cabinet level: see, for example, minutes by S. Caine 19 May, and Creech Jones 4 June, CO 852/989/3.
2. Para. 25 of the Note recommended 'guiding principles' (as summarized in para. 4 of this document) for setting the terms of public trading transactions between colonies and the UK. Para. 26 suggested 'working rules' (on price-fixing and the reservation of markets by government control) to give these principles 'greater precision'.

DOCUMENT 43

Colonial Policy in Africa: Extracts from the Diary of Sir Philip Mitchell, Governor of Kenya, May to November 1947, Mss.Afr.r.101, Rhodes House Library, Oxford

[Mitchell left Mombasa on 5 May, en route for leave in England, and arrived at Plymouth on 28 May. He left England again on 6 September, returning by air from Kenya early in November for the African Governors' Conference.]

10 May
[The 7.00 p.m. news] 'also said Mountbatten has summoned a Conference of Indian Political Leaders next week and Princes after them to tell them what we mean to do about evacuation and handing over. That is certainly the way to handle the business.'
3 June
[Listened in the evening to Mountbatten's plan for India] 'It is good sound common sense; and if they do opt for Dominion Status, a great achievement.'
11 June
[Further talks at the Colonial Office] 'Creech shows himself very friendly and anxious to help: he clearly is beginning to understand African problems. Asked me to speak to the Fabian Society and other groups and I agreed.'
8 September
[Read African Governor's Conference papers all morning] 'and cannot say that I derived much profit. But it is interesting to find the CO now advocating as the desirable and normal development the break of Col. administration into groups of Depts. under Members of the Ex. Co. and the appointment of men who are not officials to be Members – in fact generally describing the steps I took in 1945.'
9 September
'I read more papers including one on education in the Colonies which is quite good as far as it goes . . . Through all these papers there runs a rather alarming recurrent theme 'we cannot control . . .' 'we cannot prevent . . .' – ergo, laissez faire. It is high time we injected some strength and decisiveness into our affairs.'
10 September
[Read] 'the reports of the Summer School groups, on the whole sensible documents if not showing much originality or profundity.'
8 November
[Governors' Conference opened by Creech Jones who] 'spoke

for an hour and a quarter . . . dully and with little relation to realities. Afterwards Milverton and I replied shortly and gave warning about next year's conference. On procedure I had to insist that we must decide what we were going to do in 1948 and Creech gave way.'

11 November

[At the Conference] 'a very tedious time over the Colonies and international relations. Poynton,[1] a very typical bureaucrat and a man without guts or understanding droned away about proceedings in UNO and the wonderful efforts he made to get votes or support for this or that totally unrealistic – or anyhow, ineffective – resolution or project. He protested, and others with him, the greatest determination to protect British interests while at the same time describing his ideas of how to weaken or betray them. I took the line that the whole of our history showed that wisdom lay in keeping your fingers out of other people's affairs and not in trying to meddle; the Boer War came of meddling, the Union of the realisation of its folly. Robertson and others also belaboured them.[2] But I doubt if we made any impression.'

10 November

'We conferred all day, largely on dry theoretical ideas of colonial self-government totally divorced from the realities of the present day. The C.O. has got itself into a sort of mystic enchantment and sees visions of grateful, independent Utopias beaming at them from all round the world, as if there was – yet – any reason to suppose that any African can be cashier of a village council for 3 weeks without stealing the cash.

It is uphill work, but we bludgeoned them pretty severely from both sides, although the W. Africans other than Milverton are a silent lot. There is really no understanding whatever of contemporary realities in the C.O. – Creech blathered a good deal.'

12 November

[At the Conference] 'a brilliant speech by Stafford Cripps[3] . . . Cripps in answer to a question from me had said that more and more long term contracts must be made. The officials are all against, of course, and will try to sabotage that idea, and yet it is vital.'

Notes

1. Poynton, Arthur Hilton, b.1905; since 1 February 1947, Assistant Under-Secretary of State with responsibility for the departments of International Relations, Social Services, and Welfare.
2. Robertson, James Wilson, b.1899; Civil Secretary, Sudan Government, 1945–53.
3. Document 44.

DOCUMENT 44

'Speech by the Rt. Hon. Sir Stafford Cripps, KC, MP, Minister for Economic Affairs, to the African Governors' Conference on 12th November, 1947', CO 852/989/3

I make no profession to be able to assist you in your deliberations as to the lines of economic development that are most appropriate in the various Colonial territories in Africa. On that subject you have the specialised knowledge, but what I would like to do for a few minutes is to give you a summary review of our present economic position as a Commonwealth and Empire and of our prospects – not so much over the short term – as over the medium and long term.

You will, I have no doubt, have read and studied the recent statements made in the House of Commons and elsewhere which have given the details of our present situation; I need therefore only recapitulate them very shortly.

The sterling area – and indeed the rest of the non-dollar world – has got itself completely out of balance with the Dollar countries, and with the United States of America in particular.

This is partly due to an acceleration of the tendency towards unbalance which was in evidence even before the first world war, and which was much more obvious between the two wars. The rapid rise in productive capacity of the American Continent was already in those days making it difficult to balance its contribution to the rest of the world against what it took from the rest of the world.

Partly too, of course, it is due to the very great upset caused by the two world wars and the consequent setback to European productive capacity.

This lessened European productive capacity meant in effect a slower development of all those areas in Africa that are primarily dependent upon European capital goods manufactured for their capital development.

To some extent all the European countries were obliged to neglect capital development both at home and in their Colonies in their attempt to balance their overseas payments. That tendency is unfortunately accentuated by the present much higher degree of unbalance.

This unbalance is not merely or primarily in the manufactured products of the U.S.A. but also, and more importantly, in the foodstuffs and raw materials that members of the sterling group are compelled to obtain from the U.S.A., Canada or S. America (all of which must be considered as dollar countries) simply because they are not obtainable anywhere else. The degree of unbalance has risen to extraordinary levels.

The dollar unbalance in the U.S.A. has been running at over 10 billion dollars a year, and this has been balanced by every kind of artificial device such as UNRRA gifts for rehabilitation, loans and credits which have up to date enabled the flow of exports from the Western Hemisphere to be continued.

The direct trade of Great Britain with the U.S.A. has always shown a great excess of exports from over imports to the U.S.A., but before the war this was precariously balanced by the dollars we received from third parties, particularly members of the Commonwealth and Empire.

This enabled the sterling area as a whole to maintain a balance and so preserve the convertibility of sterling, thus permitting a very wide area of multilateral trade throughout the world.

Our own set-back in production consequent upon war devastation and our inability to buy foodstuffs and raw materials from the sterling area or non-dollar countries, coupled to the need of other sterling countries to buy manufactured goods from the USA, has resulted in the very heavy adverse balance of dollars running at the rate of between £600 and £700 millions a year for the sterling area.

It is the problem of righting this tremendous unbalance which now confronts us. In this regard I might mention the great importance of having prompt returns as to dollar expenditure so as to follow how the position is developing in order that immediate steps may be taken to rectify any particularly dangerous condition that is disclosed. We ourselves have laid on elaborate machinery to secure that we know from week to week how our dollar expenditure is moving and why. We want to supplement this with corresponding information from the Colonies, and you will be hearing about this through 'the usual channels'. I know you will all want to help in this matter but it is still vitally important that the great gravity of the common danger should be realised and the need for every unit in the sterling area to make the greatest possible contribution to overcoming it. In facing that problem we must have it quite clearly in our minds that this is not merely a short-term difficulty; it is one that, unless tackled fundamentally and on a long-term basis will never be solved at all. We believe that provided we can sell our goods abroad there is no insuperable difficulty in our manufacturing in this country enough goods for export to enable us to pay for all the imports that we need by the end of next year. That is within our capacity. But there remains the proviso that we can sell our goods abroad and sell them – if we want to balance our overseas payments – in the right markets.

The right markets must obviously be those from which we can get an immediate return in the form of essential foodstuffs and raw materials. This same principle of course applies to all the countries in the sterling area since we desire to make the sterling area as little dependent as possible upon supplies from the dollar area.

We must therefore not only expand our exports but at the same time we must cut down our dollar imports. This means a reduction in our total volume of imports for the simple reason that we cannot at present buy elsewhere the goods we must stop purchasing for dollars. It is only however because they come from a dollar source that we must do without them; if we could get them for sterling we could still afford to have them, because as I have said we can make enough goods to export to balance our total imports.

Our trouble is that the U.S.A. cannot take enough either raw materials or manufactured goods from the Sterling Area to anything like balance her capacity to export to that area. We must therefore, while doing all we can to increase imports into U.S.A. from the sterling area, at the same time reduce our imports from the U.S.A. If we are to maintain even the present standard of living for our people in Great Britain, we must be able to find other sources of those kinds of foodstuffs and raw materials or their equivalents, the importation of which from the Western Hemisphere we want to cut off.

We have for a long time talked about the development of Africa but I do not believe that we have realised how from the point of view of world economy that development is absolutely vital.

The economies of Western Europe and Tropical Africa are so closely interlocked in mutual trade, in the supply of capital and in currency systems that their problems of overseas balance are essentially one. Tropical Africa is already contributing much, both in physical supplies of food and raw materials and in quite substantial net earnings of dollars for the sterling area pool. The further development of African resources is of the same crucial importance to the rehabilitation and strengthening of Western Europe as the restoration of European productive power is to the future progress and prosperity of Africa. Each needs and is needed by the other. In Africa indeed is to be found a great potential for new strength and vigour in the Western European economy and the stronger that economy becomes the better of course Africa itself will fare.

It is the urgency of the present situation and the need for the Sterling Group and Western Europe both of them to maintain their economic independence that makes it so essential that we should increase out of all recognition the tempo of African economic development. We must be prepared to change our outlook and our habits of Colonial development and force the pace so that within the next 2 - 5 years we can get a really marked increase of production in coal, minerals, timber, raw materials of all kinds and foodstuffs and anything else that will save dollars or will sell in a dollar market.

But here we come up against what is a very great difficulty. All such development required the provision of large quantities of capital goods which – because of the dollar shortage – can only be obtained from Western Europe and, so far as our colonies are concerned, from Great Britain. Yet, as I have already pointed out, if we are to balance our overseas payments we must not export to countries other than those giving us an immediate return in essential goods.

These very capital goods that we shall require for colonial expansion, rails, locomotives, wagons, port facilities, bull dozers, tractors and so on are just the very goods that we require for our own rehabilitation and that are demanded by every country from whom we get foodstuffs and raw materials.

There is a very definite and sharp limit to our capacity to manufacture these capital goods in the volume of steel and of special steels that we can ourselves manufacture. That limit is today round about 14 million tons a year provided we can get enough scrap and pig iron and coal and coke. But even with 14 million tons we are some 2–3 million tons short of our requirements, bearing in mind the export task we have to carry out, some 60 per cent of which is in steel.

It is however quite probable that we shall find – indeed we expect to find – that the useful markets will not be able to absorb all the manufactured steel goods – as against the semi-finished steel – that we shall make. There will be a surplus of exports which we should have to sell either for no return at all, or to wipe off past indebtedness, or else for a return in semi luxury goods which it is not essential for us to import.

It is in this area that we shall hope to be able to find goods which can be more profitably devoted to Colonial development than to exchange for some unwanted imports.

You will however observe that there is a great uncertainty about this source of supply, which makes it extremely difficult to plan ahead.

You will be also very much concerned with the supply of consumer goods to your territories, particularly textiles of which they have been so short and which are required to reward the hard work of your producers.

We are as you know doing our utmost to increase textile production but here your people and the people at home are in competition and we can only share out between them the short supplies that exist until we can get better results from our textile industries.

Here I would like to mention the fact which may or may not be known to you that the Planning Section of the Cabinet Secretariat for which I am now responsible has had added to its terms of reference the whole subject matter of Colonial Development. This has been done because we must fit in with our own domestic investment programme that for the Colonies as well since it should really be part and parcel of the same thing.

Now that development under the Colonial Development and Welfare Act is under way and the Colonial Development Corporation has been or is about to be launched on an adequate scale it becomes essential for us to make provision for the Colonies in our programme for the manufacture of capital goods.

One of the difficulties will undoubtedly be the decision as to priorities of development. Where there are so many prospects it is difficult to choose. That matter is now under consideration and clearly we shall have to consider first those prospects which make the smallest demands upon new capital investment, and here you can most certainly help us to arrive at a wise decision. What I think is most important is that we should get right ahead with as many large scale experimental schemes as possible. These can as a rule be carried through with improvised methods which do not make great demands upon capital goods and they are essential preliminaries to any large scale development. This applies particularly to new products not hitherto used as important raw materials or foodstuffs which can be substituted for some of these materials now bought for dollars.

The development of these is bound to take time but with energetic action the time can be greatly cut down.

You may conclude from what I have said that the Government is only interested in large scale operations like the ground nut scheme in central Africa. This is not at all the case. We are interested in every method and device that will yield a few thousand tons more of any valuable crop or material. We want the small things followed up as well as the big prospects and we want the spirit of improvisation, invention and adventure to permeate the whole of our colonial economic policy. In the course of this work if it is carried through energetically we shall expect failures as well as successes. An occasional failure is the necessary price of adventurous development and we must not allow safety first to be the keynote of our work.

The situation is far too urgent for that, for the whole future of the sterling group and its ability to survive depends in my view upon a quick and extensive development of our African resources.

I have rather concentrated upon the general economic position of the sterling group because that is fundamental to our survival, but I would not have you think that I looked upon the Colonial territories as a mere adjunct to feed Britain.

It is because the future prosperity of the Colonies themselves depends upon the future strength and stability of the Commonwealth and Empire that I am convinced that their future and the happiness of their peoples can only be made secure along the lines that I have mentioned.

You will I understand be considering the question of the development of manufactures and industries in the Colonies. Though I take the view that such development is highly desirable so long as it is not pushed too far or too quickly, yet it must be obvious that with the present world shortage of capital goods it is not possible to contemplate much in the way of industrial development in the Colonies. The available steel will be better used both from a world point of view as well as from the point of view of the Colonies themselves in doing our utmost to increase the supplies of foodstuffs and raw materials.

I believe that in your hands lies the ultimate solution of our present difficulties, it is to your contribution to the righting of the world unbalance that we must look, and in order to give you the chance of success we must put behind you all that we can in the way of capital goods supplies. Time is of the essence of this solution. We hope to improvise by means of the Marshall plan or in some other way for the next 3 or 4 years but after that we must have worked out a solution of our own for the sterling area. Three or four years is a desperately short time for major developments in your areas so that there is not a moment to be lost. Our desperate need in that period is first to find ways of increasing our capital resources available for investment and secondly to invest that capital in the most profitable way so as to bring in quick results. The Colonies can make their contribution to the first by reducing demands for unnecessary current consumption and devoting some of their own earnings to capital purposes. They can contribute to the second by pushing ahead with all vigour with individual projects of development.

CABINET OFFICES

DOCUMENT 45

Palestine: Extract from Cabinet Memorandum by the Secretary of State for Foreign Affairs and the Secretary of State for the Colonies, 3 December 1947, CP (47) 320, CAB 129/22

TOP SECRET

2. *United Nations Decision*

The General Assembly of the United Nations has approved by the requisite two-thirds majority a recommendation to His Majesty's Government and the other United Nations that Palestine should be divided into two independent States, one Jewish and the other Arab, with a Joint Economic Board to link the financial and economic systems of the two States. The text of the most important part of the recommendations is given at Annex A. Other parts deal with boundaries and the city of Jerusalem. The boundaries between the two States represent on the whole acceptance of Jewish claims. Each state consists of three separate areas joined with each other by narrow corridors. The Jewish State has a very large Arab minority. The Arab State has a very small Jewish minority. Jerusalem is to be a separate territory under the United Nations Trusteeship Council.

3. One of the most important parts of the recommendations is the establishment of a United Nations Commission consisting of five representatives (Czechoslovakia, Panama, Bolivia, Denmark, Philippines). The Commission will assume authority in Palestine as we give it up and will be responsible for setting up the provisional councils of Government in each state and establishing the boundaries. If they are unable to set up the provisional councils by 1st April they are to refer back to the Security Council.

4. *Jewish and Arab reactions*

The Jews have warmly welcomed the recommendation and will clearly give their full co-operation to the United Nations Commission in setting up the Jewish State. The Arab States have refused to recognise the United Nations recommendation and are expected not to co-operate in any way with the United Nations Commission. They have for some time been threatening to take military action in Palestine and to incite disturbances there. They profess not to intend to start any trouble while the British administration is still in Palestine. The Mufti will however no doubt do his best to stir up trouble both in Palestine and outside.

5. This being the Arab attitude, it is difficult to see how an Arab State can be set up as recommended by the United Nations. The Arabs – both Arab Governments and Palestinian Arabs – are themselves divided and there will be various claims to the Arab areas of Palestine. There is very little prospect of the Arabs being willing to co-operate in working the Joint Economic Board. This might have an important effect on the economy of the whole country.

6. *Attitude of His Majesty's Government at United Nations*

The United Kingdom representatives at the United Nations, while assisting the respective Committees with factual information, have consistently taken the line that we would not comment on the substance of the partition proposal or any other proposal which was before the Assembly. Our position as regards the enforcement of this or any other settlement was, however, made abundantly clear as follows:–

(a) We would not be responsible for enforcing a settlement which was not agreed by both Jews and Arabs.

(b) If invited to participate with other United Nations in enforcing a settlement which was not agreed by Jews and Arabs, we would decide according to our idea of the justice of the settlement and the difficulty of enforcing it. (Repeated efforts have been made during the discussions at the United Nations to involve us in the implementation of United Nations recommendations. All such attempts have been resisted as this would have involved us in assuming the major role and the settlement in fact recommended is manifestly most unpopular with one of the parties.)

(c) We would in any case, failing Jewish-Arab agreement, withdraw from Palestine by 1st August, 1948.

(d) In the course of our withdrawal, our troops and administration could not be used to enforce a United Nations settlement which was not agreed by both Jews and Arabs or to support a United Nations Commission in enforcing it.

7. This neutral policy is amply justified on two main grounds:–

(a) We have tried on numerous occasions in the past to put forward solutions for the settlement of Palestine. Each one has been rejected by one side or the other, or both. We have been suspected of ulterior aims in Palestine. If we had now associated ourselves with any positive proposal, we should have diverted on to ourselves the opposition and resistance or one or both of the parties.

(b)We undertook in the mandate to establish in Palestine a national home for the Jewish people on the clear understanding that nothing should be done which might prejudice the civil and religious rights of existing non-Jewish communities in Palestine. It has proved impossible to reconcile these two objectives and we are therefore justified in laying down the mandate, which has proved unworkable. We did not undertake in the mandate to establish a Jewish or Arab State by force or to coerce either party in the interests of the other. If we were to undertake it, or to be associated in any way with the enforcement of a settlement as unpopular with one of the parties as that now recommended by the United Nations, the whole responsibility would fall on us, as the only armed forces on the spot are ours. It would thus clearly be against our interests to become involved in major repressive actions in Palestine, which would most seriously affect our whole political, strategical and economic situation throughout the Middle East and the Moslem. world.[1]

Note

1. The Cabinet discussed this paper on 4 December, and laid down the principle that 'while His Majesty's Government should do nothing to obstruct the carrying out of the United Nations' decision, British troops and the British Administration should in no circumstances become involved in enforcing it or maintaining law and order while the United Nations Commission enforced it.', C.M. 93 (47). It was also agreed to end British civil administration by 15 May 1948, and to complete withdrawal by 1 August; the United Nations Commission should arrive no earlier than two weeks before 15 May.

DOCUMENT 46

Colonial Economic Policy: Sir Philip Mitchell (Government House, Kenya) to A. Creech Jones, 6 December 1947, CO 852/989/3

Dear Secretary of State,

In view of the discussions at the recent African Governors' Conference on the subject of marketing of Colonial produce, and the fact disclosed there that at any rate in official circles in the Colonial Office views are held which appear to me to conflict with the real interests of the Colonies as well as of Great Britain, I am taking the liberty of sending you a copy of a document I produced when I was High Commissioner for the Western Pacific.[1] There is matter in it which might have to be altered in the light of subsequent events, but generally speaking I would re-write it again to-day in much the same terms. I owe you an apology for sending to so busy a man such a long document, and I can hardly hope that you will read the whole of it, but the first three or four pages, and the last, contain the gist of the matter.

I realise fully that it is to the interests of the people of Great Britain to obtain tropical produce at reasonable prices. Nevertheless, if we are to continue to sell to you we must be able to buy from you, and it is therefore essential that the disastrous gap between consumer goods prices and produce prices should be narrowed. In fact, it is continuously expanding for reasons which are as apparent to you as they are to us. If it is not possible intentionally and consciously to introduce a principle different from that of obtaining products at the lowest price which by any means the producer can be compelled to accept, then in countries with virtually no organisation of labour, or very rudimentary organisation of labour, the production will inevitably be made cheaper at the expense either of the small producer, or of the labour employed by the larger producers. Taking the broad view, therefore, it is as much to the interest of a manufacturing country such as Great Britain as it is of a producing country in the case of Colonial products, that prices should be paid which will make it possible first to escape from the low wage economy which so mitigates against consumption of goods from industrial countries, and secondly, from a level of prices to small producers which can only be obtained by selling the fertility of the soil through wrong agricultural methods.

The whole position appears to me to be the more tragic in that, during two wars, the fact that bulk buying can be organised in a satisfactory manner to the advantage of all parties has been demonstrated. Nevertheless, in spite of the views expressed by Sir Stafford Cripps and yourself at the Governors' Conference, expressions of opinion by departmental officials indicated quite clearly that they considered that the sooner we returned to the chaotic conditions that existed between the wars, the better. It does not seem to me that it has even now been realised in a good many quarters in London that those conditions were a ghastly failure, and in themselves a large part of the cause of the poverty and misery in many countries, Northern Europe included, which in the event led to the establishment of totalitarian states and to war.

However, I must not repeat the argument in this letter. I will only hope that you may be able to find time to read it, and to consider whether, as a matter of policy, it should not be laid down that these buying contracts must be based on a policy of fair standard of living to the producer and his labour, not out of any sentimental or soft-hearted wish to do good to other people at the expense of the British taxpayer, but as a matter of hard common sense in order that those from whom you buy may be able to buy from you. The incidental advantages to British merchant shipping are also not to be overlooked.

I have written in similar terms to Sir Stafford Cripps & Mr Harold Wilson,[2] sending them copies of the paper.

Yours sincerely,
P. E. Mitchell.

Notes

1. 'Post War Reconstruction – Fiji and the Western Pacific. No. 5. Note on Colonial Primary Produce Markets after the War'. February, 1944.
2. Wilson, James Harold, b.1916; President of the Board of Trade, September 1947–April 1951.

DOCUMENT 47

Local Government Policy: Extract from a Minute by A. B. Cohen, 11 December 1947, CO 847/35/47234/1/1947

I think that I ought to take the opportunity, without going into detail, to give my impressions of the work now being carried on in the various African Territories on local government as it emerges from the despatches on this file and as I have been able to gather it from discussions with officers at the summer school and elsewhere.

We can be generally satisfied with the progress being made in Kenya, Uganda and Northern Rhodesia. The despatches from the three territories . . . are documents of first-rate importance which deserve the warm commendation of the Secretary of State. Sir John Hall's policy of vigorous development of local government bodies with devolution of powers to them is particularly promising. Sir Philip Mitchell proposes to set up an African Affairs Commission which, in the circumstances of Kenya, seems to me a step warmly to be welcomed. The Northern Rhodesia despatch is more pedestrian but the work being carried out in Northern Rhodesia in the field of native administration is, I think, considering the conditions, as good as anything in Africa.

We can also be well satisfied, I think, with the state of affairs in Zanzibar and the Gambia. Sir Vincent Glenday is pushing forward vigorously with the development of local government,[1] long overdue in Zanzibar, and has responded magnificently to the stimulus we gave him on this matter shortly after he took up his appointment. His despatch of the 28th March has been followed up by another despatch with concrete proposals which have now been approved and put into effect. I think also that Mr A. Wright has the position well in hand in the Gambia.[2]

The position is not so satisfactory in Nyasaland although they fully accept the Secretary of State's views, are going to appoint a Secretary for African Affairs and a Native Courts Adviser, and are obviously reviewing their whole position. Mr A. H. Cox,[3] who is travelling with Lord Hailey, has written privately to Mr Cartland to say that things seem to have stood still in Nyasaland for a good number of years. I fear that that was also my impression. I propose to mention the matter again to Mr Colby as I am sure that some stimulus is needed in the right direction.[4]

Of the three main West African territories I feel much less qualified to judge and I shall, of course, be giving special attention to this field when I am in West Africa. I must say, however, that the despatches from the Gold Coast, Sierra Leone and Nigeria are mediocre in quality and do not give the impression that the secretariats who were responsible for writing them are organised on the right basis to deal with local government. As far as the Gold Coast is concerned at any rate, the practical performance is very much better, particularly in Ashanti, and I do not think that we really need be worried about the conduct of local govt. affairs in the Gold Coast. There has also been much good work going on in Sierra Leone and in parts of Nigeria. I must say, however, that from all I have heard I am not happy about the state of affairs in Northern Nigeria, where a fog of complacency seems to me to have been spreading, leading to inactivity in local government at the higher levels and frustration at the lower levels. Perhaps this is a false impression which will be corrected when I go there.

Generally, I feel that the three West African territories have not got down properly to the problem of organising the study and formation of policy on local government. This problem is much more difficult in West Africa than in East Africa, since one has to combine the required degree of co-ordination at the centre with the necessary devolution to Chief Commissioners. I hope to acquire some more ideas on this subject next year. Meanwhile I hope I shall not be laying myself open to the charge of an East African bias in calling attention to the fact that it is from the three territories which have had Secretaries for African Affairs, or the equivalent, for some time that we have received really good despatches on this subject.

I have left Tanganyika to the last because I am really worried about the despatch of the 8th November which Sir William Battershill told me that he wrote largely himself. It can only be described as an extremely defeatist document. In brief it says that the provincial administration is so absorbed with other questions, and particularly with economic questions, that it cannot devote the necessary time to what Sir W. Battershill agrees is its real task of encouraging local government. It also says that the African material available in Tanganyika has not yet been developed to the stage at which it can normally play the kind of part which we should like to see it playing in the sphere of local government. These depressing conclusions, in my view, do less than justice to the developments in local government going forward among the Wachagga and Wasukuma and also in other areas. Nevertheless it is undoubtedly true that the sparsity of population in Tanganyika makes the development of local government in many areas particularly difficult. I should have thought myself that it was no more difficult than, for example, in large parts of Northern Rhodesia, and I am not absolutely clear why the burden of responsibilities on the provincial administration is more pressing in Tanganyika than elsewhere. Admittedly they have the groundnut scheme which is absorbing more of the energies of Government than is perhaps generally realised. For that reason I am sure that we must not be too exacting. But I am not entirely happy at leaving things as they are described in the Governor's despatch.

I had a longish talk with Sir W. Battershill on this subject on the day before he left London. As diffidently as possible I indicated to him our disappointment at his despatch and our disquiet at the limited extent to which the ideas put forward in the Secretary of State's despatch could apparently be carried into effect in Tanganyika at the present time. I ventured to point out that in the period before the war Tanganyika had always been regarded as leading the way in African administration. Unfortunately, owing to shortage of staff and other reasons, it now seemed that Kenya, Uganda and Northern Rhodesia were all making more rapid progress. Sir W. Battershill showed that he was very sympathetic to all our ideas and he said that he had felt bound to paint the picture as it really is and not as both he and we should like it to be. I think that he is very much concerned lest, in the various proposals which we make to Governments, we try to put more on to their plate than the present organisation can carry; and I must say that I have a great deal of sympathy with his point of view. At the same time, particularly in Tanganyika, we have got to push forward. The Governor's despatch does not give us very useful material with which to face the Trusteeship Council. I told Sir W. Battershill that I thought that the Secretary of State when he saw his despatch would be rather disappointed. The question arises whether the Secretary of State should send a personal letter to the Governor on some of the points which I have made. I must confess that I am undecided on this. I can see the advantage in doing so. On the other hand, Sir W. Battershill has many anxieties at present; he has for example just agreed to a Trusteeship Council visit next year. He has a formidable task in front of him and I am not sure how much good will be done by pressing him on this particular issue. My talk may have done some good and they have a new Secretary for African Affairs. The matter is an important one and the Secretary of State may wish to have a word with us on it. Meanwhile I submit the draft despatches for approval.

ABC 11/12/47

Notes

1. Glenday, Sir Vincent Goncalves, b.1891; British Resident, Zanzibar, 1946–51.
2. Wright, Andrew Barkworth, b.1895; Governor and Commander-in-Chief, The Gambia, 1947–9.
3. Cox, Arthur Henry, b.1888; Resident, Buganda, 1932–44; retired, but employed at the Colonial Office 1947–9.
4. Colby, Geoffrey Francis Taylor, b. 1901; service in Nigeria 1925–47; Governor and Commander-in-Chief, Nyasaland, 1948.

DOCUMENT 48

'The First Aim of British Foreign Policy', Memorandum by the Secretary of State for Foreign Affairs, 4 January 1948, CAB 129/23

TOP SECRET

C.P. (48) 6
4th January, 1948

CABINET

THE FIRST AIM OF BRITISH FOREIGN POLICY

MEMORANDUM BY THE SECRETARY OF STATE FOR FOREIGN AFFAIRS

IT must be recognised that the Soviet Government has formed a solid political and economic block behind a line running from the Baltic along the Oder, through Trieste to the Black Sea. There is no prospect in the immediate future that we shall be able to re-establish and maintain normal relations with European countries behind that line. As I have explained in a separate paper these countries are dominated by the Communists, although they are only a minority in each country. Indeed we shall be hard put to it to stem the further encroachment of the Soviet tide. It is not enough to reinforce the physical barriers which still guard our Western civilisation. We must also organise and consolidate the ethical and spiritual forces inherent in this Western civilisation of which we are the chief protagonists. This in my view can only be done by creating some form of union in Western Europe, whether of a formal or informal character, backed by the Americas and the Dominions.

The Situation.

In another paper I have attempted to give my colleagues a sober and factual account of Russian policy. It is clear that from secure entrenchments behind their line the Russians are exerting a constantly increasing pressure which threatens the whole fabric of the West. In some Western countries the danger is still latent but in Germany, France, Trieste, Italy and Greece the conflicting forces are already at grips with one another. In each country the issue is still in doubt and we must act resolutely if we are to prevail. The Soviet Government has based its policy on the expectation that Western Europe will sink into economic chaos and they may be relied upon to place every possible obstacle in the path of American aid and of Western European recovery. Our course is equally clear. I have done and will continue to do all I can to bring the Marshall Plan to fruition. But essential though it is, progress in the economic field will not in itself suffice to call a halt to the Russian threat. Political and, indeed, spiritual forces must be mobilised in our defence.

The Western Union

I believe therefore that we should seek to form with the backing of the Americas and the Dominions a Western democratic system comprising, if possible, Scandinavia, the Low Countries, France, Portugal, Italy and Greece. As soon as circumstances permit we should of course wish also to include Spain and Germany, without whom no Western system can be complete. This may seem a somewhat fanciful conception, but events are moving fast and the sense of a common danger drives countries to welcome to-morrow solutions which appear unpractical and unacceptable to-day. Almost all the countries I have listed have been nurtured on civil liberties and on the fundamental human rights. The recent proceedings of the Human Rights Commission at Geneva have shown that of the eighteen States represented, all except Russia and three satellites were in substantial agreement with the British draft of an International Convention for the protection of these civil liberties and human rights. Moreover, most Western European countries have such recent experience of Nazi rule that they can apprehend directly what is involved in their loss. All in a greater or lesser degree sense the imminence of the Communist peril and are seeking some assurance of salvation. I believe therefore that the moment is ripe for a consolidation of Western Europe. This need not take the shape of a formal alliance, though we have an alliance with France and may conclude one with other countries. It does, however, mean close consultation with each of the Western European countries, beginning with economic questions. We in Britain can no longer stand outside Europe and insist that our problems and position are quite separate from those of our European neighbours. Our treaty relations with the various countries might differ, but between all there would be an understanding backed by power, money and resolution and bound together by the common ideals for which the Western Powers have twice in one generation shed their blood.

I am aware that the Soviet Government would react against this policy as savagely as they have done against the Marshall Plan. It would be described as an offensive alliance directed against the Soviet Union. On this point I can only say that in the situation in which we have been placed by Russian policy half measures are useless. If we are to preserve peace and our own safety at the same time, we can only do so by the mobilisation of such a moral and material force as will create confidence and energy on the one side and inspire respect and caution on the other. The alternative is to acquiesce in continued Russian infiltration and helplessly to witness the piecemeal collapse of one Western bastion after another.

The policy I have outlined will require strong British leadership in order to secure its acceptance in Europe on one hand and in the Dominions and the Americas on the other. Material aid will have to come principally from the United States, but the countries of Western Europe which despise the spiritual values of America will look to us for political and moral guidance and for assistance in building up a counter attraction to the baleful tenets of communism within their borders and in recreating a healthy society wherever it has been shaken or shattered by the war. I believe that we have the resources with which to perform this task.

Provided we can organise a Western European system such as I have outlined above, backed by the power and resources of the Commonwealth and of the Americas, it should be possible to develop our own power and influence to equal that of the United States of America and the U.S.S.R. We have the material resources in the Colonial Empire, if we develop them, and by giving a spiritual lead now we should be able to carry out our task in a way which will show clearly that we are not subservient to the United States of America or to the Soviet Union.

I have already broached the conception of what I called a spiritual union of the West tentatively to Mr Marshall and M Bidault, both of whom seemed to react favourably without of course committing themselves.[1] I now propose, if my colleagues agree, to ventilate the idea in public in my speech in the forthcoming Foreign Affairs Debate and thereafter to pursue it, as occasion demands, with the Governments concerned.

E. B.

1. Marshall, George C., b.1880; professional soldier, Chief of Staff of the United States Army 1939–45; Secretary of State 1947–9, and initiator of the European Recovery Programme (the 'Marshall Plan'). Bidault, Georges, b.1899; President of the French National Resistance Council 1940–5, and Minister of Foreign Affairs 1944–8; Premier, 1949–50.

DOCUMENT 49

West African Policy: A. B. Cohen to Sir J. Macpherson, 12 June 1948, secret and personal, CO 583/287/5/30453/4

I suggested to Lloyd, and he agreed, that we ought to send you immediately for your secret information a copy of the Gold Coast Commission's report, which was signed this week.[1] The report is now to be printed here and will be published probably as a Command Paper and probably about the end of July. The present intention is to publish at the same time a brief statement of Government's intentions regarding the report and Creasy, as you probably know, is flying home at the beginning of July to discuss the recommendations and the terms of such a statement with the Secretary of State.

Obviously the report when published will arouse public interest in Nigeria and this applies particularly to the constitutional chapter with its rather radical recommendations. It is for that reason specially that we have thought that you would like to see the report straight away and it would be of considerable interest to us to have any comments which occur to you on the probable reactions in Nigeria. If we could get these before the talks with Creasy timed to start on the 4th July, it would be convenient; but I do not want to put you under any obligation in this respect.

It is pretty certain that Zik will want to make capital out of the report and no doubt you will be considering this aspect of the matter.[2]

Notes

1. *Report of the Commission of Enquiry into Disturbances in the Gold Coast, 1948*, Colonial No. 231.
2. Zik: Azikiwe, B. N., see Document 39, note 2.

DOCUMENT 50

West African Policy: Extract from Sir J. Macpherson to A. B. Cohen, 28 June 1948, secret and personal,[1] CO 583/287/5/30453/4

There will certainly be lively reactions in Nigeria to the report, and as you say, it is the proposals for constitutional advance that will arouse particular interest. My first thought is that it will be assumed here, as well as in the Gold Coast, that any constitutional advance that follows upon the proposals of the Commission has been achieved as a direct result of disorder; this assumption will do great harm in leading colonial peoples to believe that advance is more certainly and more speedily achieved by violence than by constitutional means. Apart from the encouragement given to political extremists throughout West Africa the proposals in the report will cause serious misgivings amongst those in Nigeria (particularly in the North and West) who wish to see advance along different lines.

The timing of the report is very unfortunate for us in Nigeria . . . I have referred earlier in this letter to the N.C.N.C's [National Council of Nigeria and the Cameroons] attitude towards the Emirs and Chiefs. The Commission made no immediate recommendation regarding the future position of the Gold Coast Chiefs but they gave a lot of space to the criticisms made by Africans with a modern political outlook, and they did not contemplate the retention of the Gold Coast Chiefs otherwise than 'in a form which is a pale reflection of the past'. This will upset our traditional elements and encourage the extremists; and the result will not be conducive to sound progress.

At a first reading I do not think that, apart from the Constitutional proposals, there is much in the report that will cause strong reaction in Nigeria. (We are engaged in action on Nigerianisation of the Senior Service and on conditional sales. Our P.R.O. is good. And we have agreed to a swollen shoot rehabilitation subsidy which, though under criticism, is equal to the upper limit proposed by the Commission for the Gold Coast.)

The real question is what action we should take as a result of the report. I shall not attempt in this letter to deal fully with that . . . We *may* have to alter our time-table for revision of the Constitution but even if that were decided I should be averse from making any statement of our intention in advance of publication of the Gold Coast report. Our next Legislative Council meeting will begin about the 17th of August . . . We *might* avoid being put completely on the defensive by making a statement at the opening of the meeting. The N.C.N.C. will not have had much time to digest the report.

Note

1. Macpherson is replying to Cohen's letter (Document 49).

DOCUMENT 51

'The Colonial Empire and the Economic Crisis', Circular Despatch on behalf of the Secretary of State for the Colonies, 26 July 1948, T 229/220

The Secretary of State has asked me to send you the enclosed memorandum on 'the Colonial Empire and the Economic Crisis.' He sends it with some diffidence because of the considerable public discussion which has already taken place on the economic problems confronting the world and because Colonial Governors have already received a number of memoranda on the matter and have taken action to cope with some of the difficulties confronting us at the present. Nevertheless, there is some danger that without wide publicity inside the territories on the essential facts of the present continuing crisis certain misconceptions of policy may arise and, consequently, some deterioration of relations between Britain and the peoples of the territories may occur. Misunderstandings are likely if a wrong approach is made in Britain and too little emphasis is given to the place of Colonial Governments and peoples in economic expansion; or when it is expected that the Colonial public should be as alive as we are ourselves to the economic situation which has come about in the world and the particular needs of Western Europe. The public here are conscious of the heavy burden they carried in the war relative to their own resources, a burden probably heavier than that carried by any other country, and yet they must continue to face sacrifice and scarcity with the promise of more to come. They do not always find it easy to understand that other people may not fully appreciate their difficulties and sacrifices.

2. On the other hand, considering the great difference which as yet exists between the average standard of living of the British people and that of the vast majority of Colonial peoples, it is not easy for the latter to understand why the former regard themselves as making any sacrifice at all. There are here obvious seeds of discontent and unhappy relations if public pronouncements are not very carefully considered and handled. It is important that those overseas should realise that the war was concerned with the preservation of the freedom of the peoples everywhere and that the prosperity of Britain is an essential factor in promoting the well-being and economic prosperity of the Colonial peoples. Equally, while we are all

mindful of the deep rooted loyalty to Britain in the overseas territories, a false emphasis here regarding the present economic difficulties, or an attitude which assumes that economic development of the territories may be imposed as if the territories existed to meet the present shortages and difficulties of Western Europe, may prejudice good relations and increase the political difficulties in the territories. It hardly needs to be said that there is no intention on the part of His Majesty's Government to exploit the Colonial Empire for the sake of selfish United Kingdom interests or to impede in any way the political progress of the Colonial people, even if some individual statements made or action taken under pressure of present circumstances may perhaps expose us to doubt from certain types of critic.

3. The Secretary of State is convinced that we can escape most of these misunderstandings and turn the present situation to account by using the present period of crisis and trial for the whole Empire so as to demonstrate to ourselves and to the outside world that the inter-dependence of the Colonial territories and Britain is a real and powerful thing. To this end the ready interchange of information is a first necessity. I spoke earlier about the tendency on the part of the United Kingdom to assume that everybody else automatically realises this country's present difficulties and their causes. Clearly we cannot expect the fullest understanding of our difficulties from the Colonial public unless we tell them the facts, and unless this is done we ourselves at this end are largely to blame for the misconceptions and confusions which are bound to ensue. For example, people in the Colonial Empire are no doubt apt to wonder whether the United Kingdom is really in such difficulty as is made out, seeing that the Chancellor of the Exchequer is budgeting this year for a very large surplus (though admittedly at the cost of very large taxation); and they are also no doubt tempted to believe that the assistance which the United Kingdom is deriving from the European Recovery Programme puts us in 'Easy Street.' The Secretary of State feels that the Colonial Office can assist in providing material to counter any such misconceptions and to emphasise the really serious nature of the present economic position.

4. The enclosed memorandum has been prepared in the Office as a first essay in this task of 'telling the facts'. It sets out the salient facts about the present economic and financial crisis in this country and its repercussions in the Colonial field. It is,

admittedly, not intended to be a public document, and should not be quoted or referred to in any public statement. We do hope, however, that the points which it seeks to make can in one way or another be made available to the public and that, subject to any comments which you or your Advisers may have, it may be found useful as background guidance for statements in your territory.

5. We should of course be most grateful for any comments which you may like to make on the problem raised in this letter or on the memorandum itself. I do not forecast a series of regular 'bulletins' but the memorandum is intended to be a beginning of a continuing process whereby we, from the London end, will try to send periodical appreciations of the financial and economic position of the United Kingdom. One final point I would urge. The economic aspect of Colonial policy is but part of the general plan and purpose of Britain in the Colonies and in no way, in our present efforts, diminishes the importance we attach to our present and long term policies for social welfare and political responsibility. All publicity should be directed to the balanced presentation of the essential features of British policy, even if from time to time emphasis is required on one aspect or another.

(Signed) T. I. K. Lloyd

DOCUMENT 52

'Constitutional Development in Smaller Colonial Territories', Memorandum by the Secretary of State for the Colonies, 8 December 1948, CAB 134/55

SECRET
C.A. (48) 19
8th December, 1948.

CABINET
Commonwealth Affairs Committee

Constitutional Development in Smaller Colonial Territories
Memorandum by the Secretary of State for the Colonies

1. At their 8th Meeting the Committee invited me to consider, and to circulate a paper dealing with, a proposal that an enquiry should be undertaken into the question of constitutional development in the smaller Colonial territories.[1]
2. The latest general statement of our constitutional objectives is as follows:-

> The central purpose of British Colonial Policy is simple. It is to guide the Colonial territories to responsible self-government within the Commonwealth in conditions that ensure to the people concerned both a fair standard of living and freedom from oppression from any quarter. (Cmd. 7433, paragraph 3).

3. This statement embodies by implication the obvious truth that full independence can be achieved only if a territory is economically viable and capable of defending its own interests. In fact, Colonial territories can be placed in three classes:-
   (1) Those which are potentially capable of achieving full independence;
   (2) Those which can combine with others to form units capable of full independence;
   (3) Those which fall into neither of the above categories.
4. This paper is concerned chiefly with the third class. But I should point out that constitutional progress has been going on over the whole colonial field at an ever quickening pace during the last decade. These internal developments have

gone forward *ad hoc*, and their pace has depended upon social and political conditions in the individual territories and not upon extraneous considerations such as are involved when the question of granting 'Dominion Status' arises. Changes in the political institutions of a territory have sometimes followed on the recommendations of Commissions but, broadly, the individual position of each territory has been under the constant review of the Governor and the Colonial Office. Considerable thought has also been given to the grouping of territories but the ultimate constitutional status of certain of the smaller territories has not been the subject of any Enquiry.

5. My colleagues will know that some consideration was given to the grouping of territories by the Coalition Government, and much progress has been made since then. The form which grouping takes has varied according to the circumstances of each case. The principal developments are:-
   (a) *West African Council* (includes Nigeria, Gold Coast, Sierra Leone and Gambia). No executive powers, but it secures co-ordination for certain common services and regional problems (e.g. research, transport, security, etc.).
   (b) *East Africa Commission* (includes Uganda, Kenya, Tanganyika). Executive power in respect of transport, research, economic regional development, etc.
   (c) *Central Africa Council* (includes Southern Rhodesia, Northern Rhodesia, Nyasaland). Advisory council of representatives of these three governments. Develops certain common services and co-ordinates policy, e.g. labour, communications.
   (d) *West Indian Development and Welfare Organisation*, for advising and stimulating British West Indian governments. *The Caribbean Commission*, representative of U.S.A., France, Holland and United Kingdom also exists for advisory services and achieves a degree of co-operation in the Caribbean. A movement towards *federation* of the British West Indian territories is being pursued as a result of the Montego Bay Conference last year.
   (e) *South East Asia* (North Borneo, Sarawak, Brunei, Singapore and Malaya). A central government for the Malay States etc., has been achieved. A Commissioner General in South East Asia has been appointed.

(f) *South Pacific Commission* (includes Fiji, Western Pacific High Commission Territories and Kingdom of Tonga). A consultative and advisory body, comprising representatives of the Netherlands, France, United Kingdom, U.S.A., Australia and New Zealand, in matters affecting the economic and social development of the territories concerned and the welfare and advancement of their peoples.

6. Of the Colonial territories as at present organised, it is hardly likely that full self-government will be achieved under any foreseeable conditions (apart from association with other territories) by any except Nigeria, the Gold Coast, and the Federation of Malaya with Singapore. There are also territories where our aim is to promote closer union or federation in order that units capable of independence may be built up:-(a) S.E. Asia, (b) Caribbean Colonies, (c) East and Central African Territories.

7. I refer now to the smaller Colonies.

(i) *In Africa*:

(a) Gambia. Is part of the West African Council and in several services is associated with Sierra Leone.

(b) Somaliland. Has affinities with both Kenya and Aden.

(c) High Commissioner's Territories in South Africa (dealt with by the Commonwealth Relations Office).

(ii) *In Mediterranean*:

(a) Malta. Enjoys internal responsibility.

(b) Cyprus. Constitution in abeyance.

(c) Gibraltar. New constitution recently considered.

(iii) *In Indian Ocean*:

(a) Aden.) In each case minor constitutional
(b) Mauritius) changes have been made in recent
(c) Seychelles) years.

(d) Maldive Islands. A Sultanate under British protection (now under the Commonwealth Relations Office).

[(e) The Sultanate of Muscat (Oman) and the Sheikdoms of Kuwait and Bahrein ought perhaps to be included in this list. These are independent states to which British protection is afforded, through the Foreign Office.]

(iv) *Atlantic Ocean*:

(a) Bermuda and Bahamas. They have ancient constitutions conferring fairly complete local government

and are not likely to seek an alteration of status.
(b) St Helena (with Ascension and Tristan da Cunha).
(c) Falkland Islands (and Dependencies).

(v) *Pacific Ocean*:
(a) Hong Kong.
(b) Fiji. It is doubtful if Fiji should be included in this list. Administration is assisted on education and medical side by proximity of New Zealand.
(c) Western Pacific High Commission Territories (Gilbert and Ellice Islands, Solomon Islands, New Hebrides, Tonga, etc). (In the New Hebrides there is an Anglo/French Condominion).

8. I agree that some enquiry should be made into the present situation of these smaller territories and the probable trend of their future political development. Such enquiry could advise whether it is practicable or desirable to define the ultimate objective in the case of particular territories or to lay down any general principle on which policy should be based, to examine any practical steps which might be suggested for promoting healthy political progress, for mitigating the parochialism and other evils to which small and isolated communities are subject, and for giving the peoples of these territories a genuine sense of partnership in the Commonwealth. It should also take account of experiments in the way of amalgamation which have been tried in the past (e.g. Gambia and Sierra Leone, Mauritius and Seychelles), and seek to discover whether the reasons for the abandonment of these experiments hold good in modern conditions. It should consider the present political, legal and administrative structures and whether by fusion or by combination unnecessary waste may be avoided and a higher standard of efficiency attained.

9. I suggest that the enquiry should be conducted by a small working party of experts. Three should suffice: a Chairman from outside, with the Legal Adviser to the Colonial and Commonwealth Relations Offices and a senior administrative officer of the Colonial Office as members.

10. I regard it as essential that the enquiry should be conducted on a strictly confidential basis and the fact that it is taking place should not be published even in official circles. Any hint which might reach the Colonies that such an enquiry was proceeding could only raise undesirable speculations and lead to political agitation.

ACJ

Note

1. This memorandum, C.A. (48) 19, was written for the Cabinet's Commonwealth Affairs Committee, chaired by the Prime Minister, and was discussed at its meeting on 19 January 1949 (CAB 134/56: C.A. (49)1).

DOCUMENT 53

'The East African Groundnuts Scheme': Memorandum by the Minister of Food, 11 November 1949, CAB 129/37 Pt 2

SECRET
C.P. (49) 231
11TH NOVEMBER, 1949

CABINET

THE EAST AFRICAN GROUNDNUTS SCHEME

Memorandum by the Minister of Food

When I circulated the final Annual Report of the Overseas Food Corporation (C.P. (49) 210) I undertook to submit my proposals for the future development of the East African Groundnuts Scheme. The programme for the next four years prepared by the Overseas Food Corporation has been examined in detail by my officials and, although commercial considerations alone do not provide justification for its acceptance, they have recommended that it should be adopted, having regard to the wider implications mentioned in this memorandum. I have discussed the plan with the Chancellor of the Exchequer and Secretary of State for the Colonies and they are agreed that the plan should be adopted. I therefore seek the authority of my colleagues for the following proposals for the further development of the East African Groundnuts Scheme.

Reasons for the present proposals

2. It became apparent at the beginning of 1949 that original estimates (both those made in Mr. Frank Samuel's original Scheme, and in the report of the Wakefield/Rosa/Martin Mission) of the cost of clearing the African bush were so faulty that there was no prospect of attaining the original White Paper (Cmd. 7030) estimates of cleared acres within the limits of the financial resources for which the Corporation had Parliamentary authority.[1] The Corporation's first proposals (made in the light of their knowledge of actual clearing costs) envisaged a borrowing of some £67 million to clear 1,200,000 acres. But since their borrowing power is limited under the Overseas Resources

Development Act to £50 million (plus £5 million which may be borrowed on short term) the Chancellor of the Exchequer and I felt unable to accept their programme and they were asked to put forward revised proposals which kept expenditure within the limits of their borrowing powers.

The present proposals

3. The proposals which I have received from the Overseas Food Corporation are set out in the annex to this memorandum. It represents what they consider to be the most economical use of the resources available to them for continuing their development work. Briefly, what they propose is that they should be authorised to proceed with development in the period up to 1954 on the basis that by the end of that time they will have achieved the clearing of 600,000 acres at a total estimated borrowing of about £47.6 million. After allowing for the £2 million already required for the promising Queensland Sorghum Scheme this will virtually commit the present financial resources of the Corporation.
4. The Corporation propose to make the most economic use of the resources which they have available to them. This will enable them to have cleared, by the end of 1953, 90,000 acres at Kongwa, 90,000 acres at Urambo and 420,000 acres in the Southern Province. By the end of 1950 there will be cleared 90,000 acres at Kongwa, 90,000 acres at Urambo and 22,000 acres in the Southern Province. In other words, clearing has already been completed at Kongwa and will be completed in twelve months' time at Urambo. From then onwards the whole clearing effort of the Corporation will be concentrated in the Southern Province which the agricultural experts believe to be much the most promising of the three areas.
5. The Corporation's programme shows a sharp reduction in the rate at which they will require to borrow money. Their borrowing in the current year (ending 31st March, 1950) is estimated at £10,650,000 compared with £13,350,000 in 1948–49, and £8,000,000 in 1947–48. Their further requirements are:-

	£
1950–51	4,500,000
1951–52	4,000,000
1952–53	3,300,000
1953–54	800,000

In addition a further £3,000,000 are earmarked for reserves to cover the risk of losses on agricultural operations on the newly cleared lands during the development years of the scheme to 1954. The greater part of the expenditure from 1950 onwards will be for wages and local materials. The Corporation's programme therefore fulfils a further condition which the Chancellor invited me urgently to request them to provide for: it provides, that is to say, for a very rapid fall in the rate of investment of money. This rate of investment falls from £14 million a year in the first quarter of this year to £4.5 million during 1950/51. Indeed, it is only possible to come down next year to less than one-third of the peak annual investment of last year because the main capital works are at length almost completed.

Is the Corporation's plan feasible?

6. *Technical Problems*. I asked my officials to examine, in so far as they were able, the technical bases of the new plan. They report that there seems no reason why the development programme submitted by the Corporation should not be achieved within the time allowed. It is true that the programme calls for a rapid increase in the annual extent of clearing in the Southern Province where there has so far been least experience, and one naturally remembers the contrast between expectation and experience in the clearing of Kongwa. But there are substantial grounds for believing that these disappointments will not be repeated. There is available the accumulated wealth of experience at Kongwa, and at Urambo (where vegetation conditions are very similar to those in the Southern Province and where clearing has been proceeding for the last six months at the estimated speed and cost): there has been a natural increase of efficiency in the organisation and deployment of tractor operations: there have been exhaustive surveys of the initial 20,000 acres to be cleared and there is to be selective and *not* block clearing: communications in the shape of the railway (which is now running on the essential 90 mile stretch between the temporary port and the area being cleared) pipe-line, etc. have been built up in advance and the water supplies seem assured. Of course, there are still risks as there must inevitably be with any large-scale enterprise of this kind in tropical Africa. Unexpected difficulties may arise, but what is clear is that in putting forward their proposals the Corporation have been at pains fully to examine the doubtful and difficult factors and to frame their plans on realistic assumptions.

7. *The capital requirements of the new plan*. My officials are also satisfied that the programme should be capable of fulfilment

within the Corporation's borrowing powers, even if it is assumed that in some instances the Corporation have been optimistic in their cost estimates. It is, of course, impossible to make absolutely reliable estimates of all the unknowns. The Corporation estimate that their plan can be carried through by total borrowings of £47,600,000 of which £3,000,000 are earmarked as a reserve to cover the risk of loss on actual agricultural operations during the development period. My officials have checked over this calculation and, after making some adjustments which they feel reasonable but which it is not clear would be wholly acceptable to the Corporation, they conclude that the total borrowings required to complete the plan will be £48,430,000. Both estimates agree therefore that the plan can be carried through within the limit of the resources which have already been approved. And my colleagues will welcome the assurance that these new estimates are based on actual experience in East Africa to a far greater extent than has been possible hitherto. The original calculations were made without the benefit of any practical experience in the actual operations. The Corporation, in framing their new programme, have had the benefit of all the hard won and costly experience of the past three years.

8. *The earning power of the new Scheme*. What sort of asset will the Corporation have in East Africa when their development programme is completed? By the end of 1953 there will be 600,000 acres cleared and 540,000 acres will be under crop in 1954. It is a formidable task to make any reasonable estimate of what the earning power of 540,000 acres will be four years hence. The major uncertainty results from two main variables – the actual yield per acre of oilseeds, and the price of oilseeds in the years ahead. In their case the Corporation have produced their own estimate and another independent estimate has been produced by my officials.

The Corporation's Estimate

9. (a) *The Development Period.* In making their estimates on agricultural operations during the development period (1950–54) the Corporation have assumed yields of 750 lbs. per acre of both groundnuts and sunflower. They have also assumed the current price of oilseeds of £55 per ton for groundnuts and £35 per ton for sunflower seed. If they had accepted a 'safe' estimate of yields (580 lbs. per acre) and if the estimate of oilseed prices prepared by my Ministry (falling to £40 per ton for groundnuts in 1953–54) had also been used, there would be a loss on agricul-

tural operations over the four years of £4,500,000. Against this the Corporation have earmarked £3,000,000 in the belief that both pessimistic assumptions will not be fully realised simultaneously, and because they are determined to secure that the deficiency on agricultural operations in this period does not exceed this figure.

(b) *The First Post Development Year*. The Corporation's estimate for 1954–55 shows an operating profit for that year (after allowing for depreciation but not for interest or amortisation of capital) of £1,097,000. In reaching this figure they have again assumed yields of 750 lbs. per acre, of both groundnuts and sunflower. They have also again assumed the current price of oilseeds of £55 per ton for groundnuts and £35 per ton for sunflower seed. The Corporation have recognised that this profit could easily be turned into a loss if lower yields and if lower prices were assumed. But because there is hardly a limit to the assumptions which can be made for the purpose of these hypothetical calculations the Corporation retain the present prices at the yields which the experts believe will be attained, given experience.

The Ministry of Food's Estimate

10. My officials have made a calculation of what the earning power of the scheme might be in a typical post-development year – not the year 1954–55. On this assumption and allowing for yields of 750 lbs. an acre and their estimate of price of £40 per ton for groundnuts and £27 per ton for sunflower, they estimate that there will be a deficit of £775,000 per year before charging any interests and without amortisation.

The vital assumptions of yields and price

11. (a) *Yields*. The experts still maintain that average yields of 750 lbs. per acre of both groundnuts and sunflower can be attained. While they have suggested that it would be prudent not to rely on yields of more than 580 lbs. in the development period the agricultural general manager in East Africa has assured me that he has not yet found any ground for believing that the 750 lbs. per acre cannot be achieved when the scheme is fully developed and the men are experienced. Of course, like all other farmers they have to accept the hazards of the weather, but in making the estimate of 750 lbs. due regard has been paid to this factor. While as laymen we may approach the experts' figure

with caution, I cannot see any valid reason on which we can challenge their opinion.

(b) *Prices*. Forward estimates of commodity prices are always precarious and while I recognise that my own experts are as capable as anyone in making an estimate I cannot fail to stress the margin of error to which these estimates are subject. When I submitted my original proposal for this scheme my experts advised that the price of groundnuts would 'not fall below £20 per ton' this year. At the moment we have contracted to pay £53 per ton – a price even higher than that at which we were buying groundnuts in 1947. I use that illustration to show the danger of clinging too closely to a hypothetical balance sheet without regard to the uncertainty of the main assumption. On the Corporation's very favourable estimate of price the scheme will earn a margin of £1,000,000 a year; on the Ministry's more pessimistic estimate the scheme will lose £775,000 a year. There is so much uncertainty about these assumptions that no real decisive conclusions, in my opinion, can be drawn from the financial estimates. The scheme might make a surplus, or a loss, mainly according to the prices reached for the product.

Is the new scheme 'economic'?

12. One thing that is certain, however, is that the earning power of a 600,000 acre scheme will not be able to carry the overhead costs which were thought appropriate for 1,200,000 acre scheme (as was proposed a year ago) or 3,000,000 acre scheme (as originally suggested). Both the above calculations have been made on the assumption that no allowance is provided for interest or amortisation of capital. Indeed the various calculations show that it cannot even be certain, because of variable factors of price and yield, that the 600,000 acre scheme will actually earn a surplus on current account. Therefore on purely financial grounds the scheme is not at all attractive. £32,000,000 has already been spent, and a further £16,000,000 is needed over the next four years to produce an asset which cannot even be guaranteed to cover its own operating costs. My officials feel that, in view of the uncertainties about price on purely financial grounds it would not be possible to recommend the acceptance of the Corporation's plan, but they feel that the future of the scheme must be determined by references to wider considerations.

What are the alternative policies?

13. The Corporation set out in paragraph 9 of their memorandum their considered view that there are only two alternative courses of action – either to adopt the plan which they have proposed or to abandon the whole scheme forthwith. But is no middle course possible? At first sight such a middle course appears to have much to commend it. Its adoption would avoid either of the drastic alternatives postulated by the Corporation – the termination of the scheme, with all that this would involve or a further large scale programme involving the borrowing of another £15–17 million at a difficult juncture in our financial history. Would it not be better to clear in the next two years some 'minimum' economic acreage in the Southern Province (say 30,000 to 50,000 acres) and then – unless both the general financial position in the United Kingdom and the prospect of the scheme itself were brighter than now – for the Corporation to settle down for some time to operate their total holdings of say 300,000 acres in the most economic manner possible? This would give the Corporation an opportunity of testing and deciding what would be the most effective longer-term use of the cleared land and it would be in the light of their knowledge that, at a later date, the Government and the Corporation would be able to determine whether the time was ripe for further development work to be undertaken in the Southern Province. Such a view might commend a good deal of support at the present time, when we are being obliged to restrict capital investment. My officials have considered this possibility but have put forward what seem to me very cogent reasons for rejecting it.

14. Firstly, the Corporation have greatly improved the efficiency of their organisation in East Africa. They have already built up the ancillary services such as communications and workshops which will be needed for going on with comparatively large scale development work. They have available a 'striking force' of experienced staff and equipment which is capable of carrying through a clearing effort – which though small in comparison with the original plan will yet employ all their existing resources. It would obviously be wasteful to under-employ this force in what would be no more than a relatively small scale clearing operation. Moreover, a decision to curtail development work would almost certainly result in breaking the force up. It would be the signal to the able men in East Africa to seek a new job elsewhere. They would feel that the scheme had seen its death sentence. And once the team of experienced men was dissipated it would be almost impossible to build it up again.

15. And the resulting asset would have far less chance of successful and economic operation than a total area of 600,000 acres. It would burden the scheme with even greater overheads because the capital expenditure required per cleared acre would be even more disproportionate if spread over only 300,000 acres. Much the larger proportion of capital outlay in the Corporation's programme occurs during the next two years at the end of which the cleared acreage is expected to have reached 300,000 acres, and, although this expenditure is geared to a programme of 600,000 acres, it is very probable indeed that a disproportionate amount, in addition to the sums already spent on preparation, would be involved in undertaking a smaller programme.
16. Furthermore, a reduced programme would not give the scheme a satisfactory trial. It would of necessity limit development in the Southern Province. 180,000 acres would be cleared in Kongwa and Urambo and therefore there would only be the balance to be cleared in the Southern Province which is the most promising area of the three. Any chance of the scheme proving its viability would be severely prejudiced, if not lost.

What would 'closing down' mean?

17. What would be involved in a decision to 'close down' the scheme immediately? If this were done on financial grounds it would require the immediate cancellation of all contracts for the supply of equipment, the dismissal of all the staff in East Africa save those who would be required for the disposal of all equipment and the immediate cessation of all work there. It is most unlikely that more than a small proportion of the cleared land could be used by the Government of Tanganyika. The assets in East Africa would consist of a partly constructed port and nearly completed railway in the Southern Province (the purpose for which would have vanished), several considerable settlements ranging from the new town of Kongwa (which is already the second largest town in Tanganyika) and various scattered housing developments throughout the territory. These towns and townships have each considerable public works in the way of water supply, drainage, electric light and the like – none of them, in the absence of the groundnut scheme itself, would serve any visible purpose; many hundreds of miles of new roads – some, no doubt, of these would be of some use to the community, but in the absence of the groundnut scheme they would also be, to a large extent, wrongly sited: some 100,000 acres of cleared area at Kongwa in the Central Province, in what is

proving the least promising because the least well watered area of the three, 20,000 cleared acres at Urambo in the Western Province and some 2,000 cleared acres in the Southern Province. It is very doubtful whether these cleared acres on these sites would in themselves represent a workable proposition from the agricultural point of view. There can be no reason for questioning the Corporation's views that if the scheme is abandoned now there will be a loss of £30 million. And abandonment of the groundnut scheme will mean the end of the Overseas Food Corporation at a time when there is every sign that they are really taking a grip of the scheme. Mistakes have been made but the great majority of our difficulties result from the early years of the scheme before experience had been built up and when all were working to unattainable targets. The Corporation took over effective control of the scheme on 31st March, 1948, and I have been encouraged by the way in which they have overcome many of the problems which they inherited.

Can His Majesty's Government agree to a closing-down policy?

18. Is this course of closing down the scheme a policy to which the Government can subscribe? We embarked on this job with due realisation of the risks which we had to run. In my paper recommending the adoption of the scheme (C.P. (47) 10 dated 4th January, 1947) I said: 'My colleagues will see that this is a big enterprise; it has to be if it is to meet even a substantial part of our desperate need for fats. My colleagues would not believe me if I tried to pretend to them that such a scheme was free from risk. Of course, serious difficulties and delays, many of them unforeseeable, may arise in the course of a great undertaking of this sort.' It was because the risks were so high that we selected a public corporation to tackle the enterprise. An enterprise of this nature involves considerable risks and I think it would be disastrous for the prospects and prestige of public enterprise if we were to abandon the East African Groundnuts Scheme because some of the risks in the opening years have gone against it. How many of the really large business concerns have been successful right from the outset? Surely commercial experience shows that many of the really great businesses have only been built up after years of extraordinary difficulty – years without dividends, years when capital was written down – but yet successful in the end. Our policy necessarily implies that only public enterprise will be available to take the really big risks involved in opening up new

frontiers in our Colonial Empire. It is vital, therefore, that we should persevere with our efforts unless we are to discredit the very principle of public enterprise, at any rate in this field.

19. And, above all, how could we, after having spent £30 million, abandon the Scheme at this stage, before we have enough experience to judge whether it will prove a success or not? We have no grounds whatever for saying that it will fail, any more than we can 'prove' its ultimate success. We cannot use the costs during the first two years as a sound basis on which to estimate the final operating costs of the Scheme. Until we have allowed development to go on long enough for more reliable estimates of costs to be made, how can we make any real estimate of the final outcome? Surely we should lay ourselves open to every sort of criticism if we were to give up now. Not only should we be abandoning a project which had not had a chance of proving itself, but we should be dealing a severe blow to enterprise throughout the Commonwealth. For the groundnuts scheme has come to be looked upon as a prototype for this kind of large scale development.

The world needs more food

20. The Chief Scientific Officer of the Ministry of Agriculture recently gave it as his opinion that because the population of the world is increasing at the rate of 20 million a year it will be necessary to double the world's food production in the next 26 years. If we are to plan for a satisfactory food supply for the housewives of this country, and for the population of our Colonial territories, we must not try to ignore the effect which this increase in world population, coupled with a general acceptance of the fact that the pre-war standard of nutrition is unacceptable, will have on the world food situation. If we are to plan for plenty we must base our plan on increased production. This means that new frontiers must be opened up. The East African Groundnut Scheme is a pioneering effort to use modern equipment to bring marginal land into service for the production of food and if necessary other raw materials. The real need for the increased supply of food is no less urgent today than it was when the scheme was launched and to abandon it now would only make our eventual long term food problem more difficult. If we can make this project succeed we will have provided a prototype for similar developments elsewhere throughout the world. We will have developed and demonstrated a new clearing and production technique for tropical countries.

The effects of abandonment on our Colonial Territories

21. The Groundnut Scheme has become an important symbol in our Colonial Empire. It is a bold experiment to raise the economic productivity of the African territories by replacing the primitive hoe by modern mechanical agricultural machines. The output per head of the agricultural worker can be lifted substantially and so provides an economic base for the development of a higher standard of life. The work provides openings for skilled and semi-skilled labour. One of the more spectacular successes of the scheme has been the way in which it has been possible to recruit and train local labour for many skilled jobs. Men have trekked from all over Tanganyika Territory to secure jobs. The possibilities for the Africans are considerable. If we abandon all this and break up the scheme, the Africans not only in Tanganyika but throughout the whole of East Africa will suffer a great disappointment and it will be another blow for British prestige.
22. *The effect in the United States.* Some Americans have watched the development of this scheme with close interest. It represents firstly a convincing proof of our determination to develop sterling sources of food supply. Secondly it is a real demonstration of our belief in the development of our backward territories. We are hoping to take full advantage of any opportunities which may arise for United States capital investment in the British Colonies. It would greatly discourage United States help in this field if we abandoned the one really large scale food production project which we have started since the end of the war. How could we expect United States investors to take the kind of risks which we admit to be too great?
23. I feel that it is on these wider grounds of policy that our decision must be based. Our detailed estimates of probable income and expenditure are essential – but not the decisive – evidence. It is not possible to demonstrate that a 600,000 acre scheme will be able to cover its costs – but at the same time it is not possible to prove that it would lose money. The outcome depends on factors which we cannot estimate with any degree of precision. I would be the first to admit that for as far as we can see at the moment we cannot justify the scheme as a purely commercial venture in the precise sense that, allowing for the risks, it is likely to provide a rate of profit in the accepted business sense of that term. The original estimates of costs contained in the Wakefield/Rosa report were too far out for this. But I think that there is every justification for going ahead with the scheme on the sharply reduced basis now proposed when the wider aspects have been taken into account.

24. In making this recommendation that the scheme should go forward on the lines proposed by the Corporation I would ask my colleagues to bear in mind the very great differences between these proposals and those which we had when we first considered the project. The present proposals are based on three years' practical work in the bush under tropical conditions in East Africa. They are put forward by men who have now had years of experience on the job. The plans are based on lessons which have been learnt and in the sure knowledge that the administrative base to support the enterprise has been safely established. The communications, the workshops, the spare parts and all the other administrative facilities which did not exist in 1947 have now been provided. Experienced men now have the tools with which to finish the job. And the Overseas Food Corporation, although it only took over responsibility eighteen months ago, has already shown itself capable of more sustained leadership and effective organisation in East Africa than the Managing Agency.

25. I believe, however, that it is essential to strengthen the Board of the Corporation. For obvious reasons I do not want to go into details in this paper, but I will indicate orally to my colleagues the changes which I have in mind and which I have discussed with the Chancellor. I am confident that the result of these changes will be to secure a Board which will ensure not only that the approved programme is carried out with vigour but that the maximum economies in organisation are achieved.

26. In particular the strengthened Board will have to pay special attention to the pressing problem of improving the accounting arrangements of the Corporation. It is, of course, very unsatisfactory that the Auditors should have had to qualify the 1948–1949 accounts. Undoubtedly there were extenuating circumstances of considerable significance: the bulk purchase of surplus stores, difficulties of accommodation, an acute shortage of experienced staff. But some part of the failure has been due to an inadequate appreciation of the problem on the part of the Managing Agency and of the Corporation itself at the early stages. The Board is already taking emergency measures to deal with the back-log of accounts, and to strengthen its staff and overhaul its accounting organisation in East Africa. I have formally drawn their attention to the urgent importance of doing everything possible to avoid a position in which the 1949–50 accounts are also subject to qualification by the Auditors.

27. On the agricultural side I am making arrangements to broaden the advisory field on which the Corporation draws. This will ensure that all the technical matters, such as rotation and

selection of crops, are fully explored in the light of experience elsewhere, and that the experimental work is such as to yield results which can be used as a reliable guide for future plans. In particular I am arranging for regular consultation between the Corporation's experts and the Colonial Secretary's agricultural advisers whose experience will, I believe, contribute materially to the development of the Scheme on the right lines.

Summary of the problem

28. It may be helpful if, in conclusion, I endeavour to set out the essence of the problem as I see it.

(i) By the end of this financial year, the Corporation will have cleared and planted 112,000 acres and the clearing of a further 90,000 acres will be in train. The borrowings by the Corporation in the same period will have amounted to approximately £32 million. The Corporation propose that they should be authorised to proceed with further development plans over the ensuing four year period designed to bring the total cleared area up to 600,000 acres. They estimate that such a programme would involve a total borrowing of the order of £47.6 million.

(ii) The Corporation state that in their view the alternative to this programme is to close the scheme down, involving an estimated loss of £30 million.

(iii) My Department has examined the Corporation's proposals and, broadly speaking, are satisfied with the physical and financial assumptions underlying the capital development programme. But they have re-assessed the Corporation's estimate of earnings in a typical post-development year in the light of what they considered to be more realistic assumptions of price and total crop. On this basis the surplus envisaged by the Corporation would become a deficit.

(iv) They have also examined the possibility of a policy of limited liability – e.g. a four year development programme involving a total cleared area of 300,000 acres. But their conclusion is that although this would involve a modest saving of capital (say of the order of £5 million including the total cost of clearing the 300,000 acres cut from the target) the resultant net revenue would be more than halved owing to the impossibility of bringing down the operating overheads proportionately. In addition to this there would be a serious waste of the new railway and port installations built in the Southern Province. Under the Corporation's proposals these would handle the produce of 420,000 acres, whereas under a 300,000 acre scheme the acreage in that Province will be limited to 120,000 acres – i.e. there would be a reduction of 72 per cent in payable freight.

(v) The conclusion is that – quite apart from the effect of a smaller scheme on the morale of the Corporation's staff in East Africa – a limited objective would involve an uneconomic use of resources and increase the financial difficulties of the scheme.

RECOMMENDATION

29. I therefore recommend that the Overseas Food Corporation should be authorised to proceed with their revised programme to clear 600,000 acres of bush in East Africa for agricultural production by November, 1953.

J. S. [John Strachey]

Note

1. Mr Frank Samuel, Managing Director of the United Africa Company Ltd, submitted a plan for the development of groundnut production to the Secretary of State for the Colonies on 28 March 1946. This became the basis for the 'Report of a Mission to Investigate the Practicability of the Mass Production of Groundnuts in East and Central Africa' by A. J. Wakefield, CMG., D. L. Martin and J. Rosa, dated 20 September 1946 and published as an Appendix to *A Plan for the Mechanized Production of Groundnuts in East and Central Africa*, Cmd. 7030, *PP* (1946–47) X.

DOCUMENT 54

East African Groundnuts Scheme: Extract from Conclusions of a Meeting of the Cabinet, 14 November 1949, CAB 128/16

CM 66 (49) 3

The Secretary of State for the Colonies said that he was in full agreement with the recommendations made by the Minister of Food. The Scheme should not be judged from a purely commercial point of view: a substantial part of its capital outlay had been devoted to the provision of development and welfare services, which were normally the responsibility of the central Government or of the local authorities. The abandonment of the Scheme at this stage would be a major disaster for East Africa, and would involve the loss of valuable experience in the technique of economic development under tropical conditions. It seemed certain that the Government would be pressed in the debate to agree to arrangements involving closer Parliamentary control over the operations of the Overseas Food Corporation; and it would no doubt be suggested that responsibility for the Scheme should be transferred to the Colonial Development Corporation. The latter suggestion should not be accepted: the existing commitments of the Colonial Development Corporation were so heavy that it would not be able to undertake this additional responsibility . . .

The Cabinet –

(1) Approved the recommendations in C.P.(49)231 that the Overseas Food Corporation should be authorised to proceed with their revised plans to clear 600,000 acres of bush in East Africa for agricultural production by November 1953.

(2) Took note that the Prime Minister would settle with the Minister of Food the detailed changes to be made in the membership of the Board of the Overseas Food Corporation.

(3) Agreed that the Minister of Food and the Secretary of State for the Colonies should speak for the Government in the debate in the House of Commons on 21st November.

DOCUMENT 55

The USA and British Colonial Policy: Confidential Despatch from H M Ambassador in Washington to the Secretary of State for Foreign Affairs, 14 January 1950, CO 537/7136

Sir,

In my telegram No. 5896 of December 21st I reported that, like you, Sir, I had been much concerned to observe that the views expressed by British and United States representatives at the United Nations were so often in conflict on matters affecting colonial and trust territories. Having drawn attention to the danger that these differences, if allowed to continue, might seriously prejudice relations between our two countries, I suggested that we should make a strong imaginative effort both to understand the American point of view and to interpret our point of view to them so that a real 'meeting of minds' might be achieved. Shortly after this telegram was despatched Mr Sayre the United States representative at the recent meetings of the Trusteeship Council came to see me. The views which he expressed to me and which I reported to you in my Savingram No. 2 confirmed my feeling that it is of real importance to Anglo-American relations that our two Governments should try to come closer together over the colonial issue and that we for our part should make a much greater effort to make our case known to the world in general and to United States opinion in particular. I wish in this despatch to explain in rather more detail what I conceive the American attitude to be and what kind of an approach to them would in my opinion stand the greatest chance of success.

2. Anti-colonialism in the United States today is a traditional attitude rather than an active crusading force. There are of course the die-hards who will use any stick with which to beat the United Kingdom. Their hostility to Britain will be carried with them to the grave and nothing we can do will change their views. But the broad masses of the American people, including the liberals, are convinced that the supreme danger confronting their civilization is not old-fashioned colonialism but modern communism. They therefore regard the democracies of Western Europe, among whom the chief colonial powers are numbered, as their natural and indispensable allies. All too often, however, they fail to take the next step, namely to recognise that

anything which weakens the colonial powers also weakens the United States; when this thought does occur to them they are often tempted to say that the sooner Europeans lay down their self-imposed burden and stop trying to continue governing peoples who would prefer to govern themselves, the better it will be for all concerned. As a rule, however, the old prejudice against colonialism lingers under the surface, subconsciously. It expresses itself mainly in a number of sentimental ways such as a tendency to enthuse about the emergence of a new nation, like India or Indonesia. It is flattering to the American pride to regard these countries as having followed their example in throwing off the colonial yoke. The American sentiment is also seen in the extraordinary interest taken in the leaders of nationalistic movements when they visit the United States. This applies of course particularly when the visitor is a person of the eminence of Pandit Nehru but even Dr Nnamdi Azikiwe of Nigeria attracted a surprising amount of attention. The same sentiment shows itself constantly in a willingness to assume, without enquiring into the facts, that the policies of the colonial powers have not really changed much in the last two centuries, that ruthless exploitation of subject peoples is still the order of the day, and that any doubt expressed by a metropolitan government about the ripeness of its dependent peoples for self-rule is necessarily insincere. Some part of this prejudice can be dispelled as the ignorance on which it is founded is gradually dissipated. The British Information Services are doing what they can in this field but the work is slow and uphill. In this respect the power of the United Nations forum for good or for ill is considerable. There will be no hope of winning over American public opinion as long as the daily newspapers continue to report constant disagreements at the United Nations between what will inevitably be regarded as an enlightened and truly democratic United States on the one hand and a cynical selfish Britain on the other.

3. In the Administration and the State Department some of the same woolly sentimentality towards dependent peoples is in evidence. This attitude is in part due to the fact that the United States Government are not under the same compulsion as His Majesty's Government to make certain that any schemes which the United Nations seeks to impose on the colonial powers are practicable. United States officials are moreover apt to overlook their own racial problem when dealing with colonial questions since, fortunately for them, it

does not fall so readily within the purview of the United Nations. Nevertheless the orderly evolution of the self-governing sister states of the British Commonwealth is recognised, particularly in the light of constitutional changes in India, Pakistan and Ceylon, to be a striking example of the democratic genius at work. In a similar way the orderly development of backward countries is warmly welcomed especially by the State Department officials who are concerned with the containment of communism. It is gratifying to find that in the African section of the State Department, where one might expect criticism of British colonial policy, the officials who know best what we are doing are for the most part prepared to recognise that the United Kingdom now runs its colonies primarily for the benefit of their inhabitants. British policy is considered to be essentially on the right lines in that it is basically liberal and leading towards self-government. The doubt which sometimes arises is whether we are always willing to face up to the logical conclusion of our basic liberal policies. It is said that, having encouraged education in the colonies, we fail to give an educated native his natural outlet in a position of real responsibility, thus leaving him a natural prey to Soviet propaganda and turning him into an agitator instead of an administrator. It is sometimes suspected too that having laboured in the early stages to fit a colony for self-government, we try later on to retard the process so as to maintain a hold on the territory as long as possible.

4. I mentioned in my telegram No. 5896 the growing influence now exercised in the State Department by the Bureau of United Nations Affairs. Here another important factor comes into play. It is that that section of the State Department tends to adopt towards the United Nations the attitude of a doting parent whose favourite child can do no wrong. While the general public is considerably less enthusiastic over the United Nations it is I think a fact, and one which must not be overlooked, that opinion in this country does attach much more importance to making the United Nations a success and to furthering its ideas of international co-operation than does opinion in the United Kingdom. Consequently, while the United States authorities may on occasions advise the United Nations against a certain course of action, once the advice has been ignored and the action taken, the deed not infrequently becomes almost sacrosanct in American eyes because the United Nations perfomed it. What is good for the prestige of the United Nations often

comes first in importance and what is the right policy in itself has to take second place. Sometimes, especially in dependent areas affairs, an unduly short term view is taken of what will be in the best interests of the United Nations. Praise for the United Nations becomes a good in itself while criticism, however, well-meaning, is often badly misunderstood. When you, Sir, at the 1948 session of the General Assembly in Paris, expressed your fear that the Trusteeship Council might be 'degenerating into a forum for political propaganda', this was taken not so much as an attack on the abuse of the Council by the communists and their dupes but as an attack on the Council itself. Doubts arose in the American minds as to whether we really wanted the Trusteeship Council to become an effective organ of the United Nations. Conversely the reaction in United States official circles was one of genuine gratification when at New York in October 1949 the United Kingdom delegate on the Fourth Committee of the General Assembly remarked that 'all concerned in the work of the (Trusteeship) Council must have noted with appreciation in the proceedings of its most recent session a real improvement in the spirit of co-operation in which its members have conducted their joint business'.

5. We are faced therefore with two-inter-related problems. First, we have the long-term task of educating American public opinion about the realities of present-day colonial administration. Secondly we must endeavour, in a frank exchange of views with the State Department, to resolve the differences of opinion which have come to light in recent meetings of the United Nations. Mr Sayre's approach to me shows, that the State Department are as anxious as we are to improve the situation and I think it most important that we should make a forthcoming response to his and their initiative. But, as I pointed out in my telegram No. 5896, a real effort of self-interpretation and imaginative understanding of the other view will be necessary if we are to achieve success. We shall have to be prepared to expose without reticence the principles on which our colonial policy is founded and to explain, in some detail if necessary, what we are trying to achieve and what are the difficulties to be overcome. If, as I believe, these policies and principles are such as will commend themselves to the Americans we shall then be entitled to ask for their assistance in achieving our aims, not only in the United Nations but elsewhere. A narrow approach, based primarily on the need to maintain a united front against communist propaganda could not, I

believe, achieve more than a temporary alleviation of the situation. You will recall that we did in fact try such an approach early in 1949 without achieving any worthwhile result. This was, I think, partly because it looked suspiciously as if we were using the Russian bogey in order to avoid facing the issues themselves and partly because the Americans did not (and do not) think that the methods we follow in the Trusteeship Council are always the best means of defeating Soviet propaganda.

6. If we are to make genuine headway with the United States Government it is essential that a large measure of understanding be reached between us. To achieve this aim we might, I suggest, proceed on the following lines:-

(a) We should reiterate clearly to the State Department the fundamental aims of British colonial policy, giving convincing evidence that it is our aim to work in the interests of the inhabitants themselves and to lead them towards self-government in as orderly and speedy a manner as possible. We should make it clear that, when we are satisfied that a colony is ready and able to stand on its own feet, it is not our policy to flinch from the final award of complete self-government.

(b) We should give the United States Administration, not as a matter of right but as a gesture of our confidence in them, a frank account of the progress being achieved in the colonies. We should give an equally frank account of the difficulties we are encountering, saying what, if anything, the United States could do to help in overcoming them. This account should be sufficiently detailed to carry conviction. We should be prepared to discuss difficulties such as Administrative Unions (especially Tanganyika) since these are the points which the Americans have very much in mind and which cause misundertandings.[1] It would also be useful to include figures in order to drive home once more the point that so far as we are concerned colonial exploitation has long been dead.

(c) We should reaffirm our willingness to accept and to encourage the use of private capital from the United States in development programmes in the colonies. Some months ago we received an approach from the United States Chamber of Commerce asking whether His Majesty's Government favoured the participation of private capital in the Colonial Empire. The rather lukewarm reply which we made to this proposal (see Mr Berthoud's letter UR 9026/4995/98 of the 31st December, 1948) must I feel have given rise to a certain amount of suspicion. It is felt here that there must be something sinister behind our attitude or we should be a good deal keener than we are. It may be that not much United States capital could in fact be attracted to colonial enterprises. In that case it is unnecessary as well as damaging to pour cold water on the idea.

(d) We should offer a fuller and more obviously enthusiastic support for the Caribbean Commission and the South Pacific Commission.[2] We should do our best to provide stronger representation at the meetings of those bodies on something nearer the scale adopted by the Americans themselves. In particular we should be careful always to include in our representation persons with a definite standing among the people of our territories as well as someone in touch with current United States feeling. We need to convince the Americans that we are not merely participating half-heartedly in these two Commissions to the least possible extent while our real aims lie elsewhere, for example in the federation of the British colonies in the Caribbean area. It is worth noting that according to a statement by Mr Warren Austin,[3] President Truman is himself very much interested in the Caribbean area. Mr Austin who is leaving on the 26th January on a goodwill tour of the main Caribbean Islands, says that Mr Truman has a 'vision of development' for the islands which would include a ferry system which would connect the United States with 'that string of Caribbean pearls'. If the United States decided to do anything about Mr Truman's dream it is quite likely to act through the Caribbean Commission.

(e) We should be willing not only to accept but to encourage publicity for our colonial policies. It would for example be valuable if we could adopt a more forthcoming attitude towards such proposals as that which was recently put forward by the State Department for a policy statement on the activities of the Caribbean Commission. It would not matter much from the point of view of Anglo-American relations if the statement was to some extent window-dressing; we should give at all events the appearance of being in step with the United States and of being equally liberal in our ideas without serious cost to ourselves. I cannot stress too emphatically the importance of this aspect. United States spokesmen will not risk falling seriously out of line with United States public opinion on these issues however unrealistic and sentimental it may sometimes be. One of the most promising lines on which to work is to attempt to win the approval of United States public opinion by frequent (even if somewhat unsubstantial) announcements of joint action by the United States and the United Kingdom in this field. Joint announcements get better publicity here and are less suspect than statements put out by ourselves.

(f) We should offer to help the United States win over the non-communist vote in the United Nations. To this end we should be willing on occasions to accept with good grace resolutions of which we do not perhaps wholly approve rather than oppose them head-on. It would be helpful too if we could sometimes adopt the devices of voting for resolutions, while making suitable reservations, rather than abstaining. The Americans cannot understand why we do not see how much harm we are doing ourselves in the eyes of world opinion by instructing our Delegation to vote, for example, against a resolution favouring equal opportunities in matters relating to education. They realise that we did so on the technical grounds that the Special Committee was not competent to deal with such matters but they feel that this attitude not only provides excellent propaganda for the Russians but alienates the other non-administering powers. The Americans also think that our rigid attitude about the proposal to fly the United Nations flag in the Trust Territories was unnecessary and misconceived. Admittedly a line must be drawn somewhere and I am certainly not suggesting that we should vote in favour of resolutions which are fundamentally unsound or contrary to the Charter. To do so would of course lose us all respect. But short of the point where we really have to disagree we should offer willing cooperation rather than reluctant compliance. In these matters appearance counts for a great deal.

7. I suggest that our first step should be to seek to arrange early and frank exploratory talks with the State Department, at a reasonably high level. This would not only give the Americans an opportunity to explain their misgivings, but would also give us a chance to put forward our own suggestions for a rapprochement. We may well discover that in many cases

we do not need so much to modify our policies as to explain to the United States where their misgivings are based on a misunderstanding of our position. As a sequel to these talks it might be desirable at a later stage for a senior official to come out from London to clear up any special points of difference which may be uncovered. We may also need to be sent detailed information on particular topics. In any case I would hope that this Anglo-American exchange of views would be the beginning of a continuous process of keeping each other informed of what we are each trying to achieve in this important and delicate field.

8. Simultaneously we should, I suggest, take active steps both in this country and elsewhere to ensure that the United Kingdom case is better known and understood by public opinion. It should be borne in mind however that it serves little purpose simply to prove to the American public that our attitude at the United Nations is legally correct. The kind of material that is needed in order to impress them are facts and figures demonstrating that the British colonies are advancing economically, socially and politically in a manner which would do credit to many an independent nation. When I have been able to consult the Head of the British Information Services, who is at present out of Washington, I may have suggestions to offer on this aspect at a later date. Meanwhile you may care to consider whether some of the points mentioned in paragraph 6 above in connection with an approach to the United States Administration, could not also be used as a foundation on which to build up a case for presentation to the American public.

9. It is important to notice that almost everywhere in the State Department a clear distinction is drawn in our favour between British and French colonial administration. The French system is sometimes described by State Department officials as one under which a few natives only receive a thorough training in France and are then sent back to their own countries as puppet rulers who can be depended upon to act more ruthlessly than any Frenchman in the interests of metropolitan France. At the same time the masses of the people in French colonial possessions are, it is alleged, deliberately kept without education in order to discourage political evolution in all its stages. Holding these views, Americans sometimes deplore what they describe as a tendency on our part to make common cause with the French in the United Nations as though our colonial policy were tarred with the same brush as theirs. Indeed, the comment has

been heard from responsible officials of the Dependent Areas Division of the State Department, that in spite of their inferior record the French have often succeeded in creating a better impression in the Trusteeship Council than we have. Were it not for the over-riding importance of maintaining stability in Western Europe, I think it probable that the State Department would by now have taken more active steps to press the French to alter their ways. In these circumstances I believe it would be unwise to associate ourselves too closely with the French, or for that matter the other African Colonial Powers, in any approach we may make to the State Department in an effort to reach an understanding about colonial and trusteeship matters.

10. I am sending copies of this despatch to the Chancery at Paris, and to the United Kingdom Delegation to the United Nations at New York.

I have the honour to be, with the highest respect, Sir,
Your most obedient, humble servant,

(SIGNED) OLIVER FRANKS.

Notes

1. Tanganyika's status since the First World War as an international mandate had always created difficulties for any suggested administrative union of the East African territories.
2. Caribbean Commission: a joint advisory body established in March 1942 by Britain and the USA, as a result of the Lend-Lease negotiations. South Pacific Commission: established in 1947, as the result of an agreement negotiated and signed by representatives of Australia, New Zealand, France, the Netherlands, the UK and the USA, in Canberra 28 January– 6 February 1947.
3. Austin, Warren Robinson, b.1877; United States Senator for Vermont 1931–46, and Ambassador to the United Nations, June 1946–January 1953.

DOCUMENT 56

Central African Territories: Memorandum by A.B. Cohen, 16 March 1950, DO 35/3588

SECRET

Relations of the Two Rhodesias and Nyasaland

1. The arguments in favour of some form of closer constitutional association between the two Rhodesias and Nyasaland are:-

   (1) From the broad Commonwealth point of view the creation of a solid British bloc of territories in Central Africa would make it easier to resist economic and political pressure from the Union of South Africa and to prevent the undue spreading of South African ideas northwards. At the same time the existence of a strong unit in Central Africa would probably tend to ease relations with the Union in the future.
   (2) From the strategic, economic and communications points of view there would be great practical advantages in establishing a stronger inter-territorial organization in Central Africa. The planning of these matters on a regional basis represents accepted policy and our current troubles over transport in Central Africa are an illustration of the difficulty of using the transport facilities to the best advantage while more than one Government is responsible. U.K. Ministers have on a number of occasions, including the recent talks with Mr Beadle,[1] recognised the practical advantages of some form of closer association in Central Africa.
2. The arguments against closer association are:-
   (1) There are certain major differences between Southern Rhodesian and U.K. policy towards Africans. The Southern Rhodesian Government have no definite plans for the participation of Africans in the central political life of the Colony. There is an industrial colour bar against Africans in Southern Rhodesia in certain areas and in respect of certain trades. With regard to the second point it must be admitted that on the Rhodesia Railways and the Copperbelt in Northern Rhodesia there is effectively at present an industrial colour bar. This has always existed on the railways, which are managed from Southern Rhodesia, and was forced on the managements of the copper mines by the white trade union during the war at a time when production of copper could not be endangered. The colour bar is not recognised by the Government in Northern Rhodesia. The Government has encouraged the formation of African trade unions and will continue

in its efforts to find some means of bringing the colour bar in Northern Rhodesia to an end in spite of the formidable difficulties. In spite of the major differences in Southern Rhodesian policy towards Africans referred to above, Southern Rhodesia's efforts for African advancement, particularly in agricultural matters, have been excellent, as has been recognised by many outside observers.

(2) Africans in Northern Rhodesia and Nyasaland are almost unanimously opposed to amalgamation or even federation with Southern Rhodesia. It would certainly be necessary to consult with African opinion through the African Representative Councils in the two Territories and the Provincial Councils before any final decision could be taken by His Majesty's Government to agree to any form of closer association with Southern Rhodesia. His Majesty's Government is, of course, under no obligation necessarily to accept African views and, if a scheme could be devised which His Majesty's Government regarded as fair, it would be reasonable for this scheme actually to be recommended to Africans. But it would be most difficult to proceed with any scheme in the face of strong African opposition. It must be noted in this connection that any scheme which subordinated Northern Rhodesia and Nyasaland to Southern Rhodesia would be objected to not only by Africans in the two northern Territories, but also by Europeans. This is a point which is often ignored by Southern Rhodesian proponents of closer union.

(3) Any scheme which failed to safeguard African interests in Northern Rhodesia and Nyasaland or which subordinated these two Territories to Southern Rhodesia in a unitary self-governing state would be strongly objected to by opinion in this country and would be similarly criticised internationally.

3. The most recent positive step in the direction of closer association between the Central African Territories was taken in 1944, when it was decided to set up the present Central African Council to promote the closest possible co-operation between the three Territories in matters of common interest. This Council has achieved a considerable amount and it is generally agreed that its Secretariat has been most useful to the three Territories. But Southern Rhodesian Ministers have criticised the Council itself on the two contradictory grounds that it is purely consultative and that it infringes on the prerogatives of the Southern Rhodesian Parliament. The main reason why the Council has been less successful recently than in its earlier years has been the unwillingness of Southern Rhodesia Ministers to work its machinery properly and

to recognise that for the purpose of wider co-operation in Central Africa Southern Rhodesia must be prepared to accept some derogation from its full right of independent action, just as the European countries do for example in O.E.E.C. and members of the United Nations do in that body and the specialised agencies. Underlying the attitude of Southern Rhodesia Ministers is the thought that so long as an inter-territorial body such as the Central African Council exists His Majesty's Government in the U. K. may use its existence as an argument against some form of closer association.

4. In the talks last November with Mr Beadle, Mr Noel-Baker and Mr Creech Jones asked that the Southern Rhodesia Government should provide His Majesty's Government with their views on three points:-

(1) the limitations which they see in the existing machinery of the Central African Council;
(2) their views on some form of political association short of closer amalgamation;
(3) their views on the establishment of an effective body to deal with economic co-operation should closer political association not prove possible.

Mr Beadle suggested that after these views had been sent to His Majesty's Government a conference should be called by His Majesty's Government to discuss the problem with representatives of the three Territories (including unofficial representatives from Northern Rhodesia and Nyasaland). This suggestion was favourably received, but U.K. Ministers said that they would first wish to obtain the information from Southern Rhodesia.

5. At the end of January it was agreed at the Central African Council that an inter-territorial organisation was necessary, but the Southern Rhodesia Ministers gave notice that they would not be prepared to continue membership of the Central African Council as at present constituted after a period of twelve months had elapsed. A committee of the Council was set up to examine the existing machinery and alternatives to it and to make recommendations to the three Governments. This committee has already met and presented its report to the three Governments. The report has not yet been received in London, but it will presumably provide the information about the Central African Council for which His Majesty's Government has asked (see paragraph 4 (1) above).

6. As regards the answers to questions (2) and (3) in paragraph 4 above, Sir Godfrey Huggins has stated that answers will be

prepared after consultation with the elected members of the Northern Rhodesia Legislative Council. It is thought possible that a proposal will be put forward for the amalgamation or federation of Southern Rhodesia and the whole of Northern Rhodesia except Barotseland (the native state in the north-west part of Rhodesia which is in special treaty relations with His Majesty's Government). Nyasaland would also under this proposal be left out. The proposal is, of course, quite unacceptable. A close integration of the major part of Northern Rhodesia, including the Copperbelt, with Southern Rhodesia would be opposed by Africans generally in Northern Rhodesia just as much as the amalgamation or federation of the whole Territory. Barotseland would be deprived of the necessary financial support. If this proposal is put forward by Sir Godfrey Huggins in London, it will, it is suggested, be necessary to make it clear that it would not be acceptable to His Majesty's Government.

7. It is suggested that in the solution of this problem the following three principles should be accepted:-

(1) On practical grounds much would be gained by some form of closer association between the three Central African Territories.
(2) Any scheme must be such as would safeguard the interests of the African people of Northern Rhodesia and Nyasaland and not in any way prejudice their advance. Equally a scheme must be such as His Majesty's Government could wholeheartedly recommend to the Africans for acceptance.
(3) We should avoid giving the impression to Southern Rhodesia Ministers that there is no chance of His Majesty's Government agreeing to any form of closer association. Otherwise there is a danger of encouraging the tendency towards isolation which has shown itself in the recent unwillingness of Southern Rhodesia Ministers to work the Central African Council and in some of the statements made by Sir Godfrey Huggins in his speech at Gatooma last December. (No doubt Sir Godfrey Huggins was talking for political effect rather than on conviction; he has always been a good Central African). There is also the danger that a negative attitude on the part of His Majesty's Government might eventually lead Southern Rhodesia in the direction of a closer association with the Union of South Africa.

8. With these principles in mind it is suggested that the line to be taken by Ministers in the forthcoming discussions with Sir Godfrey Huggins might be as follows:-

(1) Ministers should, it is suggested, adhere to the line taken by Mr Noel-Baker and Mr Creech Jones in the talks with Mr Beadle, namely that the next step is for Southern Rhodesia to provide His Majesty's Government in the U. K. with their views as to the existing limitations of the Central African Council and as to possible forms of closer political or economic association. It is important that Sir Godfrey Huggins should not succeed in avoiding the necessity of submitting these views.
(2) Ministers might frankly recognise the practical advantages of some form of closer association.
(3) They might say to Sir Godfrey Huggins that, in order to have any chance of acceptance, a scheme of closer association between the three Territories would require to satisfy Parliament in the United Kingdom that African interests in the two northern Territories would be safeguarded and to satisfy the Africans themselves. In the view of H.M.G. in the U.K. it is very unlikely that any scheme would satisfy either Parliament or Africans if it sought to fuse the two northern Territories into Southern Rhodesia or completely to subordinate their Governments and Legislatures, over the whole or the greater part of the field of administration, to some federal authority. It might be suggested, therefore, that further examination of the problem should address itself to studying a scheme under which inter-territorially [sic] executive machinery would be established for the existing inter-territorial services and others which have been under consideration but have been rejected by Southern Rhodesia (this would cover railways, air communications, currency, meteorology, research and perhaps certain other matters of common interest). Appropriate machinery for legislation on these subjects or at any rate for close consultation with the Legislatures of the three Territories could also be considered. Under such a scheme the Central inter-territorial executive and legislative or consultative machinery would derive its authority and finance from the three Central African Governments and legislatures and would not be a federal authority super-imposed on them. If a scheme on these lines could be devised, it might perhaps be possible for Parliament in the U.K. to be persuaded to agree to some arrangement regarding their responsibility towards the inter-territorial services which would not infringe against Southern Rhodesia's self-governing status.
(4) Ministers might suggest to Sir Godfrey Huggins that after the information referred to in paragraph 4(1) above had

been supplied to His Majesty's Government in the U.K., a conference of officials of the U.K. Government and the three Central African Governments might be held in London for the purpose of narrowing the issues for further discussion by the Governments and preparing an analysis of the problem and recommendations for a solution.

(5) If this conference were fruitful it should be followed by another conference, also in London, at which U.K. Ministers would be prepared to discuss the whole problem with Southern Rhodesia Ministers and representatives of the Governments and Legislatures of Northern Rhodesia and Nyasaland. The conference of officials should be regarded as purely preparatory to this conference, but the final decision by the Governments whether to hold the main conference should await the outcome of the preparatory conference and there should be no publicity of the intention to hold the main conference until this decision had been taken.

9. The following points may be made on the above suggestions:-

(1) For the last eighteen months His Majesty's Government in the U.K. have deliberately refrained from taking the initiative in this matter and have left it to those in Central Africa who are in favour of closer association of the Territories to put forward their proposals for consideration. The results have so far been negative. The Victoria Falls Conference produced a scheme which, besides being half-baked, would clearly have been unacceptable not only to His Majesty's Government in the U.K., but also to the European as well as the African inhabitants of Northern Rhodesia and Nyasaland. A scheme for amalgamating or federating Northern Rhodesia and Southern Rhodesia, less Barotseland, if it is put forward, would be equally unacceptable to His Majesty's Government and at any rate to African opinion in Northern Rhodesia. The Southern Rhodesian Government and Mr Welensky in Northern Rhodesia have had great difficulty in agreeing on terms of reference for further study of the problem locally. Mr Beadle admitted this in the talks last November and his purpose in discussing the matter with U.K. Ministers was to find out how far His Majesty's Government would be prepared to go. Similarly Mr Welensky introduced a motion in the Northern Rhodesia Legislature asking His Majesty's Government to take the initiative in the matter. The Chief Secretary of the Central African Council has also urged that His Majesty's Government should take the initiative.

It is suggested that there are good grounds for His Majesty's Government taking the initiative at this stage, but this must be done in such a way as to safeguard African interests and to avoid alarming African opinion. Hitherto the U.K. Government and the Southern Rhodesia Government have been working separately on this problem and the solutions coming from Southern Rhodesia have so far been quite unacceptable to H.M. Government in the U.K. What seems to be required now is to bring the parties together, but at the same time to make it clear what H.M. Government in the U.K. regards as the limits to any scheme of closer association at the present time. The suggestions in paragraph 8(4) and (5) for a preparatory and a main conference in London are designed to bring the parties concerned in this problem together in devising a solution to it. The suggestion in paragraph 8(3) that H.M. Government should indicate broadly the lines on which they think that further studies should proceed is designed to safeguard African interests and if possible to set limits within which an attempt to devise a solution should be made.

(2) The proposal in paragraph 8(3) that any form of closer association should be limited to the subjects which are dealt with inter-territorially, with certain others which have already been considered for inter-territorial action, is based on suggestions made by Sir Gilbert Rennie,[2] the Governor of Northern Rhodesia, who believes that it might be possible to arrive at some solution in this way.

(3) If the main conference proposed in paragraph 8(5) takes place, it will be necessary for African representatives to be included in the Northern Rhodesia and Nyasaland delegations. It may be desirable to make this point clear to Sir Godfrey Huggins, if the suggestion for a conference is put forward.

Notes

1. Beadle, Thomas Hugh William, b.1905; Minister of Justice and Internal Affairs, Southern Rhodesia.
2. Rennie, Gilbert, McCall, b. 1895; service in Ceylon, Gold Coast and Kenya, 1920–47.

DOCUMENT 57

Constitutional Development in South-east Asia: Extract from Minutes of the Fifteenth Commissioner General's Conference held at Bukit Serene on 7th June 1950,[1] CO 537/5970

SECRET

ITEM 1 CONSTITUTIONAL DEVELOPMENT

(a) Tempo of transition to Self-Government

The Commissioner General reviewed the developments and stated that hitherto they had been working on the assumption that the strict merits of the case, and the best interests of the peoples of Malaya, required a transition period of a generation, say 25 years, before the peoples of Malaya would be ready for complete self-government. This assumption, he said, was until recently generally accepted by all responsible Asian leaders. In London at the end of 1948, Dato Onn had said that he thought a period of about twenty-five years would be necessary.[2] To Malayan Chinese and Indian leaders, and the more conservative Malays, this conception had been wholly acceptable. Dato Onn had, however, recently revised his views, and now spoke of a term of about fifteen years. The Dato thought that the process must be speeded up, and there is now a tendency among all responsible Asian leaders to accept the view that the transition to self-government will have to be accelerated.

2. *The Commissioner General* went on to say that in his opinion the process of development towards self-government will inevitably be accelerated by factors over which we shall have little or no control. These factors are: –

(i) Within the next five or ten years a new generation of Malayan leaders will be coming to the fore, whose influence will be in favour of quickening the pace. He was thinking of students now in the United Kingdom, Australia and the University of Malaya. Many of them will come into politics and the administration and will want to move at a faster pace towards self-government than the present more conservative leaders have been contemplating. These new leaders will have the support of the politically conscious. Though large sections of the masses will not support them, as they are not interested in politics, they will not raise any opposition and the influence of the new generation of leaders in political circles five years hence is bound to be a factor favouring the acceleration of the pace towards self-government.

(ii) The climate of opinion outside Malaya is likely to influence the pace of transition. Malaya, (with British Borneo) and Indo China are the only non-self-governing territories in South East Asia, and Indo China is likely to move towards complete self-government in the next two years. Malaya will then be left alone as a dependent territory, and the pressure of Asian opinion and also world opinion as expressed through U.N.O. will be irresistible upon Asian leaders in Malaya. If agitation in the direction of self-government is started, whatever the merits of the case may be, we shall have to agree, in conformity with local opinion, to a speeding up of the transition, extending the period as long as we wisely can to ensure the peoples are as fit as possible for the change. We must be mentally prepared, therefore, to accept a quickening of the pace, and if we were to resist the pace of change we should lose the present support of Asian leaders. It is vitally important that we should keep in step with them on this matter. We should not however, commit ourselves to a definite period of time.

(iii) When the Emergency is ended it will be of vital importance to retain the support of the politically conscious people; if we lose that we should have them, and world opinion, against us. The secret of success is in pursuing a policy that always carries the agreement of the local Asian leaders, exercising our influence to slacken the pace, so that they may have time to fit themselves for their responsibilities, but accommodating ourselves to the requirements of the situation. We must be in harmony with Asian leaders so that there is no discernable [sic] difference in views on which world opinion can take sides against us.

3. *The High Commissioner* thought the Commissioner General's analysis was correct, and emphasised the importance of keeping in step with Asian opinion in this matter. He thought it important that we should not set a time limit in which to satisfy the demands for self-government. It would be a great mistake to do so politically despite the apparent advantages. If Asian leaders spoke of a certain period, well and good, but it would be politically impossible for us to do

so. He said he was not clear what self-government in Singapore meant. In the case of the Federation the State Governments rule themselves. The policy is to link up the Federation and Singapore, and if that is to be done what form will self-government take in Singapore? If we conceived of Singapore developing separately from the Federation as a strategic outpost of the Commonwealth like Malta there was a danger of handing it over to the control of the Chinese. At what stage of development should we aim at the fusion of the two territories? His view was that it would have to come at a comparatively late stage, and they had still a long way to go in the Federation before public opinion would be ready to demand a constitutional link with Singapore. It was important to prevent the gap from widening between Singapore and the Federation.

4. *The Governor of Singapore* said that it was important to know whether we should encourage the transition towards self-government, or try to put a brake on the pace. It is much easier to retard development at an early stage. At a later stage when elected members have executive responsibilities it would be a much more difficult matter to do so. Should it be decided that the ultimate aim was the fusion of the two territories it would be possible to plan both administrative needs and political progress accordingly. The possibility of linking the two territories will be much easier if the Federation carries out a policy of decentralisation, Singapore could then fit into the structure as a City State, with complete control over its local affairs, its defence and external affairs being controlled by a central authority. It would be helpful if decentralisation on those lines could therefore proceed in the Federation.

5. *The Governor of Singapore* explained that political advance in Singapore was proceeding differently from that in the Federation. In Singapore they were concentrating on consolidating the electorate so that the elected leaders would have the full support of the people, and could later take up executive responsibility with the people's support. The Governor understood that the Federation felt it necessary that executive responsibility should devolve on its leaders at an early stage rather than wait for members to become responsible to their electorate, because the advance to self-government through elections would come too slowly to satisfy the aspirations of their political leaders.

6. *The Commissioner General* thought it a great mistake to contemplate Singapore developing separately from the Fed-

eration. It is predominantly a Chinese city and might choose to dispose of itself in the international scene according to the wishes of the Chinese majority, and might even become a satellite of China. To his mind this was unthinkable. Singapore was vital to the Federation both economically and strategically. Clearly the aim must be to bring Singapore into closer association with the Federation on a mutually satisfactory basis, so that Singapore could not be disposed of by its Chinese majority without the agreement of the Federation. A loose Federation of Malaya and Borneo would add a counter-poise to the Chinese element. He agreed with the views of the High Commissioner and Governor that Singapore must develop in union with the Federation.

7. *The Governor of Singapore* said that Singapore could not in fact exist independently. If it attempted so to exist it would fall under the influence of China, India or Indonesia and therefore the sooner they could move towards fusion with the Federation the better.

8. *The Secretary of State* said that this analysis had been very clear and helpful and corresponded with his own impressions during his tour. The old assumption that 25 years would be necessary before self-government could come was based on an estimate of the time needed to train the local peoples to the extent compatible with the responsibilities of self-government. This was a sound assumption if we were living in a normal peaceful world, but with conditions as they are today and especially in view of the control of China by the Communists, the tempo would have to be increased. It would be unrealistic, unsafe and perhaps disastrous to work on the basis that 25 years was still available to us to accomplish the transition to self-government. He stated that two separate groups of people had asked that the terms of the Prime Minister's statement about British intentions in Malaya should be made more specific. There were, firstly, Europeans and Chinese who thought we ought to say that we do not propose to leave Malaya under 25 years. He suspected that their reason was that they realised the demand for self-government was growing and that it would have to be satisfied before 25 years and they wished to prevent this by a declaration. The other group who pressed for a statement of this kind were students, although they wished for something more precise for very different reasons. They thought that a time limit of 10/15 years should be set to enable the steps towards self-government to be planned. The Secretary of State thought it likely that the

young intelligentsia, many of them perhaps natural orators, might well play a bigger part than we anticipated in the political developments of the next ten years. He thought it dangerous to adhere to the old assumption and that we would be wise to accept the conclusion that the period for transition is likely to be a shorter, rather than a longer one.

9. *The Secretary of State* said that the crucial stage would come when the Emergency was ended. The Trades Unions in the Federation, especially, had made it clear that they were looking for advances when the Emergency was over and he thought we must be ready then to make very substantial advances in the political, economic and social standards of the people. The Trades Unions particularly look for advance in economic and social security, and he hoped that it would be possible for plans to be ready in the not too-distant future which would give a real indication of what is to come when the Emergency is over. He agreed that it was very important to keep in touch with Asian leadership, with students and Trades Union leaders. His impression was that the Trades Unions at present support the Government enthusiastically in the Emergency. The alternative to the present leadership is a more leftist one or worse. Self-government had a definite meaning for the Trade Unions in the way of better wages, and improved standard of living, increased opportunities and above all a promise of social security.

10. The second matter of importance to the Trades Unions was their request for an adviser from the U.K. Trade Unions to give them further guidance. They had asked for Mr F. Dalley whom they would like out here for several months.[3] They also wanted facilities for adult education and he hoped it would be possible to help them by providing such facilities, and showing them that we were anxious to meet their needs. There had been a great advance in the lot of the masses at the end of the two world wars and he felt that the peoples of Malaya would look for a similar advance at the end of the Emergency. We must be ready with plans to meet their aspirations.

11. *The Secretary of State* said that he was more concerned about Singapore than the Federation. In the Federation, the people had roots; and although racial differences were more apparent on the surface in the Federation than Singapore, Singapore had a large and growing rootless proletariat. He wondered how great was the influence of the present political leaders with the masses in Singapore. If a crisis developed in our affairs with China, he thought it unlikely that the

present leaders would have the support of the masses (as against the pull of Chinese nationalism.) The *Governor of Singapore* agreed with this view. The *Secretary of State* also thought Singapore Trade Unions needed more help than those in the Federation: they needed a central council, and if there was any dissension among them we should help to resolve it. There were also vital defence considerations in Singapore, and he agreed the Colony could not be left to independence on its own but he was doubtful when the fusion would become possible. Meantime, he wondered whether it would be possible to satisfy the political ambitions of Singapore through increasing the measure of self-government in the Municipality. Speaking with the Municipal Commissioners, who seemed to him to be a better cross-section of the peoples of Singapore than the Legislative Counsellors, the Commissioners had expressed their desire to achieve complete municipal self-government, and the granting of city status to the municipality. He appreciated that it would be impossible to grant a charter until the City had a complete self-government with an elected Mayor, but he wondered if political aspirations in Singapore would be satisfied by the grant of self-government on the municipal level. The dominant thought in his mind was to be ready after the emergency so that we could give the people tangible evidence that we had a better alternative to offer.

12. The *Commissioner General* agreed as to the importance of maintaining the closest contact with students. The present University students were moderate and wise. With regard to the demand for adult education he stated that the Peoples Education Association was already doing excellent work in Singapore and would shortly be starting work in the Federation. Perhaps assistance might be forthcoming from the U.K. to help the P.E.A. to spread its influence. The *Commissioner General* said that he did not think that the grant of full self-government to the Municipality would satisfy the ambitions of the politically conscious people in Singapore. If they thought we were playing down the development of self-government in the Colony Councils by offering limited self-government to the Municipality it would certainly create an unfavourable reaction. A solution for political advance must be found in associating Singapore with the Federation in the advance towards self-government.

13. *The Governor of Singapore* stated that he was investigating the possibility of an Advisory Commission being sent out from the U.K. to advise on municipal development and the

relationship between the Municipality and the Rural Board. It was likely that the Municipal Commissioners would pass a resolution asking for such a commission. Data, he said, was already being collected for a social security scheme in the Colony. The work of the P.E.A. was of the greatest value to the labouring classes as it provided an avenue of self-advancement which made a great appeal to them.

14. After further discussion on the need for a Trade Union Council in Singapore and the difficulties in the way, it was considered that if Mr Dalley could be persuaded to come out he would be able to help in resolving the present difficulties and assist in the establishment of a Trades Union Council.

15. *The Commissioner General* said that political advance must be worked out between the Government and Asian leaders to enable them to agree on a common policy, and he suggested that he, the High Commissioner and the Governor might meet informally with four or five Asian leaders from the Federation and Singapore in an endeavour to reach agreement on the lines of political development which could then be put before the Councils and public opinion. No one would be committed and an informal body such as proposed would stimulate thought and discussion, and lead to eventual action towards self-government. It would include a European and leaders of all communities, and would meet quite informally.

16. *The High Commissioner* said whatever solution was agreed upon for the fusion of the Federation and Singapore they had a very long way to go in the Federation before they would be ready for it. He was agreeable to and favoured the setting up of a very informal and flexible 'study group'. The *Commissioner General* said that it might be premature to try to bring the leaders of the Federation and Singapore together at once and suggested they might meet separately at first. He confirmed that the C.L.C. would continue,[4] but he thought that it would not be an altogether appropriate body to handle political developments concerning the relations between the Federation and Singapore. The *Governor of Singapore* agreed that it was necessary to try and bring the leaders of the Federation and Singapore together. The discussion by Singapore leaders of the 'member system' had made them realise the necessity for both territories keeping in step.

The *Commissioner General*, the *High Commissioner* and the *Governor* agreed to meet at an early date to have further talks on the possible functions of the C.L.C. in regard to the political issues reviewed today.

Notes

1. This conference was held at MacDonald's headquarters at Bukit Serene, Johore Bahru (across the causeway from Singapore) and was attended by, amongst others, James Griffiths, Sir Henry Gurney (High Commissioner, Malaya), Sir Frank Gimson (Governor, Singapore) and Sir Hilton Poynton (Deputy Under-Secretary, Colonial Office).
2. Dato Onn bin Jaafar was founder-president of the United Malays National Organization, the major Malay party, between 1946 and 1951.
3. Author, with S. S. Awberry, of *Labour and Trade Union Organisation in the Federation of Malaya and Singapore* (Kuala Lumpur: 1948).
4. The Communities Liaison Committee: an unofficial grouping of Malayan community leaders.

DOCUMENT 58

Native-born Administrators and the Colonial Civil Services: Memorandum by the Secretary of State for the Colonies, 17 July 1950, CAB 129/41

CONFIDENTIAL
C.P. (50) 171
17*th July*, 1950

CABINET

EMPLOYMENT OF NATIVE BORN ADMINISTRATORS IN THE HIGHER GRADES OF COLONIAL CIVIL SERVICES

MEMORANDUM BY THE SECRETARY OF STATE FOR THE COLONIES

At the Cabinet's meeting on 11th May (Con. (50) 30th Conclusions, Minute 6), I was invited to submit a memorandum indicating what steps were being taken to introduce an adequate proportion of native-born administrators into the higher grades of the Colonial Civil Service, particularly in African and other colonies which are progressing towards self-government.

General

It has long been recognised that self-government in the Colonial territories will not be a reality until the administrative and executive machinery of government is operated by the people of the country. Most of the junior ranks of the Colonial civil services are already filled by locally born officers. Progress in increasing local appointments to the higher grades has inevitably varied in different territories. The desirability of such appointments is taken for granted. The limiting factor is the supply of suitably qualified local candidates who can take over the work without undue sacrifice of efficiency. The best way of attacking the problem, therefore, is to increase the sources of supply.

2. During the post-war years, particularly in West Africa, Malaya and the West Indies, there has been great progress in the provision of higher and technical education facilities, and further important developments in those territories are taking place.

3. In all Colonial territories there are scholarship schemes to enable students to train for posts of higher responsibility in

Government Service. In addition £1 million has been allocated under the Colonial Development and Welfare Act, 1945 for similar scholarships. For the most part scholarships are tenable in the United Kingdom, but when possible scholars are placed at Universities or other institutions of higher education in the Colonial territories. Scholarships are granted to candidates already in Government service as well as to applicants straight from the schools. In awarding these scholarships care is taken to use them so as to encourage Colonial people to qualify themselves in branches of knowledge which will be of practical value in the economic and cultural progress of their communities. At present there are 1,713 Colonial students at Universities and 2,480 at non-university institutions in the United Kingdom; of these 1,500 are Colonial Government or Colonial Development and Welfare Scholars; the rest are private students, many of whom will take up higher grade Government posts. Details of those students holding Colonial Scholarships are given in Appendix A.

There are also special schemes for Colonial Service training (details are given in Appendix B) some of which are designed to enable members of the public services to qualify for higher appointments. A separate allocation of £1½ million has been made for this purpose under the Colonial Development and Welfare Act.

4. In the following paragraphs details are given of the steps being taken to introduce native-born officers into the higher ranks of the Colonial Service in all the African territories and those other Colonial territories which are moving towards self-government. Throughout this memorandum reference to 'officers in the higher ranks of the Colonial Service' includes both administrative officers in the strict sense and those holding professional and technical posts, such as accountants and auditors, agricultural and forestry officers, customs officers, education officers, electrical, civil, mechanical, marine and mining engine[e]rs, labour officers, legal and judicial officers, surveyors and medical and veterinary officers.

West Africa

5. There has been a rapid increase in the last three years in the number of appointments of Africans to the higher ranks in the West African Colonies, and this rate of increase is being steadily accelerated. In Nigeria there are at present 364 (as against 26 in 1938 and 172 in 1948) Africans in the higher ranks as compared with some 1,800 expatriates; in the Gold Coast the corresponding figures are 276 (as against 17 in 1928, 31 in 1938 and 98 in 1948) and 1,100; in Sierra Leone the figures in 1949 were 54 and 417. It

will, however, be some time before there are enough qualified Africans to fill a majority of the higher posts in any of the West African Colonies.

6. Since 1948 the reports of local Committees or Commissions on the Africanisation of the higher civil service in Nigeria, the Gold Coast and Sierra Leone have been accepted by the Governments concerned. It is now officially recognised that expatriate candidates should only be recruited for Government posts when no suitable and qualified African is available, and that the policy of Africanisation should be pursued as rapidly as is consistent with the maintenance of present standards of efficiency.

7. In Nigeria, Public Service Boards with a majority of unofficial members were set up in 1949 with the object of selecting candidates for higher civil service posts and for scholarship and training schemes. Departmental selection boards have also been established to recommend junior officers for training and for promotion to the higher ranks. An Assistant Civil Service Commissioner for Nigeria is posted in London; he is specially concerned with the recruitment into the civil service of Nigerians who are undergoing training in the United Kingdom. Up to February 1950, 243 scholarships or training awards had been made and provision of £250,000 for the three year period 1948–1951 has been made to meet the cost of scholarships and training for higher posts.

8. The progress of Africanisation of the Government Service of the Gold Coast was reviewed in 1949 by a Select Committee with a majority of African members, and recommendations for further Africanisation were made. These recommendations included the appointment of an African Commissioner for Africanisation whose duties would include the co-ordination of recruitment and scholarship policy. The further recommendation for the appointment of a Commission of Enquiry into the organisation of the whole Gold Coast service is now being implemented. In the Gold Coast 626 Government scholarship awards have been made since 1947.

9. In Sierra Leone, the Africanisation Committee recommend, as a short-term policy, the employment of suitable Africans from the junior grades in higher posts. The Committee's main recommendation was however concerned with measures for training suitable candidates by means of scholarship schemes. Ninety Government scholarships for overseas higher education courses have already been granted since 1947.

10. Facilities for higher education at University level have been developed in Nigeria and the Gold Coast since the end of the war and in 1948 a University College was established in each territory. The University College at Ibadan in Nigeria now has Faculties of Arts, Science, Medicine and Veterinary Science, and there are at present 295 students. The University College of the Gold Coast has departments of theology, philosophy, geology and economics and there are over 100 students. It is being developed as rapidly as possible, on the recommendation of the Africanisation Committee, to produce the highest possible number of graduates for the Africanisation programme. Faculties of Agriculture will be opened in both Colleges in October 1950 and in the course of the next few years each of the Colleges will provide facilities for degree course training for about 600 students. The two Colleges expect eventually to accommodate 2,000–3,000 students each.

11. Colleges of Arts, Science and Technology for higher technical education are also to be established shortly in Nigeria and the Gold Coast. They will provide, *inter alia*, courses in engineering, building and surveying, accountancy, telecommunications, agriculture, forestry, veterinary science and secretarial and commercial practice. Within a few years, there will be about 600 students in the Nigerian College and 300 (eventually there will be 2,000) in the Gold Coast College. The students will come not only from the schools but also from the public services, and the colleges will take over much of the training now carried out by Government Departments. In Sierra Leone, Fourah Bay College is being reconstituted. It will continue to provide certain degree courses and in addition will establish training facilities similar to those proposed for the Nigerian and Gold Coast Colleges. There are at present over 200 students; eventually there will be 1,200.

12. It is the University Colleges and the new Colleges of Arts, Science and Technology which will in the future supply a large proportion of qualified candidates for appointment to the higher ranks in the West African Colonies.

Other African Territories

13. With one exception in Tanganyika, there are no African officers holding higher administrative, professional or technical posts in any of the African territories outside West Africa. There are, however, a number of Africans carrying out important executive functions in all the East African territories, though they do not occupy posts which would otherwise be filled by

Europeans. In Nyasaland, Northern Rhodesia and Somaliland, the policy of the local governments is first to educate Africans to fill the more responsible clerical posts. In the Somaliland Protectorate a number of Somalis have been appointed to the junior grades and the policy for the immediate future is to provide training to fit them for appointment to the middle grades, *e.g.*, a few Somalis have recently been appointed as Administrative Assistants.

14. These East and Central African territories were in an exceedingly primitive state when they first came under British rule some fifty years ago, and the provision of adequate educational facilities has been and remains an enormous problem. It is, therefore, not surprising that there are no Africans in the higher Governments posts. More primary schools and some secondary and vocational schools are however now being built. At Makerere College, courses of University 'intermediate' standard, open to students from all East African territories, are available in Arts, Science, Education, Medicine, Agriculture and Veterinary Science; certain courses for London University degrees are also now available. All the Colonial Governments grant scholarships for higher education to qualified students; these scholarships are for the most part tenable in University institutions in the United Kingdom. Many of the successful students may be expected to qualify for higher posts in Government Service. It will, however, be many years before appreciable numbers of qualified Africans with the necessary standards of integrity and the sense of responsible public service will be ready to hold senior Government appointments.

West Indies

15. About 50 per cent. of the higher posts in the administrative services in the West Indies are held by West Indian-born officers (in Barbados, the percentage is as much as 60). A very large number of medical, legal and technical posts are also held by West Indians. Expatriate officers are only appointed when West Indians of suitable quality are not available.

16. The policy of appointing West Indian officers in the higher grades is well established and increasing numbers are being appointed.

17. The local governments also grant scholarships to students and serving officers with a view to appointing successful scholars to the higher ranks of the Colonial Service. These scholarships are tenable for the most part in the United Kingdom and

Canada, but also, where suitable courses are available, at the University College of the West Indies.

18. Teaching at the University College of the West Indies began in 1948, and there are now Faculties of Medicine and Science, and a Faculty of Arts will be opened in October 1950. There are at present 70 students, but it is hoped that there will be as many as 2,000 when the College has been fully established.

Singapore and Malaya

19. The latest figures available show that, in the highest division in the Federation of Malaya Government Service, there were 181 substantive and acting posts filled by local officers, representing approximately 15 per cent. of the establishment. The corresponding figures in the Singapore Government Service were 102 and 23 per cent. In addition, the Malayan Civil Service, which is confined to high-grade administrative officers occupying the more senior appointments in both territories, had 30 Malays representing approximately 12 per cent. of the total membership.

20. In Singapore a Public Service Commission has now been established to advise on training, recruitment and promotion of local candidates, and it is the declared ultimate aim of Government policy to fill all senior posts by local appointments. In the Federation a Select Committee of Enquiry has been set up to examine the structure of the Public Service. The appointment of Malays is being encouraged by the promotion of suitable officers, by direct recruitment and by scholarship schemes although progress has been delayed in part by the reluctance of the Malay Rulers to consider the admission of non-Malays (*e.g.*, Malayan-born Chinese) to senior posts.

21. In 1949, the University of Malaya was formally constituted. The University has faculties in Arts, Science and Medicine (including Dentistry). There are at present approximately 650 students, and it is hoped that the University will eventually provide higher education for 1,000 students.

22. Facilities for higher technical education in Malaya are provided at the Technical College, Kuala Lumpur. This College provides three-year courses of study in Civil, Mechanical, Electrical and Telecommunications Engineering, and in Surveying. At present there are approximately 200 students attending the College, but when new buildings, now in course of erection, are completed, it is hoped to provide courses for up to 700 students.

Hong Kong

23. In Hong Kong there are 395 higher civil service posts, of which 51 are at present held by local officers, mostly in the educational, medical, nursing and other professional services. There is one local-born member of the Administrative Service.

24. In correspondence concerning a Bill to authorise the appointment of a Public Services Commission the Governor expressed the opinion that for some years to come the majority of Hong Kong vacancies in the higher posts would have to be filled from the United Kingdom; he emphasised in particular the difficulty of finding good local material for the Administrative Service and the Police.

25. The University of Hong Kong, which was opened in 1912 and which has faculties of Medicine, Engineering, Arts and Science, had an enrolment of 638 students for the year 1949–50. It is hoped to expand the capacity of the University shortly and also to increase the number of subjects provided for. Courses in building and wireless telegraphy and engineering are provided by the Technical College.

Other Territories

26. (*a*) *Cyprus*.—In Cyprus most of the junior posts and a third of the middle grade posts (*e.g.*, District Judge, District Medical Officer, District Commissioner, &c.) are filled by local-born officers. In the higher posts there are six local-born officers (all in legal and judicial posts) and 34 expatriates.

27. There has been little recent progress towards increasing the number of local-born officers, but the Governor is about to recommend a reduction in the total number of expatriates.

28. In the ten-year period 1946–1956, 150 scholarships will be granted for candidates who will fill Government posts on the successful completion of their training. All but fourteen of those so far awarded are tenable in the United Kingdom. A number of scholars have already been appointed to posts in the Government service, but the majority will not qualify until later in the period.

29. (*b*) *Mauritius and Seychelles*. Local officers have already largely replaced expatriates, and now occupy 75 per cent. and 40 per cent. respectively of the senior appointments in these two territories. No further rapid development is to be looked for in this direction, though there will be a gradual increase in these proportions as technically qualified officers gain further adminis-

trative experience. Scholarships for higher and technical education overseas are provided from local revenues and from Colonial Development and Welfare funds.

30. (*c*) *Fiji*. In Fiji there is one native-born head of a government department; there are also two Fijian Administrative Officers and seven other native-born officers who hold higher rank posts.

31. In Fiji and the Western Pacific High Commission territories, approved C. D. and W. schemes providing scholarships for secondary and university education will increase the numbers of locally-born persons who will in future be qualified for higher appointments.

Conclusion

32. From this survey it will be gathered that progress is being made all along the line in encouraging the flow of Colonial people into their own civil services. The key to the problem is education, not merely at the higher level but at all levels. The developments in the Colonial educational services during the last twenty-five years are now beginning to bear fruit, and the supply of suitably qualified Colonials for the higher posts will greatly increase as time goes on. But there is also a continuous increase in the demands of the territories for higher staff as the activities of government broaden out in proportion to the social and political progress of the Colonial communities. In the Colonial field as a whole, therefore, we shall for very many years to come need considerable numbers of qualified men and women from Britain and other parts of the Commonwealth.

J. G.

APPENDIX A

Colonial Students studying in the United Kingdom and Southern Ireland during the Academic Years 1947–50

These figures represent the total number of Colonial Government and local C.D.W. scholarship students in these years

	1947–48	1948–49	1949–50
West Africa—			
Gambia	3	4	7
Gold Coast	130	185	241
Nigeria	83	117	156
Sierra Leone	17	21	24

East and Central Africa—			
Aden	...	8	11
*Kenya	55	76	95
Northern Rhodesia	2	4	7
Nyasaland	...	...	3
Tanganyika	6	9	6
Uganda	10	16	15
Zanzibar	2	4	3
Far East—			
Hong Kong	24	17	11
Malaya	33	60	64
†Singapore	...	...	22
West Indies—			
Bahamas	2	4	3
Barbados	14	12	11
Bermuda	4	4	6
British Guiana	25	32	30
British Honduras	4	6	7
Jamaica	61	67	61
Leeward Islands	12	10	10
Trinidad	49	58	58
Windward Islands	35	33	32
Mediterranean—			
Cyprus	40	38	55
Gibraltar	13	14	14
Malta	10	15	14
Other Territories—			
Falkland Islands	...	...	...
Fiji	...	...	1
Mauritius	31	39	45
Seychelles	1	...	2
	666‡	853‡	1,014‡

* The figures for Kenya include Government ex-servicemen's bursaries, Kenya High School, Prince of Wales and Government Indian High School bursaries.

† No separate figures were kept for Singapore before 1949–50; in previous years the figure is included with Malaya.

‡ There are 1,500 at present in this country.

APPENDIX B

Schemes for Colonial Service Training

1. Reference is made in paragraph 3 of the paper to the £1 million C.D.W. scholarship scheme (1946–56), open to candidates from all the Colonial territories, under which scholarships for higher edu-

cation are being granted to potential officers of the higher grades of the Colonial Service; and to the £1½ million scheme, also financed from C.D.W. funds, for training members of the Colonial Service. Details of these are given in paragraphs 2 and 3 respectively, below.

2. *Scholarships for Potential Colonial Servants.*—These scholarships are in addition to those provided by Colonial Governments. They cover subjects such as Agriculture, Arts, Medicine, Engineering, Law, Science, Veterinary Science, Surveying and Administration. Details are given below of such scholarships in respect of the territories mentioned in the memorandum:—

	1947	1948	1949	*Total*
Gold Coast	1	5	14	20
Nigeria	14	11	14	39
Sierra Leone	5	2	3	10
Tanganyika	5	6	5	16
Kenya	3	5	3	11
British Somaliland	2	7	...	9
Nyasaland	1	7	...	8
Northern Rhodesia	2	5	4	11
Uganda	3	8	4	15
Malaya	7	7	11	25
Singapore	2	4	2	8
Hong Kong	6	4	4	14
West Indies	10	20	16	46

3. *Training of Officers in the Colonial Service.*—In the training schemes for members of the Colonial Service financed from C.D.W. funds, special provision is made to enable members of the public services of the Colonial territories to qualify for higher appointments, while the Special Course for Colonial Administrative Service Cadets is open to those selected in the Colonies themselves for appointment to this Service. The following table shows the numbers, small as yet, who have attended the Administrative Cadet Course since its inception in 1946:—

	1946–47	1947–48	1948–49	1949–50	1950–51
Fiji	2	...	Nil	1	...
Malaya	2	...	Nil	...	1
Nigeria	...	3	Nil	1	...
Cyprus	...	1	Nil	1	...
Sierra Leone	...	...	Nil	...	1

Courses in Agriculture, Forestry and Education qualifying for appointment to the respective branches of the Colonial Service are also open to locally domiciled men (and women, in the case of the Education courses). Special arrangements have been made to modify the courses to suit the needs of men and women from Colonial territories so that they can benefit most from them and from their stay in this country.

4. Officers of the Colonial Service with between 2½ and 10 years' Service are brought to this country for a two- or three-term course (study leave) at Oxford, Cambridge or London University. Locally-appointed officers join in these courses side by side with their colleagues from this country.

Locally-domiciled Officers attending the 'Second' Colonial Service Course

	1948	1949	1950
Gold Coast	1	1	2
Nigeria	2	2	5
Zanzibar	...	...	2
Malaya	2	2	6
West Indies	4	7	9
Seychelles	...	2	...

5. In addition to the 'Second' Colonial Service Course several other courses of instruction providing professional training for serving officers in various branches of the service have been arranged during the past eighteen months. These courses are also open to locally-domiciled officers, who are being nominated in increasing numbers. The main courses of this kind and the numbers of locally-domiciled officers who have attended and are now attending are shown in the following summary:—

	1949	1950 (to date)
Labour Officers Course	16	10
Survey	3	6
Police College	2	9
Police Training for Gazetted Rank (started 1950)	...	12
Police Attachments and Specialised Courses	11	14
Civil Aviation	3	6
Nursing	...	3
Income Tax	1	3
Prison Officers Course (started 1950)	...	3
Customs	8	11
Trades Union	2	2
Totals	46	79

6. On these particular courses locally-domiciled officers now represent nearly one-third of the total number of attendances. The large majority of the officers come from West Africa, the West Indies and the Federation of Malaya. Most of these courses are assisted from the £1½ million Colonial Development and Welfare allocation referred to in paragraph 3 of this Appendix.

DOCUMENT 59

'A Survey of Communism in Africa', Extract from a Paper by the Research Department, Foreign Office, secret, August 1950, CO 537/5263

Conclusions

33. It is remarkably difficult, and even dangerous, to generalise about Communist trends in Africa. Apart from the striking differences of race, of social evolution and political development encountered everywhere, the remoteness of much of the continent and the sparseness of communications make the collection of accurate information a formidable problem. At present the territories about which least is known are the Belgian Congo, parts of French Equatorial Africa, French Somaliland and Mozambique.
34. A careful study of the considerable volume of information examined between October, 1948, and June, 1950, does, however, point to the conclusion that, although the 'colonial campaign' directed by the Kremlin and carried out by Prague, Paris and, to a lesser extent, London, has been intensified over the past year, in the continent as a whole Communism in the strict sense is making no headway. Indeed, the overall picture is one not of progress but of stagnation and even retrogression.
35. Signs of such regression are most noticeable in French territory. In Morocco, Algeria and Tunisia the small Communist Parties have definitely lost ground over the past three years and continue to make no progress, although the Communist hold on the Algerian trade unions remains serious. In French West Africa the R.D.A. [Rassemblement Démocratique Africain] can still claim to be the most powerful native Communist movement in the continent; but it has certainly suffered an overall decline since 1947, due to the activities of rival parties, the stiffened attitude of the French Administration and the unwillingness of the rural masses – among whom it had a remarkable initial success – to accept its revolutionary doctrine and violent methods or to tolerate its heavy financial demands. This decline, which has been accelerated by the defection of certain prominent leaders, is clearly reflected in the party's consistent loss of seats at local and metropolitan elections. In the Ivory Coast, for example, where it has always been, and remains, strongest, it now

holds only 12 of the 45 seats in the *Conseil Général*, as compared with 27 in January, 1949. There are indications that the recent intensive efforts of the party's leaders may have brought about some increase in membership, particularly in the Ivory Coast, but in the other territories of French West Africa the R.D.A. is suffering from a serious shortage of funds, which has led to a reduction of activity. In French Equatorial Africa, apart from the Middle Congo, the R.D.A. appears to have failed to make any significant progress since its establishment.

36. Elsewhere in the continent, with the exception of the Union of South Africa, where the Communists had tightened their hold on the Native, Coloured and Indian labour elements, there have been no indications of Communist gains. The reverses suffered by the Communists in French territory have been paralleled, to some extent, in former Italian territory, particularly in Somalia and Eritrea, where the Communist Parties have now dwindled into insignificance. As mentioned earlier, Communist influence in British territories is still very slight, and no gains of any importance have been noted over the past year. It is particularly encouraging that there was no trace of Communist inspiration behind the serious strikes in the Gold Coast (January, 1950) or Nigeria (November, 1949). It is thought that recent police action has considerably weakened the two main Egyptian Communist groups.

37. It is as yet impossible to forecast what will be the effect of the dissolution of the Communist Party in South Africa. Until this happened, it could be said that the areas of greatest Communist influence were parts of French West Africa, particularly the Ivory Coast, and, to a lesser extent, the non-European areas in the cities of the Union of South Africa. The three parties of French North Africa – the only remaining Communist Parties in the continent – despite their comparative weakness, are also clearly of importance. As might be expected, in all these areas Communism is mainly confined to the larger towns.

38. There are several factors operating against Communist expansion in Africa. The first is, perhaps, the general backwardness of most of the continent with its widespread illiteracy and deeply rooted superstitions. The hostility of most of the influential tribal leaders – a generalisation that applies to Arab North Africa as well as to the 'Black' area – and the disinclination of the rural masses to accept the revolutionary doctrine of Communism are further factors of

some importance. In the Arab countries the influence of Islam is a considerable counter-force, but in parts of French West Africa, particularly the Niger and Sudan territories, the R.D.A. has made surprising headway among the Moslems, especially the extremists of the 'hamallist' sect. Throughout French territory the Communists have been opposed by the established nationalist movements – as in North Africa – or – as in French West and Equatorial Africa – by the various political groups preaching regional solidarity that have sprung up in opposition to the R.D.A. with its policy of embracing all peoples and tribes throughout French 'Black' Africa. In the Union the Communists have had to face the counter-thrust of the Afrikaner nationalist movements. Finally, official opposition, often involving drastic suppressive measures, has generally proved an effective damper both in the case of established movements and parties (e.g., those of the French territories and Egypt) and of partly-penetrated subversive groups, as in Spanish and Portuguese territory.

39. Against these obstacles must be set, chiefly, the expansion of industry, which is fostering a drift from the rural areas to the towns, and the spread of education. The increasing number of Africans who study in Europe clearly gives cause for some anxiety, especially when considered in conjunction with the Kremlin's 'colonial campaign' directed, in the main, through such organisations as the I.U.S. [International Union of Students], the W.F.D.Y. [World Federation of Democratic Youth], the W.F.T.U. [World Federation of Trade Unions], and the W.I.D.F. [Women's International Democratic Federation]. A further intensification of the colonial campaign must be expected and the Kremlin can doubtless be relied upon to exploit any incipient unrest in colonial or other territories. It seems doubtful, however, to judge by present trends, whether doctrinaire Communism will make substantial headway in the continent as a whole.

DOCUMENT 60

Colonial Resources and Defence Policy: Extracts from Minutes written in the Colonial Office, August 1950, on a Draft Memorandum by J. C. Morgan, CO 537/5324

Mr Martin
Mr Cohen
Mr Paskin

4. As you know, the O.D.C. memorandum (O.D.C. (49) 47) on 'The Role of the Colonies in War' sets out, with some precision, the part which Colonial Forces may be expected to fulfil in a major war. Mr Morgan has taken this paper as the basis for his proposals,[1] on the assumption that the cold war situation demands the adoption of measures on the lines of, though perhaps falling short of, the programme set out in O.D.C. (49) 47. It seems clear . . . that, until recently, there was little prospect that the War Office would contemplate the increased use of Colonial troops on this basis; the rigid financial ceiling imposed on United Kingdom defence expenditure would have made this, in their view, a wasteful use of their available financial resources. In the new situation resulting from the Korean war, however, it seems likely that in future manpower may be an even more serious limiting factor than finance, and Defence Department feel that it is incumbent on the Colonial Office, not so much to press for greater use of Colonial manpower, as to ensure that the Chiefs of Staff give proper consideration to the arguments for and against such extended use on the basis of adequate information.
5. The argument in the attached draft memorandum (which is not, I think, brought out as clearly as it could be) is that there are directions in which Colonial troops might be used in the present cold war situation—

   (a) In substitution for United Kingdom troops at present engaged on garrison duties in Colonial territories.
   (b) As part of the Commonwealth strategic reserve.
   (c) In active operations, e.g. in Malaya or Korea.

   As regards (a), the present disposition of United Kingdom troops employed on garrison duties is set out in paragraph 4 of the draft memorandum; I should be grateful for the views of Assistant Under-Secretaries concerned on the specific suggestions made in the second part of that paragraph. I feel some doubt, for instance, whether it would be appropriate to station coloured West Indian troops in Gibraltar.

As regards (b), the suggestion here, which is not very clearly explained, is that existing Colonial Forces, particularly of course the African Forces, should be substantially expanded so that it would no longer be necessary to earmark United Kingdom troops as an ultimate reserve for the maintenance of internal security in the Colonial territories. Under this proposal the Forces in East and West Africa would be substantially increased, and the threat to internal security would thereby be diminished in the sense that the larger forces thus made available could be used either within their own area or for service outside their own area. The United Kingdom reserve, relieved in this way of their residuary responsibility for internal security in the Colonies, would thus become wholly available for other cold war postings.

As regards (c), the argument is that, in view of the increasing strain on United Kingdom manpower involved in the present attempt to increase our defence preparations with a minimum of interference with the process of economic recovery, the time has come to consider seriously whether Colonial troops might be used in actual operations.

6. It is obvious that the Colonial Office is not in a position to weigh up all the relevant factors in this question. But we can make constructive proposals for the Chiefs of Staff to consider against the wider background. But the first step is to consider the broad political implications of proposals on the lines summarised in the preceding paragraph, since we obviously do not want to turn down ultimately, on political grounds, proposals which we ourselves had originally put forward. Broadly, this means that the problem must be considered under two main heads—

(1) Whether, in conditions falling short of a major war, there is political objection to sending Colonial troops from their own territory for service elsewhere for any one of the three purposes set out under (a), (b) and (c) above.

(2) Whether political difficulties are likely to arise from the use of Colonial troops drawn from another Colonial territory as part of operations under (a), (b) or (c) above.

7. Mr. Morgan will be available to provide, in discussion, any further information that may be needed.

S.E.V.L. [S. E. V. Luke]
1.8.50.

* * *

Reference (1) in paragraph 6 of Mr Luke's minute, I do not think there would be any objection to taking local troops from Malta or Cyprus for use elsewhere, provided of course that the liability to service overseas is clearly stated as a condition of enlistment and that, as regards existing Maltese Units, no compulsion is applied to men who did not volunteer on this understanding. Delicate questions of the scale of overseas allowances appropriate would have to be satisfactorily settled first: Maltese are touchy about differentiation between themselves and people from the United Kingdom in this respect. It would be undesirable to put forward any very firm proposals without first consulting the Governors. (Sir Gerald Creasy will be here from the 8th – 29th August and it is probable that Sir A. Wright will be paying a short visit in the second half of September.)[2]

As regards (2) in the same paragraph of Mr Luke's minute—

Gibraltar. There would be considerable objection to the employment of coloured troops from the West Indies; but I do not think that a similar difficulty would arise in connection with the employment of Maltese or Cypriots provided that the fullest opportunities had first been given to Gibraltarians. (Sir K. Anderson,[3] who is coming on a short visit to the United Kingdom, will be available for consultation on the 14th August if desired.)

Malta. I agree with Mr Morgan's statement in his paragraph 4. No question of bringing Colonial troops from elsewhere need arise and there would certainly be objections to stationing coloured troops in the Island as a part of the strategic reserve.

Cyprus. I do not know the authority for Mr Morgan's statement 'that not more than one battalion' is necessary for internal security and local defence; but certainly this is the minimum and the minimum could be supplemented by resurrecting the Cyprus Regiment. There would be considerable political objections to bringing coloured troops from elsewhere either for garrison duties or as part of the strategic reserve; but this would not necessarily apply in the event of active operations. I agree with Mr Morgan's remark that 'there are good political grounds for considering the raising of a Cypriot force to be desirable': we have of course only just disbanded the one we had.

J.M.M. [J. M. Martin]
2.8.50

* * *

I have considerable doubts about a good deal of the memorandum opposite. As far as the African Territories are concerned I do not think that there is much to be done either under (a) or (c) of paragraph 5 of Mr Luke's minute. I am pretty sure that African troops could not without political and many other difficulties be used to garrison any other Colonial Territories. Equally I think that there would be political and other difficulties in using troops from other Colonies to help maintain internal security in the African Territories. It would certainly be most undesirable for East African troops to be used for internal security purposes in West Africa or West Africans in East Africa. It must also be remembered that both in East and West Africa if there were serious and continuing trouble U.K. troops might have to be brought in; this applies particularly in East Africa with plural communities. Increased numbers of African troops might not have the same effect.

I do not believe that it would be found profitable to use African troops either in Malaya or Korea.

Increased numbers of African troops could admittedly be raised as a strategic reserve, although, as the paper points out, they are not suitable for service in all parts of the world. I am, however, doubtful whether we should be justified in confidently stating that so far as numbers are concerned as many African troops could be raised for duties elsewhere as were raised during the war. In the first place it would be far more difficult to raise troops in peace time (even under a cold war) than it was in wartime. In the second place demands of economic development, etc. might well interfere. Any statement on this point should, I think, be very much more guarded than the draft.

A.B.C. [A. B. Cohen]
2/8/50

* * *

So far as Malaya and Hong Kong are concerned it is a little difficult to think in terms of the future in the midst of such pressing preoccupations in the present and the very immediate future. For example, it would be the merest possible guesswork to suggest that in 'Malaya and the Far East' it might be possible to raise one Infantry Brigade for general Colonial service. It is quite certain that, for so far into the future as we can possibly see, all the local forces which it will be possible to raise in this territory will be required for service there.

It is equally impossible even to guess at what would be a 'normal' garrison for Hong Kong if and when the present emergency should come to an end.

As regards the employment in Malaya and Hong Kong (even in active operations) of Colonial forces [from] elsewhere (even if and when there are any to be spared from elsewhere) I should say quite positively that black troops would be inacceptable [sic] in both these territories.

It is perhaps conceivable that forces from the Western Pacific might be acceptable in Malaya or Hong Kong and we are about to consult the High Commissioner in Malaya on this point. But quite apart from the ethnological aspects of the matter the obvious answer for the High Commissioner to give in present circumstances is that, if H.M.G. can find the money to raise a Fiji battalion for service in Malaya, a much better use of that money would be to expedite the raising of a further battalion of the Malay regiment.

J. J. P. [J. J. Paskin]
9th August, 1950

* * *

Sir Thomas Lloyd

The War Office clearly have no particular wish to make greater use of Colonial troops for cold war defence purposes, and I do not think that this attitude is surprising, in view of the rigid ceiling hitherto imposed on defence expenditure. In the new situation resulting from the war in Korea, it is possible, I feel, that manpower may become a more serious limiting factor than finance, and that the time may therefore come, even in a situation falling short of world war, when the War Office may wish to make greater calls on Colonial manpower. For the present, however, the views of Assistant Under-Secretaries on this question, as set out in the three minutes above, are so discouraging that I do not think that there would be any advantage in pursuing the question further on the lines suggested in Mr Morgan's draft memorandum . . . In general, the conclusion that I draw from this discussion is that, under present conditions, the major contribution that Colonial Governments can make in the field of Commonwealth defence is to maintain security forces adequate to cope with any foreseeable internal disorder; and that we should therefore concentrate our attention on maintaining a steady pressure on Governors and Colonial Governments to do everything possible to bring up their Police Forces in particular to an adequate state of efficiency. This policy can best be pursued in the form of the follow-up to the Inspector-General's reports, and I shall be putting forward separately proposals under this head in a few days.

S.E.V.L. [S. E. V. Luke]
14.8.50.

Notes

1. Morgan, John C., b.1910; Principal Secretary, Defence and General Department of the Colonial Office, since 1947.
2. Wright, Sir Andrew Barkworth, b.1895; Governor and Commander-in-Chief Cyprus, 1949–54.
3. Anderson, General Sir Kenneth Arthur Noel, b.1891; Governor and Commander-in-Chief Gibraltar, 1947–52.

DOCUMENT 61

Central African Territories: Minute by P. C. Gordon Walker, 5 October 1950, PREM 8/1307

Prime Minister,

Closer Union in Central Africa

I am submitting this minute in consultation with the Secretary of State for the Colonies who agrees in its terms.

I attach a copy of a telegram which was sent to you in my absence by Sir Godfrey Huggins on the 12th August. In it he proposes, as a sequel to discussions held in London last November with Mr Beadle, then Southern Rhodesian Minister of Justice, that a conference of officials should be held in London as early as possible to consider the means of overcoming the difficulties hitherto experienced in promoting the closer association of the three Central African territories. He does not, indeed, supply the views of his Government which Mr Beadle was asked to obtain, and confines himself to suggesting as a basis for discussion, a list of functions that might be undertaken by a common organisation.

Mr Griffiths and I are convinced that the proposal to hold a conference of officials should be accepted. We are already committed, by Mr Noel-Baker's statement in the House on the 15th December last,[1] to further discussion of the subject with the three Governments when they so desire. Apart from that, we see great advantages in subjecting this difficult issue to a joint discussion (for the first time) with official representatives of the three African Governments. The calling of the conference will remove the frequently heard reproach that His Majesty's Government are indifferent to the problem and have nothing to offer but destructive criticism of proposals that emanate from Central Africa for the closer association of the territories. Although we see no possibility of satisfying those Southern Rhodesian aspirations that look towards amalgamation with the northern territories we think it of prime importance to the future of the whole area to promote as far as practicable the association of Southern Rhodesia with her northern neighbours; the danger, accentuated by the steady increase of Afrikaner immigrants, that she may turn to association with the Union of South Africa is very real.

It will be necessary at the conference for the United Kingdom,

Northern Rhodesian and Nyasaland officials to have constantly in mind the special responsibilities of His Majesty's Government with regard to Northern Rhodesia and Nyasaland and the attitude of Africans in the two territories who are suspicious of closer political association with Southern Rhodesia. We are very conscious of the difficulties of the problem, and we do not see any prospect at present of complete political integration of the three territories. We hope however that a conference of officials, who should be free to examine the matter in all its aspects, will provide the Governments concerned with a full and objective survey and may succeed in formulating acceptable proposals for closer association between them in the ordering of matters of common concern. Our officials would also hope to bring home to the Southern Rhodesian officials, and through them to their Government, that the difficulties are not of our making but that there are real limitations imposed by the nature of the problem.

I attach a draft telegram which we propose, if you agree, to send to Sir Godfrey Huggins, telegrams to the same effect being sent to the other two Governments. It deals with the time for holding the conference (which we contemplate as being in next March), the terms of reference, and the text of an early announcement. You will see that this draft announcement makes the point that African opinion in Northern Rhodesia and Nyasaland will be consulted on any proposals which emerge from the conference.

I am sending a copy of this minute to the Secretary of State for the Colonies.

[minuted] I approve[2] CRA
6.x.50

Notes

1. *Hansard Parliamentary Debates* (1948–9) vol. 470, cols 2884–8.
2. The decision to hold the conference of officials was announced by James Griffiths in the House of Commons, 8 November 1950, *Hansard Parliamentary Debates* (1950–1) vol. 480, cols 946–51.

DOCUMENT 62

Constitutional Development in East Africa: Extract from Conclusions of a Meeting of the Cabinet, 20 November 1950, PREM 8/1113

CM (50) 76th Conclusions

1. The Cabinet had before them a note by the Secretary of State for the Colonies (C.P.(50)270) covering the draft of a statement which he was proposing to make in the House of Commons on constitutional development in East Africa.

THE SECRETARY OF STATE FOR THE COLONIES said that for some time past there had been a growing feeling of anxiety and unrest throughout East Africa, which was due partly to the policies of the South African Government, partly to the fact that European settlers in East Africa were tending to turn for encouragement to that Government, and partly to the pace of recent constitutional change in West Africa. It had been suggested that a conference should be held to discuss the constitutional problems of East Africa; but he did not favour that course, which would tend to suggest that the problems of the various territories in East Africa could all be solved on similar lines. He preferred to continue to deal separately with the different problems of the various territories; but he thought there would be advantage in making a single statement of policy enunciating the general principles on which the Government were proceeding.

In discussion doubts were expressed about the expediency of making a general statement on these lines. The dependent territories in East Africa were in varying stages of constitutional development, and the problems arising from a mixture of races were more acute in some than in others. This fact was bound to be blurred if the Government made a single statement of policy applying to them all. Moreover, language applicable to all these territories was not likely to be specially apt to any. Secondly, was it not undesirable to offer a statement of policy in respect of a selected number of areas in East Africa at a time when there was increasing need to consider the problems of Africa as a whole? Thirdly, in so far as the statement dealt with economic development, was it wise to appear to be treating these territories in isolation from the general problem of securing economic assistance for under-developed countries throughout the world?

The following points were also raised on the wording of the draft statement—

(a) The language of paragraph 2(iii) might be thought to place undue emphasis on the paternal aspect of Colonial responsibilities. It might be preferable to recast this in terms of assistance towards the economic development of these territories.

(b) The reference to 'other sections of the community' in paragraph 2(iii) would be more appropriate to Kenya than to other territories, such as Uganda. These words might perhaps be omitted.

(c) Was it necessary, in paragraph 2(iv), to add the warning that some time would pass before self-government could be fully established in these territories? It was the general view of the Cabinet that in any such statement as this it would be expedient that such a warning should be included.

(d) In paragraph 2(iv) it might be preferable to speak of 'developing', rather than 'allowing', reasonable freedom of action by local governments.

(e) The appeal for co-operation, in paragraph 2(v), was out of place in what purported to be a statement of principles. If included at all, it should be placed as a separate paragraph at the end of the statement. There was, however, much to be said for omitting this appeal altogether.

THE PRIME MINISTER, summing up the discussion, said that there seemed to be general agreement that before any such statement of policy was made the problem should be further considered – particularly in relation to Government policy in respect of other parts of Africa and to current discussions in the United Nations on racial problems in Africa.

The Cabinet—

Invited the Commonwealth Affairs Committee to consider, in the light of the Cabinet's discussion, the proposed statement of policy (set out in C.P.(50)270) on constitutional development in East Africa.[1]

Note

1. This discussion by the Cabinet significantly affected the shape of the statement finally made to the House of Commons on 13 December 1950, *Hansard Parliamentary Debates* (1950–1) vol. 482, cols 1167–9.

DOCUMENT 63

'Closer Association in Central Africa'. Memorandum by the Secretary of State for the Colonies and the Secretary of State for Commonwealth Relations, 3 May 1951, PREM 8/1307

SECRET

C.P. (51) 122
3rd May, 1951

CABINET

CLOSER ASSOCIATION IN CENTRAL AFRICA

MEMORANDUM BY THE SECRETARY OF STATE FOR THE COLONIES AND THE SECRETARY OF STATE FOR COMMONWEALTH RELATIONS

We circulate herewith, for the consideration of our colleagues, the Report of the Conference of officials recently held in London to consider the question of the closer association of the Central African territories of Southern Rhodesia, Northern Rhodesia and Nyasaland (Annex II).[1] The substance of the Report is summarised in the following paragraphs. There is no question of committing ourselves at this stage to a final view on the proposals of the Conference and we do not ask our colleagues now for a decision on the substance of the recommendations. But we do recommend, for the reasons given below, that His Majesty's Government

(1) should, if the other Governments concerned agree, publish the Report for general information; and

(2) should, without being committed to acceptance of the proposals in the Report, commend them in general terms for the careful consideration of all the peoples concerned as embodying a constructive approach.

We should, of course, propose to report further to the Cabinet when there has been time for public discussion of the proposals both here and in the Territories.

Review of recommendations of the recent Conference

2. The question of the closer association of the three British

territories in Central Africa has been under discussion for many years. It has recently become more urgent; and last year it was decided to hold a conference of senior officials of all the Governments concerned, to re-examine the problem and endeavour to formulate proposals that might be generally acceptable. This was announced in Parliament on 8th November.

3. The Conference took place during March. Its Report (Annex II), which is addressed to all four Governments, was unanimous on all points. The Conference also agreed on the terms of a Confidential Minute, to be addressed by each team of officials to its own Government, setting forth certain considerations not suitable for publication (Annex I).

4. The Report (paragraph 35) reaches the definite and unanimous conclusion that 'closer association between the three territories ought to be brought about, and that the need for this is urgent[']. The reasons for this conclusion are set forth under the headings 'Economic' (paragraphs 25–26), 'Strategic' (paragraph 27), 'Communications' (paragraph 28), 'Administrative' (paragraphs 29–30), 'Moral and Social' (paragraph 31), and 'The urgency of the problem' (paragraph 32). In the Confidential Minute closer association is held to be the only effective means of countering the increasing pressure of the Union of South Africa on the Central African Territories.

5. While thus decisively recommending closer association, the Report adds: 'But in any scheme of closer association certain conditions must be fulfilled. Account must be taken both of Southern Rhodesia's self-governing status and of the special responsibilities of His Majesty's Government in the United Kingdom towards Northern Rhodesia and Nyasaland. Political progress for Africans must be maintained and Africans must be enabled to play an appropriate part, according to their qualifications, in the Government and the political institutions to be established. At the same time, until their partnership with Europeans becomes fully effective, there must be adequate provision in the constitution for African welfare and advancement. Finally, the unit of government which is established for the Central African territories must be able to stand on its own feet economically; and it must be autonomous financially.' The detailed recommendations in the Report are designed to satisfy these conditions.

6. The Report rejects amalgamation and recommends that association should be on a federal basis; in paragraphs 35–45 it gives reasons for this and for the belief that on such a basis

adequate safeguards for the interests of Africans can be provided. Subject to these safeguards, the federal Government would have full responsibility within the sphere allotted to it under a Ministerial system and with a federal Legislature. The federal subjects would include defence, external affairs, immigration (but *not* land settlement and alienation), economic development planning, customs, posts and telecommunications, railways, and civil aviation. The authority of the Centre, however, would be limited to the specified subjects declared to be 'federal,' and the whole sphere of government in all three territories would, apart from these specified subjects, remain with the Governments and Legislatures of the territories constituted as at present. The Territorial subjects would include all those matters that are most closely related to the life of the African inhabitants: for example, African education, health, agriculture, land and settlement questions, local government and native administration generally, police, mines and labour. In respect of all subjects not made federal the relationship of each territory to the United Kingdom Government would remain exactly as it is now and African political development would go forward as at present in the two territories. (The Conference assumed that the federal State would come, and Southern Rhodesia would remain, within the scope of the Commonwealth Relations Office, while Northern Rhodesia and Nyasaland would remain within that of the Colonial Office. There would be the closest consultation between the two Offices in all important questions affecting Central Africa.)

7. Thus in all matters most closely affecting Africans existing safeguards would remain unaltered and the control of the Colonial Office in respect of Northern Rhodesia and Nyasaland would continue as at present. But in federal matters (*e.g.*, customs or railways) decisions would have to be taken affecting African interests. To meet this the proposals provide, in the federal field, for African representation in the Legislature; for an African Affairs Board including an African member from each Territory (with the duty of scrutinising all projected federal legislation which, if the Board considered it detrimental to African interests, could not be brought into force without the approval of the United Kingdom Government); and for a Minister for African Interests in the federal Cabinet (with power to defer executive action proposed by the federal Government, if he considered it detrimental to African interests, pending reference to the United Kingdom Government who could, if they thought it necessary, refuse agreement to such action). The

Minister for African Interests would be appointed and dismissed not by the Prime Minister of the federal Government, but by the Governor-General acting in his discretion and then only with the approval of the Secretary of State; the Minister would thus be responsible through the Governor-General to the United Kingdom Government.

8. To secure co-ordinated planning over Central Africa as a whole, to minimise friction between the federal and territorial authorities, and to promote from the outset a habit of co-operation rather than rivalry, the proposals (paragraphs 53–56, 70, and 77) provide, in the spheres of economic and development policy and of finance, for the establishment of consultative machinery through joint federal-territorial bodies.

Our Conclusions and Recommendations

9. For the reasons given in paragraph 4 above and particularly because of the need to counter South African pressure, we are satisfied that closer association is urgently desirable in the interests of the Territories (including those of the African inhabitants) and of the Commonwealth. The scheme put forward appears to us to be constructive and workable; whether it can be brought into force will depend on the reactions to it of European and African opinion in the Territories and to that we will revert below. We do not at present ask our colleagues for decisions on the specific recommendations; we will therefore confine our comments on these to certain points affecting the safeguards for African interests.

10. His Majesty's Government in the United Kingdom have special responsibilities towards the African inhabitants of Northern Rhodesia and Nyasaland, which they have an inescapable obligation to fulfil. The safeguards proposed in the Report are necessarily different, within the limited federal field only, from the existing methods of exercising our responsibilities in respect of the two northern Territories; but we see no reason why they should not be effective. And it is noteworthy that they would apply to the Africans in Southern Rhodesia, who would thus acquire, again in the federal field, safeguards which they have not now.

11. The linchpin of the proposed federal safeguards is the 'Minister for African Interests'. Though a member of the federal Cabinet, and appointed to it as a Member of the federal Parliament (from those nominated thereto to represent African interests), he would be outside the ordinary political field and would

be appointed with the approval of, and be ultimately responsible to, the United Kingdom Government. The arrangement is certainly unusual, but we do think it would be workable and we regard it as an essential part of the scheme. It is only by being within the Cabinet that the guardian of African interests could be fully effective; and a Minister appointed – ostensibly to protect African interests – on ordinary party grounds would not necessarily be an adequate safeguard.

12. It should be recognised that if the Southern Rhodesian Government agree to the scheme recommended they for their part will be accepting, within the range of subjects proposed to be made federal, the reimposition (through the safeguards already referred to) of a measure of control from London which would amount to an appreciable curtailment of Southern Rhodesia's present degree of independence. From their standpoint this would be a very severe concession which it would require a great effort to commend to their Legislature and con[s]tituents. His Majesty's Government in the United Kingdom would also be making an important concession, although only within the limited federal field, in respect of our responsibility for Northern Rhodesia and Nyasaland; but we should at the same time secure powerful safeguards within this field for African interests. We should also gain the acceptance by Southern Rhodesia of the representation of African interests in the federal Legislature – a most important and a new step for Southern Rhodesia. In the allocation of seats in the federal Legislature between the three territories, we understand that it only just proved possible – with no margin – to find a basis that the members of the Conference felt might be capable of acceptance by their respective Governments. Indeed, it seems evident that, as regards the main lines of the recommendations, there is very little scope for manœuvre, and that any attempt on our part to push the Southern Rhodesians still further would probably wreck any hope of securing a practical outcome.

13. Amalgamation being ruled out (paragraph 38 of the Report), the only form of closer association worth considering is federation; and it is therefore a choice between federation and doing nothing. If we do nothing, and so prevent the Southern Rhodesians from linking with their northern neighbours, they will inevitably tend more and more to look southwards. The absorption of Southern Rhodesia into the Union would then probably be only a matter of time. If Southern Rhodesia were absorbed, Northern Rhodesia, through its geographical position

and economic circumstances, would be exceptionally vulnerable to Union pressure and eventual absorption and it is most doubtful if Nyasaland, at present a backward territory, could in those circumstances stand out against encroachment by the Union.

14. That the danger is real and urgent can be seen by a perusal of paragraphs 5–8 of the Confidential Minute. Afrikaner infiltration into both Southern and Northern Rhodesia is proceeding apace – at present the flow of immigration from the Union is almost double of that from the United Kingdom. Not all the immigrants from the Union are Afrikaners, and not all the Afrikaners have strong political views; but those who do obviously form a base for the extension of Nationalist South African influence. There has always been an appreciable minority body of opinion in Southern Rhodesia which would not be averse from incorporation into the Union, and indeed we have just heard from Southern Rhodesia of a reported movement there for the formation (under local Afrikaner auspices) of a new political party with incorporation as its main plank. The rejection of closer association would enable this party to increase its influence.

15. Our task must in fact be to take every possible step to induce Southern Rhodesia to look northwards rather than southwards and to strengthen those in Southern Rhodesia who favour a more liberal policy towards Africans. Much progress has been made by Southern Rhodesia in recent years in services for the benefit of Africans and a more liberal attitude is developing, particularly among settlers from this country since the war; we must do everything we can to encourage this process. In the absence of an organised African public opinion in Central Africa, the most effective counter to Union influence is the attachment to the British connection of a large section of the Europeans in all three Territories. By forging a constitutional link between them and creating a strong Central African block we shall at once put Central Africa in a better position to resist Union pressure and strengthen the British connection.

16. Economically the Union overshadows Central Africa, and if the Central African territories were to encounter a serious slump in production or the export of their products the danger of the economic attraction to – and pressure from – the Union would be aggravated. A Central African block, forming a strong economic unit, would be in a better position to resist this pressure than three separate units.

17. It will be a difficult and delicate matter to enable these vital considerations to play a part in convincing Parliamentary and public opinion here of the need for positive action to keep Southern Rhodesia out of the Union. They cannot well be stated publicly by United Kingdom Ministers. We shall have, by one indirect means or another, to endeavour to bring them to the notice of influential quarters in the Press and of others, including certain members of the Parliamentary Labour Party, who will seek to lead public opinion. We must aim at persuading those who are concerned for the welfare of Africans that if we do nothing – with the consequence of driving Southern Rhodesia into the Union – we are likely to expose the welfare of the Africans to much greater dangers than any that may arise from the pursuit of closer association, specially if the latter includes the important safeguards embodied in the Conference's proposals.

18. The Governments concerned, including our own, have given assurances that before any decision is taken to bring about closer association adequate opportunity will be afforded for public discussion of any proposals that may be put forward. This can only be done on the basis of a set of concrete proposals. For this reason the Conference has framed its Report in a form suitable for publication. We recommend that, if (as expected) the other Governments agree, the Report should be published here for general information in the form of a White Paper early in June, shortly after the Secretary of State for the Colonies returns from East Africa.[2] (Two separate documents that provide relevant background – a factual survey of the territories and a comparative survey of native policy – would be published at the same time.)

19. In addition to publishing the Report, we consider that His Majesty's Government should also (on the broad lines of the draft statement at Annex III) commend it in general terms for the careful consideration of all the peoples concerned as embodying a constructive approach.[3] As no decisions would be taken until after public reactions have been obtained, this would in no wise conflict with our undertakings.

20. In the public discussion of the proposals in Central Africa the crucial factors are likely to be the attitude of Europeans in Southern Rhodesia and of Africans in Northern Rhodesia and Nyasaland; the latter is bound powerfully to affect the reaction

in this country and in Parliament. Vocal African opinion in the northern Territories has expressed itself as opposed to closer association with Southern Rhodesia and the conference recognised (paragraph 20) that this is a serious obstacle to closer association. But the Conference took the view that in the last resort the African reaction in the northern Territories would depend on the nature of the scheme put forward. They thought it unlikely that Africans would withdraw their opposition to amalgamation, but they felt that, provided that some form of closer association could be designed containing adequate provision for African representation and adequate protection for African interests and provided that the services more intimately affecting the daily life of Africans were outside the scope of a federal Govenment, Africans might well come to realise the very substantial advantages of closer association from their point of view.

21. It is fairly certain that Africans do not at present realise that it is only by setting up a strong Central African block that Union influence, which they greatly fear, can be effectively countered. It is clearly most desirable that before His Majesty's Government in the United Kingdom have to make final decisions they should be fully aware of African opinion in the northern Territories; it is equally desirable that there should be opportunity for full discussion of the proposals between representatives of His Majesty's Government in the United Kingdom and Africans in the northern Territories and Europeans, as well, of course, as the three Central African Governments. The matter is of such importance to Central Africa and the Commonwealth as a whole that we think that, if this proves practicable, we should both proceed to Central Africa during the summer recess after there has been sufficient time for consideration of the proposals by the public for the purpose of such discussions.[4] A Conference could then be held in which we should take part and which would settle the form of the proposals which the Governments would formally sponsor for the consideration of the Legislatures and the public in Central Africa and, of course, of Parliament here. The holding of such a Conference, whether here or in Central Africa, could of course only be decided upon with the agreement of the Governments concerned, and subject to the approval of our colleagues we propose to seek this forthwith. In our view it is most important that the intention of holding such a Conference and if possible of a visit by ourselves should be referred to in the announcement accompanying the publication of the proposals; this would discourage public opin-

ion in the Territories, whether European or African, from reaching premature conclusions, pending our visit, either for the acceptance or rejection of the proposals or particular features of them pending the opportunity of discussion with ourselves.

J. G.
P. C. G. W.

Notes

1. The conference of officials was held at the Commonwealth Relations Office between 5 and 31 March 1951.
2. The report was published on 13 June 1951: Cmd. 8233 *Central African Territories: Report of Conference on Closer Association London, March 1951, PP* (1950–1) X.
3. A statement was made by the Secretary of State for the Colonies on 13 June, *Hansard Parliamentary Debates* (1950–1) vol. 488, cols 2315–21.
4. James Griffiths and Patrick Gordon Walker attended the second Victoria Falls Conference 18–21 September 1951.

Biographical Notes

Acheson, Dean G. (1893–1971). Lawyer; private secretary to L. D. Brandeis; associate justice US Supreme Court 1919–21; Under-Secretary of Treasury May–November 1933; Assistant Secretary of State 1941; Under-Secretary of State 1945–7; Secretary of State 1949–53.

Amery, Leopold S. (1873–1955). MP (Unionist) 1911–45; Assistant Secretary War Cabinet and Imperial War Cabinet 1917; on staff of War Council, Versailles, and personal staff of Secretary of State for War 1917–18; Parliamentary Under-Secretary for the Colonies 1919–21; Parliamentary and Financial Secretary to Admiralty 1921–2; First Lord of Admiralty 1922–4; Secretary of State for the Colonies 1924–9; Secretary of State for Dominion Affairs 1925–9; Secretary of State for India and Burma 1940–5.

Anderson, John (1882–1958). KCB 1919, 1st Viscount Waverley 1952. Entered Colonial Office 1905; secretary to Northern Nigeria Lands Committee 1909; secretary to West African Currency Committee 1911; Permanent Under-Secretary of State Home Office 1922–32; Governor of Bengal 1932–7; MP (Nationalist, Scottish Universities) 1938–50; Lord Privy Seal 1938–9; Home Secretary and Minister of Home Security 1939–40; Lord President of the Council 1940–3; Chancellor of the Exchequer 1943–5; Chairman Port of London Authority 1946–58.

Attlee, Clement R. (1883–1967). 1st Earl Attlee 1955; MP (Lab.) 1922–55; Parliamentary Private Secretary to Leader of Opposition 1922–4; Parliamentary Under-Secretary of State for War 1924; Chancellor of Duchy of Lancaster 1930–1; Postmaster General 1931; member Indian Statutory Commission 1927; Deputy Leader Labour Party in House of Commons 1931–5; Leader of Opposition 1935–40; Lord Privy Seal 1940–2; Secretary of State Dominion Affairs 1942–3; Lord President of the Council 1943–5; Deputy Prime Minister 1942–5; Prime Minister 1945–51; Minister of Defence 1945–6; Leader of Opposition 1951–5.

Battershill, William D. (1896–1959). KCMG 1941; military service in India and Iraq 1914–19; Ceylon Civil Service 1920–8; Assistant Colonial Secretary Jamaica 1929–35; Colonial Secretary Cyprus 1935–7; Chief Secretary Palestine 1937–9; Governor Cyprus 1939–41; Assistant Under-Secretary of State Colonial Office 1941–2; Deputy Under-Secretary of State 1942–5; Governor Tanganyika 1945–9.

Baxter, George H. (1894–1962). Entered India Office 1920; Financial

Secretary 1933–43; Assistant Under-Secretary of State for India 1943–7 and for Commonwealth Relations 1947–55; Chairman Conference on Closer Association in Central Africa March 1951; visited Central Africa for Victoria Falls Conference September 1951.

Bevin, Ernest (1881–1951). General Secretary Transport and General Workers Union 1921–40; member General Council of TUC 1925–40; MP (Lab.) 1940–51; Minister of Labour and National Service 1940–5; Secretary of State Foreign Affairs 1945–51.

Bourdillon, Bernard H. (1883–1948). KBE 1931; Indian Civil Service 1908–17; service in Mesopotamia and Iraq 1918–29; Colonial Secretary and Chief Secretary Ceylon 1929–32; Governor Uganda 1932–5, Nigeria 1935–42, (Governor-General-designate Sudan 1940); member Colonial Economic Development Council; Director of Barclay's Bank DCO, and of Barclay's Overseas Development Corporation.

Burns, Alan C. (1887–1980). KCMG 1936; colonial service in Leeward Islands 1905–12, Nigeria 1912–24; Colonial Secretary Bahamas 1924–9; Deputy Chief Secretary Nigeria 1929–34; Governor British Honduras 1934–40; Assistant Under-Secretary of State Colonial Office 1940–1; Governor Gold Coast 1941–7; acting Governor Nigeria 1942; Permanent British Representative UN Trusteeship Council 1947–56.

Caine, Sydney (b. 1902). KCMG 1947; Assistant Inspector of Taxes Inland Revenue 1923–6; entered Colonial Office 1926; secretary West Indies Sugar Commission 1929; Financial Secretary Hong Kong 1937; Assistant Secretary Colonial Office 1940; member Anglo-American Caribbean Commission 1942; Financial Adviser to Secretary of State for Colonies 1942; Assistant Under-Secretary of State 1944 and Deputy Under-Secretary of State Colonial Office 1947–8; 3rd Secretary Treasury 1948; Head UK Treasury and Supply Delegation, Washington 1949–51; Chief, World Bank Mission to Ceylon 1951; Vice Chancellor University of Malaya 1952–6; Director London School of Economics 1957–67.

Cameron, Donald C. (1872–1948). KBE 1923; colonial service in British Guiana 1890–1904, Mauritius 1904–7, Nigeria 1908–24 (Chief Secretary 1921–4); Governor Tanganyika 1925–31 and Nigeria 1931–5.

Campbell, John (1874–1944). Kt 1925; Indian Civil Service 1897–1922; Financial Officer University of London; Vice Chairman Greek Refugee Settlement Commission 1923–7 and 1929; Economic and Financial Adviser to Colonial Office 1930–42.

Cartland, George B. (b. 1912). Kt 1963; colonial service Gold Coast 1935; Colonial Office 1944–9; editor *Journal of African Adminis-*

tration 1945–9; secretary London African Conference 1948; served in Uganda 1949–62 (Chief Secretary 1960, Deputy Governor 1961); Registrar University of Birmingham 1963–7; Vice Chancellor University of Tasmania 1968–77.

Churchill, Winston L. S. (1874–1965). KG 1953; MP (C) 1900–4, (Lib.) 1904–18, (Coalition Lib.) 1918–22, (Constitutionalist) 1924–31, (C) 1931–64; Under-Secretary of State Colonies 1906–8; President Board of Trade 1908–10; Home Secretary 1910–11; First Lord of Admiralty 1911–15; Chancellor Duchy of Lancaster 1915; Minister of Munitions 1917; Secretary of State for War and Air January 1919–February 1921, Air and Colonies February–April 1921, and for Colonies until October 1922; Chancellor of Exchequer 1924–9; First Lord of Admiralty 1939–40; Prime Minister and Minister of Defence 1940–5; Leader of Opposition 1945–51; Prime Minister October 1951–April 1955 (resigned) and Minister of Defence October 1951–January 1952.

Clauson, Gerard L. M. (1891–1974). KCMG 1945; oriental scholar; transferred from Inland Revenue to Colonial Office after retirement from Army 1919; Assistant Secretary 1934; Assistant Under-Secretary of State 1940–51; member UK Delegation to Hot Springs Conference 1943, etc.; Chairman International Wheat Conference 1947 and International Rubber Conference 1951; retired 1951; Chairman Pirelli Ltd. 1960–9.

Cohen, Andrew B. (1909–1968). KCMG 1952; transfer from Board of Inland Revenue to Colonial Office 1933; served in Malta 1940–3; Assistant Secretary 1943; Assistant Under-Secretary of State and head Africa division 1947; Governor Uganda 1952–7; Permanent British Representative UN Trusteeship Council 1957–61; Director-General Department of Technical Co-operation, London 1961–4; Permanent Secretary Ministry of Overseas Development 1964–8.

Cranborne, Viscount born **Robert A. J. Gascoyne-Cecil** (1893–1972). Viscount, 1942; 5th Marquess of Salisbury 1947, MP (Unionist) 1929–41; Parliamentary Under-Secretary of State Foreign Affairs 1935–8; Paymaster General 1940; Secretary of State Dominion Affairs 1940–2; Secretary of State for Colonies 1942; Lord Privy Seal 1942–3; Secretary of State Dominion Affairs 1943–5; Leader House of Lords 1942–5, 1951–7; Lord Privy Seal 1951–2; Secretary of State for Commonwealth Relations 1952; Lord President of Council 1952–7, resigned over colonial affairs.

Creasy, Gerald H. (1897–1983). KCMG 1946; entered Colonial Office 1920; accompanied Secretary of State to Ceylon and Malaya 1928 and to West Africa 1935; Principal Private Secretary to Secretary of State 1937–9; seconded to Ministry of Supply 1939–42; Assistant Under-Secretary of State 1943; Chief Secretary

West African Council 1945–7; Governor Gold Coast 1948–9 and Malta 1949–54.

Cripps, R. Stafford (1889–1952). Kt 1930; barrister 1913; MP (Lab.) 1931–50; Solicitor-General 1930–1; British Ambassador to Russia 1940–2; Lord Privy Seal and Leader House of Commons 1942; Minister of Aircraft Production 1942–5; President Board of Trade 1945; Minister for Economic Affairs 1947; Chancellor of Exchequer 1947–50.

Dawe, Arthur J. (1898–1950). KCMG 1942; entered Colonial Office 1918; secretary Malta Royal Commission 1931 and mission to Malta 1933–4; Assistant Secretary 1936; Assistant Under-Secretary of State 1938; Deputy Under-Secretary of State Colonial Office 1945–7.

Eden, R. Anthony (1897–1977). KG 1954; 1st Earl of Avon 1961; MP (C) 1923–57; Parliamentary Private Secretary to Secretary of State Foreign Affairs 1926–9; Parliamentary Under-Secretary of State for Foreign Affairs 1931–3; Lord Privy Seal 1934–5; Minister without Portfolio for League of Nations Affairs 1935; Secretary of State for Foreign Affairs 1935–8, for Dominion Affairs 1939–40, for War 1940, for Foreign Affairs 1940–5, also Leader House of Commons 1942–5; Deputy Leader of Opposition 1945–51; Secretary of State for Foreign Affairs and Deputy Prime Minister 1951–April 1955; Chairman OEEC 1952–4; Prime Minister April 1955–January 1957.

Franks, Oliver S. (b. 1905). KCB 1946; Baron (life peer) 1962; academic career until 1939 when temporary civil servant Ministry of Supply; Permanent Secretary Ministry of Supply 1945–6; Provost Queen's College, Oxford 1946–8; British Ambassador at Washington 1948–52; Chairman Lloyds Bank Ltd 1954–62; Provost Worcester College, Oxford 1962–76; served on various government committees including being chairman Falkland Islands Review 1982–3.

Gater, George H. (1886–1963). Kt 1936; local government service from 1912 culminating in Clerk to the London County Council 1933–9; Permanent Under-Secretary of State Colonial Office, February 1940; seconded to Ministry of Home Security and Ministry of Supply 1940–2; Permanent Under-Secretary of State Colonial Office 1942–7.

Gent, G. Edward J. (1895–1948). KCMG 1946; entered Colonial Office 1920; assistant secretary to Indian Round Table Conference 1930; Assistant Secretary Colonial Office 1939; Assistant Under-Secretary of State and head Eastern Department 1942–6; Governor Malayan Union 1946–8 and High Commissioner Federation of Malaya February–July 1948.

Gordon-Walker, Patrick C. (1907–1980). Baron (life peer) 1974;

tutor Christ Church, Oxford 1931–40; MP (Lab.) 1945–64 and 1966–74; Parliamentary Private Secretary to H. Morrison 1946; Parliamentary Under-Secretary of State Commonwealth Relations 1947–50; Secretary of State Commonwealth Relations 1950–1; Secretary of State for Foreign Affairs 1964–5; Minister without Portfolio 1967; Secretary of State Education and Science 1967–8.

Griffiths, James (1890–1975). MP (Lab.) 1936–70; Agent Llanelly Labour Party 1922–5; President South Wales Miners Federation 1934–6; Minister of National Insurance 1945–50; Secretary of State Colonies 1950–1; member National Executive of Labour Party 1939–59 and chairman 1948–9; Deputy Leader and Vice-Chairman Parliamentary Labour Party 1956–9; Secretary of State Wales 1964–6.

Hailey, W. Malcolm (1872–1969). 1st Baron 1936, KCSI 1922, entered Indian Civil Service 1895; member Governor-General's Executive Council (Finance and Home Depts) 1919–24; Governor Punjab 1924–8 and United Provinces 1928–30, 1931–4; Director African Research Survey 1935–8; member Permanent Mandates Commission of League of Nations 1935–9; head Economic Mission to Belgian Congo 1940–1; chairman Colonial Research Committee 1943–8.

Halifax, 1st Earl of Halifax 1944, born **Edward F. L. Wood** (1881–1959). 1st Baron Irwin 1925, 3rd Viscount Halifax 1934, MP (Unionist) 1910–25; held government office 1921–35 including Parliamentary Under-Secretary of State for Colonies 1921–2 and Minister of Agriculture 1924–5; Viceroy of India 1926–31; held various offices in National Government 1932–40 culminating in Secretary of State for Foreign Affairs 1938–40; British Ambassador at Washington 1941–6.

Hall, 1st Viscount 1946, born **George H. Hall** (1881–1965). Checkweigher, local agent South Wales Miners Federation 1911–22; MP (Lab.) 1922–46; Civil Lord of Admiralty 1929–31; Parliamentary Under-Secretary of State for Colonies 1940–2; Financial Secretary to Admiralty 1942–3; Parliamentary Under-Secretary of State for Foreign Affairs 1943–5; Secretary of State for Colonies 1945–6; First Lord of Admiralty 1946–51; Deputy Leader House of Lords 1947–51.

Huggins, Godfrey M. (1883–1971). KCMG 1941, 1st Viscount Malvern 1955; medical training and practice in England; general medical practitioner in Southern Rhodesia 1911–21; Member Legislative Assembly 1923–58 (Federal 1953–8); Minister of Native Affairs 1933–49; Minister of Defence 1948–56; Prime Minister Southern Rhodesia 1933–53; Prime Minister Federation of Rhodesia and Nyasaland 1953–6.

Hull, Cordell (1871–1955). Tennessee Volunteer Infantry in

Spanish–American War 1898 and served in Cuba; judge in Tennessee 1903–7; member US House of Representative 1907–21 and 1923–31; US Senator from Tennessee 1931; resigned as Senator on appointment as Secretary of State (March 1933–November 1944) (resigned); US delegate to UN Conference at San Francisco 1945; Nobel Peace Prize 1945.

Jones, Arthur Creech (1891–1964). Executive member London Labour Party 1921–8; executive member Fabian Society; MP (Lab.) 1935–50 and 1954–64; member Colonial Office Educational Advisory Committee 1936–45; Parliamentary Private Secretary to Minister of Labour and National Service (E. Bevin) 1940–5; Chairman Fabian Colonial Bureau and formerly of Labour Party Imperial Advisory Committee; Vice-Chairman Higher Education Commission to West Africa 1943–4; Parliamentary Under-Secretary of State for Colonies 1945–6; Secretary of State for Colonies 1946–50.

Lewis, W. Arthur (b. 1915). Kt 1963, economist; recruited to Colonial Office 1941; temporary Principal Board of Trade 1943; Colonial Office 1944; Professor of Political Economy University of Manchester 1948–58; part-time member Board of Colonial Development Corporation 1951–3; various UN consultancies 1952–8; Principal University of West Indies 1959–62 and Vice-Chancellor University of West Indies 1962–3; chairs at Princeton University 1963–83.

Lloyd, Thomas I. K. (1896–1968). KCMG 1947; Assistant Principal Ministry of Health 1920; transferred to Colonial Office 1921; secretary Palestine Commission 1929–30; secretary West India Royal Commission 1938–9; Assistant Secretary 1939; Assistant Under-Secretary of State 1943; Permanent Under-Secretary of State Colonial Office 1947–56.

Luke, Stephen E. V. (b. 1905). KCMG 1953, Assistant Clerk House of Commons 1930; entered Colonial Office 1930; seconded to Palestine 1936–7; secretary Palestine Partition Commission 1938; Under-Secretary Cabinet Office 1947–50; Assistant Under-Secretary of State Colonial Office 1950–3; Comptroller for Development and Welfare in the West Indies, and British Co-Chairman of Caribbean Commission 1953–8; Commissioner for preparation of West Indies Federal Organization 1956–8; Senior Crown Agent for Overseas Governments and Administrations 1959–68; Interim Commissioner for West Indies 1962–8; Director Pirelli Ltd, etc. 1968–76.

Lyttelton, Oliver (1893–1972). 1st Viscount Chandos 1954, MP (C) 1940–54; President Board of Trade 1940–1; Minister of State in Middle East and member War Cabinet 1941–2; Minister of Production and member War Cabinet 1942–5; President Board of

Trade and Minister of Production May–July 1945; Chairman Associated Electrical Industries Ltd; Secretary of State for Colonies 1951–4; Chairman AEI Ltd and subsidiaries 1954–63.

MacDonald, Malcolm J. (1901–1981). MP (Lab.) 1929–31, (Nat. Lab.) 1931–5, (Nat. Govt) 1936–45; Parliamentary Under-Secretary of State for Dominion Affairs 1931–5; Secretary of State for Dominion Affairs 1935–8 and 1938–9; Secretary of State for Colonies 1935 and 1938–40; Minister of Health 1940–1; UK High Commissioner in Canada 1941–6; Governor-General British territories in South-east Asia 1946–8; Commissioner General in South-east Asia 1948–55; UK representative on South-east Asia Defence Treaty Council 1955; British High Commissioner in India 1955–60; leader British Delegation and Co-Chairman International Conference on Laos 1961–2; Governor Kenya 1963; Governor-General Kenya 1963–4; British High Commissioner in Kenya 1964–5; British Special Representative in East and Central Africa 1966–7; Special Representative of HMG in Africa 1967–9.

Macleod, Iain N. (1913–1970). MP (C) 1950–70; Conservative Party Secretariat 1946; head Home Affairs Research Department of Conservative Party 1948–50; Minister of Health 1952–5; Minister of Labour and National Service 1955–9; Secretary of State for Colonies October 1959–October 1961; Chancellor of Duchy of Lancaster and Leader of House of Commons 1961–3; Chairman Conservative Party Organisation 1961–3 and Joint Chairman 1963; editor *The Spectator* December 1963–December 1965; Chancellor of Exchequer June 1970.

Macmillan, M. Harold (b. 1894). 1st Earl of Stockton 1984; MP (Unionist) 1924–9, 1931–45, (C) 1945–64; Parliamentary Secretary Ministry of Supply 1940–2; Parliamentary Under-Secretary of State for Colonies 1942; Minister Resident at Allied HQ in North-west Africa 1942–5; Secretary for Air 1945; Minister of Housing and Local Government 1951–4; Minister of Defence October 1954–April 1955; Secretary of State for Foreign Affairs April–December 1955; Chancellor of Exchequer December 1955–January 1957; Prime Minister January 1957–October 1963.

Macpherson, John S. (1898–1971). KCMG 1945; Malayan Civil Service 1921–37, seconded to Colonial Office 1933–5; Nigeria 1937–9; Chief Secretary Palestine 1939–43; head British Colonies Supply Mission in Washington and member Anglo-American Caribbean Commission 1943–5; succeeded Stockdale as Comptroller for Development and Welfare in West Indies and British Co-Chairman Caribbean Commission 1945–8; Governor Nigeria 1948–54; Governor-General Federation of Nigeria 1954–5; Chairman UN Visiting Mission to Trust Territories in Pacific; Permanent Under-Secretary of State Colonial Office 1956–9.

Martin, John M. (b. 1904). KCMG 1952; entered Dominions Office 1927; seconded to Malayan Civil Service 1931–4; secretary Palestine Royal Commission 1936–7; private secretary to Prime Minister 1940–5 (principal private secretary 1941–5); Assistant Under-Secretary of State Colonial Office 1945–56; Deputy Under-Secretary of State 1956–65; High Commissioner Malta 1965–7.

Mitchell Philip E. (1890–1964). KCMG 1937; served in Nyasaland 1912–19 and Tanganyika 1919–35 (Chief Secretary 1934–5); Governor Uganda 1935–40; Political Adviser (on conquered Italian territs. in Africa) to Wavell; British Plenipotentiary in Ethiopia and Chief Political Officer (rank of Major-General) to G.O.C. East Africa; Governor Fiji and High Commissioner Western Pacific 1942–4; Governor Kenya 1944–52.

Mountbatten, Louis F. A. V. N. (1900–79) Lord Louis 1917, Viscount 1946, 1st Earl of Burma 1947, Admiral of the Fleet 1956; midshipman 1916; Captain HMS *Kelly* 1939; Chief of Combined Operations 1942; Supreme Allied Commander in South-east Asia 1943–6; Viceroy and Governor-General of India March–August 1947; Governor-General in India August 1947–June 1948; naval command Mediterranean 1948–9; Board of Admiralty 1950–2; C.-in-C. Mediterranean 1952–4; First Sea Lord and Chief of Naval Staff 1955–9; Chief of Defence Staff and Chairman Chiefs of Staff Committee 1959–65; assassinated by Provisional IRA.

Moyne, Walter E. Guinness, (1880–1944). 1st Baron 1935, MP (Unionist) 1907–31; held minor government offices 1922–4 and 1924–5; Minister of Agriculture and Fisheries 1925–9; Financial Mission to Kenya 1932; chairman West India Royal Commission 1938–39; Parliamentary Secretary Ministry of Agriculture 1940; Secretary of State Colonies 1941–2; Deputy Minister in Cairo 1942–January 1944; Minister-Resident in Middle East January–November 1944; assassinated by Stern Gang.

Noel-Baker, Philip J. (1889–1982). Baron (life peer) 1977. League of Nations secretariat 1919–22; MP (Lab.) 1929–31, 1936–70; Parliamentary Private Secretary to Secretary of State for Foreign Affairs 1929–31; Joint Parliamentary Secretary Ministry of War Transport 1942–5; Minister of State Foreign Office 1945–6; Secretary of State for Air 1946–7; Chairman Labour Party 1946–7; Secretary of State for Commonwealth Relations 1947–50; Minister of Fuel and Power 1950–1; Nobel Peace Prize winner 1959.

Parkinson, A. C. Cosmo (1884–1967). KCMG 1935. Entered Admiralty 1909; transferred to Colonial Office 1909; Assistant Secretary 1925; Assistant Under-Secretary of State 1931; Permanent Under-Secretary of State Colonial Office 1937–40; Permanent

Under-Secretary of State Dominions Office 1940; acting Permanent Under-Secretary Colonial Office 1940–2; seconded for special duty in the colonies 1942–4; retired 1944; re-employed as adviser on reorganization of Colonial Service 1945.

Paskin, J. John (1892–1972) KCMG 1954, transferred from Ministry of Transport to Colonial Office 1921; Assistant Secretary 1939; Principal Private Secretary to Secretary of State for Colonies (MacDonald and Lord Lloyd) 1939–40; Assistant Under-Secretary of State Colonial Office 1948–54.

Pedler, Frederick J. (b. 1908) Kt 1969. Entered CO 1930; seconded to Tanganyika 1934; secretary Commission on Higher Education in East Africa and the Sudan 1937, to Lord Privy Seal 1938, to Lord Hailey in Africa 1939 and in the Congo 1940; Chief British Economic Representative Dakar 1942; Financial Department Colonial Office 1944; joined United Africa Co. 1947, Deputy Chairman 1965–8; Director, Unilever 1956–68, etc.

Pethick-Lawrence, Frederick W. (1871–1961) 1st Baron 1945, MP (Lab.) 1923–31, 1935–45; Financial Secretary to Treasury 1929–31; member Indian Round Table Conference 1931; Secretary of State India and Burma 1945–7; Deputy Chairman Commonwealth Parliamentary Association UK branch 1945–52; member Political Honours Scrutiny Committee 1949–61.

Richards, Arthur F. (1885–1978) KCMG 1935, 1st Baron Milverton 1947, Malayan Civil Service 1908–30; Governor North Borneo 1930–3, Gambia 1933–6, Fiji (and High Comr West Pacific) 1936–8, Jamaica 1938–43, Nigeria 1943–7; part-time director Colonial Development Corporation 1948–51, etc.

Rogers, Philip (b. 1914) KCB 1970. Entered Colonial Office 1936; private secretary to Governor of Jamaica January–December, 1939, to Permanent Secretary Dominions Office 1940; to Permanent Secretary Colonial Office 1940–2, to Secretary of State for Colonies 1946; Assistant Secretary 1946–53; Assistant Under-Secretary of State Colonial Office 1953–61; thereafter served in Department of Technical Co-operation, Cabinet Office, Treasury, Civil Service Department and Department of Health and Social Security where he was Permanent Secretary 1970–5.

Roosevelt, Franklin D. (1882–1945) member New York Senate 1910–13; Assistant Secretary Navy 1913–20; Governor of New York 1929–33, 32nd President (Democrat) of the USA 1933–7, 1937–41, 1941–5, and re-elected for 1945–9.

Seel, George F. (1895–1976) KCMG 1950. Transferred from Air Ministry to Colonial Office 1922; secretary Rhodesia–Nyasaland Royal Commission 1938–9; seconded to Ministry of Information 1939 and Ministry of Supply 1941–2; Assistant Under-Secretary of State Colonial Office 1946–50; Comptroller for Development and Welfare in West Indies and British Co-Chairman Caribbean Commission 1950–3; Senior Crown Agent for Oversea Governments and Administrations 1953–9.

Stanley, Oliver F. G. (1896–1950). MP (C) 1924–50; Parliamentary Under-Secretary of State Home Office 1931–3; Minister of Transport 1933–4; Minister of Labour 1934–5; President Board of Education 1935–7; President Board of Trade 1937–40; Secretary of State for War 1940; Secretary of State for Colonies 1942–5.

Stockdale, Frank A. (1883–1949) KCMG 1937. Government agricultural scientist in West Indies 1905–12; Director of Agriculture Mauritius 1912–16 and Ceylon 1916–29; Agricultural Adviser to Secretary of State for Colonies 1929–40; Comptroller for Development and Welfare in West Indies 1940–5; Co-Chairman Anglo-American Caribbean Commission 1942–5; Adviser on Development Planning, Colonial Office 1945–8; Vice-Chairman Colonial Development Corporation 1948.

Strachey, E. John St. L. (1901–1963). MP (Lab.) 1929–31; resigned from Parliamentary Labour Party 1931; MP (Lab.) 1945–63; Parliamentary Under-Secretary of State for Air 1945–6; Minister of Food 1946–50; Secretary of State for War 1950–1.

Swinton, Viscount, born **Philip Cunliffe-Lister** (1884–1972). 1st Viscount 1935, 1st Earl 1955, KBE 1920. MP (Unionist) 1918–35; President Board of Trade 1922–3, 1924–9, 1931; Secretary of State for Colonies 1931–5; Secretary of State for Air 1935–8; Chairman UK Commercial Corporation 1940–2; Cabinet Minister-Resident in West Africa 1942–4; Minister for Civil Aviation 1944–5; Chancellor of Duchy of Lancaster and Minister of Materials 1951–2; Deputy Leader House of Lords 1951–5; Secretary of State for Commonwealth Relations 1952–5.

Truman, Harry S. (1884–1972). Judge, Jackson County Missouri 1922–34; US Senator (Democrat) for Missouri 1934–45; elected Vice-President of USA for 1945–9; 33rd President of the USA on death of Roosevelt 12 Apr 1945 until 1949 and re-elected 1949–53.

Wavell, Archibald P. (1883–1950). KCB 1939, 1st Viscount 1943, Field-Marshal 1943, 1st Earl 1947; gazetted to the Black Watch 1901; active military service before 1920 in South African War, India, Western Front and Middle East (staff of Allenby); worked at War Office and as staff officer in inter-war period; Commander, Palestine 1937; C.-in-C. Middle East 1939–41; C.-in-C. India 1941–3; Supreme Commander South-west Pacific January–March 1942; Viceroy and Governor-General India 1943–February 1947.

Welensky, Roy (b. 1907) Kt 1953. Joined railway service (Rhodesia) 1924; member National Council of Railway Workers Union; formed Northern Rhodesian Labour Party 1941; Director of Manpower Northern Rhodesia 1941–6; Member Legislative Council Northern Rhodesia 1938; Member Executive Council 1940–53; Chairman Unofficial Members Association 1946–53; Minister of Transport, Communications and Posts, Federation of Rhodesia and Nyasaland 1953–6; Leader of the House and Deputy Prime Minister 1955–6; Prime Minister and Minister of External Affairs 1956–63, and also Minister of Defence 1956–9.

Williams, Owen G. R., (1886–1954) entered Inland Revenue 1910; transferred to Colonial Office 1911; Assistant Secretary 1926–46; retired 1946.

Select Bibliography

ADAMTHWAITE, ANTHONY, 'Britain and the World, 1945–9: The View from the Foreign Office' *International Affairs*, 61, 2 (Spring 1985) pp. 223–35.

ALBERTINI, RUDOLF von, *Decolonization: The Administration and Future of the Colonies, 1919–1960* (New York: 1971).

BARTLETT, C. J., *The Long Retreat: A Short History of British Defence Policy, 1945–70* (London: 1972).

BULLOCK, ALAN, *Ernest Bevin: Foreign Secretary, 1945–*1951 (London: 1983).

CARLTON, DAVID, *Anthony Eden: A Biography* (London: 1982).

CARTLAND, GEORGE, 'Retrospect', *Journal of Administration Overseas*, XIII, 1 (January 1974) pp. 269–72.

CELL, J. W., 'On the Eve of Decolonization: the Colonial Office's Plans for the Transfer of Power in Africa, 1947', *Journal of Imperial and Commonwealth History*, VIII, 3 (May 1980) pp. 234–57.

CHAMBERLAIN, M. E., *Decolonization: The Fall of the European Empires* (Oxford: 1985).

COHEN, SIR ANDREW, *British Policy in Changing Africa* (London: 1959).

COHEN, MICHAEL J., *Palestine, Retreat from the Mandate: The Making of British Policy 1936–45* (London: 1978).

CONSTANTINE, STEPHEN, *The Making of British Colonial Development Policy 1914–1940* (London: 1984).

COWEN, M., 'Early Years of the Colonial Development Corporation: British State Enterprise Overseas during Late Colonialism', *African Affairs*, 83 (January 1984) pp. 63–75.

DARBY, PHILLIP, *Britain's Defence Policy East of Suez 1947–1968* (London: 1973).

DARWIN, JOHN, 'Imperialism in Decline? Tendencies in British Imperial Policy between the Wars', *Historical Journal*, 23 (1980) pp. 657–79.

FIELDHOUSE, D. K., 'The Labour Governments and the Empire–Commonwealth, 1945–51' in Ritchie Ovendale (ed.) *The Foreign Policy of the British Labour Governments, 1945–1951* (Leicester: 1984).

FLINT, JOHN, 'Planned Decolonization and its Failure in British Africa', *African Affairs*, 82 (July 1983) pp. 389–411.

FLINT, JOHN, 'Scandal at the Bristol Hotel: Some Thoughts on Racial Discrimination in Britain and West Africa and its Relationship to the Planning of Decolonisation, 1939–47', *Journal of Im-*

perial and Commonwealth History, XII, 1 (October 1983) pp. 74–93.
GALLAGHER, J. *The Decline, Revival and Fall of the British Empire* (Cambridge: 1982).
GIFFORD, PROSSER, and LOUIS, WILLIAM ROGER (eds) *The Transfer of Power in Africa: Decolonization 1940–60* (Yale: 1982).
GOLDSWORTHY, DAVID, *Colonial Issues in British Politics, 1945–1961: From 'Colonial Development' to 'Wind of Change'* (Oxford: 1971).
GRIMAL, HENRI, *Decolonization: the British, French, Dutch and Belgian Empires* (London: 1978).
GUPTA, P. S., *Imperialism and the British Labour Movement, 1914–1964* (London: 1975).
GUPTA, P. S., 'Imperialism and the Labour Government of 1945–51', in J. M. Winter (ed.) *The Working Class in Modern British History* (Cambridge: 1983).
HARRIS, KENNETH, *Attlee* (London: 1982).
HOLLAND, R. F., *European Decolonization, 1918–1981: An Introductory Survey* (London: 1985).
HOLLAND, R. F., 'The Imperial Factor in British Strategies from Attlee to Macmillan, 1945–63', *Journal of Imperial and Commonwealth History*, XII, 2 (January 1984) pp. 165–86.
LEE, J. M. *Colonial Development and Good Government: A Study of the Ideas Expressed by the British Official Classes in Planning Decolonization, 1939–1964* (Oxford: 1967).
LEE, J. M., '"Forward Thinking" and War: the Colonial Office during the 1940s', *Journal of Imperial and Commonwealth History*, VI, 1 (October 1977) pp. 64–79.
LEE, J. M., and PETTER, MARTIN, *The Colonial Office, War, and Development Policy: Organisation and the Planning of a Metropolitan Initiative, 1939–1945* (London: 1982).
LOUIS, WILLIAM ROGER, *Imperialism at Bay 1941–1945: The United States and the Decolonization of the British Empire* (Oxford: 1977).
LOUIS, WILLIAM ROGER, *The British Empire in the Middle East 1945–1951: Arab Nationalism, the United States, and Post-war Imperialism* (Oxford: 1984).
MANSERGH, NICHOLAS, *The Commonwealth Experience. Volume Two: From British to Multiracial Commonwealth* (London: 2nd edn, 1982).
MEREDITH, DAVID, 'The British Government and Colonial Economic Policy, 1919–1939', *Economic History Review*, XXVIII (1975) pp. 484–99.
MOORE, R. J., *Churchill, Cripps and India, 1939–45* (Oxford, 1979).
MOORE, R. J., *Escape from India: The Attlee Government and the Indian Problem* (Oxford: 1983).

MORGAN, D. J., *The Official History of Colonial Development*, 5 vols, (London: 1980).

MORGAN, KENNETH O., *Labour in Power 1945–1951* (Oxford: 1984).

MORRIS-JONES, W. H., and FISCHER, GEORGES (eds) *Decolonization and After: The British and French experience*, (London: 1980).

NORDMAN, C. R., 'The Decision to Admit Unofficials to the Executive Councils of British West Africa', *Journal of Imperial and Commonwealth History*, IV, 2 (January 1976) pp. 194–205.

PEARCE, R. D., *The Turning Point in Africa: British Colonial Policy 1938–48* (London: 1982).

PEARCE, R. D., 'The Colonial Office in 1947 and the Transfer of Power', *Journal of Imperial and Commonwealth History*, X, 2 (January 1982) pp. 211–15.

PEARCE, R. D., 'The Colonial Office in 1947 and the Transfer of Power in Africa', *Journal of Imperial and Commonwealth History*, X, 2 (January 1982) pp. 211–15.

PEARCE, R. D., 'The Colonial Office and Planned Decolonisation in Africa', *African Affairs*, 83 (January 1984) pp. 77–93.

PERHAM, MARGERY, *The Colonial Reckoning* (London: 1961).

PORTER, A. N., 'Iain Macleod, Decolonization in Kenya, and Tradition in British Colonial Policy', *Journal for Contemporary History*, 2 (1975) pp. 37–59.

ROBINSON, R. E., 'The Journal and the Transfer of Power 1947–51', *Journal of Administration Overseas*, XIII, 1 (January 1974) pp. 255–8.

ROBINSON, R. E., 'Sir Andrew Cohen: Pro-consul of African Nationalism', in L. H. Gann and P. Duignan (eds) *African Pro-Consuls* (Stanford: 1978) pp. 353–64.

ROBINSON, R. E., 'The Moral Disarmament of African Empire 1919–1947', *Journal of Imperial and Commonwealth History*, VIII, 1 (October 1979) pp. 86–104.

ROBINSON, R. E., 'Andrew Cohen and the Transfer of Power in Tropical Africa, 1941–1951', in W. H. Morris-Jones and G. Fischer (eds) *Decolonization and After*, pp. 50–72.

SHORT, ANTHONY, *The Communist Insurrection in Malaya, 1948–60* (London: 1975).

SMITH, RAYMOND, and ZAMETICA, JOHN, 'The Cold Warrior: Clement Attlee Reconsidered, 1945–7', *International Affairs* 61, 2 (Spring 1985) pp. 237–52.

SMITH, T. (ed) *The End of Empire: Decolonisation after World War II* (Lexington, Massachusetts: 1975).

SMYTH, R., 'Britain's African Colonies and British Propaganda during World War II', *Journal of Imperial and Commonwealth History*, XIV, 1 (October 1985) pp. 65–82.

STOCKWELL, A. J., *British Policy and Malay Politics during the Malayan Union Experiment, 1942–1948* (Kuala Lumpur: 1979).

STOCKWELL, A. J., 'British Imperial Policy and Decolonization in Malaya, 1942–52', *Journal of Imperial and Commonwealth History*, XIII, 1 (October 1984) pp. 68–87.

TARLING, NICHOLAS, '"A New and Better Cunning": British Wartime Planning for Post-War Burma, 1942–3', *Journal of Southeast Asian Studies* 13, 1 (March 1982) pp. 33–59.

TARLING, NICHOLAS, '"An Empire Gem": British Wartime Planning for Post-War Burma', *Journal of Southeast Asian Studies* 13, 2 (September 1982) pp. 310–48.

TARLING, NICHOLAS, 'Lord Mountbatten and the Return of Civil Government to Burma', *Journal of Imperial and Commonwealth History*, XI, 2 (January 1983) pp. 197–226.

THORNE, CHRISTOPHER, *Allies of a Kind: The United States, Britain and the War against Japan, 1941–1945* (Oxford: 1978).

TOMLINSON, B. R., *The Indian National Congress and the Raj, 1929–42: The Penultimate Phase* (London: 1976).

TOMLINSON, B. R., *The Political Economy of the Raj. 1914–47: The Economics of Decolonization* (London: 1979).

TOMLINSON, B. R., 'The Contraction of England: National Decline and Loss of Empire', *Journal of Imperial and Commonwealth History*, XI, 1 (October 1982) pp. 58–72.

TOMLINSON, B. R., 'Indo-British Relations in the Post-Colonial Era: The Sterling Balances Negotiations, 1947–49', *Journal of Imperial and Commonwealth History*, XII, 3 (May 1985) pp. 142–62.

Index